Fashion in Art

The Second Empire and Impressionism

John Moore Stratford upon Avon 23.2.97

Fashion in Art

The Second Empire and Impressionism

Marie Simon

Epilogue by

Vivienne Westwood

ZWEMMER

English edition first published in 1995 by Zwemmer
an imprint of Philip Wilson Publishers Ltd
28 Litchfield Street,
London WC2H 9NJ

First published by Editions Hazan,
35/37 rue de Seine 75006 Paris, France
in 1995 under the title
Mode et Peinture Le Second Empire et L'Impressionisme
by Marie Simon

ISBN 0 302 00658 3

Designed by Sylvie Raulet
Jacket designed by Atalante
Translated by Edmund Jephcott
Printed and bound in Italy.

CONTENTS

Introduction

In the second half of the nineteenth century Baudelaire, following Stendhal's example, offered a redefinition of beauty. In contrast to beauty as an absolute ideal, Baudelaire revealed and extolled its relative aspects, completely overturning existing artistic opinion. To express this new aesthetic he chose fashion as his standard. Raising it aloft as a symbol of modernity, he ascribed to fashion a value it had not hitherto had, and was not to retain in the century to follow.

The importance the poet attached to fashion at first seems surprising. However, it was in tune with a general preoccupation among poets, writers, painters and theoreticians at that time. Since 1830 fashion had exerted a fascination which stirred reflection and fired enthusiasm. It was part of a current of exciting new ideas which included Lavater's theories on physiognomy, discoveries in the field of natural sciences, and occultism. Among the myriad discoveries of the nineteenth century, fashion asumed an important place; it became a topic for thought and research as it was now a subject commented on in the Press. For the first time, fashion journals and prints provided a means of diffusion and a focus for discussion. In the second half of the century the advent of photography completed the means available for the study and comparison of fashions. Until then, painting had been our only source of information. From the nineteenth century onwards we have a much fuller picture of the origins and movements of fashion, of the value the art world attached to it and of its influence on painting.

This enthusiasm for fashion reached its peak in the second half of the century. In addition to its economic importance and traditional function, fashion assumed a symbolic value: it embraced and explained everything. And, above all, its links with art were noted and exploited for the first time. Painters and art critics, following in Baudelaire's footsteps, even went so far as to attribute to it an essential role in the revolution in art and the rise of modernism. The connections established between fashion and painting during the Second Empire and the Third Republic made this an exceptional period. But to see the full importance of these connections we must first be aware of the economic role of fashion at that time.

During the upheavals of the French Revolution fashion, like all other signs of ostentatious wealth, was a prime target. The late eighteenth century saw a sweeping change in the way fashion was perceived and understood, and this was consolidated in the nineteenth century. From now on, men were to dress themselves in a coat and long trousers, and abandon, in the course of the century, the colour and preciosity of the ornate, fitted, even clinging attire they had previously affected. Though dandies offered some resistance, most men saw their personalities dissolved in the melancholy dark suit, that 'uniform, desolate livery bearing witness to equality'. The long-trousered suit had existed before the crisis whose symbol it became. It appeared in England, several

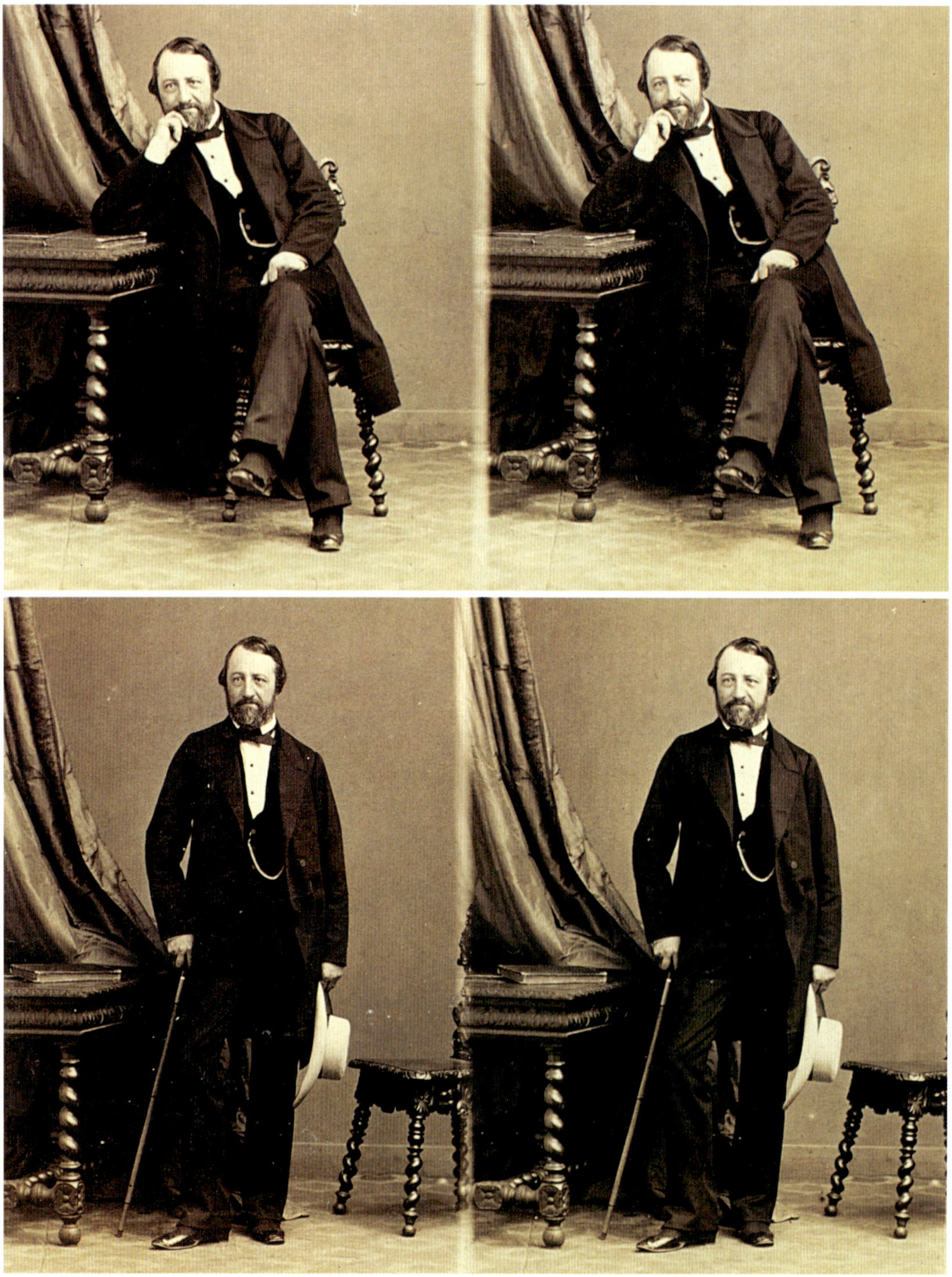

Disdéri, Portraits of a man, *no date. Musée d'Orsay, Paris.*

decades before the French Revolution, both in the dress of the commercial classes and in sporting outfits worn by aristocrats on their country estates. From the early 1760s it was associated with the ideas of liberty, patriotism, virtue, the spirit of enterprise and virility, while the elaborate coats then fashionable came to signify aristocratic decadence. Around 1790 these ideas spread throughout British and French society, and the black suit was widely adopted.

Luxury and frivolity became the prerogative of women. Men delegated to them the outward display of wealth and idleness characteristic of the old ruling class. From then on the wife became the main indicator of a couple's social status. Whereas, in the eighteenth century, sartorial contrasts had expressed class antagonisms, in the nineteenth they bore witness to a polarisation of men and women. This decline in the importance of male fashion has persisted until today. It is one of the legacies of the nineteenth century.

Another legacy, no less important, concerns production and distribution. The second half of the nineteenth century saw the development of the ready-made garment, the ancestor of our ready-to-wear industry, and the emergence of haute couture. Both these developments were supported by the rise of industrialisation[1] and of the commercial market.[2] In addition, thanks to the new political stability in France, the Second Empire was the start of an era of unprecedented prosperity. The court, aware of the advantages flowing from the cultural pre-eminence of Paris, especially as regards fashion, re-established a court life in which luxury and consumption were vigorously encouraged.

Reversing their eclipse by the bourgeoisie under Louis-Philippe and reverting to Napoleonic principles, the sovereigns supported weavers and manufacturers. Thus, the Empress Eugénie wore 'political clothes', brocade dresses intended to support the Lyons silk industry, and tried to initiate a 'court costume'. In its second issue in 1853, the Moniteur de la mode disseminated the 'court costume designed by Jules David in the presence of the Empress and ladies of her House'. This comprised a French-style coat and knee-breeches for men, and for women a court cloak with a train two metres long fastened to the waistband.[3]

Sartorial competition at the balls at the Tuileries or the receptions at Compiègne and Fontainebleau was fierce and stimulating. The example of Lillie Moulton, wife of an American banker who had moved to Paris in the reign of Louis-Philippe, who took ten chests of dresses with her for a week's stay at Compiègne, is eloquent on this point! This ostentation naturally favoured the emergence of haute couture. When Charles Frederick Worth founded his own fashion house in 1858, he knew that its success depended on adoption by the court. He therefore sent his wife to see the audacious Princesse de Metternich, with sketches and a proposal to make a dress of her choosing for a price she, the princess, would decide. The princess launched the couturier's career at the Tuileries ball and Fontainebleau. In the small world of the court Worth's rise was swift.[4] He dressed the whole of high society and became the exclusive supplier of lavish gowns to the empress (for soirées, fancy-dress balls, receptions, and official visits).

Worth is regarded as the founder of haute couture. He certainly managed to establish a new stature for the couturier: that of an all-powerful artist of genius, temperamental but adored. To clients who had been in the habit of giving orders he taught obedience and respect, while flattering their vanity and giving them the feeling of having been indulged. To this audacity he added that of having his wife, attired in Worth dresses, parade about as a living advertisement; he then built on this by employing living mannequins almost identical to his clients, thus laying the foundations of the fashion catwalk.

However, for the manufacturing and administrative side of his business, he undoubtedly drew on his experience at the Gagelin firm of 'novelties and ready-made dresses' which he had joined as an assistant in the late 1840s, becoming a partner in 1853. It was, paradoxically, ready-made garments that were his inspiration in setting up a system that aimed to produce the exact opposite. Fashion design and the ready-to-wear trade were closely interlinked in the nineteenth century, when the two ideas did not have the distinct connotations they have today. In the *Bottin professionnel* (trade directory) of 1871–2, the same firm is sometimes listed under both headings, 'couture' and 'novelties and ready-made clothing'. The couturier Pingat, for example, was classified as a maker of ready-to-wear garments. As for Jacques Doucet, he illustrates the transition from one activity to the other. His parents had a shop selling lace, ready-made lingerie and gentlemen's shirts. When he joined the family firm in 1871, a department for ready-made dresses was added to the women's lingerie. Doucet developed the dressmaking side and on his father's death, in 1898, the firm became a direct competitor of Worth.

In trying to establish a history of garment-making in the nineteenth century, we should go back to the origins of the ready-to-wear industry. It seems to have been initiated by 'novelty shops' (meaning, since the eighteenth century, shops selling fabrics and shawls). After the end of the Restoration period (1814–30), they offered, in addition to their materials and imported shawls, 'ready-mades', that is jackets or overcoats, paletots (short overcoats) and mantelets (capes) that did not need precise fitting, as well as lingerie items. These garments were either made in workshops attached to the shops, or bought from wholesale manufacturers. The most important of these shops were Le Petit Saint-Thomas founded in 1810 (altered and enlarged up to 1840), La Belle Jardinière founded in 1824, Le Bonhomme Richard founded in 1828, and A la Ville de Paris founded in 1841. Before 1870 these shops did not sell dresses.[5]

The great stores which came into being under the Second Empire (except Les Trois Quartiers, founded in 1827–9), took over the formula of the novelty shops (indeed,

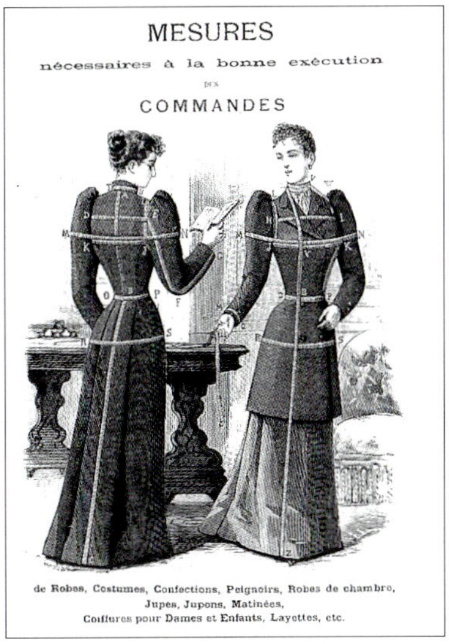

Le Bon Marché, *'Measures necessary for the satisfactory execution of orders', winter 1891 (left).*

Le Journal des jeunes filles, *town outfit, 1 October 1869 (right).*

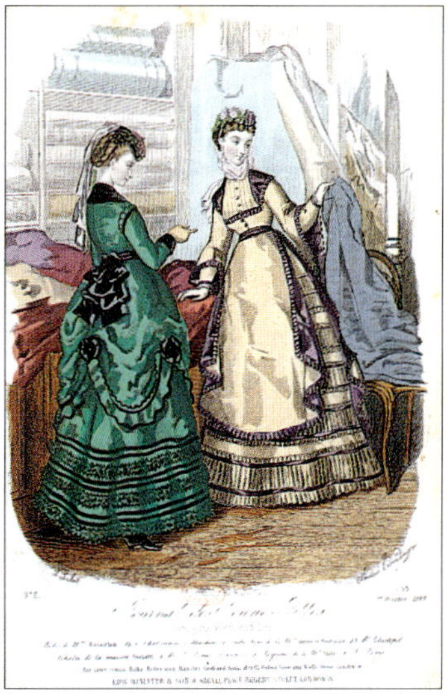

some of them used this name at first), but supplemented the materials and ready-made clothes with utensils, decorative items – the whole range of goods offered by the large store. They developed ready-to-wear jackets and coats, and later fitted garments, especially robes, or ladies' costumes (skirt and jacket made of the same material). They offered many 'semi-ready-mades' (pre-fitted garments) which the customer adjusted herself to her own measurements. The best-known of these great stores were Le Bon Marché, founded in 1849; Le Louvre, 1855; Le Printemps, 1865; and La Paix 1869.

Very quickly, a typology of these great shops emerged: Le Louvre was the most chic, La Samaritaine had a popular clientèle, Le Printemps drew its young customers from the petty bourgeoisie and middle class; as for Le Bon Marché 'it smacks somewhat of the provinces', Zola commented in his preliminary notebooks for *Au Bonheur des dames.*

The ready-to-wear industry continued to grow and prosper throughout the century, thanks in particular to exports. For a very long time France was the only country to represent the fashion industry at the universal exhibitions, which only emphasized the leading role Paris had long played in matters of fashion and taste.

Couture differed from the ready-to-wear shops in that it offered made-to-measure garments. But, like the novelty shops, couturiers could also sell materials or fancy goods (which were sometimes their main source of income). They could also make ready-made garments, which they sold as exclusive designs to the great stores. Couture and the ready-to-wear industry used the same means of publicity and dissemination: they were mentioned in the Press, in a veiled form of publicity, journalists having special relationships with this or that house.[6] In the provinces, both types of firm distributed patterns and models by mail. (Worth himself was to disseminate some of his patterns

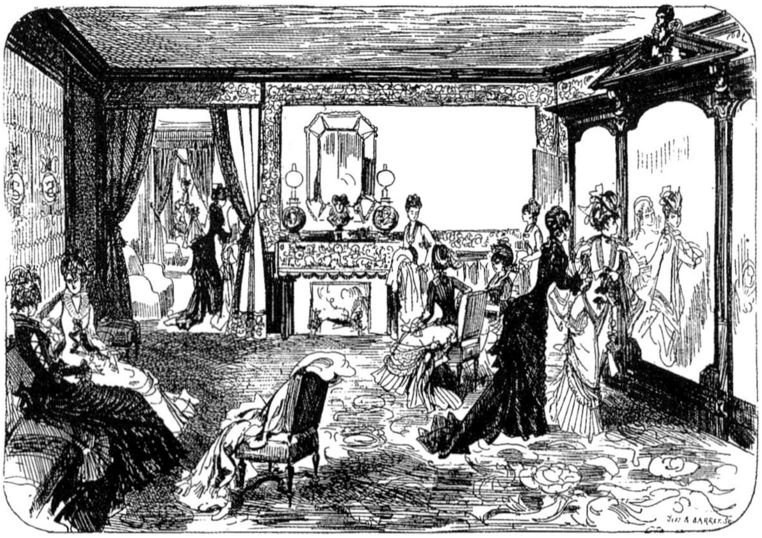

La Vie parisienne, *the showrooms of the fashion designer Sporck (dresses and ready-madeclothes), 1875.*

through *Le Printemps*, a short-lived journal, and in the American magazine *Harper's Bazar).* Worth's innovation was to use the same suppliers that he had worked with at Gagelin, buying materials wholesale directly and ordering exclusive designs from the suppliers. In this way he could offer a choice of pre-designed models (as for ready-to-wear); but these could be adapted into unique garments. Arrogantly flaunting his artistic status, he eclipsed couturiers such as Mesdames Roger, Camille or Palmire who, though enjoying a certain discreet renown, would never have dreamed of being held up as examples. In this way he was quickly able to demand exorbitant prices. In 1871 a parisienne of average means could dress herself very respectably for 1,500 francs a year; but at Worth, that was the price of the least expensive of day dresses. The annual amounts spent at his house varied between 10,000 and 100,000 gold francs (a worker earned 1,250 francs a year).

The great stores, betraying their envy of Worth even while shunning him, used his name in their publicity. In 1869 La Paix, established in the 'new Opéra quarter', boasted of offering 'ravishing costumes in no way inferior to those of Worth'.[7] As for Le Louvre, it thought it necessary to assert that its ready-made and gown departments 'do not copy fashion: they create it, from the most modest garment to the court gown and the gala costume'. In these attempts by the big stores to widen their clientèle and embellish their image, the leading role played by couture can be clearly seen. Fashion was created within an élite for whom wealth was more important than membership of a particular class. Worth's clients were recruited from high society, but also from the demi-monde of actresses and expensive kept women.

Ready-to-wear clothing was really only a threat to couturiers working for the middle classes. The traditional way of producing a dress in close collaboration with the client remained largely their preserve. This was done both with the aid of patterns found in fashion journals or noticed and remembered, and by using fashion designs bought by couturiers from professional designers (the forerunners of our designers). Protection of designs was only introduced relatively late, so that advertisements such as the following could be read in the columns of the press:

> I realize there are some women whose means do not allow them to have all their gowns made by such eminent houses [referring to a renowned couturière, Mme Camille]. But at the start of every season they can, if they will believe me, have a dress designed and made for them at Mme Camille's; then, at home and under their own direction, they will have their own simpler dress made up using this excellent pattern.[8]

This suggestion of employing both Mme Camille's expensive services and a small home dressmaker looks like a desperate attempt to resist the rise of the novelty shops.

All these ways of producing garments which, as we have seen, were more interconnected than it at first seems allowed a democratisation of fashion. Even if fashion was the prerogative of an élite to begin with, it spread progressively through all classes of society.[9] More and more, in the course of the century, the great stores gave wider access to elegance and brought greater uniformity of dress. This phenomenon, fostered and encouraged by the press, was a major factor in the fascination that fashion held for people at that time. Intellectuals saw in it a symbol of a new society with which they would henceforth have to reckon.

This society, which appropriated fashion for itself, turned in a parallel gesture towards painting, especially the portrait. In gaining access to these two former prerogatives of the aristocracy it showed the same consuming desire, but also the same ambivalence. At the same time as it assumed these aristocratic ideals abolished by its fathers, it knew it was grasping at something already lost for ever. This common attitude towards both emblems of aristocratic life explains, in part, the subtle links which formed between them. The interplay of reciprocal influences set up between fashion and painting during this period is a phenomenon quite unique in the history of art.

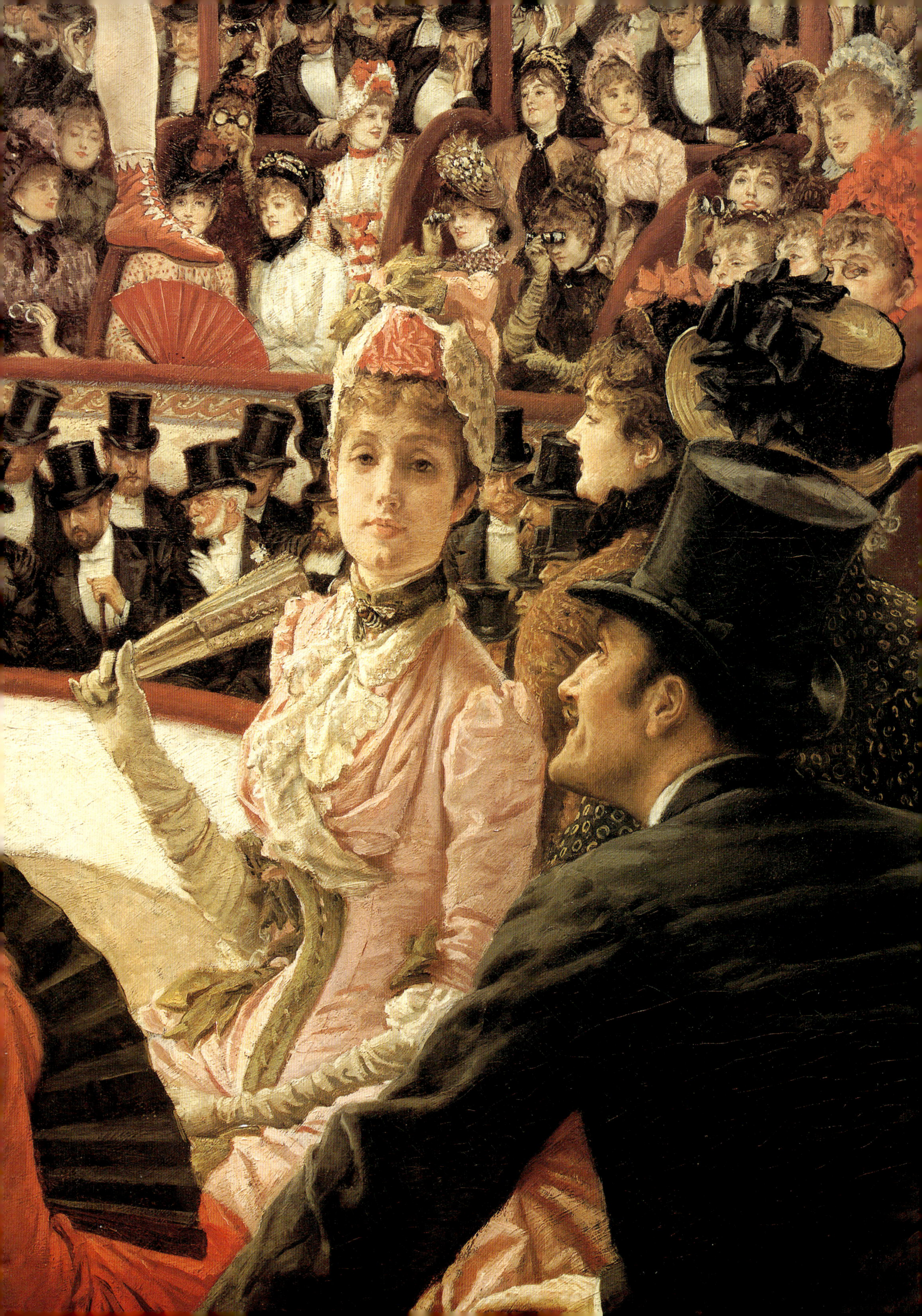

Chapter One

For Women, Dress is the First of the Arts

James Tissot, The Sportswomen, *1883–1885 (detail).*
Museum of Fine Arts, Juliana Cheney Edwards Collection, Boston.

Woman and fashion, an indivisible whole

We instinctively think of fashion as a feminine concern. Yet the supposedly natural abstention of men from coquetry and ornamentation is a product of the French Revolution and of the nineteenth century. Before this feminisation, men and women paraded on an equal footing. In the course of the nineteenth century, woman appropriated the whole of fashion to herself. It seems to us that she did so in an exaggerated way, as if fulfilling a duty, such were the social pressures and material constraints upon her. However, what we are presenting as an aberration certainly was not experienced as such, except by a few moralists who, in any case, were more vociferous in Germany, Great Britain and America than in France.

Fashion therefore took on a new social significance. In rejecting all manifestations of luxury, men were no less preoccupied with the place and esteem accorded to them within society. Women were to provide them with a foil. Not being subjected to the constraints of work, a woman could surround herself at leisure with delicate, cumbersome and imposing finery. This could be a signboard for her wealth, 'a fashion of vain display...a mark-up of value that could be assessed at the Stock Exchange'.[1] Her appearance was a guide to the affluence of her household, for 'while men do battle for fortune, women's only resource is to go out on the pretext of squandering their husbands' financial conquests'.[2]

The woman, the social and worldly double of her husband, was thus on permanent display. As if to compensate for being thereby reduced to a pure reflection, an ostentatious image of luxury devoid of a soul, she disembodied herself, turned herself into an immaterial being venerated by writers and painters, an archetype simultaneously dreamed of and inaccessible. The fetishistic passion harboured by the heroes of Balzac or Flaubert for certain items of feminine costume, whether it is Frédéric Moreau admiring the display windows of lace merchants or jewellers and dressing his beloved in his imagination, or 'Charles {Bovary}, who could not stop himself touching over and over again her comb, her skirts, her shawl...', is no doubt a sign of sublimation:[3]

> Which poet, in depicting the pleasure caused by a beautiful woman, would dare to separate the woman from her costume? Where is the man who...has not enjoyed, in the most disinterested manner, a woman's artfully composed attire, and has not taken away an image of it inseparable from the beauty of its wearer, making of both, the woman and her dress, an indivisible whole?[4]

A self-portrait by Eva Gonzalès perfectly illustrates this revelation. Whereas Manet had painted a portrait of his pupil as a free and strong-willed artist (1869–70, London, National Gallery), she chose to reveal herself as Romantic and feminine. Her dress, with

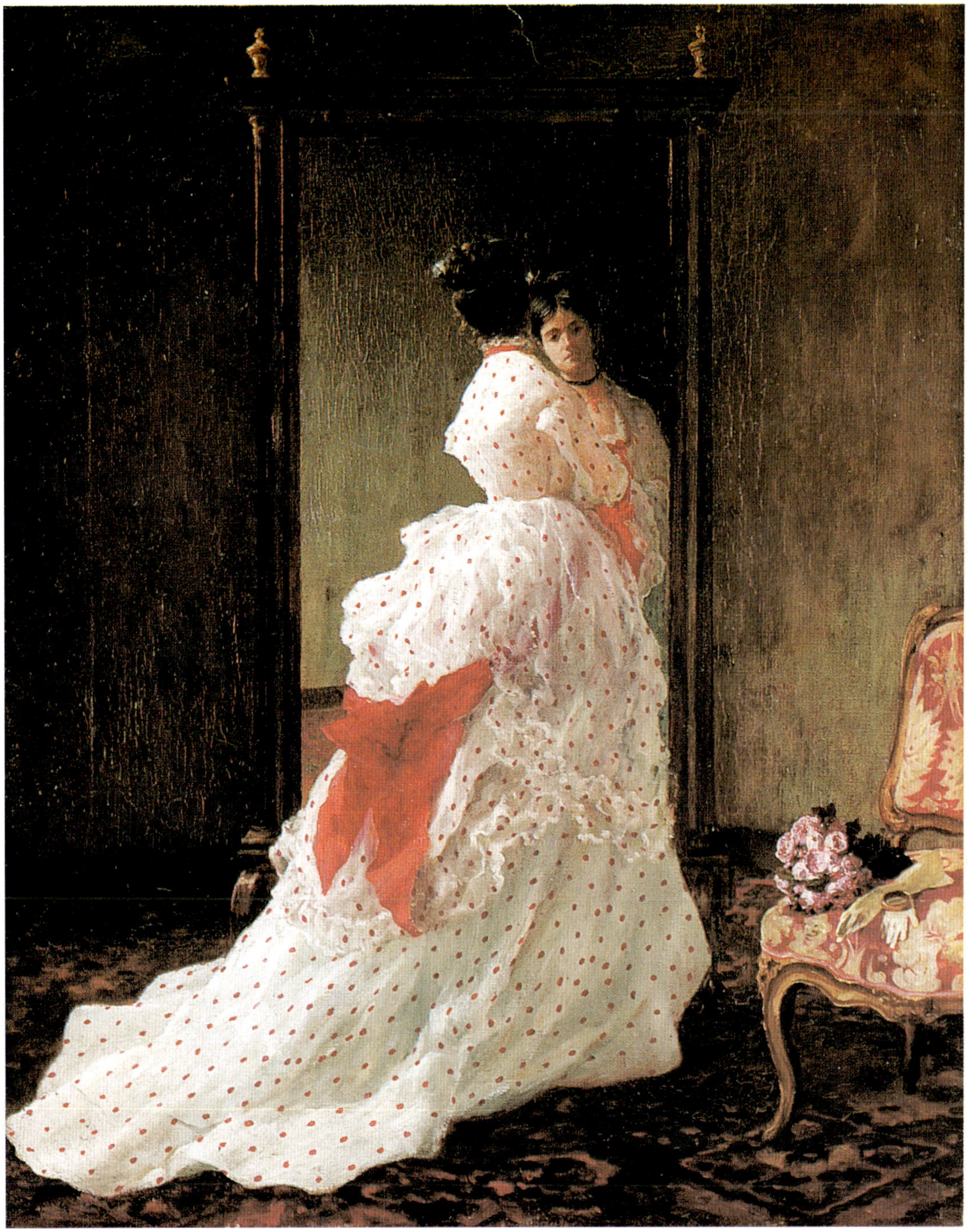

Eva Gonzales (attributed to), Self-portrait, *no date. Private Collection.*

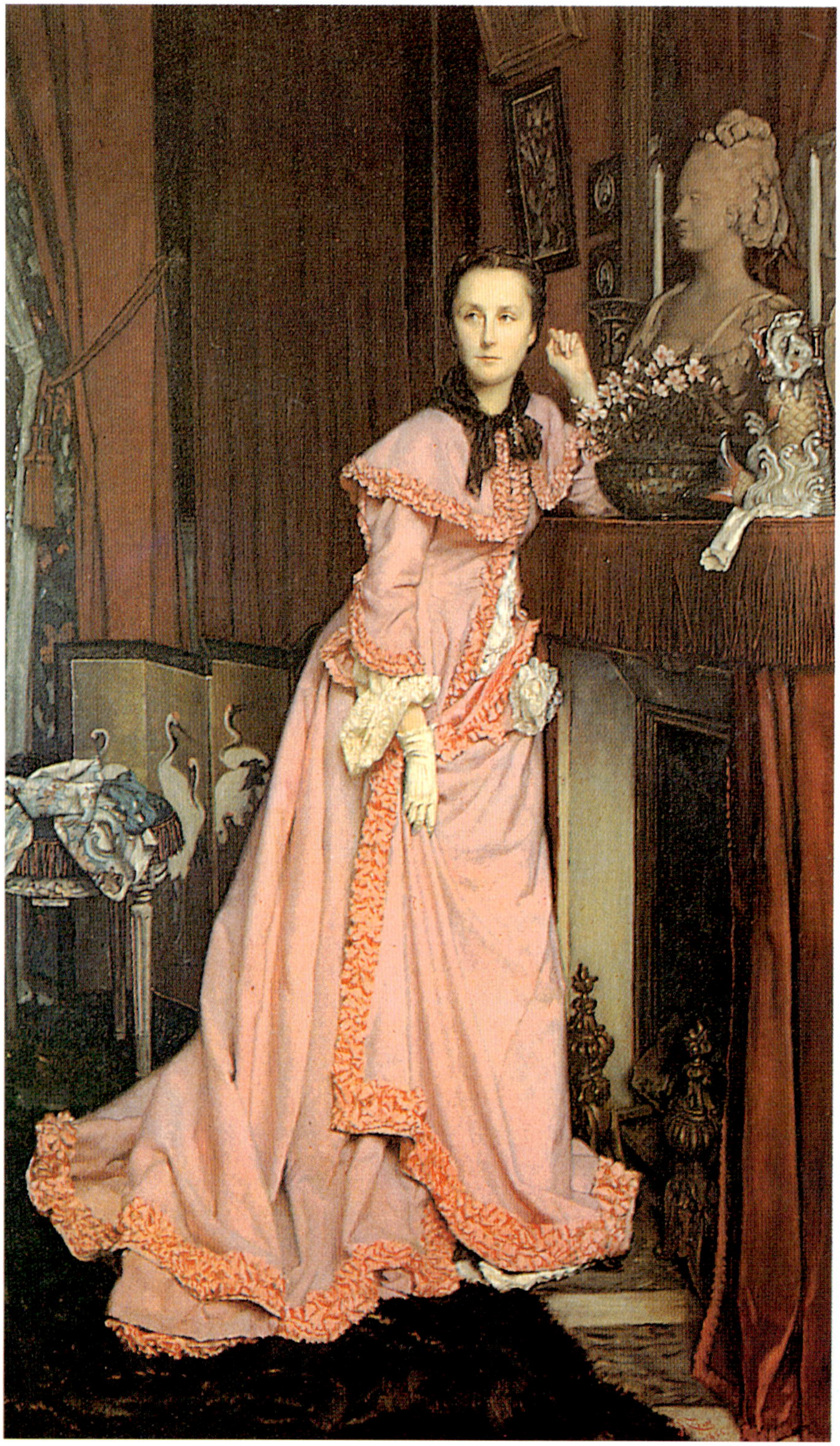

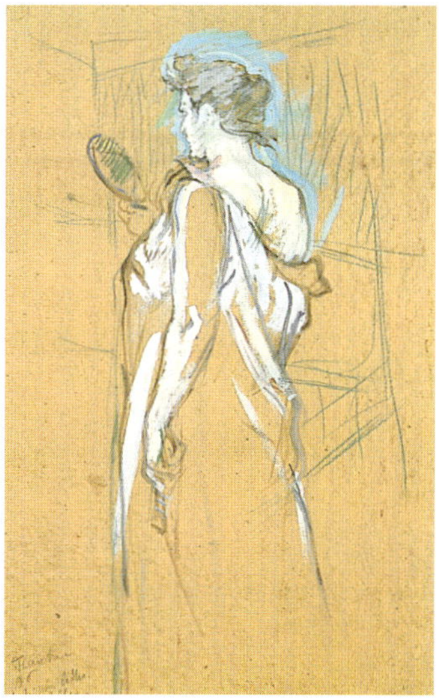

Henri de Toulouse-Lautrec, Study for Elles: The Hand-mirror, *1896. Private Collection (left).*

Catalogue of the Magasins du Louvre, *négligés, winter fashions, 1888–1889 (right).*

James Tissot, The Marquise de Miramon, née Thérèse Feuillant, *1866. Private Collection (facing page).*

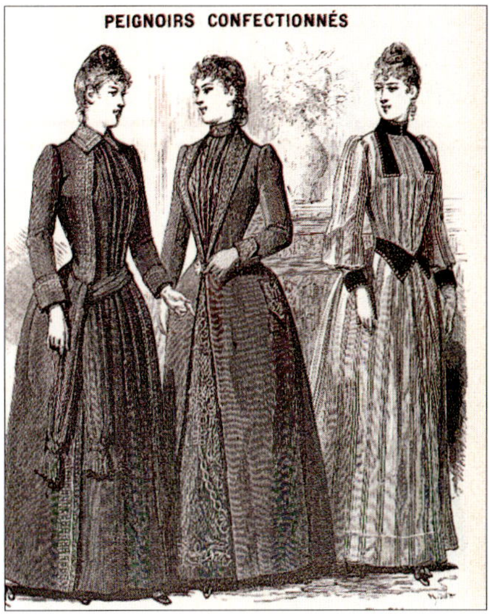

the red bow of her bustle, catches the eye and then leads our gaze towards the discreet reflection of her face in the mirror. The artifice of the mirror is not used, as in many self-portraits, to give an exact, 'photographic' image of the painter. Here, it points rather towards an archetype of woman. Paradoxically, what Eva Gonzalès shows first of herself is: 'All that artificial harmony wich the woman has imposed on her features, and that she checks each day in the mirror before venturing out, to make sure it is still in place...' (Proust, *A l'Ombre des jeunes filles en fleurs*).

The comedy of dress

Sartorial rites

This female society which existed on appearances was caught up in something akin to a religious cult. It was a cult with constricting sartorial rites which imposed a hectic timetable. Indeed:

> A fashionable woman who wishes to be well dressed in any situation must have all she needs to make seven or eight changes of clothing in a day: her dressing gown in the morning, her riding costume for the promenade, her town costume if she goes out on foot, her visiting clothes if she goes out in her carriage, her dinner dress and her evening or theatre robe. This is not an exaggeration, and her attire is further complicated in summer, at the seaside, by bathing costumes, and in autumn and winter by hunting and skating costumes, if she enjoys sharing these healthy exercises with men.[5]

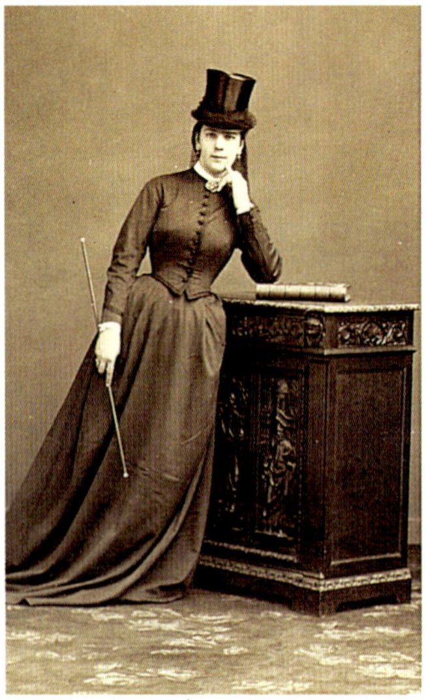

Disdéri,
Madame de Bélianis, *1865.*
Musée d'Orsay, Paris
(left).

Fashion engraving by Jules David, 'Her Majesty the Empress in Amazon costume', *no date. (right).*

Giuseppe de Nittis, Return from the Bois de Boulogne, *1878.*
Museo Civico Revoltella, Galleria d'arte moderna, Trieste
(facing page).

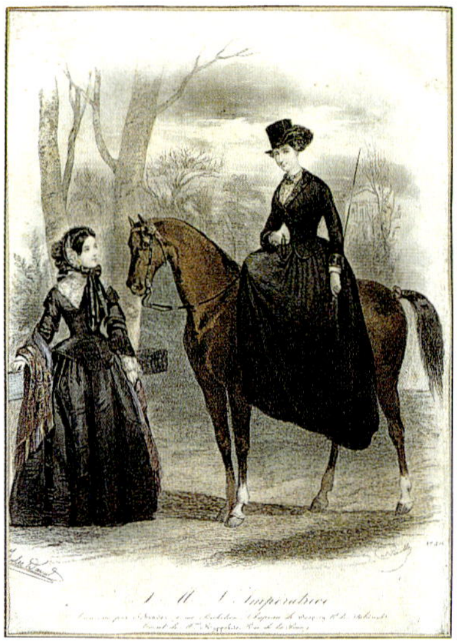

In the first hours of her day, a woman put on a luxurious peignoir – or house-coat – embellished with bows, lace and crimped flounces. This indoor robe grew more and more sumptuous until it became a truly elegant form of attire in which to receive visits from intimate friends. But for a long time this practice met with resistance.

> Women who wore a négligé at home were long viewed with disapproval. This mode of dress was judged severely, and was only allowed to be worn while dressing, or for visiting church after sickness or childbirth. Apart from those uses, the peignoir was thought indecent, and no respectable woman would consent to wear this appurtenance of gallantry.[6]

In painting, it was audacious to depict this sphere of feminine intimacy. To depict a woman in her nightdress, while washing or dressing or, less bluntly, in her morning house-coat, showed either a desire to ignore social rules by moving towards realism (as in Manet, Caillebotte, Morisot, Lautrec), or to be deliberately provocative by harking back to the seductions of the previous century (as in Stevens, Tissot, Madrazo y Garreta). The peignoir, as we shall see, was one of the items of dress most heavily charged with meaning for painters.

After that, a woman would choose a fitted suit of dark material, her riding costume, if she indulged in that sport with its very British form of chic; in that case she would either own a horse or hire one at the Bois de Boulogne. To depict women on horseback was a sure sign of Parisian sophistication in a painter. A fashion print signed Jules David (Compiègne, Musée du Second Empire) shows the empress in a riding habit. De Nittis excelled at these evocations of society life, but Manet, too, showed an

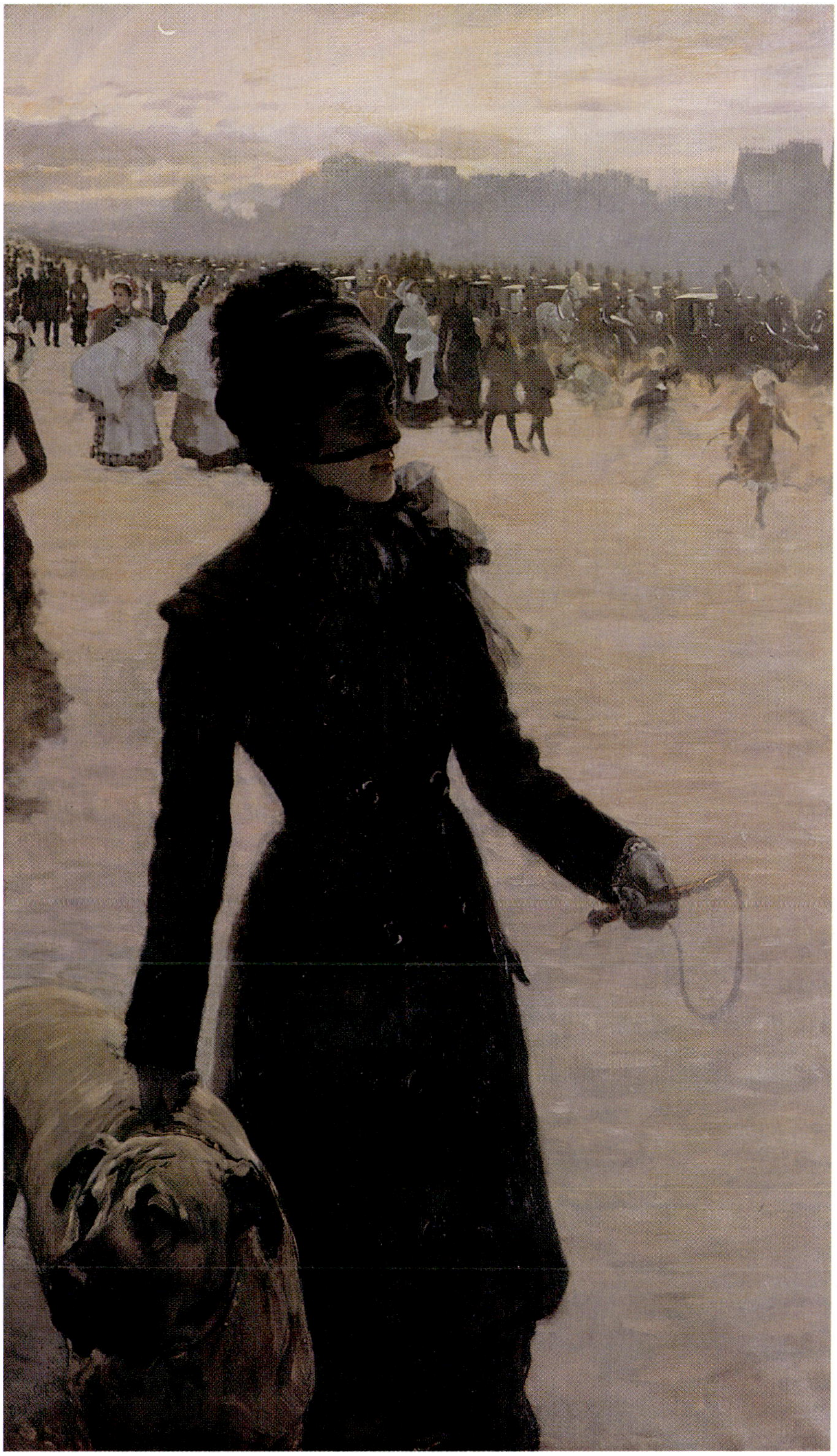

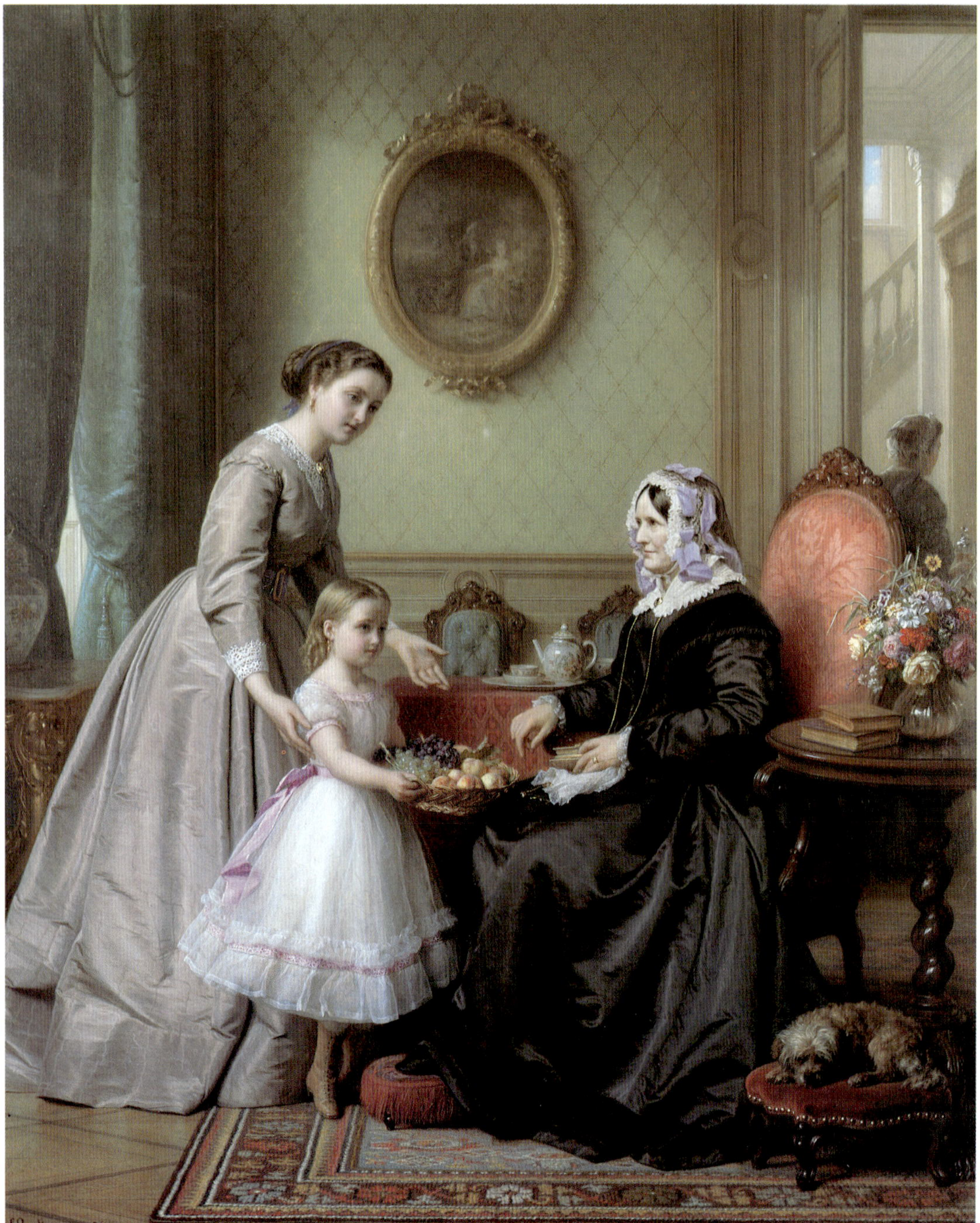

Joseph Laurens Dykmans, Interior, *1867. The Victoria and Albert Museum, London.*

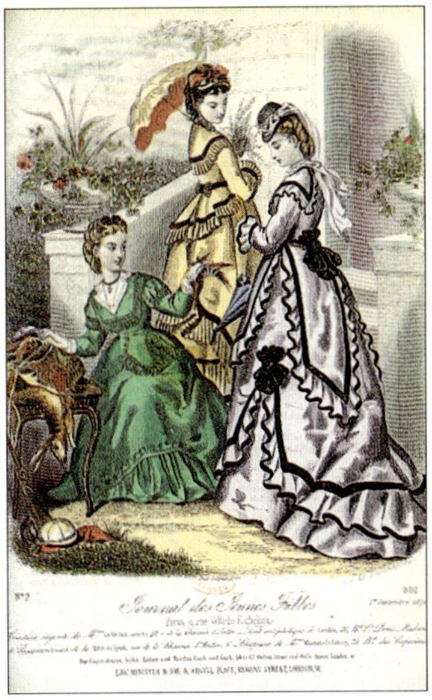

Le Journal des jeunes filles, *indoor outfit, outdoor outfit and town outfit, 1 September 1870 (left).*

La Revue de la mode: *In the Wood, 1889 (right).*

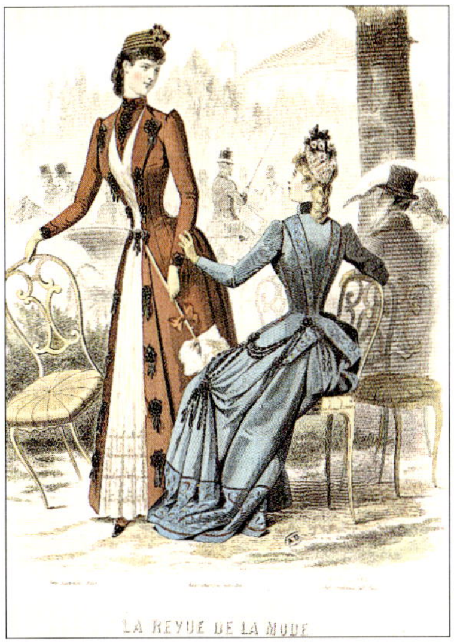

unexpected attachment to them. A town outfit enabled a lady to make her morning outings and pay visits to 'intimates'. This day dress was distinguished by 'simplicity and a kind of chasteness';[7] it was 'correct, without superfluous ornaments', and was accompanied only by a matching hat and gloves.

Social visits in the afternoon (between three o'clock and half-past five) required a costume that was one note higher on the scale of sophistication. The choice of accessories was governed by the type of visit: social visits, ceremonial visits (New Year's Day, engagement, condolences, etc. and so on. These nuances of dress are imperceptible to us, ignorant as we are of this scale of etiquette. We can easily identify a 'courtesy visit paid to a person of higher rank', thanks to an ostentatious train. We also need to know that violet was appropriate for young engaged girls, and that it was better to wear 'only plain dresses, or those protected by an apron, in the street',[8] that it was polite to keep on one's shawl and hat during a ceremonial visit which offered neither the time nor the privacy needed to 'consult a mirror in order to adjust your hair, or to be helped in straightening your shawl'.[9]

The late afternoon was the time for another ritual, that of the promenade at the Bois de Boulogne, the Champs-Elysées or the Tuileries. For that occasion one had to wear a town dress, that was different again, depending whether the outing was on foot or by carriage. The victoria or barouche, the 'pedestal of eccentricity',[10] allowed an abundance of flounces, knots, lace, flowers and even gems, on an outfit almost as lavish as that required for a social visit;[11] this outfit was not allowed to be 'set down on the pavement'. Under no circumstances could a woman going out during the day infringe two basic rules: to wear a hat (a bareheaded woman was a member of the lower orders), and to cover the shoulders. Bare shoulders were reserved for evening attire which,

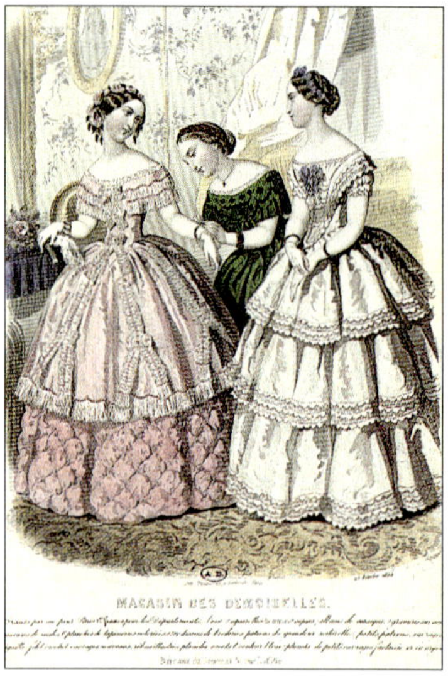

Le Magasin des demoiselles, *outfit for a ball, outfit for an evening party or the theatre, outfit for a ball or grand evening party, February 1854 (left).*

Disdéri, Madame Bonnet, *1859. Musée d'Orsay, Paris (right).*

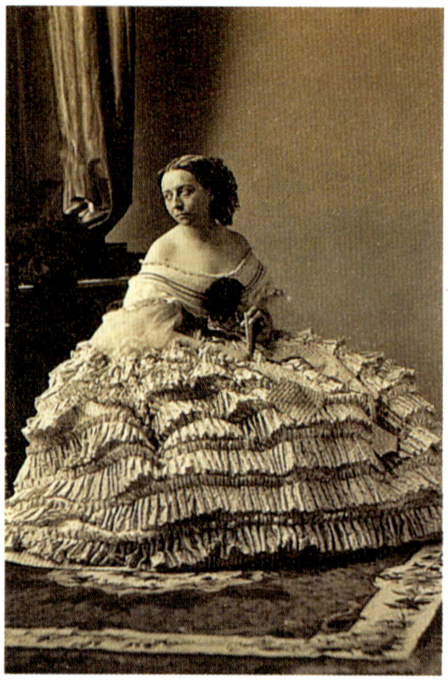

unlike daytime dress which tended towards 'increasing enclosure', followed the opposite tendency towards greater exposure. Here, too, there was a complex array of possibilities, depending on whether one was going to the theatre, to the Opéra, to a small or large dinner party, to a soirée or to a ball. For a dinner or a *soirée*, gowns were not *décolleté*, shoulders were never exposed, and dress had to be relatively sober with regard to trimming and flowers. Colours had symbolic value: 'Very young ladies choose colours of every soft nuance: "Finland sky", faded pink, etc., or pure white. Older women first wear red, then yellow, and finally black.'[12] In 1870 Jules Claretie, as if to echo Marguerite d'Aincourt in the preceding quotation, commented as follows on Charles Chaplin's portrait of Mme D., who was no doubt wearing one of those 'faded pink' dresses:

> Misfortune has decreed that the sitter is –how shall I put it without offending anyone? – more 'mature' than that of M. Jalabert. The age of M. Chaplin's subject is no longer really suited to these half-childish disguises. I am aware that the lady is powdered, still attractive and has adorable pink hands. But her dress is pink too, her fan is blue and her soft colours are slightly out of place.[12]

A praiseworthy attempt at tact on the critic's part, towards one of fashion's victims.

> A large dinner party, being generally followed by a reception, usually requires women to be in full evening dress; that is to say, their hair is embellished with diamonds, flowers or lace, but never a hat; a *décolleté* dress with short sleeves is worn; and sometimes a scarf, a cape or a fur stole may be thrown over the shoulders.[14]

With this costume– the ball gown –lavishness and *décolletage* knew no limits.

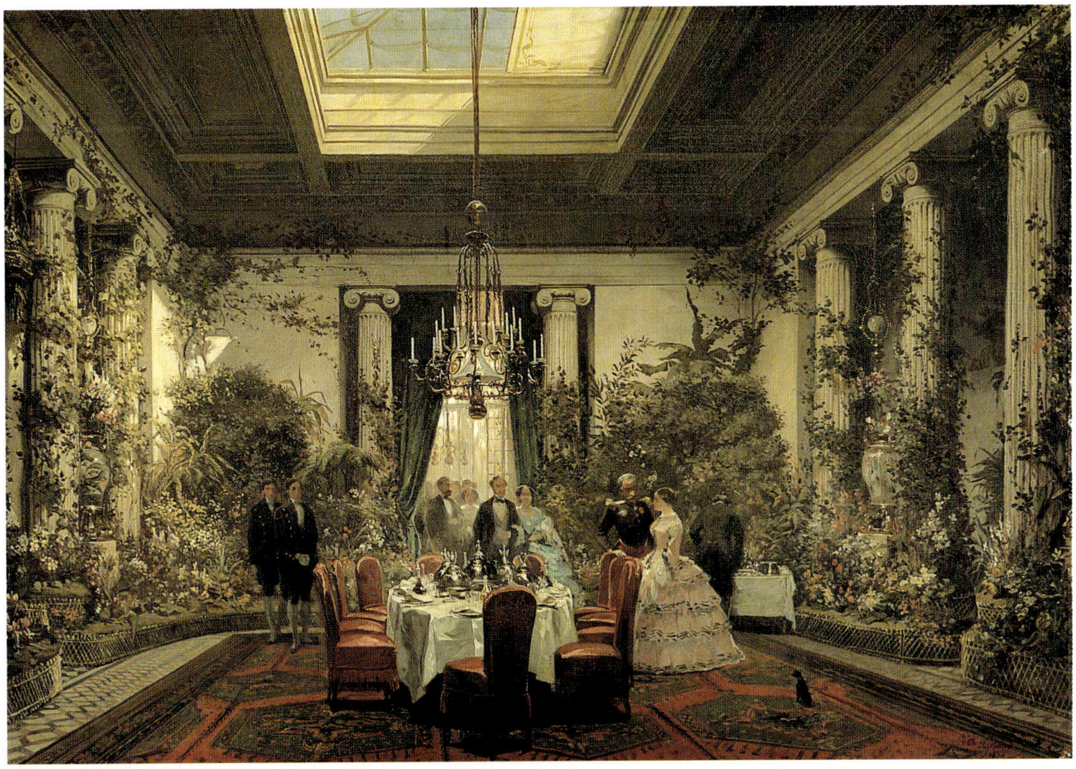

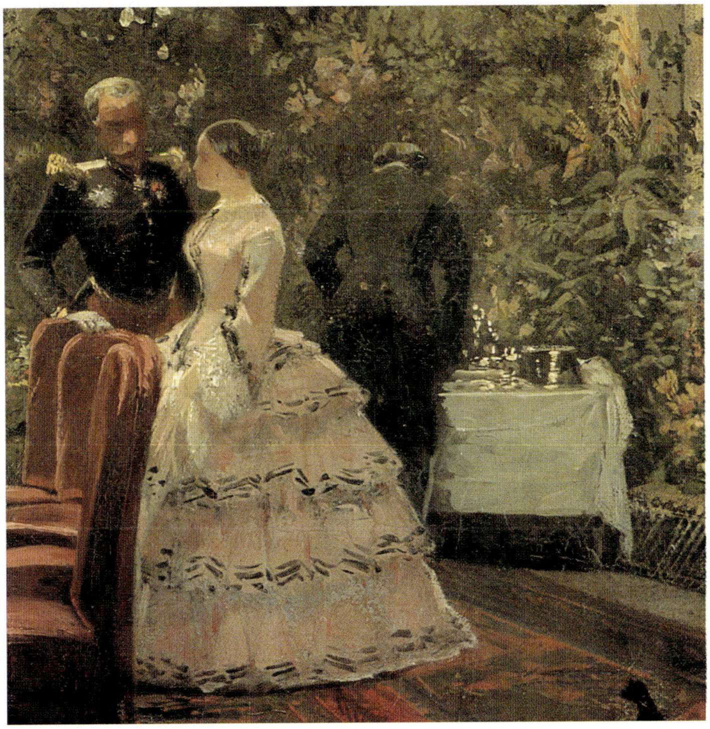

Charles Giraud,
Princess Mathilde's
dining-room, *1854*.
Musée du Second Empire,
Château de Compiègne.

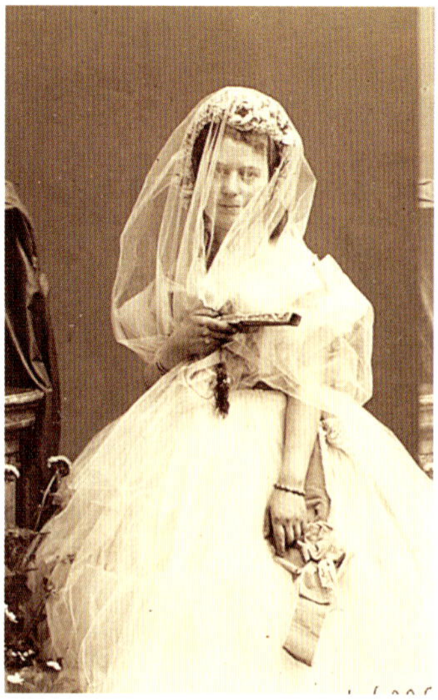

Disdéri,
Madame Huteau, *1859,*
Musée d'Orsay, Paris
(left).

Disdéri,
Madame Bartoleomucci, *1862.*
Musee d'Orsay, Paris
(right).

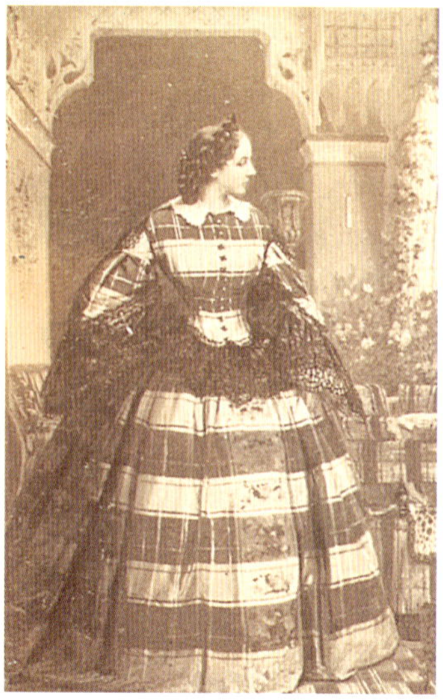

> Extreme elegance and supreme luxury are perfectly in order in the evening...It is essential for ball gowns to be very *décolleté* (skin fully exposed); short sleeves or none at al ...every rich material, all kinds of lace, all colours and all shades may be worn.[15]

From the 1860s, feathers or garlands of fruit or flowers adorned hair styled in elaborate chignons or falling artfully in ringlets. Just as one did not go out without a hat during the day, at a ball in the evening a woman whose hair was not carefully styled would have appeared very improper. A peculiarity of the Second Empire was its predilection for blond or red hair, in contrast to the passion for brunettes in the Romantic era. In 1837 Théophile Gautier dreamed of 'writing, contrary to the tendency of the time, a blonde novel or even, if it were possible, a redhead novel'.[16] This is probably an example of the frequent tendency within fashion for one excess to provoke its opposite; or it may reflect the influence of the fair hair of Empress Eugénie. All the women of the day dreamed of being ash-blondes, bleaching their hair with hydrogen peroxide. Nestor Roqueplan, a journalist and editor-in-chief of *Le Figaro*, even drew up a classification of shades of blonde which was prolix to say the least:

> From a tawny blond, slightly roseate where the corneous substance emerges from its root, to the king of blondness, rutile...which enriches the sunbeam, multiplying it with a prismatic play of light, the colour of the river Pactole, *rutili fontes*, and of the conquest of the Argonauts, *rutili pellis*, preferred by Titian, Veronese and Tintoretto.[17]

In 1864 the celebrated *demi-mondaine* Cora Pearl started a fashion for redheads. For a brief period women even reverted to the fashions of the *ancien régime* by powdering their hair. The vogue for false hair, too, was at its height in the second half of the nineteenth century.

This sophistication of dress, these exercises in dressing-up, went on uninterrupted throughout the year. Even in summer, at the seaside, the hectic rhythm was maintained.[18] One can readily imagine that these extensive wardrobes consumed large budgets. But rather than failing to conform, women fell back on dissimulation. Thus, the Press which addressed the lower-middle and middle classes was full of advice and stratagems for safeguarding an old dress or inventing dresses capable of adaptation:[19]

> Supposing that, for example, you have a dress of velvet, satin, faille or wool, black or any other colour, depending on your situation. If this dress is fresh, add a pretty adornment, a muslin and lace flounce sewn under the hem of the skirt, gloves matching the tint of the dress as closely as possible (excepting black ones); with this dress, depending on the richness of the cloth, you can wear light or half-tint gloves: that's all you need for your visiting outfit. You wish to use the same dress for a gala dinner, a soirée? Open it up as much as possible, embellish it with a pleated front, a ruff around the neck and a piece of lace laid flat below the ruff and forming a frill against the bodice.[20]

The search for variety of ornamentation was very symptomatic of fashion in the nineteenth century, which overloaded a basic form of relatively constant volume (fitted bodice, wide skirt) with details that created extra volumes, giving the impression of excrescences on the basic form.

The theatres of fashion

There are certain places where fashion is the focus of attention (for the French, until 1993, such a place was the Cour Carrée, the site of the fashion catwalks). In the nineteenth century such places, where the general public was on parade, were the principal means of diffusing new fashions. Journalists and couturiers frequented them to study the latest eccentricities. Conversely, couturiers sometimes sent a woman dressed by them to stroll there as a living advertisement. Descriptions of costumes 'seen' 'at the races', 'at the Opéra', 'at the Tuileries ball', or even 'at Mass', were essential to fashion reporting, other sources of information being the latest lines studied at couturiers' houses. These reports were never accompanied by illustrations, so that the reader needed to have some imagination if she was to picture the dresses evoked. Is this why the language was so precise and detailed, and why the descriptive approach seemed diametrically opposed to our own? One cannot fail to be surprised when

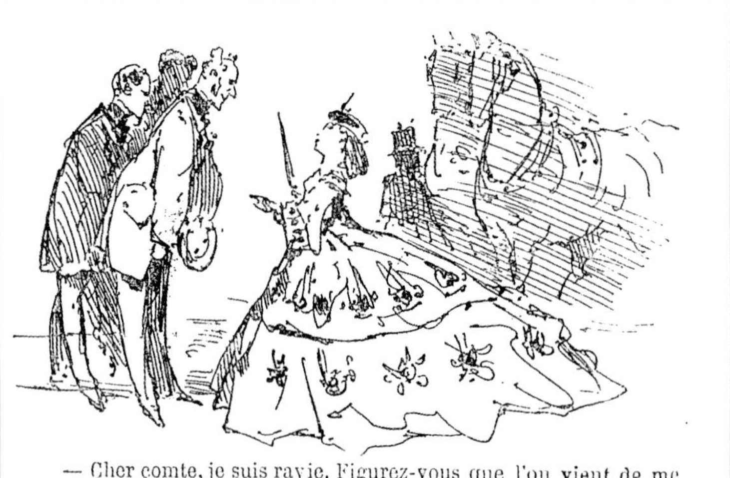

La Vie parisienne, *'Dear Count, I am delighted. Can you imagine, I have just been taken for a cocotte', 29 October 1864.*

looking at a nineteenth-century print and the accompanying commentary. At first sight, the text does not seem to bear any relation to the image. This distortion is the result of the mode of description, which invariably proceeds from top to bottom, starting with the hat and bodice and moving down to the skirt, and gives priority to detail before arriving at the general. Our contemporary eye first sees a silhouette, unencumbered by the perception of details and accessories. To describe a sleeve before stating the type of garment to which it belongs (tailored suit or dress), following a figure of speech not unlike synecdoche, is investing the detail with a significance the garment as a whole might be unable to sustain.

On the other hand, women had the privilege, now vanished, of being able to adopt a fashion as soon as it came out. There was no time-lag in the season: fashions were created, worn and admired simultaneously. The strategic places where fashions were shown were widely accessible, but one had to be there at the right time, on the right day and at correct hour.[21] Since the beginning of the century the Bois de Boulogne had been a marvellous observation post; there was a daily performance, proceeding from the Champs-Elysées to the Etoile and finishing at the lake, where the congested carriages allowed the observer, like Maxime and Renée in La Curée, to 'undress at leisure the women displayed in the nearby coupés and landaus'.[22] Many society painters, such as Lami, De Nittis and Boldini, tried to capture the fleeting, elegant atmosphere of these open-air salons, whereas the Impressionists (excepting Manet) turned to the anonymity of the street, both by inclination but also because they were not part of the fashionable milieux.

In general, the season took the following course: after the return of Parisian ladies who had spent the autumn at their châteaux in the country, it began gently with the

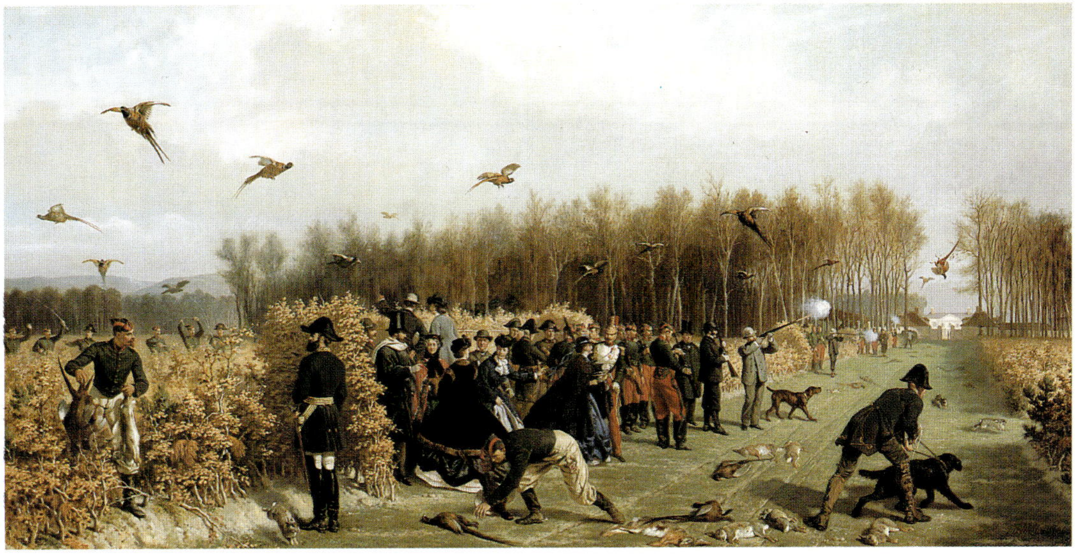

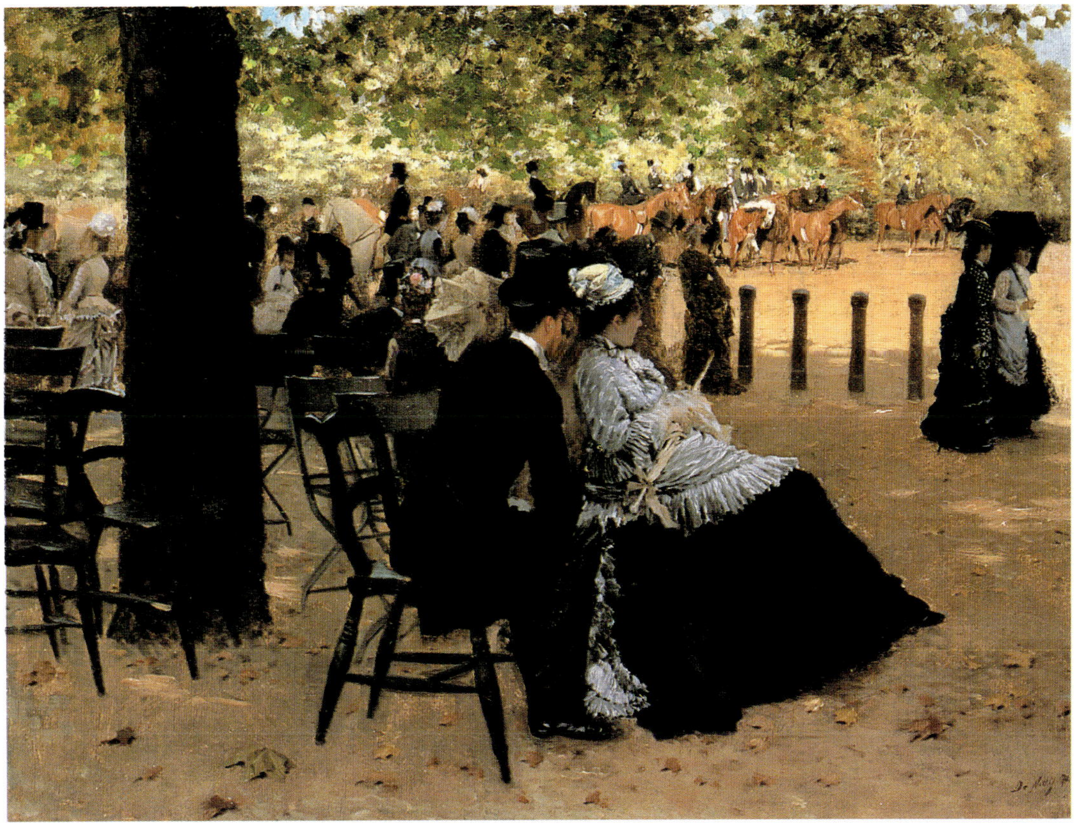

Ange Louis Janet-Lange, The Pheasant-shooting party, *no date. Musée du Second Empire, Château de Compiègne (above).*
Giuseppe De Nittis, At the Races, *1874. Private Collection (below).*

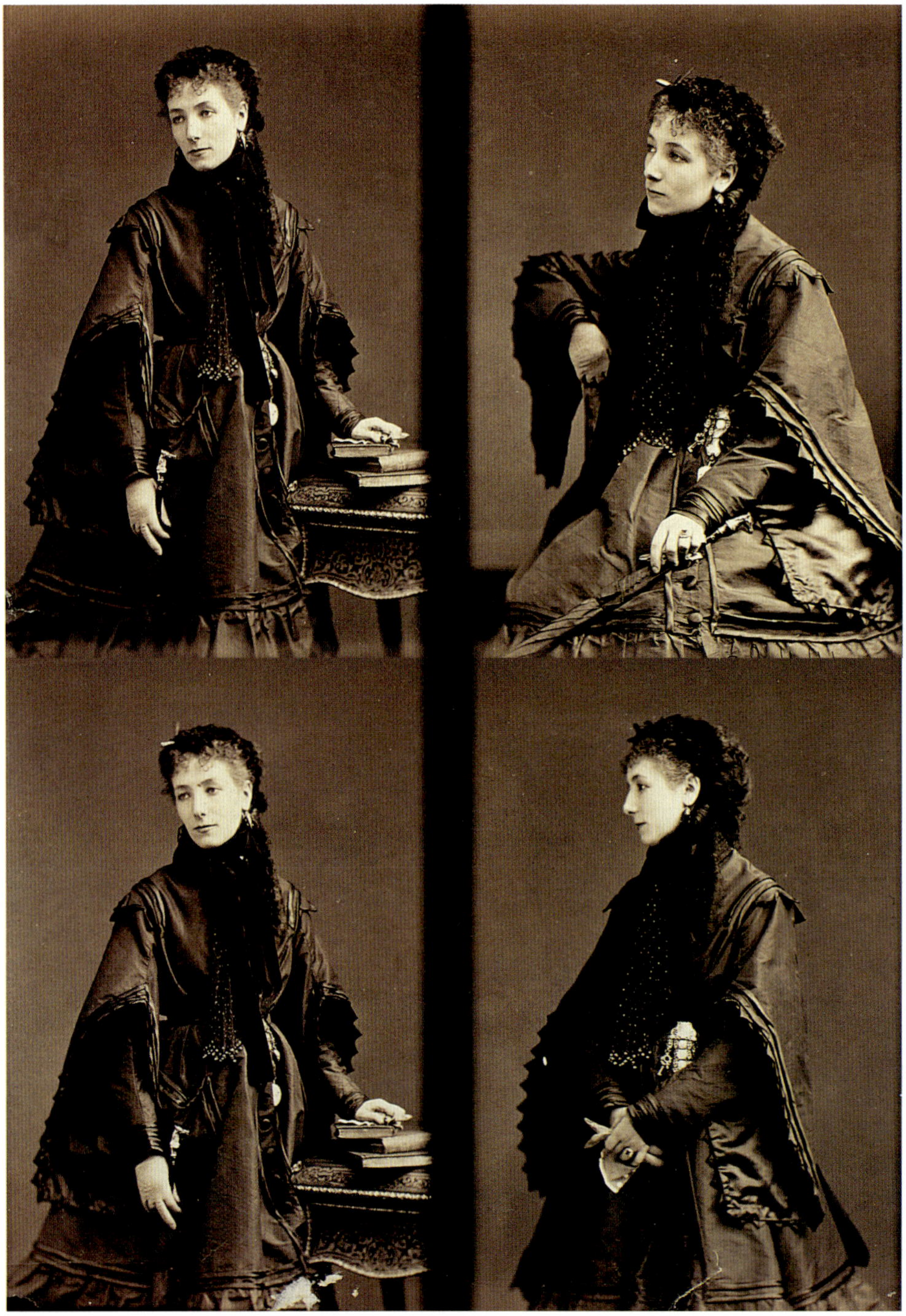

Disdéri, Sarah Bernhardt, *no date. Musée d'Orsay, Paris.*
Le Petit Courrier des dames, *Two Women by a race-course, 3 June 1854 (facing page,left).*
La Mode illustrée: *theatre fashions,1879 (facing page, right).*

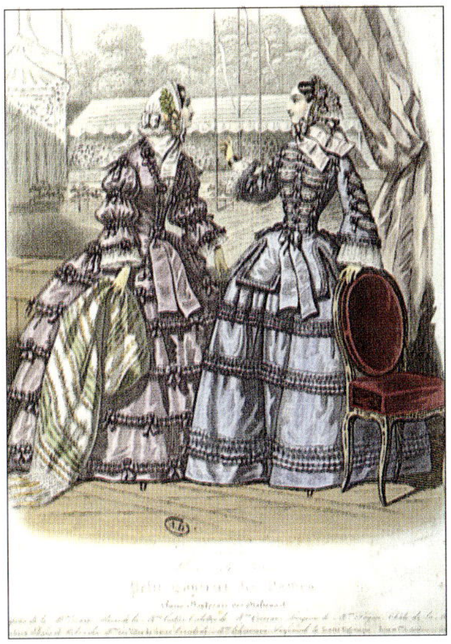

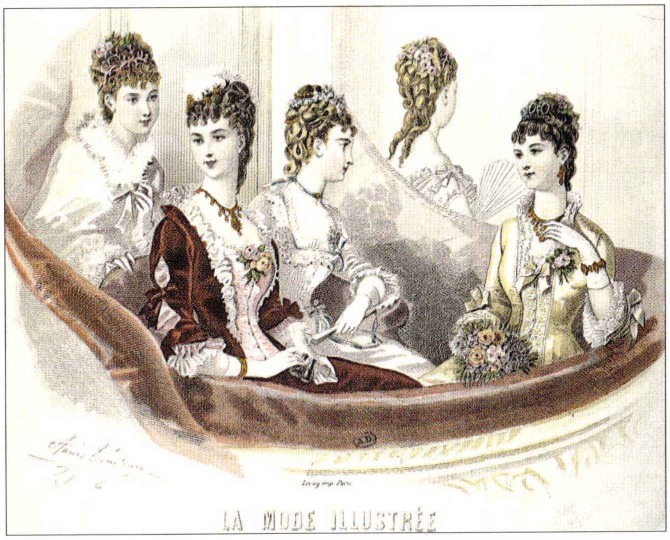

official reception at Compiègne and the October and November balls. The most important month was January, with the Grand Bal des Tuileries and the first masked ball at the Opéra. From late March to late May the spring fashions were launched at the races at Longchamp and at the Jockey Club at Chantilly. The major steeplechase at Auteuil in June set the trends for the summer. However, the races became more and more the preserve of the *demi-monde*, high society preferring the intimacy of fashionable soirées. Then, to follow fashion from July to early September, one had to move to 'the waters' (Trouville, Spa, Baden, Dieppe, or, at the end of the century, Biarritz and Monaco).

In addition to these main events of the season, the balls and salons of the great ladies, the exhibitions and entertainments, indeed the whole of society life was a subject of study and a pretext for parade. The theatre gradually took on a special role: fashion was displayed not only in the auditorium but on stage, especially after the start of the Third Republic. In modern plays by Octave Feuillet or Victorien Sardou, Sarah Bernhardt was dressed by Worth and Réjane by Doucet. Fashion quite naturally took over the place most advantageous for its display, the place where human dreams and desires were enacted.[23]

The great bluffers

If actresses created fashion, they nevertheless had serious rivals: society women. These women with solidly established social positions – the Comtesse de Pourtalès, Princesses Mathilde, Radziwill and Sagan – acquired the gift of dressing well by birth. That they had access to the latest styles is beyond question. However, good taste required them to show some moderation with regard to fashion. 'A society woman is one who knows how to dress with a certain elegance, without being too far behind or to far ahead of the current mode.'[24]

Propriety 'applauds the woman of good sense and good taste who does not rush to follow new fashions, considers their likely duration before adopting them, and chooses and modifies them successfully in keeping with her size and figure'.[25] To pay too much attention to fashion would amount to a 'disregard for their class status of mythological proportions'.[26] The *demi-monde* of cocottes (kept women), actresses, social upstarts and *cocodettes* (women who have lost their social position through the scandal of a divorce or an affair), was not cramped by the strict rules of morality. It had the brazenness and freedom to launch a new style with aplomb. This phenomenon is clearly evoked in Zola's *Nana*:

> When she rode along the boulevards in her carriage, the crowd turned and said her name with the excitement of a populace saluting its sovereign, while she, reclining in her airy attire, smiled gaily...Supple as an eel, her scanty dress seeming both artful and negligent, exquisitely elegant, she had the highly-strung distinction of a pedigree cat. With the aristocratic haughtiness of vice she set her foot defiantly on Paris as its all-powerful mistress. She set the tone, and the great ladies imitated her.[27]

High society and the *demi-monde*, therefore, were jealous rivals. *La Vie parisienne* (an emancipated society journal) of 1863 gives a humorous description of an encounter between a society lady and a former actress at a fashion house they both patronized (Worth, no doubt). After spying on each other nervously, they each asked the shop-girl where the other came from. When she heard the reply, 'the Marquise's face lit up. What did this insolent beauty matter to her, now that she knew she would never have to meet her? Perhaps the actress had guessed her thoughts, for she gave her a big, challenging smile. Who said that she needed to go into society to compete with the noble Marquise?'[28]

High society, the *monde*, was sure of its rights, as fashion was still regarded as a prerogative of the aristocracy; but it sometimes hankered after the 'forbidden fruit' of an easy seduction. As for the *demi-monde*, fashion gave it a new feeling of power, and of strongholds to be taken.

Between these two spheres floundered the bourgeois wife who aspired only to a genteel mode of life modelled on that of the aristocracy. Terrified of committing the gaffe that would expose her, she devoured etiquette manuals in her efforts to learn the social syntax that came so naturally to the class which imposed it and was so baffling to her:

> Two women dressed in the same way will involuntarily betray their difference of blood. The manner of wearing a hat tilted more or less backward [is revealing]; it is

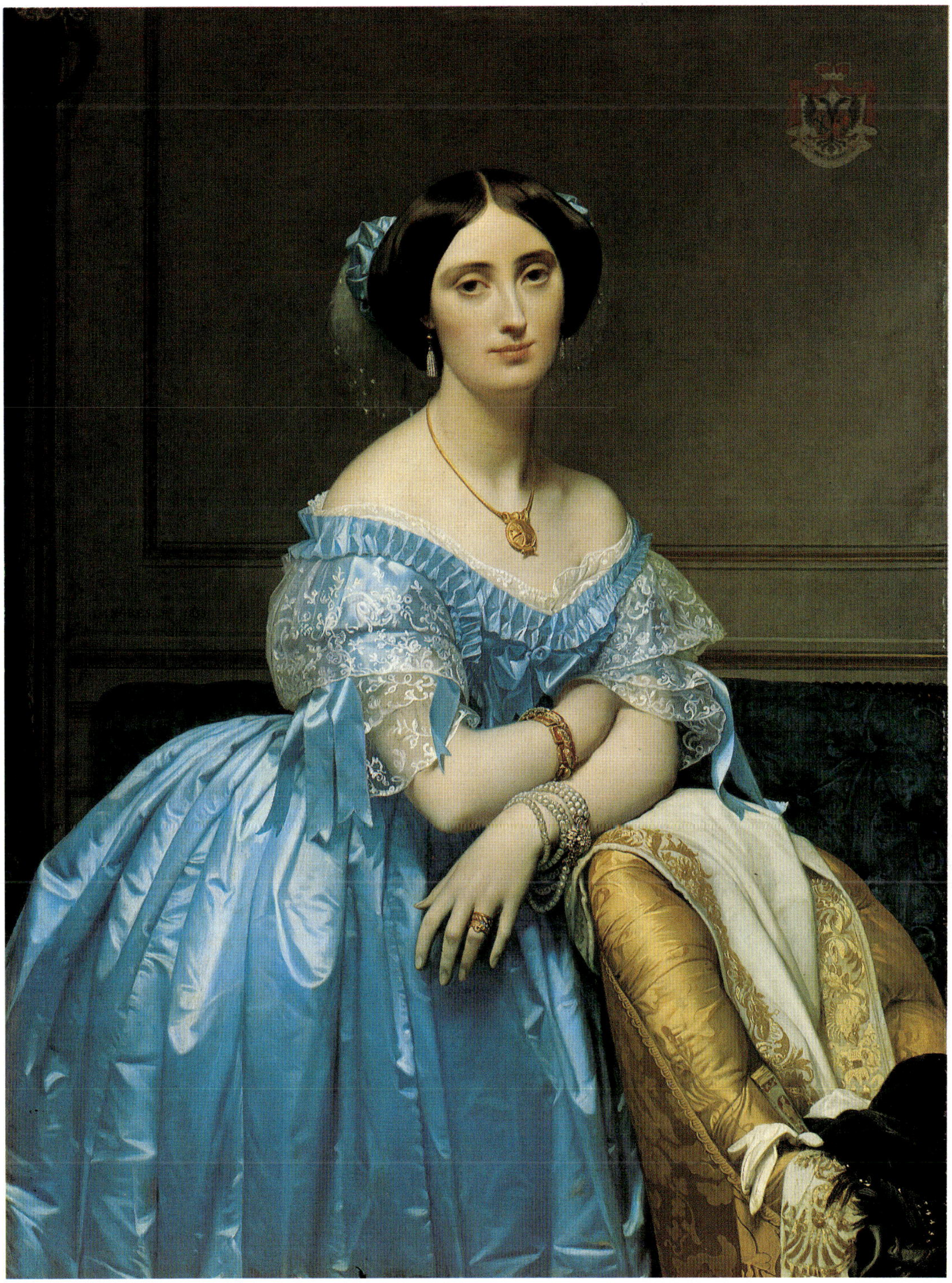

Jean-Auguste-Dominique Ingres, The Princesse de Broglie, *1853.*
The Metropolitan Museum of Art, New York (detail, page 38).

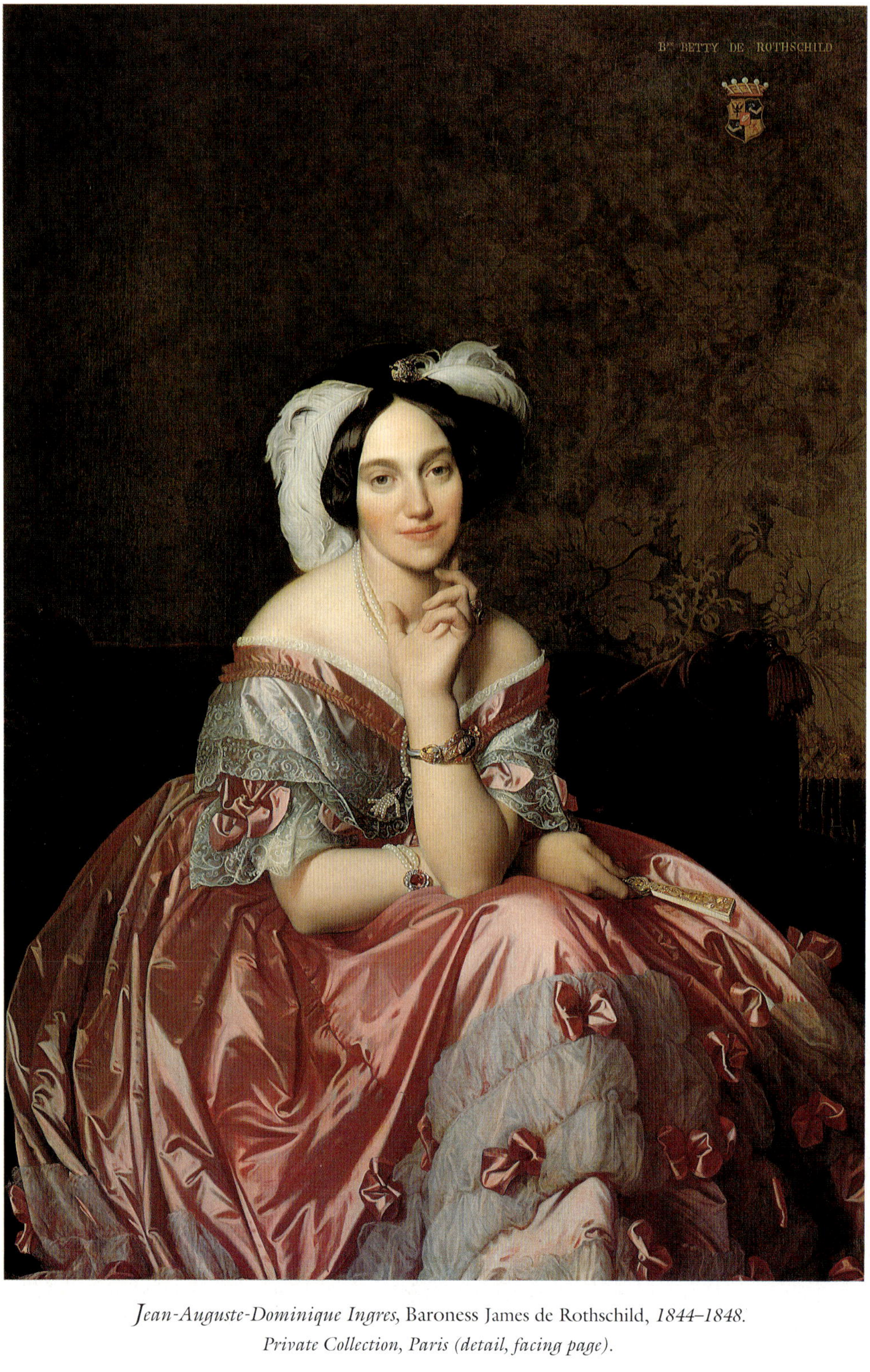

Jean-Auguste-Dominique Ingres, Baroness James de Rothschild, *1844–1848.*
Private Collection, Paris (detail, facing page).

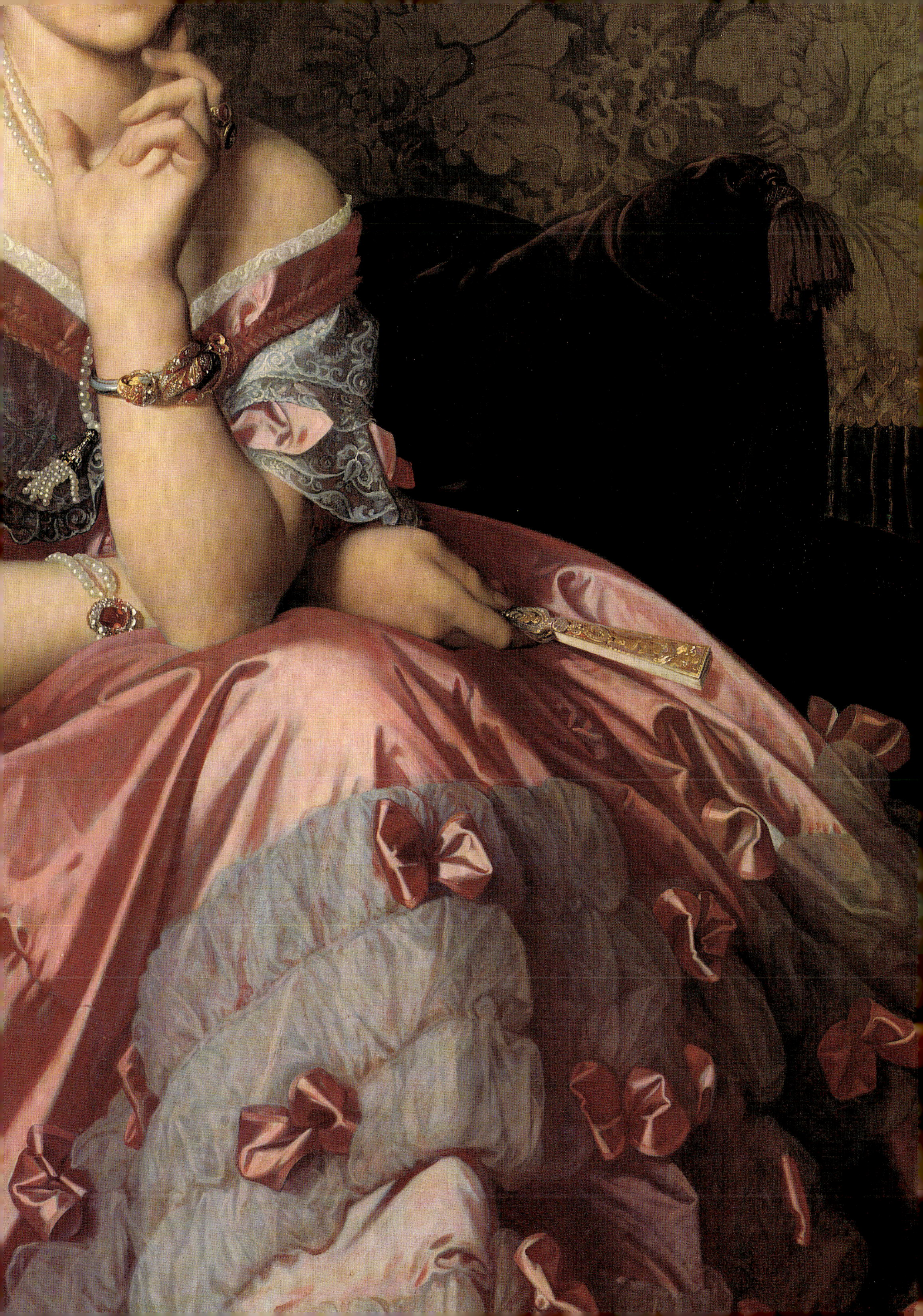

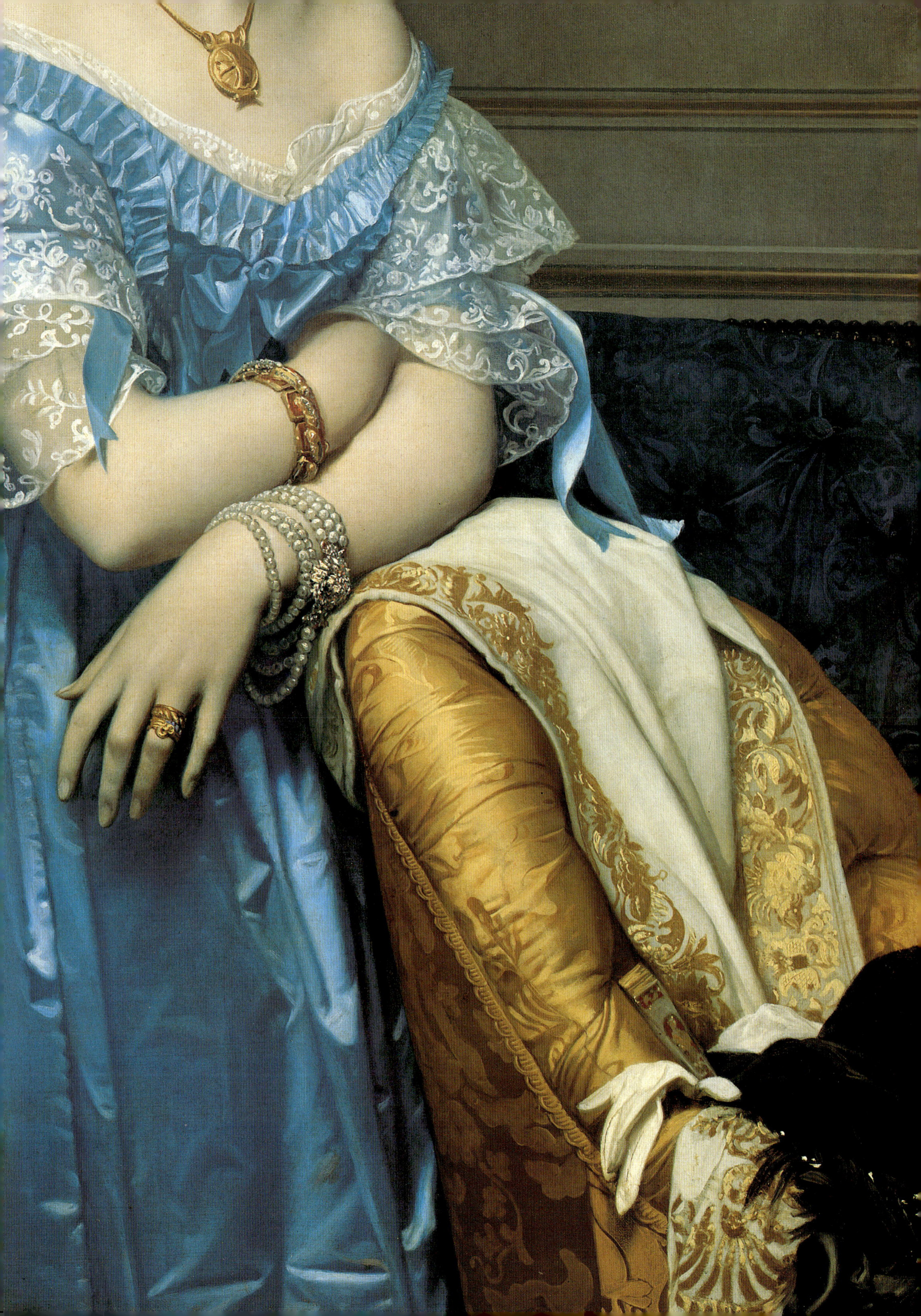

> no less difficult to wear a mantelet or to step down on to the pavement. The manner of holding a handkerchief is an indelible sign to which so many women aspire and only a single class among them can carry off as a *grande dame*. All this forms an indestructible inheritance which a woman of high society has received from her mother
> and will leave to her children, an intangible vengeance which everyone has seen begin and no-one will see end.[29]

Does painting, and especially the portrait, reveal these 'differences of blood'? It is instructive to compare two roughly contemporary female portraits by Ingres, the *Portrait of the Baronne de Rothschild* (1848, private coll.) and that of the *Princesse de Broglie* (1853, New York, Metropolitan Museum of Art, Lehman Coll.). Despite the sitters' apparent membership of the same class, do the portraits reveal two different ways of presenting oneself in society?

The two women are wearing ball gowns which are extremely similar. They have the same form of *décolleté*, the same sleeves embellished with lace and ribbons, the same satin material, pink for the Baronne de Rothschild and blue for the Princesse de Broglie. Each of them wears jewellery: for the Baronne, a pearl necklace and bracelet on her right arm and a silver bracelet encrusted with precious stones on her left; for the Princesse, a rather simple gold necklace adorned with a medallion in the shape of the Maltese cross, a bracelet of gold and jewels less extravagant and of a more irregular size than those of the Baronne, and another of pearls (replacing, incidentally, two rattan bracelets which appear in the black-lead drawing belonging to the Comte d'Haussonville) and, finally, a pair of earrings.

In his *Voyage à travers l'exposition des Beaux-Arts de 1855*, Edmond About gives us a description of the Princesse de Broglie:

> Madame la Princesse de Broglie is refined, delicate, elegant to her fingertips...a marvellous incarnation of nobility. Her pose alone would reveal her descent even if the delicacy of her features did not give it away. Around this exquisite beauty the painter has omitted nothing that could heighten its effect. He has signed both her dress and her furnishings, that exterior *toilette*. The satin of her robe, the gems, the lace and the marabou feathers in her hair have a Chinese precision and an English elegance. M. Muller has been highly praised for his skill in painting silks. But when one has seen the dress of Mme la Princess de Broglie, all M. Muller's silks look as if they had been bought second-hand at a market stall.[30]

What gives rise to this feeling of a 'marvellous incarnation of nobility'? Edmond About insists it is the sitter's pose; the Princesse de Broglie's body is in three-quarter view, her arms delicately crossed and resting on the back of an armchair on which have been cast a gold-embroidered white shawl, a fan and a black hat or opera cloak adorned with feathers (these last details are difficult to read). The Baronne de Rothschild is also in three-quarter view, with her head facing us, but her pose is different, more coquetish.

She sits cross-legged, her left hand against her throat, in a gesture close to that of the Comtesse d'Haussonville in her portrait by Ingres (1845, New York, Frick Collection). She has the intent, absent-minded look of someone who has been suddenly distracted from a conversation.

Her position places in the foreground the hem of her dress with three ruffled tulle borders decorated with satin bows, which are seen as scattered points at each side of the painting. By attracting our gaze this skirt draws us closer to the sitter, whereas the Princesse de Broglie dominates the beholder, commanding distance and respect. The hem of her skirt is not seen, so that there is no superfluous ornamentation to distractthe eye. Another element, apart from the satin bows, underlines the relative frivolity of the Baronne's dress, while giving it a certain ponderousness. This is the hat she is wearing, a large black hat with white feathers which, compared to the delicate, airy marabou feathers, looks out of place, almost in bad taste, and certainly incongruous: hats were excluded from the ballroom, hair being embellished with bows, garlands and so on. This impression is further underlined by the similarity of the women's hair, both in style and colour. Is Ingres telling us, in these three almost extraneous details of costume (slightly more complicated jewellery, tulle bows and ruffles, an indiscreet hat), of the sometimes overdone luxury and coquetry of a social class? The 'exterior toilette' formed by the furnishings also speaks of the difference: on one hand the heavy, garnet-red velvet of Mme de Rothschild, on the other the luminous yellow damask of the Princesse de Broglie.

THE WELL-BRED LADY

Codes of dress redefined new distinctions. They were a means of both recognition and exclusion: recognition of members of the same society, exclusion of those (even if they were part of it) who had not perfectly mastered the social syntax.

In *Les Parisiens comme ils sont*[31] Balzac defined the new social scale. At the top is the 'woman of distinction...descended from the ranks of the nobility or pushed up from the bourgeoisie'; she is 'the one who knows'. Then come the *demi-monde* and the social upstarts, flashy and flamboyant; then, she who 'does not know': the bourgeoise, bundled up in her dress and 'admirably versed in the redundancies of *toilette*'. Finally, the woman from the provinces, 'recognisable by the scantiness of detail in her person and dress', is at the bottom of the scale of fashion, which she adopts when it is at least three years out of date.

The very definite social geography of Paris allowed these differences to be located in specific districts. As Mme Emile de Girardin noted in 1839: 'The chaussée d'Antin proposes, the faubourg Saint-Honoré adopts, the faubourg Saint-Germain consecrates and the Marais executes and buries.'[32] The chaussée d'Antin, the financial quarter, was inhabited by rich bourgeois women and cocottes whom their husbands were launching in society. The women of the chaussée d'Antin displayed a certain 'sartorial panache as an effect of wealth', while taking care not to lapse into the extravagance of the upstarts of the faubourg Saint-Honoré[33] The faubourg Saint-Germain, by contrast, was the haven of the old aristocracy where good taste was indicated by a sober disinterest in fashion (note in this connection Proust's disappointment at finding the Duchesse de Guermantes preoccupied by her ball dress, a sign of 'forgetting her native grandeur'; or the encounter between the Duchesse and the Princesse de Guermantes at a *soirée* at the Opéra: 'One had the impression that the Duchesse, who was said to poke fun at what she called her cousin's exaggerations, had guessed that the Princesse ... was to wear that evening one of those toilettes which the Duchesse considered to be "fancy dress", and that she had meant to give her a lesson in taste.')[34] Here, too, Mme de Girardin gives us valuable insight:

> If an elegant lady from the chaussée d'Antin goes to a ball held by a banker of the former rue du Mont Blanc attired in a dress adorned with eight flounces...the eight flounces will be envied by the rival dresses which only have four, five or six. To have eight flounces is to say: I do things more grandly than you, I am elegant to the eighth degree...But suppose, on the other hand, that this lady, before arriving at the ball, pays a visit...to pure faubourg Saint-Germain...can you imagine the effect of those eight flounces in a world so noble and charitably reasonable? Those eight flounces will cause a scandal, such gaudy attire will offend everyone's good taste.[35]

It is worthwhile disentangling the reality from the fantasy that underlies this kind of discourse. These codes of etiquette, the assertions in manuals or the Press, were written for the most part by women from the aristocracy and addressed to the lower-middle or middle class, or to upstarts such as the 'elegant lady from the chaussée d'Antin'. They accentuated and embellished a distinction that was becoming less and less obtrusive, in a way which could only disconcert their readers. In an attempt to restrict access to an elegance which was being more and more widely shared, the aristocracy consented to an alliance with the upper bourgeoisie (as Balzac shows very clearly) in order to ensnare their common rival in the labyrinth of a prolific, demanding wardrobe.[36]

And, indeed, how could one not feel disconcerted by so many different styles of

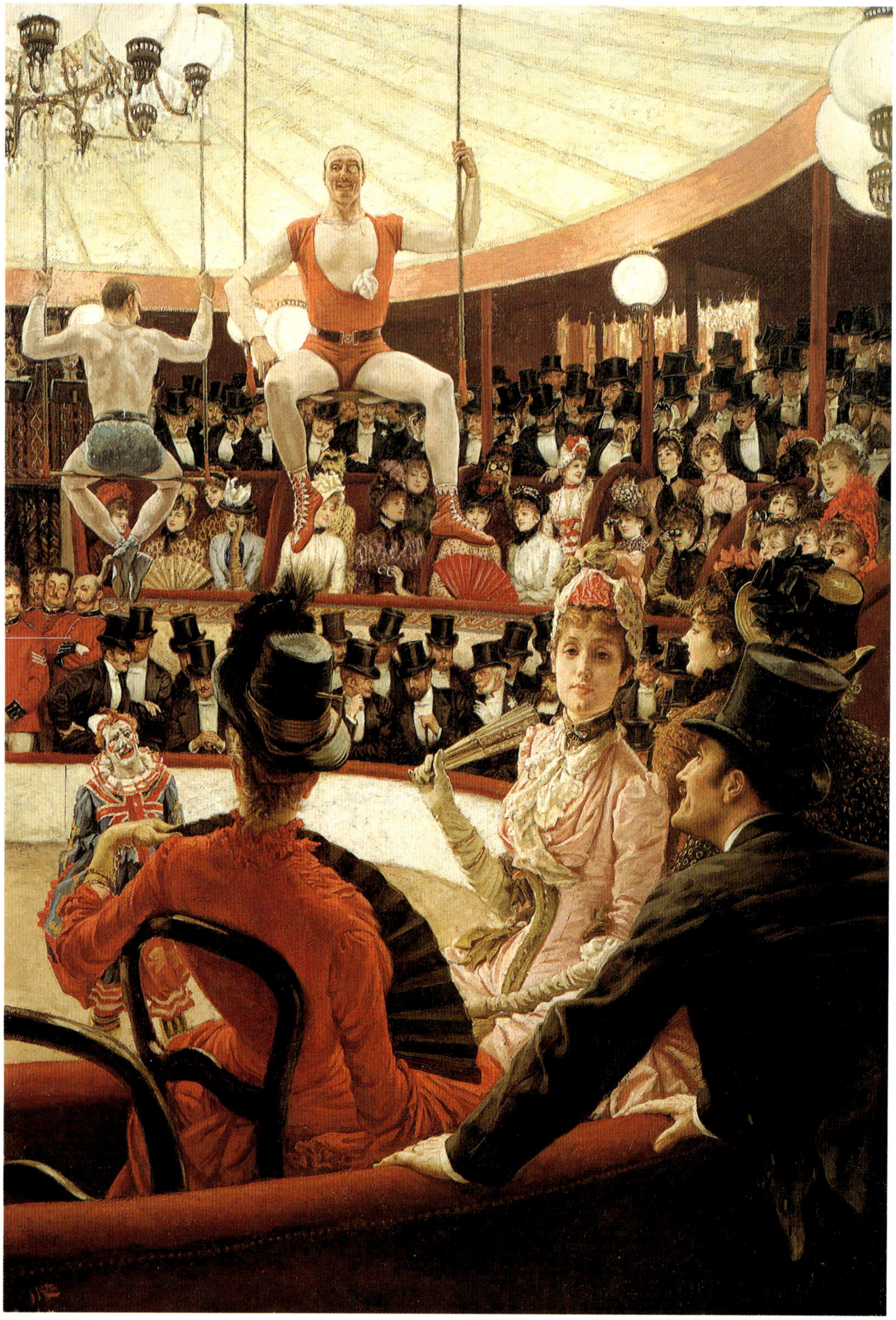

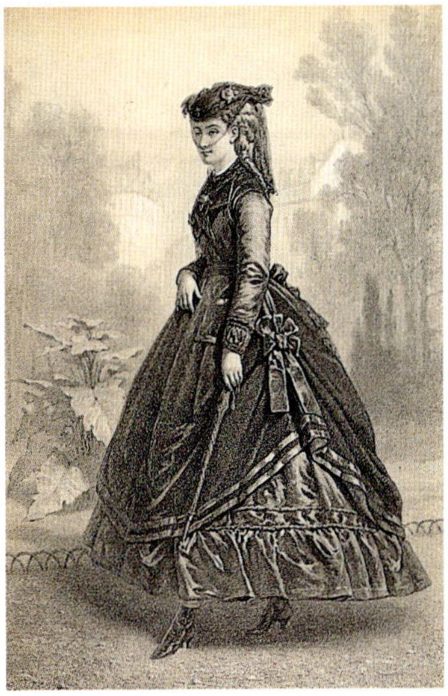

James Tissot,
The Sportswomen,
1883–1885.
Museum of Fine Arts,
Juliana Cheney Edwards
Collection, Boston
(facing page).

La Foulhouze,
La Cocodette,
no date
(left).

Le Moniteur de la mode,
Ball outfit and visiting
clothes, 1853
(right).

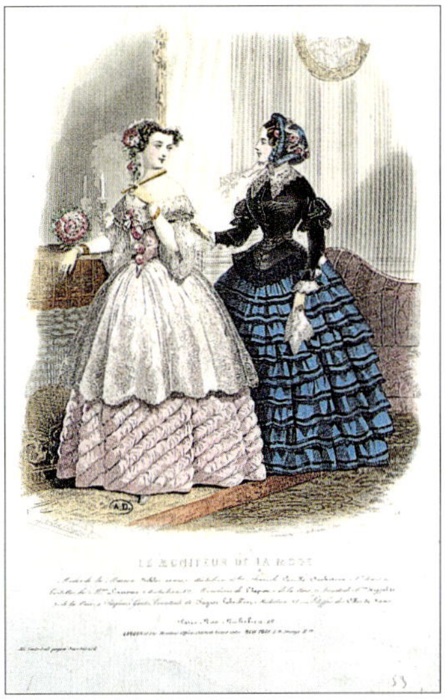

dress, so many signs threatening to give one away and cause one's ruin? The nineteenth-century woman was beset on one side by fear of the flashy excesses of the cocotte and on the other by the timorous, ridiculous drabness of the provincial. Poor woman from the provinces, always informed about Paris fashions one year late,[37] and thus inevitably out of fashion, while also being recognisable, according to the Goncourts, by her 'flustered and eternal fear of ridicule'.[38] Baudelaire, in *La Fanfarlo*, gives a fine evocation of these poor provincial creatures floundering in the trammels of social convention: Mme de Cosmelly is abandoned by her husband for an actress (another cliché of the time), *La Fanfarlo*. She tells the hero of the novel about the revolutions she has instigated in her wardrobe to bring her husband to his senses.

> Instead of the dark, simple dresses that used to please his eye, I have worn giddy, sumptuous outfits like theatre women. I, the chaste spouse he came to seek in an impoverished château, have paraded before him in the clothes of a courtesan, I have made myself witty and skittish when my heart was breaking. I spangled my despair with tinsel smiles. Alas! He saw nothing. I put on rouge, Monsieur, I put on rouge! As you see, it's a commonplace story, the story of all unhappy women, a novel of the provinces![39]

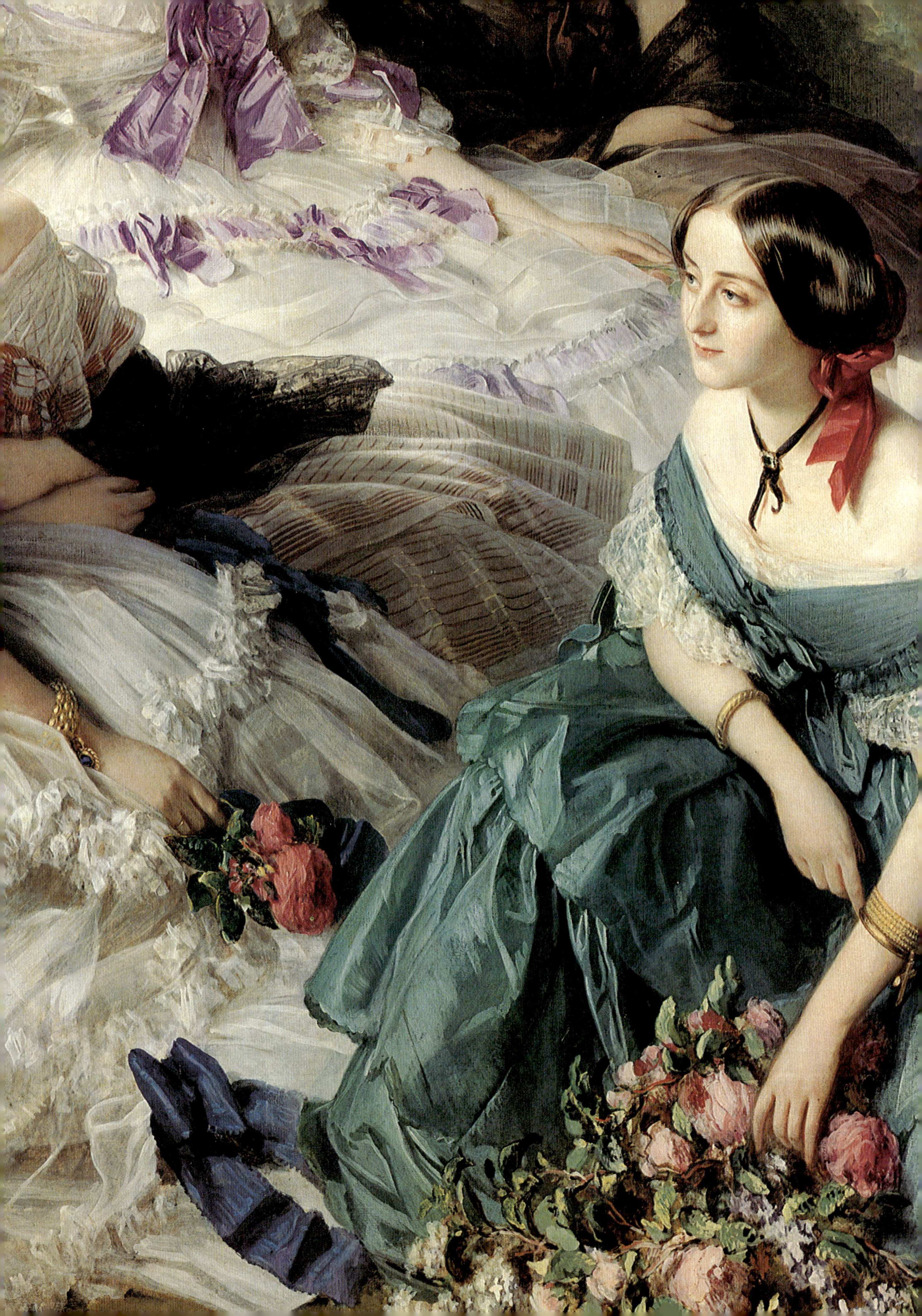

The crinoline 1850–70

Feminine costume began the nineteenth century in emphatic style with a total transformation of fashion. At that time, high-waisted, supple, simplified dresses, inspired by the art of ancient Greece, were evolving towards a new freedom. This line, following the body more closely, had not been seen since the fifteenth century. However, with the restoration of the Bourbons in 1814 fashion did an about-turn, reverting to the conventional (reassuring?) combination of a fitted bodice and a voluminous skirt. This basic form remained unchanged throughout the latter part of the century.

From 1850 to 1900 three main silhouettes were developed within this framework: the crinoline, the bustle and the bell skirt. This amplitude was eclipsed only once in a brief interval between 1876 and 1882, when a more clinging style was adopted. Each of the three shapes underwent developments and modifications, and there were also some innovations: the princess style (a dress in one piece adopting the shape of the moment, crinoline or bustle), the short skirt (down to the ankle, but controversial nevertheless!), the *costume-tailleur* (tailored jacket over a long skirt) and baggy trousers (part of the cyclist's outfit).

Apart from these variations, fashion was characterized by rigidity. Many authors have underlined the fact that it was corseted, closed, enveloping, but it could not exactly be called modest. It was also distinguished by a certain Baroque quality. It was ornamental, massive, excessive in the exaggeration and incongruity of its forms. It was embellished with acid or dark colours, often in clashing combinations; and it was strongly tinged with artificiality. Yes, it was thoroughly Baroque, and probably had to be if it was to be so thoroughly scrutinized, analyzed and admired.

The crinoline expanded, took over completely, then shrank again during the first two decades of the second half of the century. This longevity was against all expectations, since, quite apart from its main detractors (humorists, doctors, moralists, etc.), many fashion chroniclers had pronounced it ridiculous and predicted its early demise. Despite these reservations, the crinoline went through three different developments: first it spread out to the sides, like the hoop petticoats of the eighteenth century; then it extended backwards; finally, it was gathered up in a cone.

The word *crinoline* originates from a sixteenth-century fabric made of horsehair mixed with cotton or linen. It was used for petticoats after 1840. The uncomfortable material was quickly abandoned, but bequeathed its name to the ringed skirts of 1850, then to the 'hooped cage' of 1856. Monsieur Tavernier, the inventor of the 'cage', that curious metal skirt, is said to have been inspired by the iron and glass structure of the Crystal Palace, erected in London by Joseph Paxton for the Great Exhibition of 1851. Whether or not that was so, Tavernier was considered a man of progress, since apart

Chapter Two

'Paris Novelties': A Little Catalogue of Fashion from 1850 to 1900

Franz-Xaver Winterhalter,
The Empress Eugénie and her maids of honour, *1855 (detail).*
Musée du Second Empire, Château de Compiègne.

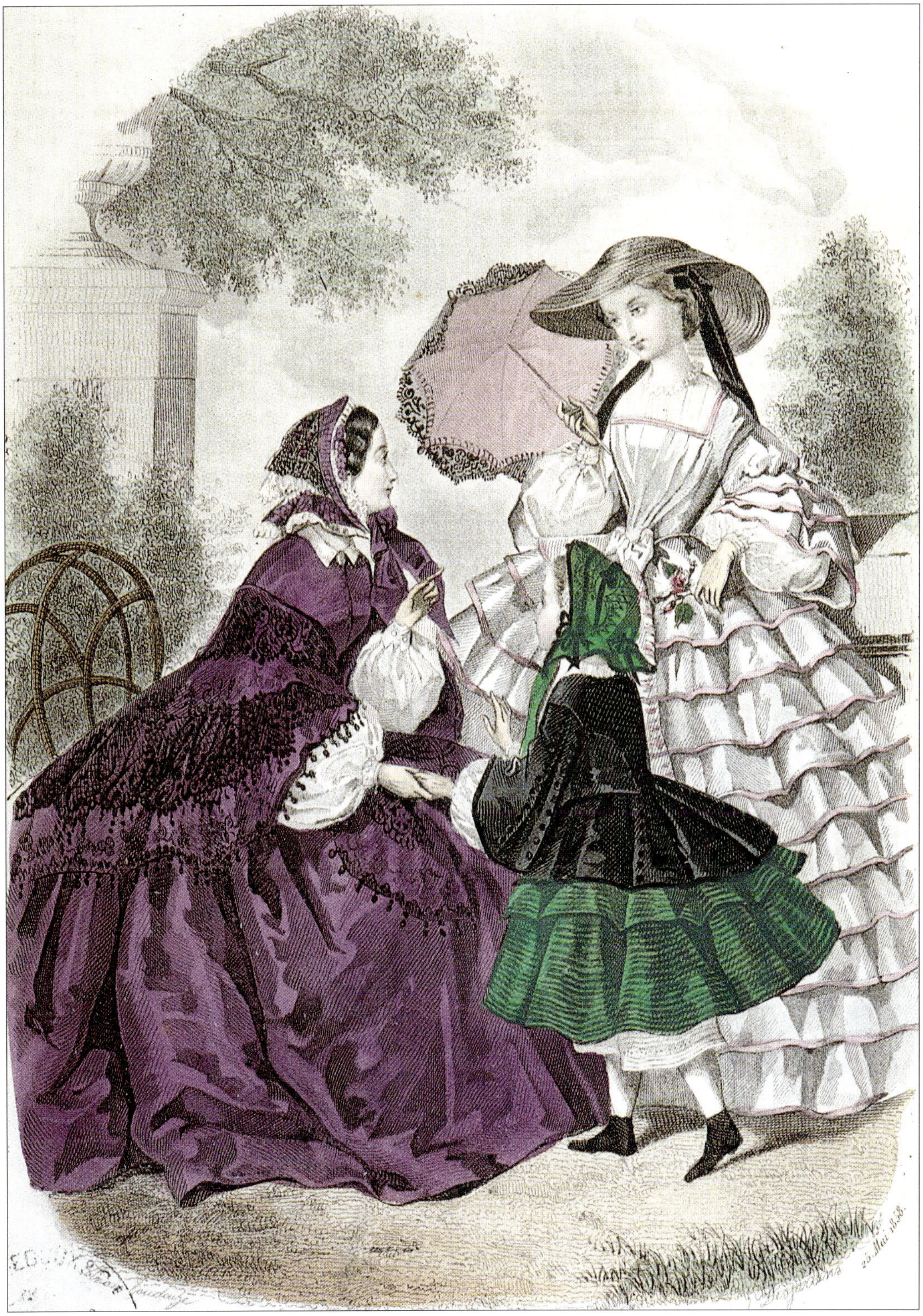

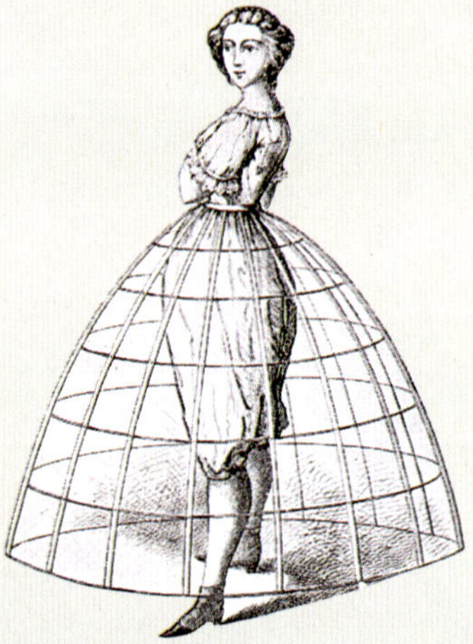

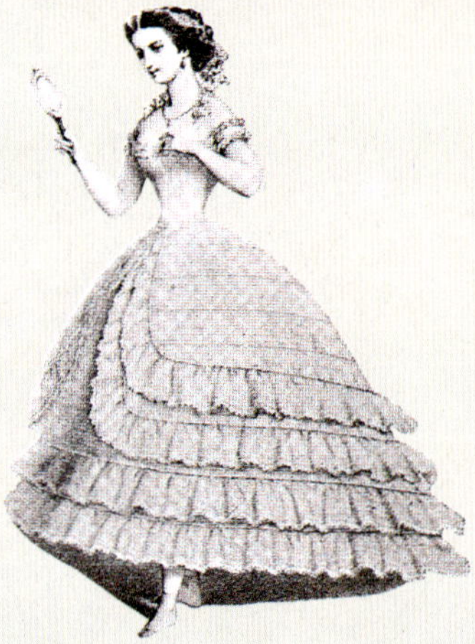

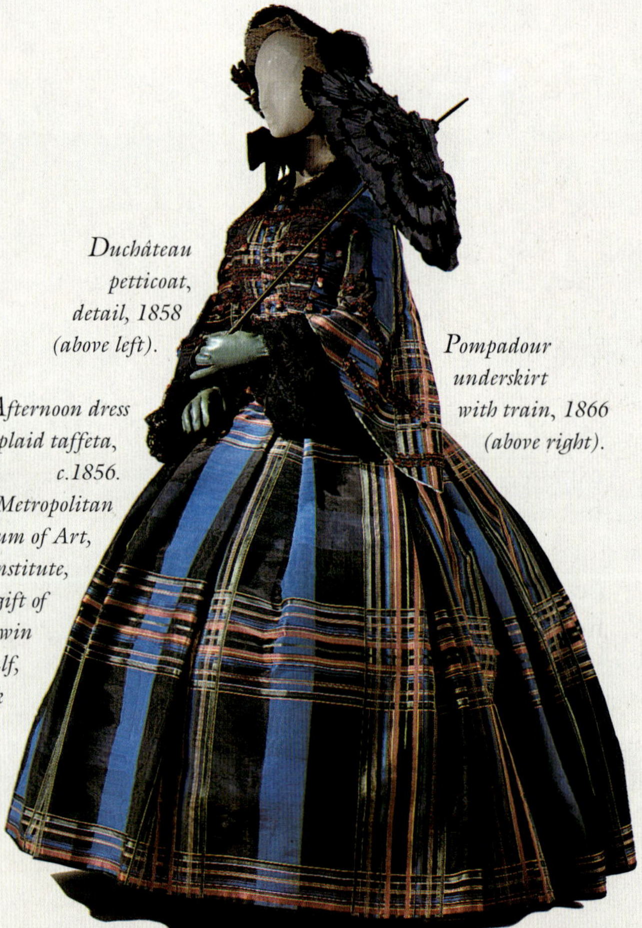

Duchâteau petticoat, detail, 1858 (above left).

Pompadour underskirt with train, 1866 (above right).

Afternoon dress in plaid taffeta, c.1856. The Metropolitan Museum of Art, Costume Institute, gift of Mrs Edwin R. Mitcalf, New York (right).

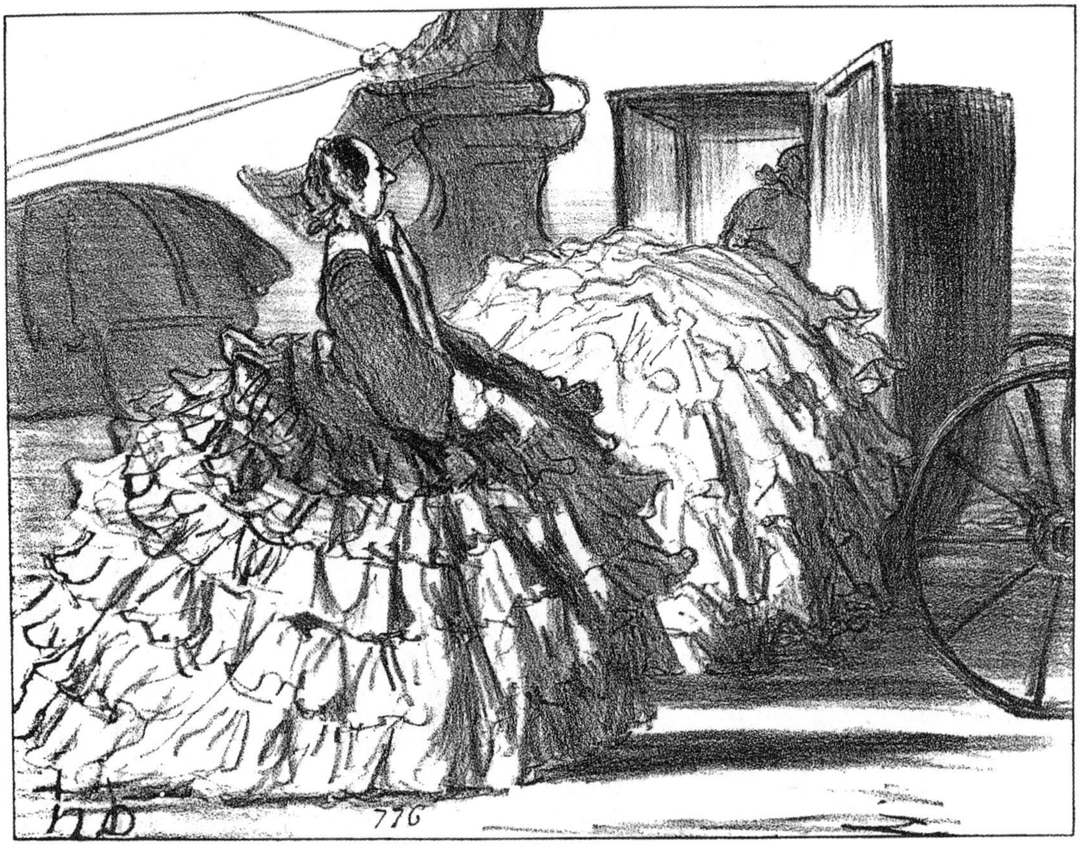

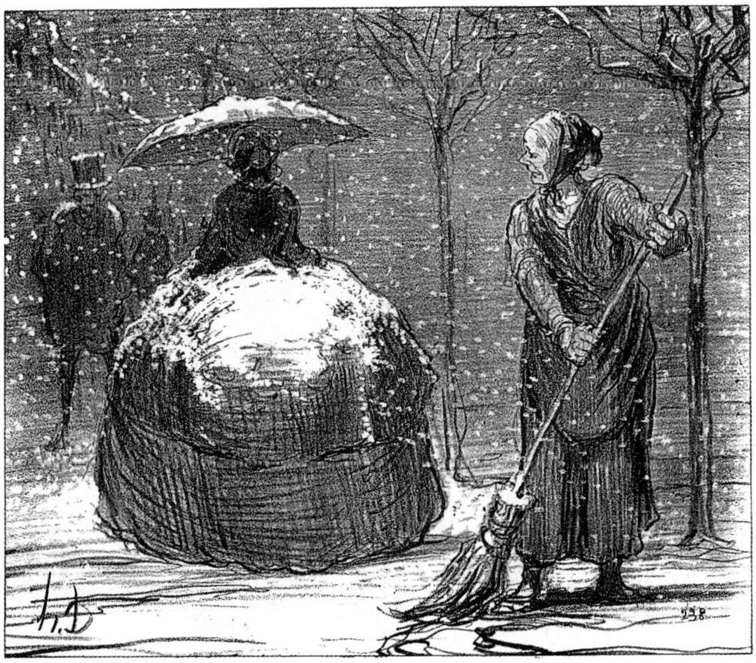

Le Magasin des demoiselles, *town fashions for ladies and young girls, 25 May 1858 (facing page).*

Honoré Daumier, 'Ladies of the demi-monde without demi-skirts', *drawing no. 190 of the series 'Actualités' for* Le Charivari, *11 May 1855 (above).*

Honoré Daumier, 'Charming lady, should one sweep you away?', *drawing no. 1 of the series 'Winter sketches' for* Le Charivari, *13 November 1858 (left).*

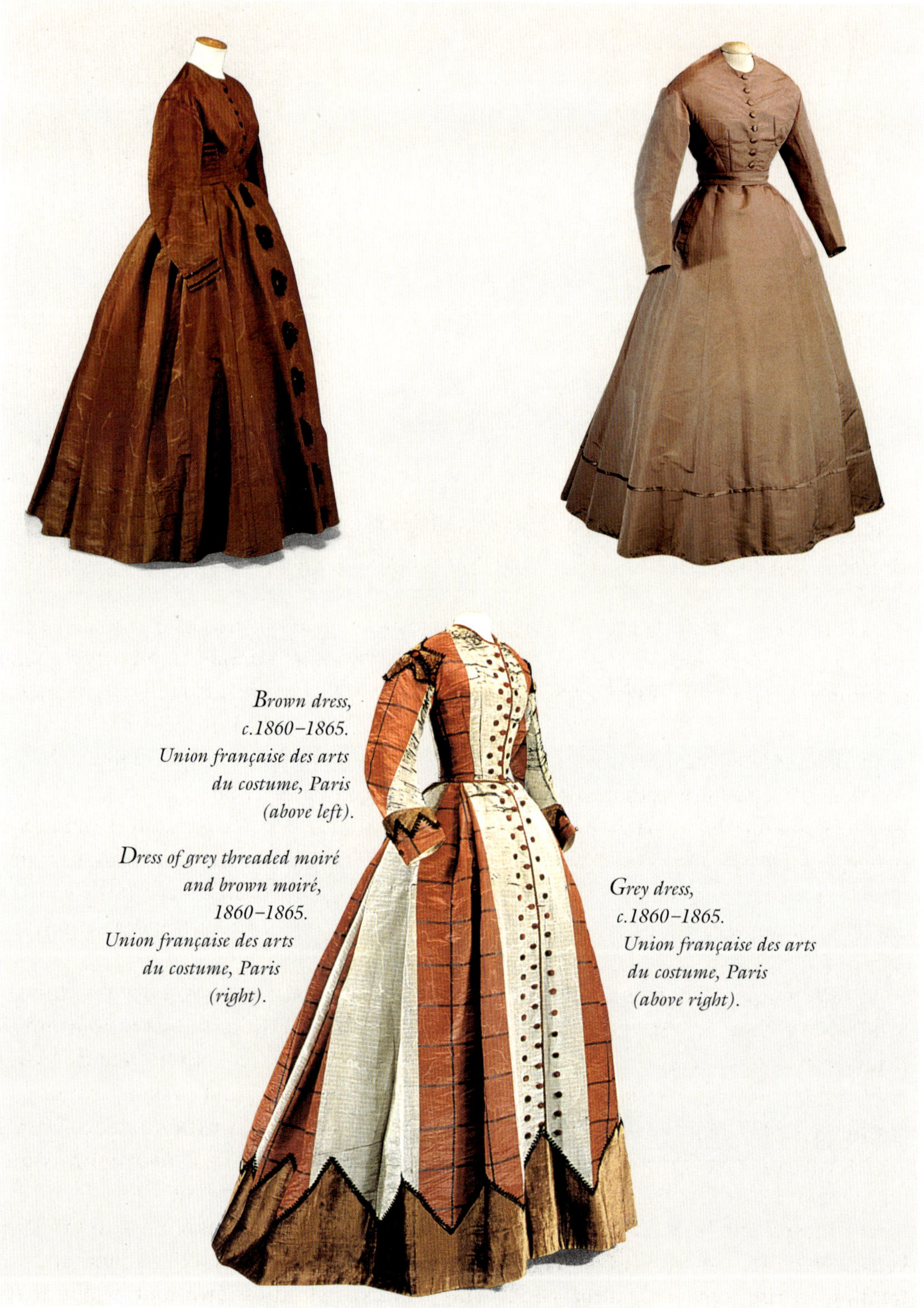

Brown dress, c.1860–1865. Union française des arts du costume, Paris (above left).

Dress of grey threaded moiré and brown moiré, 1860–1865. Union française des arts du costume, Paris (right).

Grey dress, c.1860–1865. Union française des arts du costume, Paris (above right).

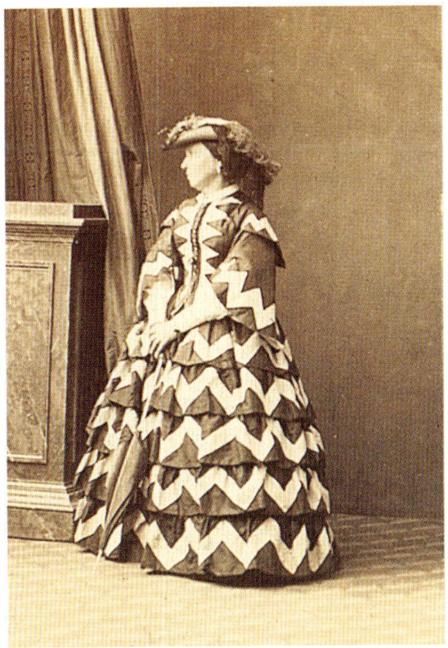

Disdéri,
Madame Aubert,
no date.
Musée d'Orsay, Paris
(left).

A crinoline shop,
c. 1862
(right).

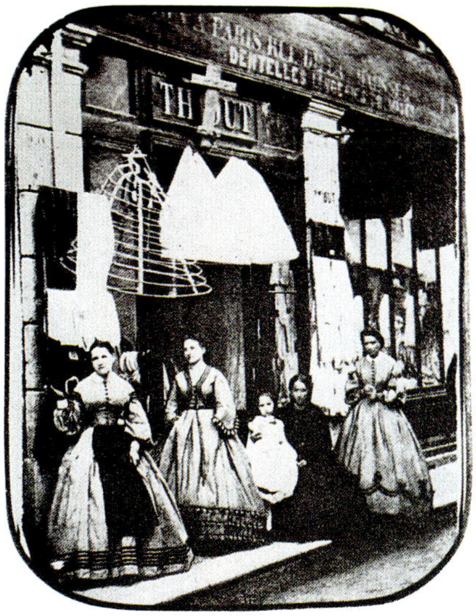

from considerably lightening the skirt by eliminating the numerous petticoats, his frame could be expanded almost without limit. Its maximum circumference was reached in 1858.

It became impossible at that time for a man to give his arm to a woman. There was talk of widening doorways, and caricaturists, the most famous among them being Daumier, delighted in showing travellers suffocated by skirts in railway compartments, capsizings caused by a fatal gust of wind or the selective malice of turnstiles. Moralists were shocked by the amount of cloth these skirts required: tens of metres, further augmented by the flounces which were much in vogue up to 1860.

Paralleling this expansion, sleeves widened in pagoda fashion from shoulder to elbow, to the point of bursting. Bodices ended in a point below the waist and were often embellished with little basques. The shawl and mantelet were indispensable adjuncts to this silhouette, as was a bonnet with front brim, a bavolet and wide knotted strings.

The materials used were taffeta, faille and *poult-de-soie*, printed with flowers, stripes and checks. The first synthetic dyes appeared during the Second Empire: mauvein was discovered in England in 1856 and fuchsine at the same time in Lyons. Hence the vogue for violet, by turns 'pansy' or 'Alpine violet', and jarring colours. The apotheosis of the crinoline is undoubtedly the rather sour portrait of the *Empress Eugénie and her maids of honour*, painted by Winterhalter in 1855 (Compiègne, Musée du Second Empire).

Changes occurred in the 1860s. The volume of the skirt was shifted towards the back, narrow sleeves appeared, the waistline was no longer pointed but round and was tending to rise, especially after 1864. The princess-style dress (without a join at the

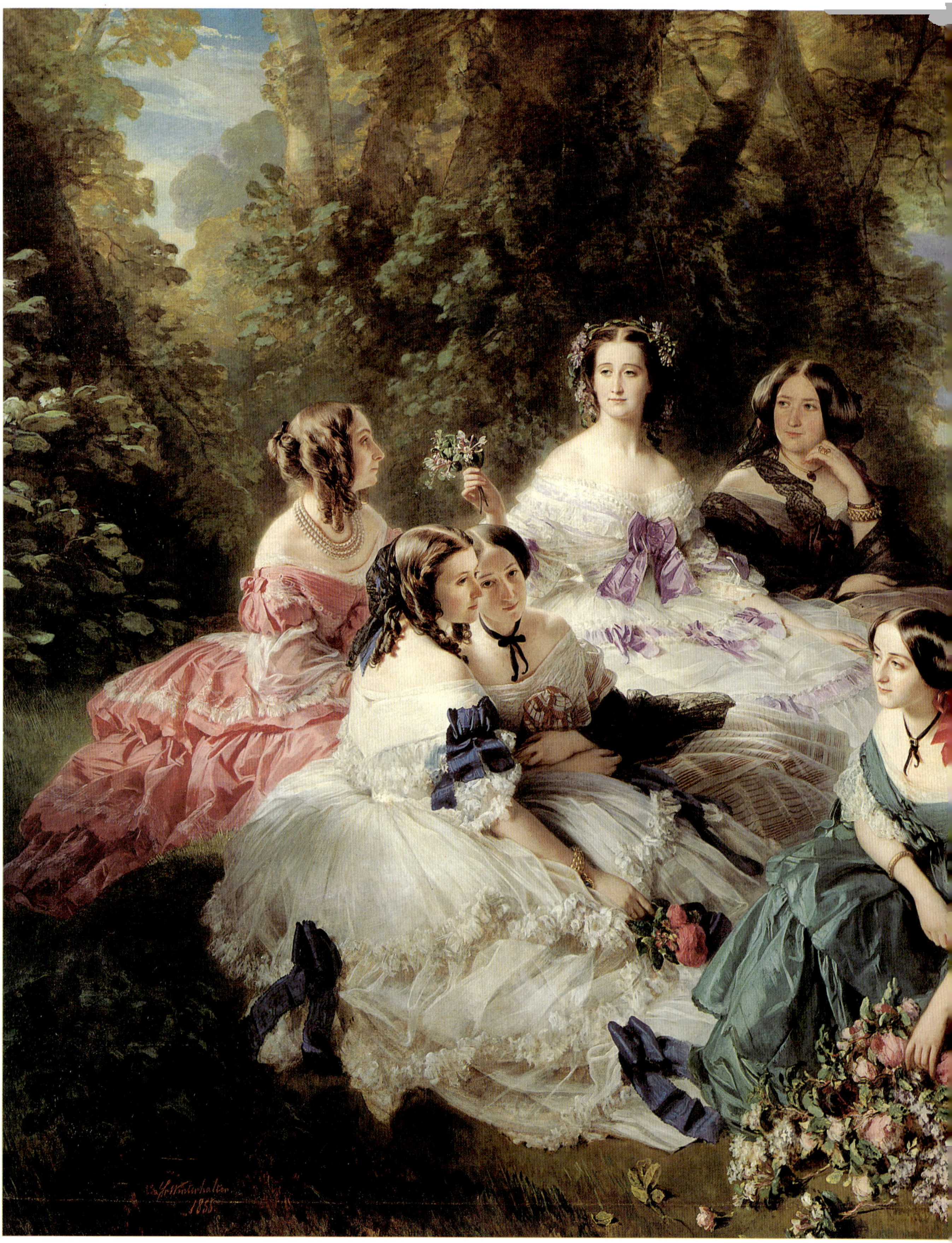

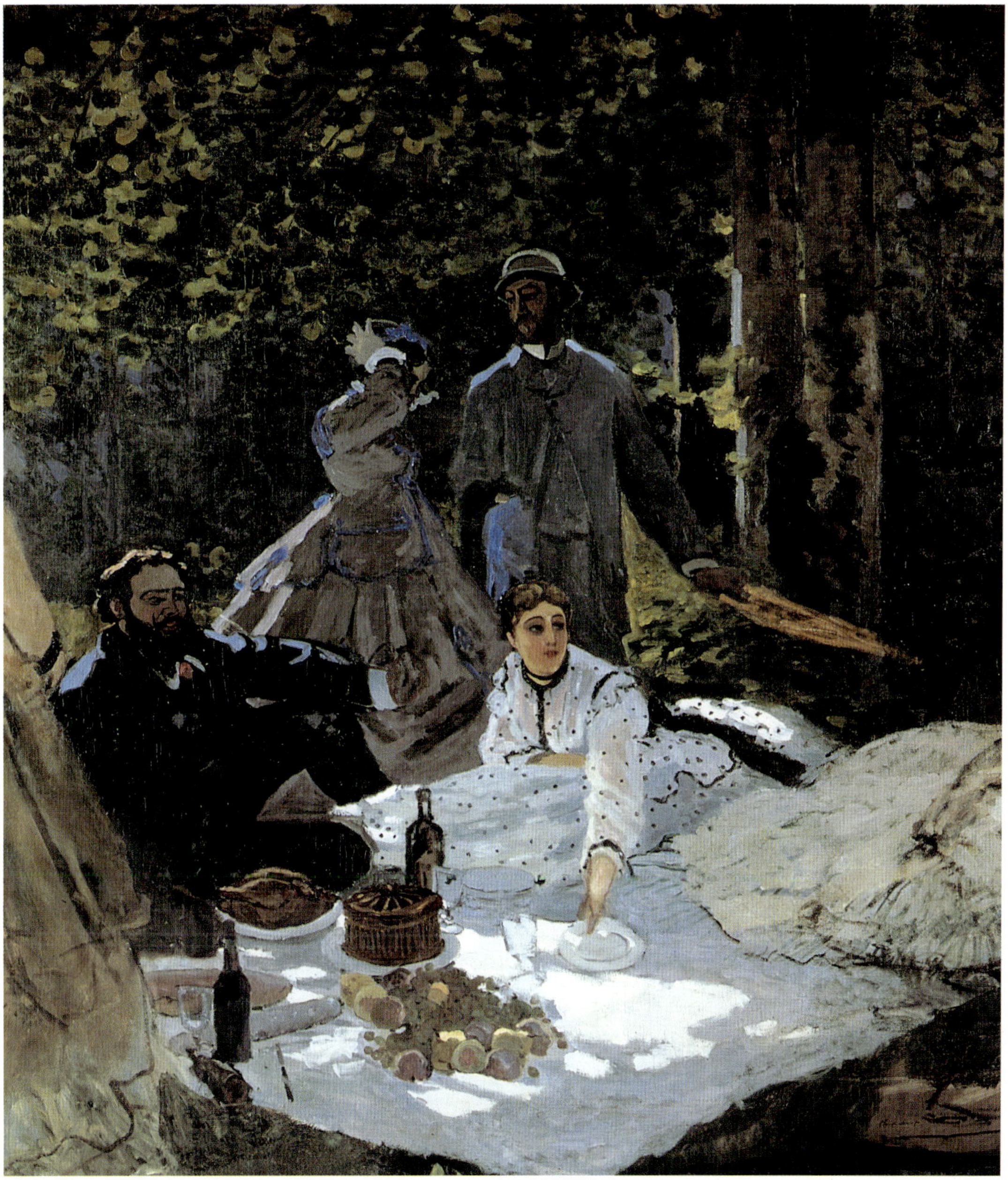

Claude Monet, Le Déjeuner sur l'herbe, *central part, 1865–1866. Musée d'Orsay, Paris.*

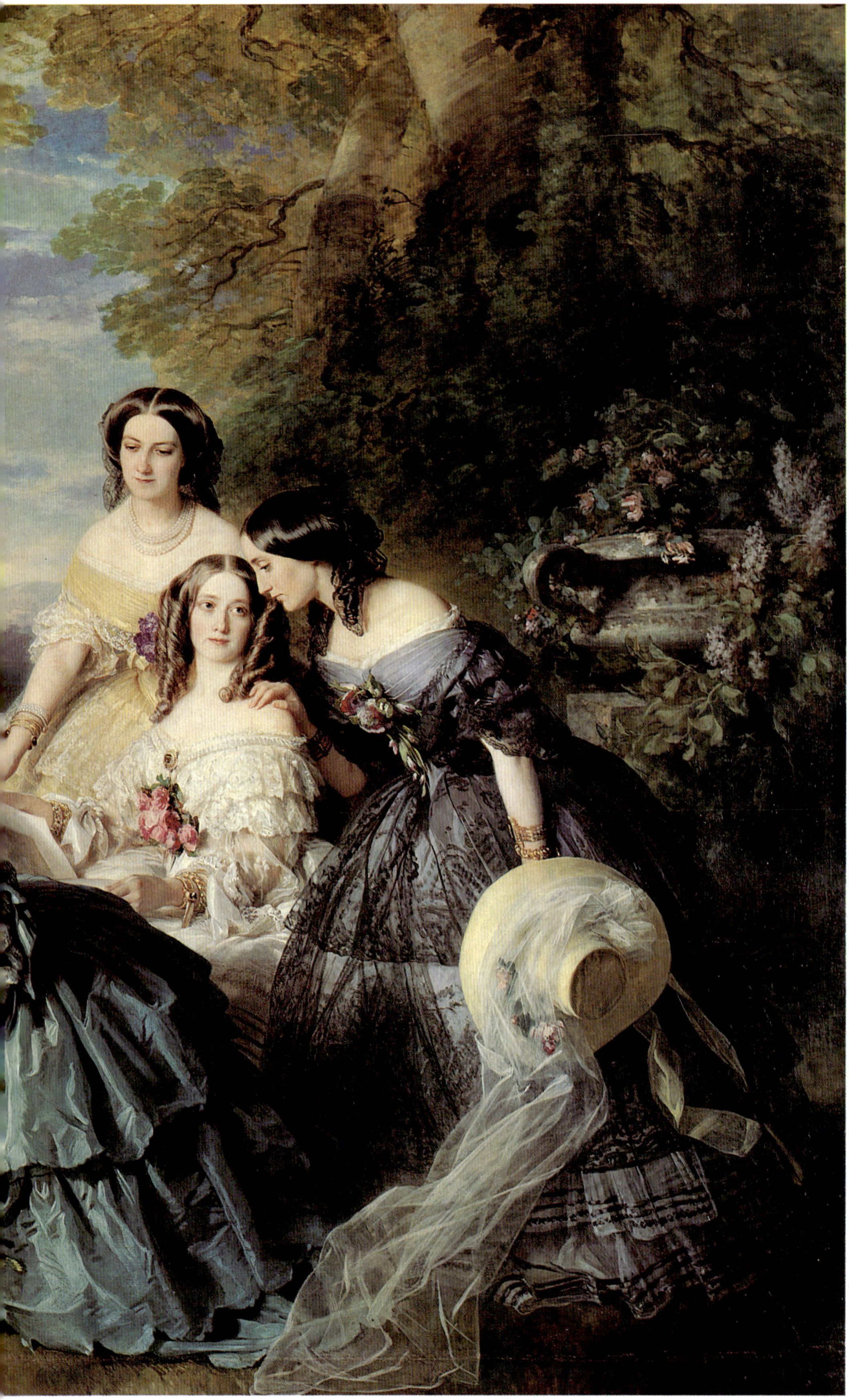

Franz-Xaver Winterhalter,
The Empress Eugénie and her maids of honour, *1855.*
Musée du Second Empire, Château de Compiègne.

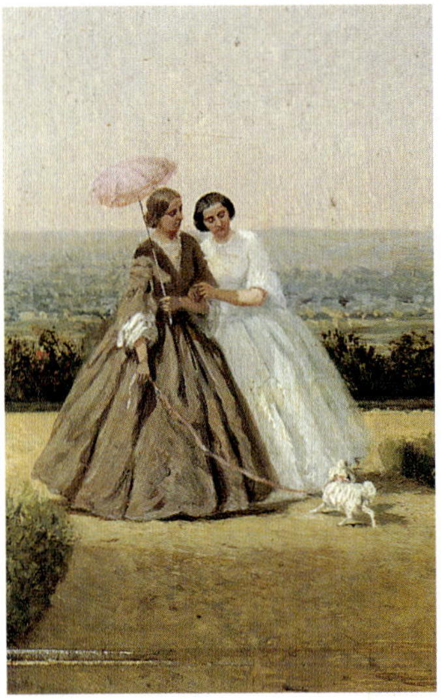

Martial Potemont,
Women in a Garden
(detail), undated.
Musée du Second Empire,
Château de Compiègne
(left).

After Auguste Toulmouche,
Forbidden Fruit,
Salon de 1865
(right).

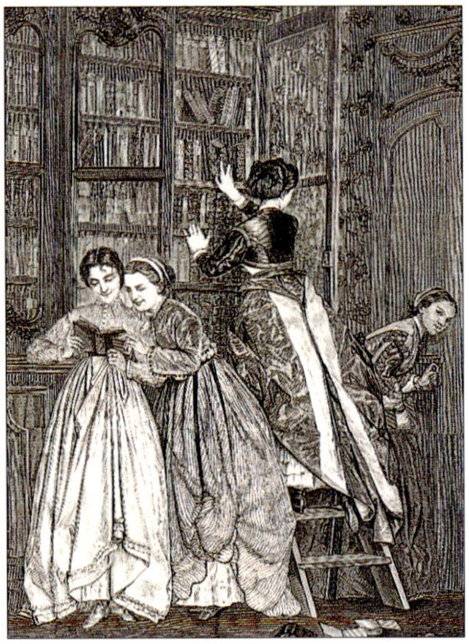

waist) was created. 1864 was also the year of the appearance of square-cut *décolletés*, sashes with free ends and small hats worn higher on the head.

The more and more widespread use of the sewing machine encouraged an abundance of applied ornaments: passementerie, geometrical designs, braids; from now on materials tended to be plain, but heavily decorated. These dresses with geometrical patterns were favoured by the Impressionists (see Monet's *Le Déjeuner sur l'herbe*, 1865–6, or *Women in a garden*, 1866–7, Paris, Musée d'Orsay).

A turning-point was reached in 1865: the volume of the skirt began to shrink. The cumbersome crinoline, sweeping the ground, had conclusively demonstrated its impracticality. Ankle-length skirts became popular and the skirt was doubled. An overskirt, lifted at the hem by loops, created a new decorative effect with contrasting colours and materials. From 1869–70 this overskirt was draped with a polonaise, a kind of apron at the front with two puffs at the back. A new shape began to appear, often as high as the small of the back: the bustle was about to be born.

A variety of coats continued to be worn and the paletot was superseding the mantelet. Hats, growing smaller and smaller, projecting forward above the brow and embellished with flowers and lace, accentuated this conical silhouette. Acid colours, lilac, maize, peacock green, pink and sky-blue, were in vogue.

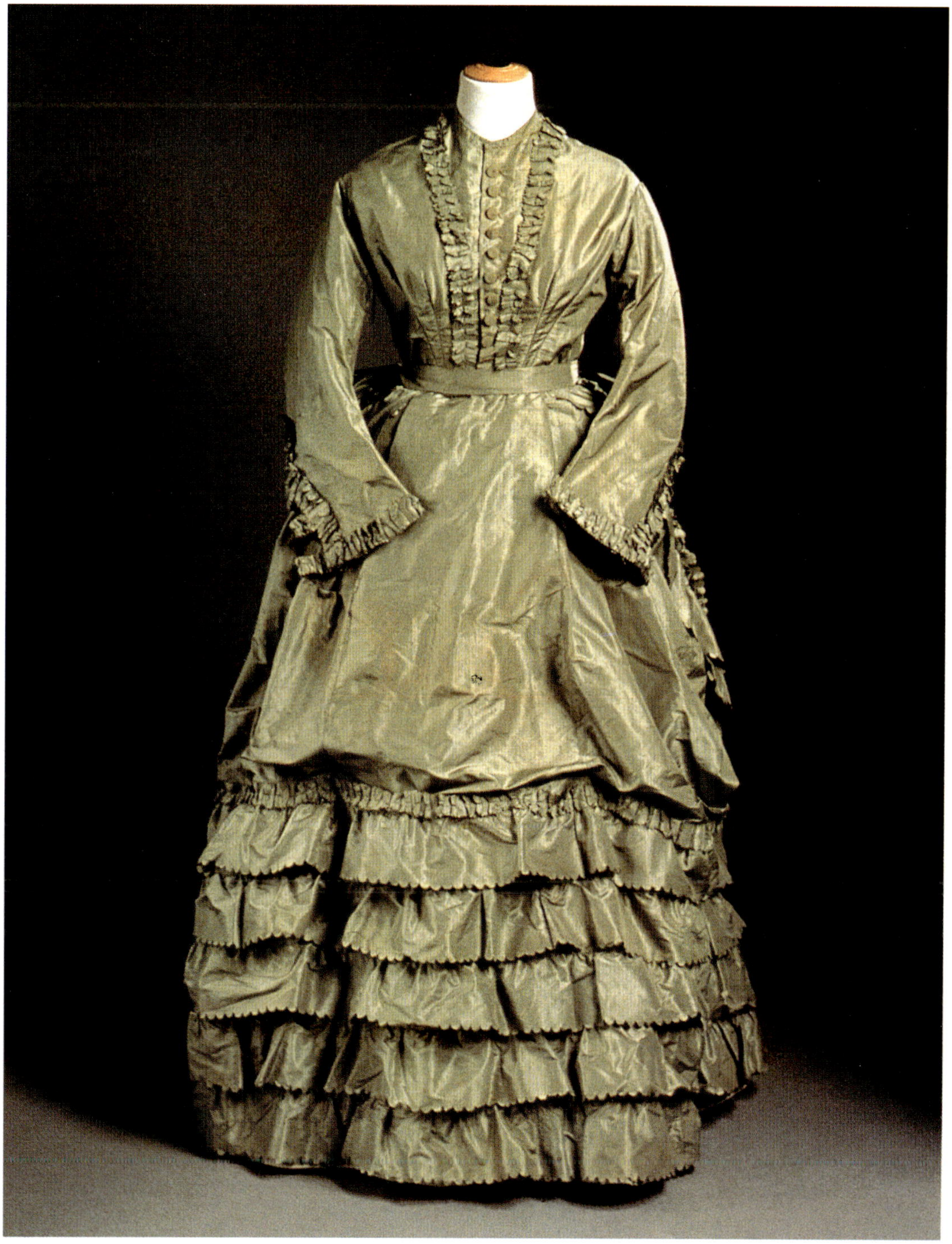

Dress of green-grey shot taffeta, c. 1870–1875. Union française des arts du costume, Paris.
James Tissot, The Branch of Lilac, *1875. Private Collection, London (facing page).*

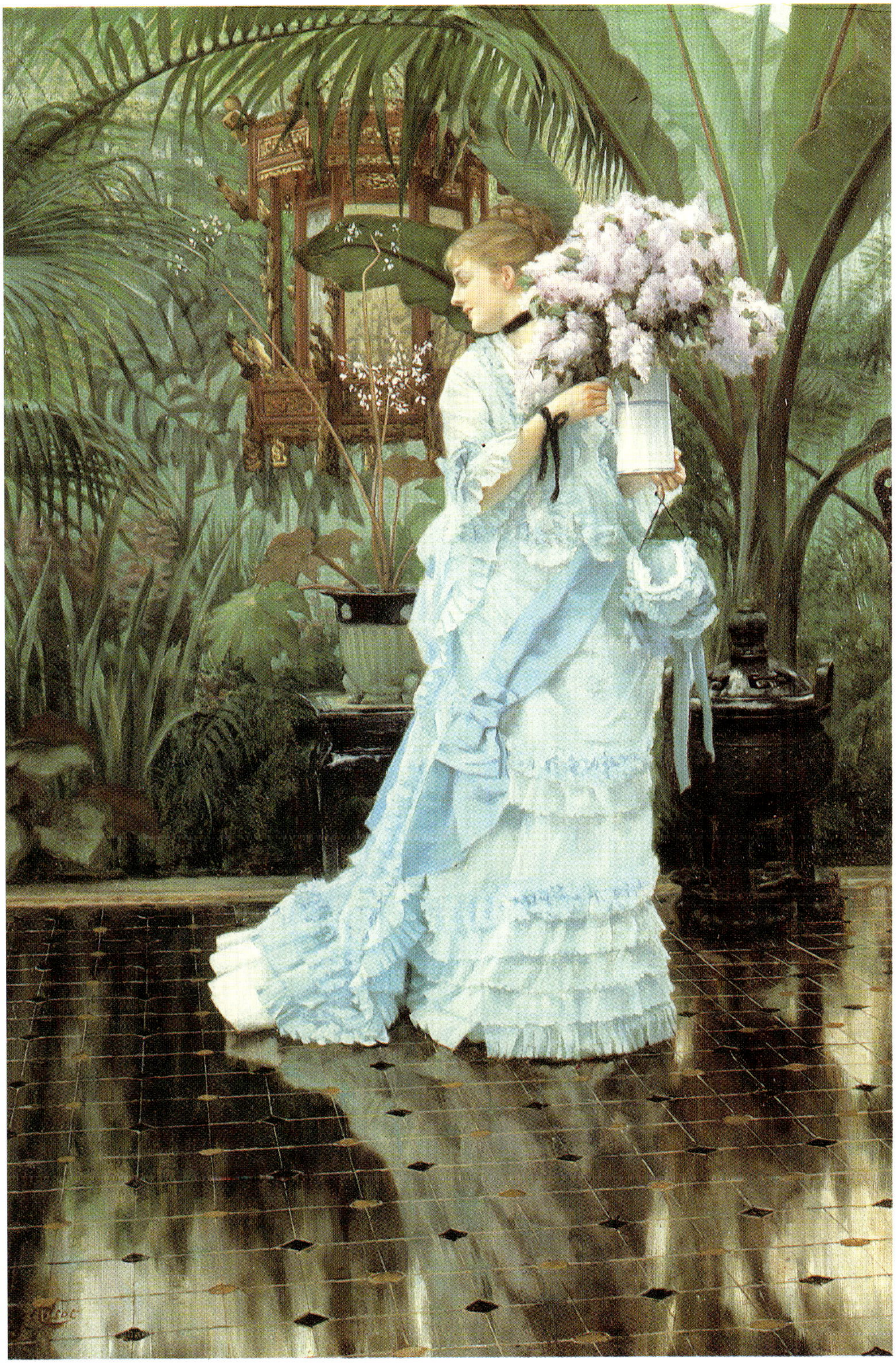

The bustle: from the tournure to the strapontin, 1870–1888

The 'tournure', 1870–75

The polonaise was a transitional garment bridging the gap between a voluminous skirt that formed a circle and a new, semicircular volume, the bustle or *tournure*. The bustle skirt was flat at the front but was fitted at the back with half-hoops, sometimes tensioned by cords. This 'crinolinette', as it was sometimes called at first, accentuated the curve of the back and supported drapery. This took the form of a puff and was either removable, hooked to the waist, or was formed by a second skirt lifted by internal cords. It was sometimes supported by pads. Here, again, caricaturists never failed to ridicule this ungraceful 'false behind'. Nevertheless, it was certainly less inconvenient than the crinoline: there was a system allowing it to be swung to one side when sitting down.

The sleeves of dresses were long and narrow, but ended in small pagodas or double cuffs. Sometimes, as a decade earlier, they formed large pagodas starting at the shoulder. The waist was slightly higher than its normal position. *The Portrait of Madame Hartman* by Renoir (1874, Paris, Musée d'Orsay) shows one of the most widespread variants of the skirt, the *tablier* (apron), draped in horizontal folds at the front, gathered at the back to form a large knot and finishing in a train. The underskirt is made of pleated flounces, the bodice and undersleeves are of lace. Renoir did not hesitate to show the model directly from the side, although this angle of view did nothing to lighten the profile. It is very possible that he was himself aware of this ponderousness, for he told Ambroise Vollard, when asked which kind of dress he preferred to paint: 'to tell the truth, what I like best is the nude woman; but if I have to paint her dressed, the dress I prefer is the princess style. It gives women that sinuous line which is so pretty.' We seem a good way from that ideal!

Décolletés were often cut straight across the bust, over a *guimpe* with a collar and small revers for daytime and bordered with lace or ruching in the evening. V-shaped necklines were also in fashion, and oval *décolletés* were still used in the evening, competing equally with low square-cut openings. Small short sleeves and a train completed the definition of the ball-gown. The materials were serge, Sicilian (a kind of wool or silk poplin) and satin. The rather strident colours varied from blue (sky, drake), green (bronze, olive) to garnet, pink and mauve.

Ready-made dresses were based on the paletot and on striped or check costumes; the corsage had an 'officer' collar or a tailored collar, and was worn with a bustle skirt. Hats became a little higher and receded to show the hairline. Bonnets, much in vogue from 1830 to 1850, were hardly worn, except in the morning with a négligé, or by elderly women.

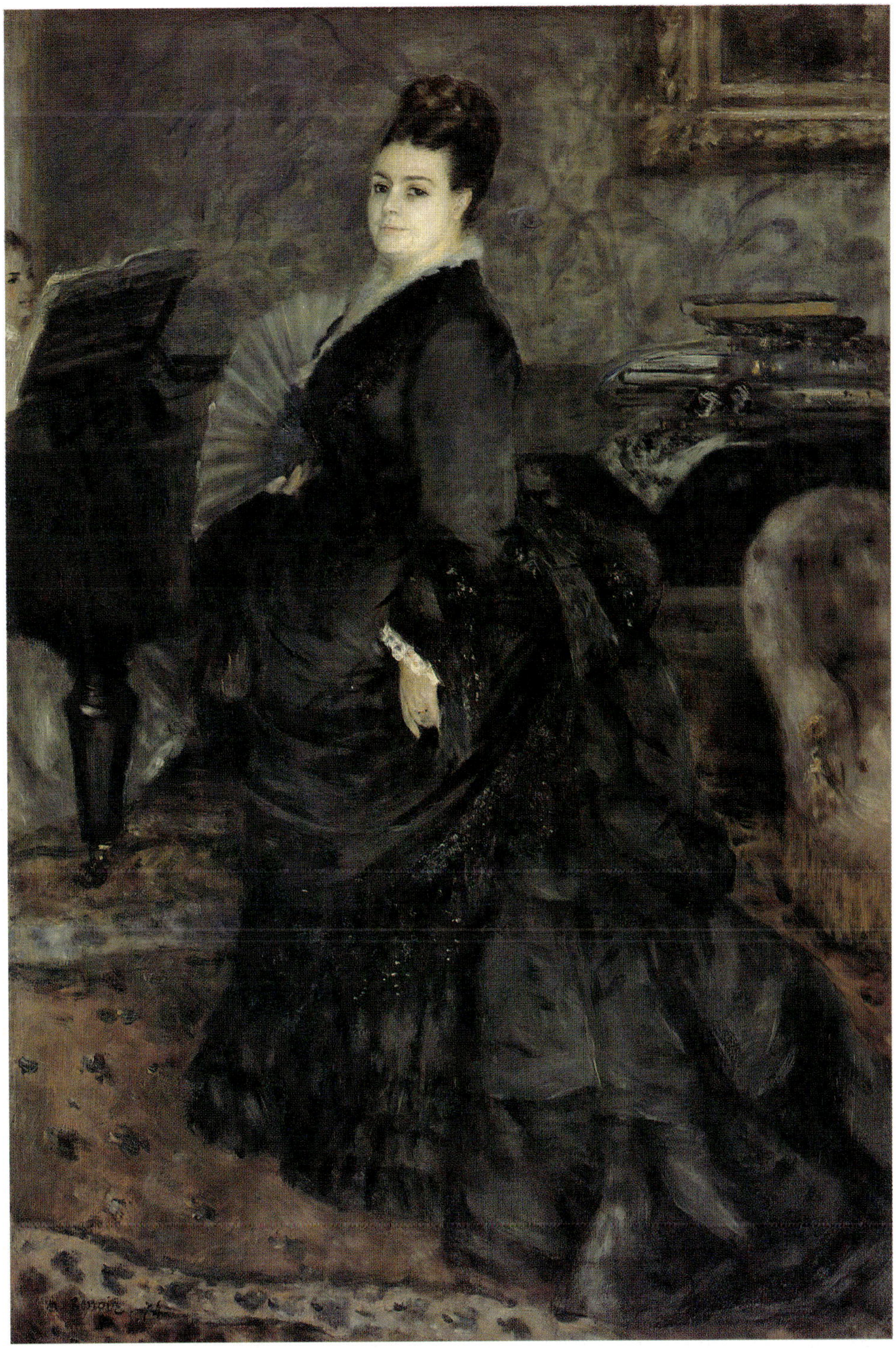

Pierre Auguste Renoir, Portrait of a Woman, *or* Portrait of Madame Hartmann, *1874. Musée d'Orsay, Paris.*

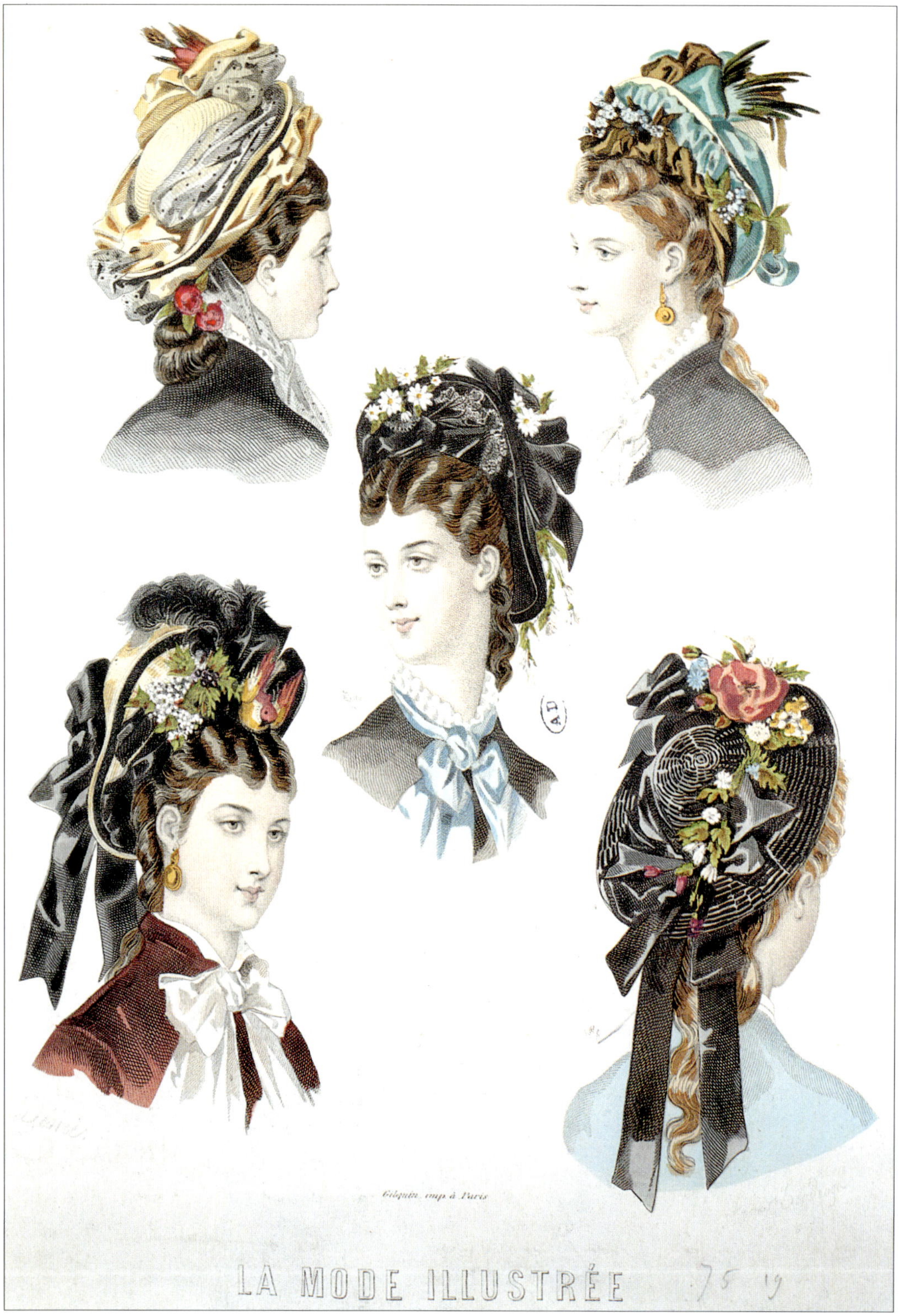
Gilquin imp à Paris
LA MODE ILLUSTRÉE

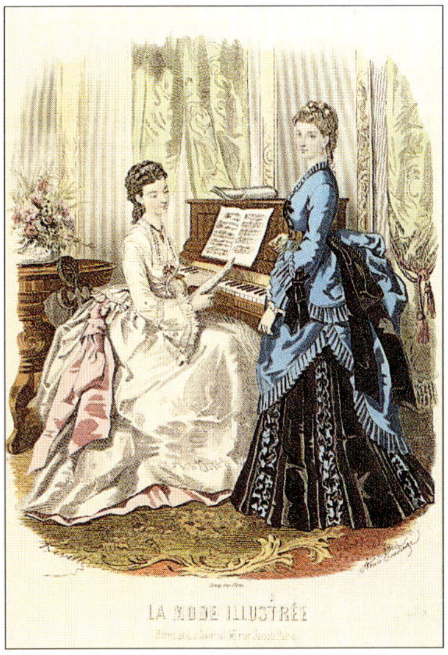

La Mode illustrée: *display of hats, 1875 (facing page).*

La Mode illustrée, *1872 (left).*

La Mode illustrée, *1875 (right).*

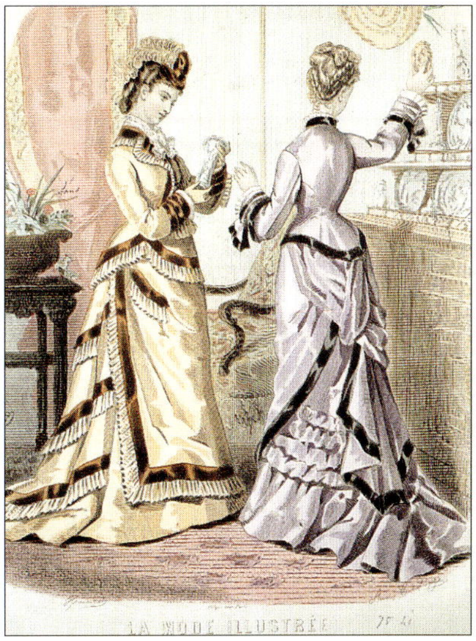

Fashion in these years was unbelievably complex. The architecture of the bustle is surprising in itself, but around and beside the bulge there developed an superabundant ornamentation of pleats, ruffles and flounces attached in all directions by bows, sashes, buttons. As if that were not enough, fringes, ruching, strips of velvet and contrasts of colour and fabric (light and dark, plain and striped for the bodice and sleeves) were superimposed on this hybrid composition of 'diverse pieces badly joined together'.[1] The exuberance of this style earned it the name *tapissier* (tapestry maker). Later, it was thought vulgar, mannered and decadent. However, there was something touching in its loudness and its eagerness to show off its *savoir-faire.*

The long-limbed line, 1876–82

During a brief interlude in this evolution, starting in 1876, the bustle subsided and, from 1877 to 1881, disappeared or was worn very low on the hips. A new long, even lanky silhouette was born. The bustle already showed stout women in an unflattering light, and during the 1880s the clinging style offered no refuge to the fuller figure. The corsage moulded bust and hips; the loose drapes started lower down, encircling the legs in a cylindrical form. When not decorated with horizontal drapes, the skirt was flat or striped with small vertical pleats accentuating a tree-trunk effect. The hemline was flared to form a small corolla or train. Contrasting fabrics were still used but became somewhat more complex, being cut in vertical strips to give the effect of a double dress. They were also used to form very low, V-shaped *décolletés*, simulating false jackets over shirt fronts. The line of the bodice went down to a point far below the waist. Sleeves were narrow, necklines straight-across or V-shaped. Ornamentation was still required, with bows, buttoning and borrowings from male dress: tailored collars, lapels, waistcoats

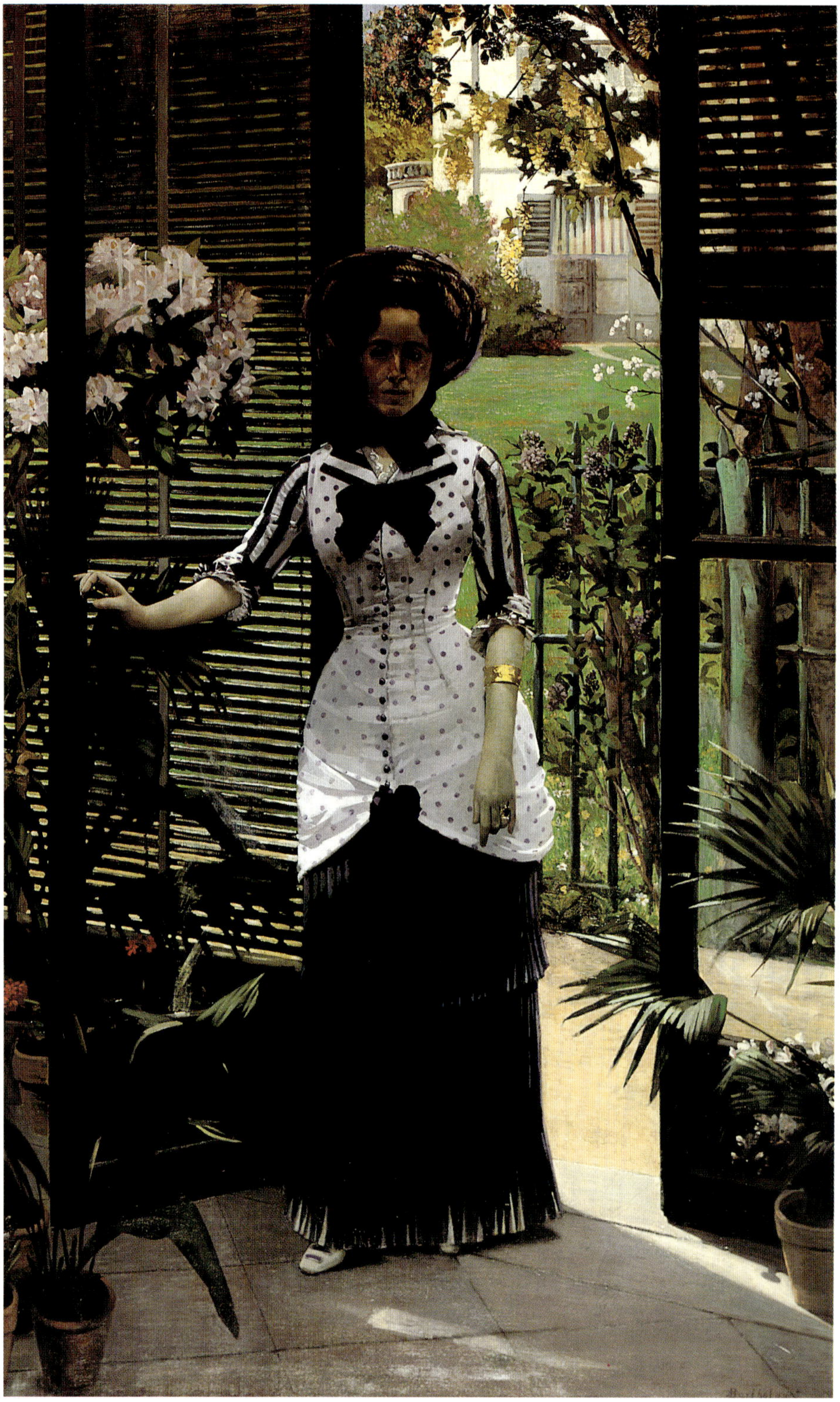

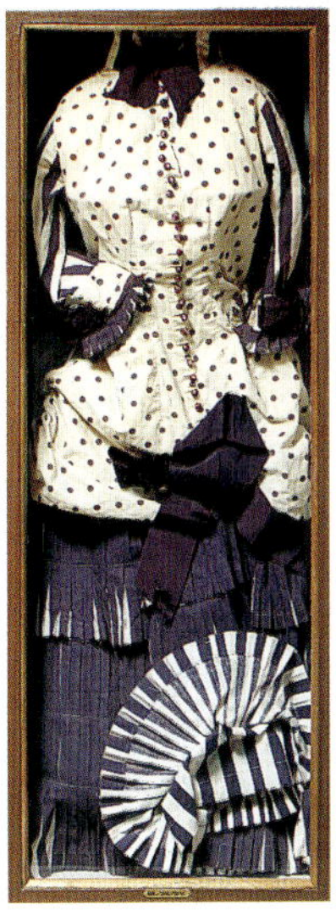

Albert Bartholomé,
Madame Bartholomé *or*
In the Conservatory, *1881.*
Musée d'Orsay, Paris
(facing page).

Dress worn by Madame Bartholomé in the painting by Albert Bartholomé,
Madame Bartholomé *or*
In the Conservatory, *1880.*
Musée d'Orsay, Paris.

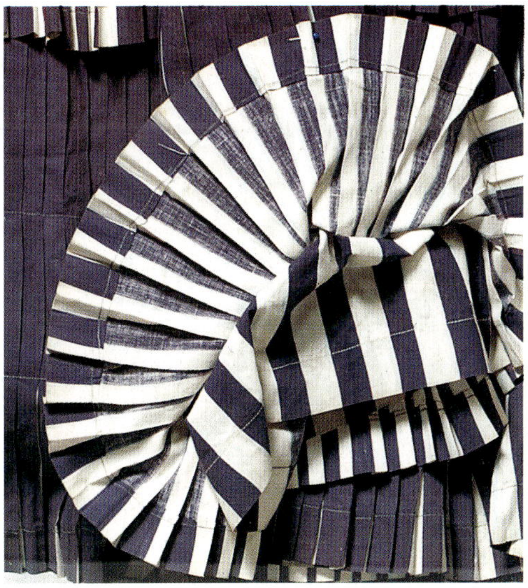

and so on. Ready-made dresses were also long and narrow, trimmed with fur or fringes. Fabrics were cashmere and materials in such colours as pink, blue-grey, beige, maroon and sapphire were used for contrast.

The *Portrait of Madame Bartholomé* painted by her husband, recently acquired by the Musée d'Orsay, may be dated to the 1880s. The museum also owns the young woman's dress. It is a summer *toilette* in printed cotton, playing on pretty contrasts of violet and white dots and stripes, and on the optical effect produced by a violet pleat with white spaces. Only a light drape embellishes the hem of the tunic, which is adorned at the back by a large flat bow in violet grosgrain. The small hat with strings that start at the nape of the neck and are knotted under the chin was to be very popular until the end of the century. The other style of hat much in vogue was the *capote* (bonnet), which left the ears and nape of the neck uncovered and helped to elongate the silhouette. This enchanting dress was carefully preserved by the painter and his heirs, in memory of his wife, who died tragically soon after the painting was finished. Prospérie, daughter of the Marquis de Fleury, died at the age of twenty-eight. She and husband were an elegant, fashionable couple, friends of Raffaëlli, Cassatt, Huysmans and Jeanniot. After her death, Bartholomé's career took a decisive turn, as the memorial he carved for his wife marked the start of his brilliant career as a sculptor.

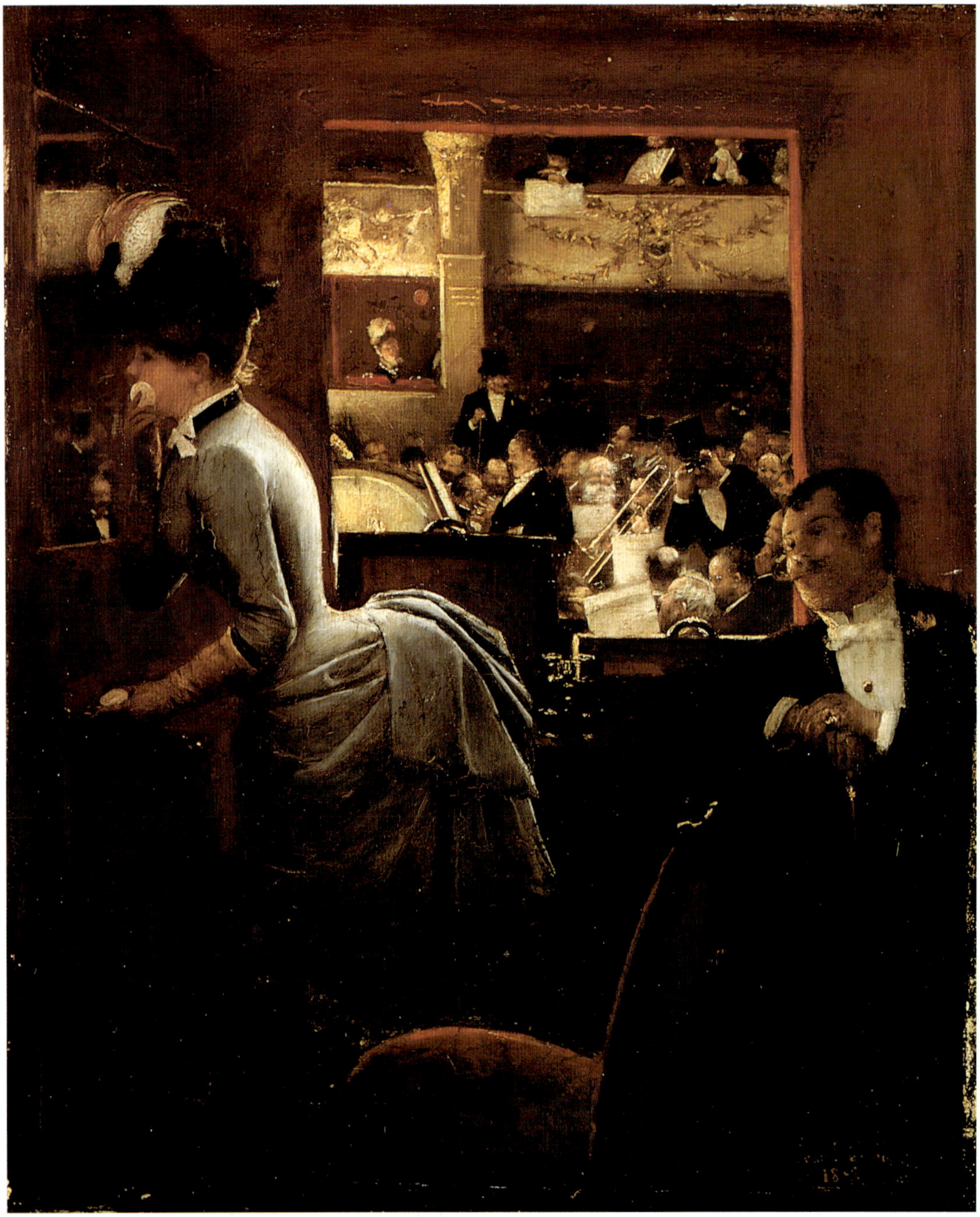

Jean Béraud, The Stalls-box, *1883. Musée Carnavalet, Paris.*

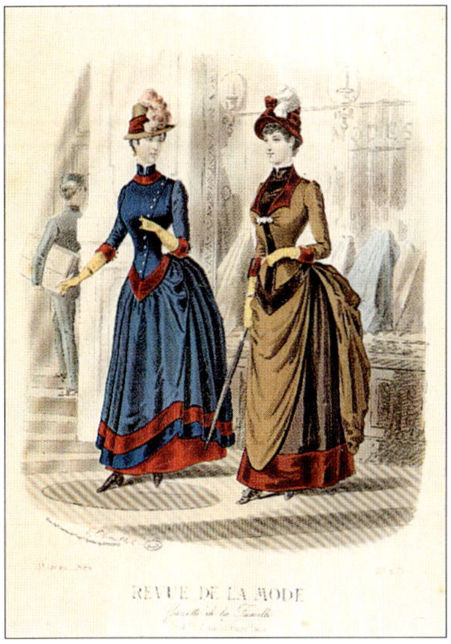

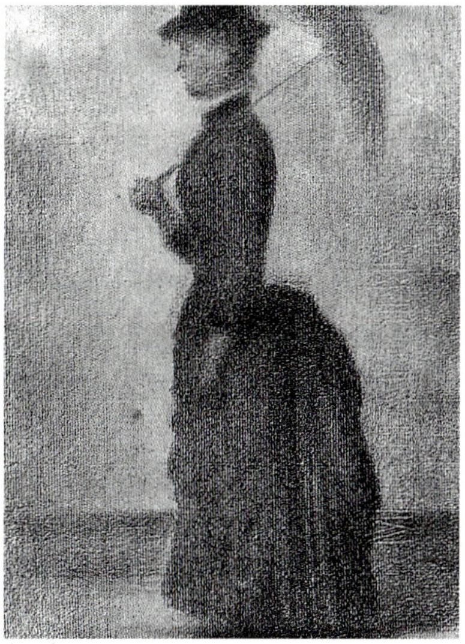

La Revue de la mode: *town fashions, 1884 (left).*

Georges Seurat, Lady strolling with a parasol *(study for* La Grande Jatte), *The Museum of Modern Art, New York (right).*

The 'strapontin' 1883–88

In 1882 knots or drapery perched on the buttocks prefigured the return of the bustle. And return it did, in 1883, in a still more extravagant form: the *strapontin*. This term referred, in a theatrical analogy, to a structure of articulated hoops that could be raised against the back of a chair, and then swung back into place as soon as one got up. The term *strapontin* also referred to the curious 'armchair' shape given to the silhouette by the very prominent volume jutting out at right angles at waist height.

In *La Grande Jatte* (1883, Art Institute of Chicago), Seurat accentuated this geometrical regularity of the female silhouette, but there is nothing incorrect in his depiction. The small hat shaped like a truncated cone exactly resembles those in fashion prints, as do the fitted, uplifted breastplate bodice and the large folds at the back of the dress. *The stalls-box* (*La baignoire*) by Jean Béraud (1883, Paris, Musée Carnavalet) shows exactly the same outfit. The chair in the foreground, the square opening of the theatre box and the *baignoire* in the background form lines and angles which seem to comment on the naive, ridiculous extravagance of feminine fashion, as does the slightly mocking expression of the man on the right.

Skirts grew wider, no longer fitting tightly around the legs. The train had disappeared and the tip of the shoe could be glimpsed. The bodice was still a fully fitted 'breastplate', often pointed at the bottom. Sleeves were narrow and could extend somewhat above the line of the shoulder. The neck was enclosed in an 'officer' collar. The fashion was for bodice-jackets with lapels, opening on plain shirt-fronts of a different colour, or vertical drapes, or, again, lace flounces. Another characteristic of these bodices was their asymmetry: sometimes a scarf was draped diagonally from one

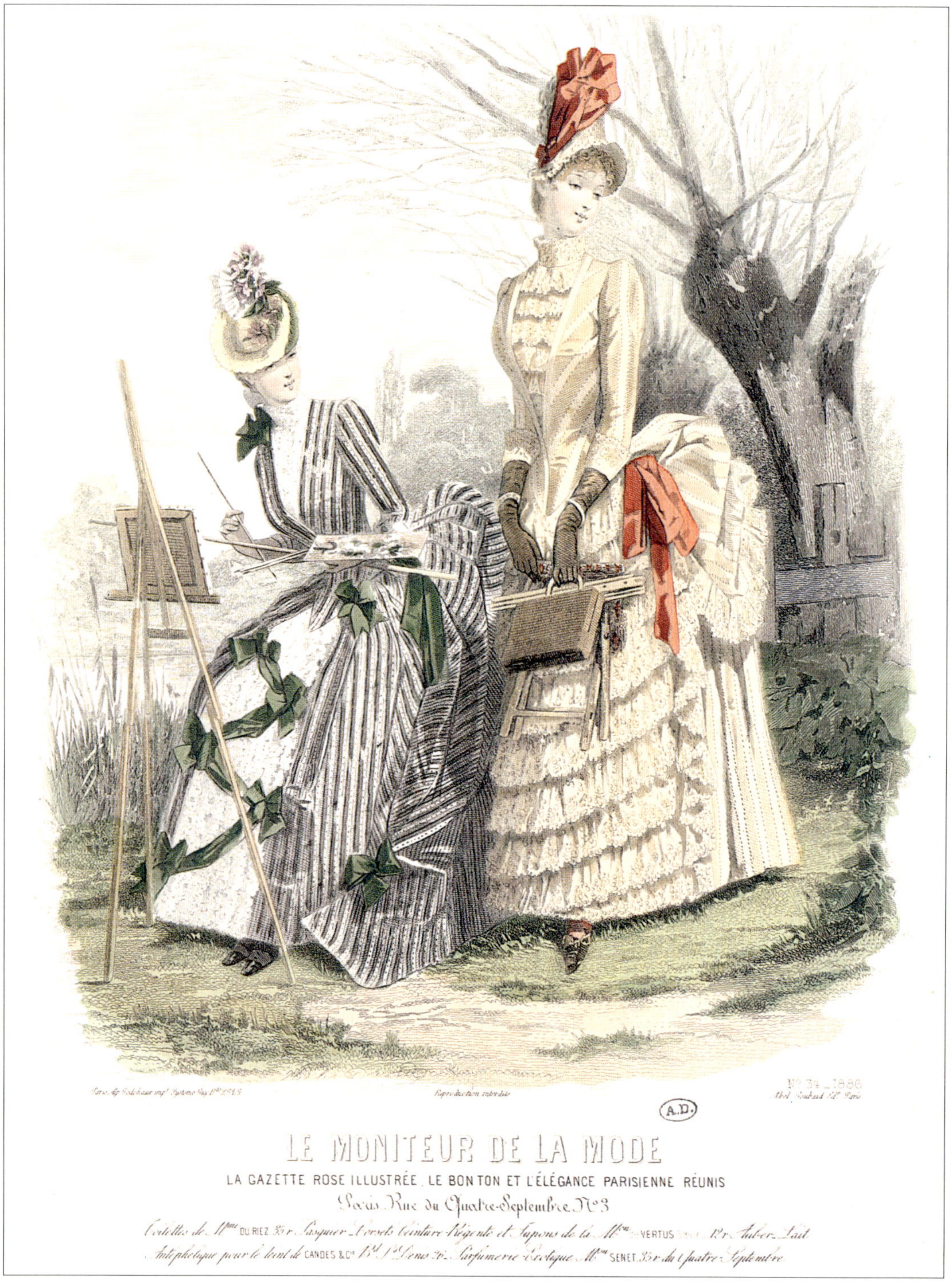

La Moniteur de la mode, *fashions for walking out, 1886.*

shoulder, reaching the waist at the opposite side; or else a lapel on one side and a strip of embroidery on the other formed a deep V-shape. This liking for asymmetry was also seen in skirts: the petticoat was covered both by a somewhat shorter apron, often arranged to one side, and by a tunic or hoop petticoat with horizontal drapes. The skirt was sometimes straight-down on the left and embellished with a draped flap on the right. The princess dress was open over a decorative petticoat; the decoration was with velvet ribbons, lace and jet. Coats also took on an asymmetrical form, with a short back above the bustle and long flaps reaching to the feet at the front. The *cache-poussière* (dust-coat) and *redingote* (long tailored coat), which stopped just above the hem of the skirt, were highly successful. From now on materials were heavy, often brocaded or striped, and were combined in clashing colours (salmon and dark khaki, pale pink and tobacco-colour). The materials were grogram, velvet, satin and, for the summer, surah, vicuña (a light wool fabric) and faille. The colours in vogue were heliotrope (mauve), garnet, ruby, moss green, dark blue and chestnut. These deep colours were to remain in favour until the end of the century. Hats were very tall and narrow (in which case they were adorned with plumes and drapes) or, on the contrary, large and wide-brimmed (trimmed with birds, flowers, ostrich feathers).

The Bell Skirt and the Leg-of-Mutton Sleeve 1889–96

The third silhouette characteristic of the Belle Epoque appeared in about 1889–90. The bust now superseded the skirt as the focal point. The strapontin disappeared once and for all and draped skirts gave way to a simple, bell-shaped skirt, while all the extravagance was concentrated on the corsage and the sleeves.

The first sketch of this silhouette dates from between 1889 and 1891. As in the 1880s, the line was extremely fine and long. The waist was pulled in, often by a corselet belt, ending in a point. The skirt was straight and smooth. Sleeves were given new attention: small flounces rose above the shoulder line, or swags of material created volume at the top of the sleeve. A balloon sleeve extending to the elbow was progressively evolved. To accentuate its visual presence and its volume, it was of a different colour to the rest of the dress or its trimming. The 'officer' collar continued to be worn, and square yokes down to mid-bosom were introduced. To create a slender silhouette princess dresses and long coats, often opening wide over the dress, were worn. Ornament became more moderate. Lace, jet, *entre-deux* (beaded insertions) and sable were more discreetly used. The materials and colours were still those of the preceding period (brocade, velvet, faille, vicuña; 'cress', 'brick', 'aubergine', 'Nile green'). Hats were either small bonnets perched on chignons, or flat hats elongated into a vizor.

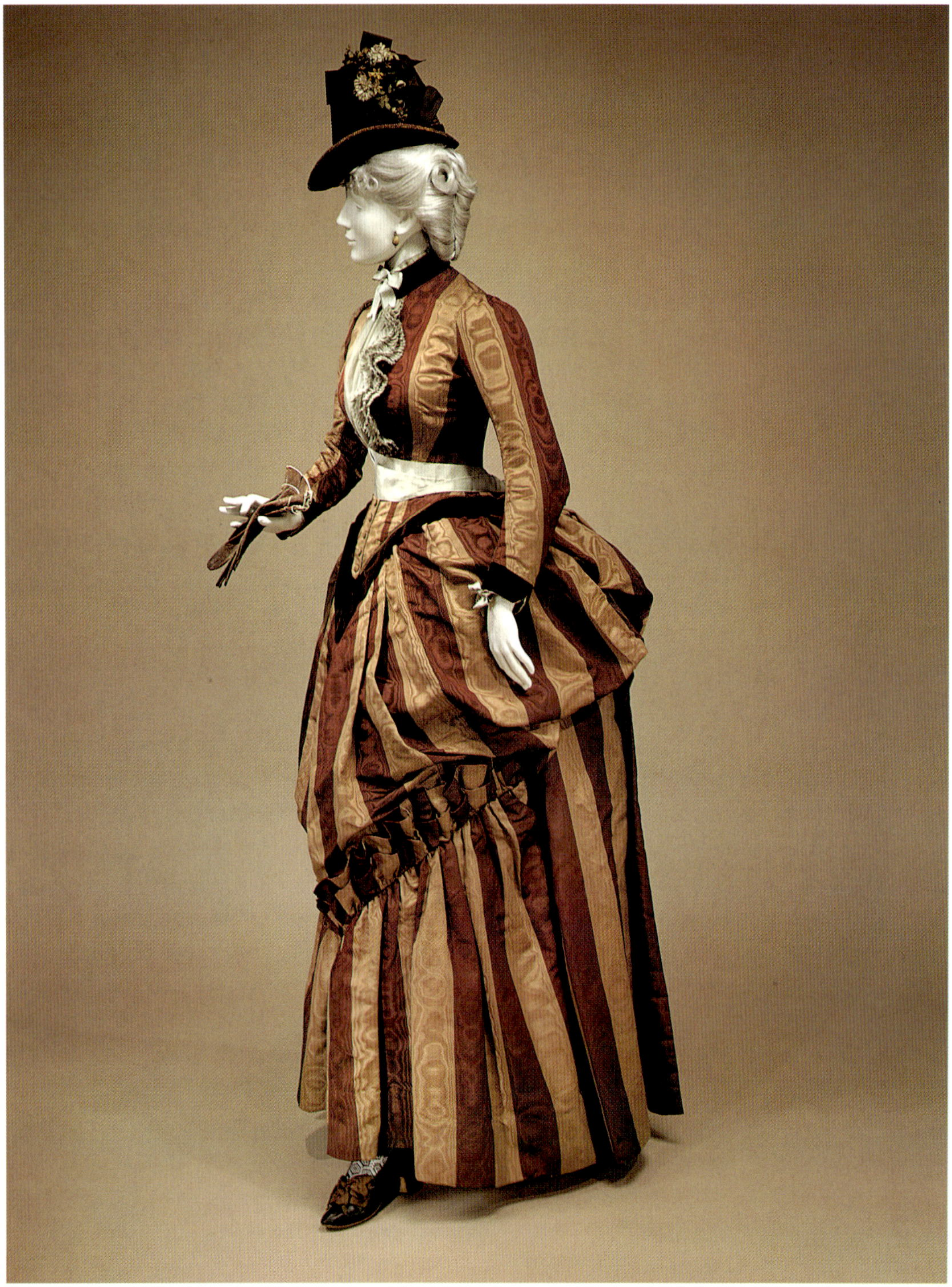

Day dress, signed Worth, c.1888. The Brooklyn Museum, New York.

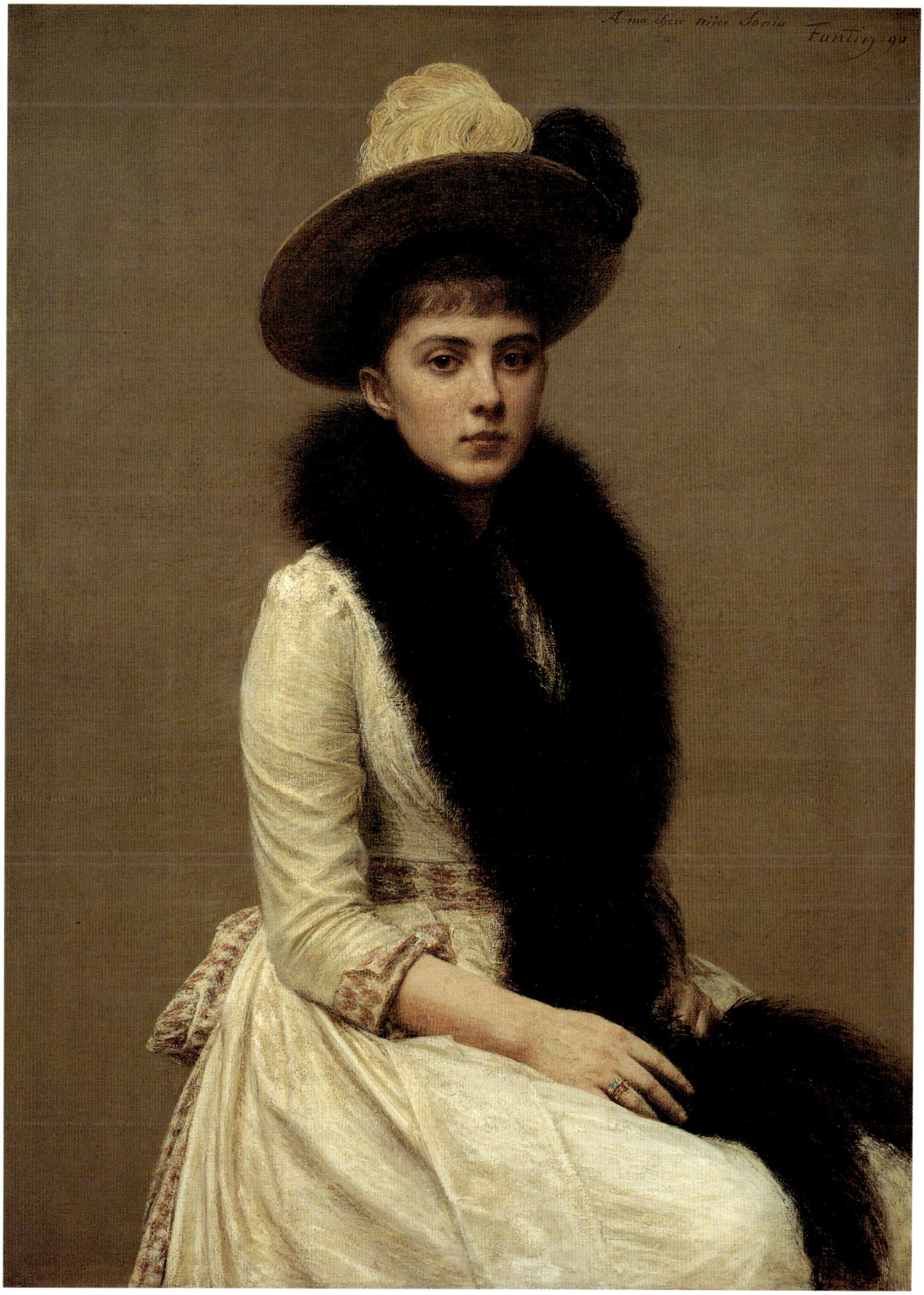
A ma chère nièce Sonia
Fantin 90

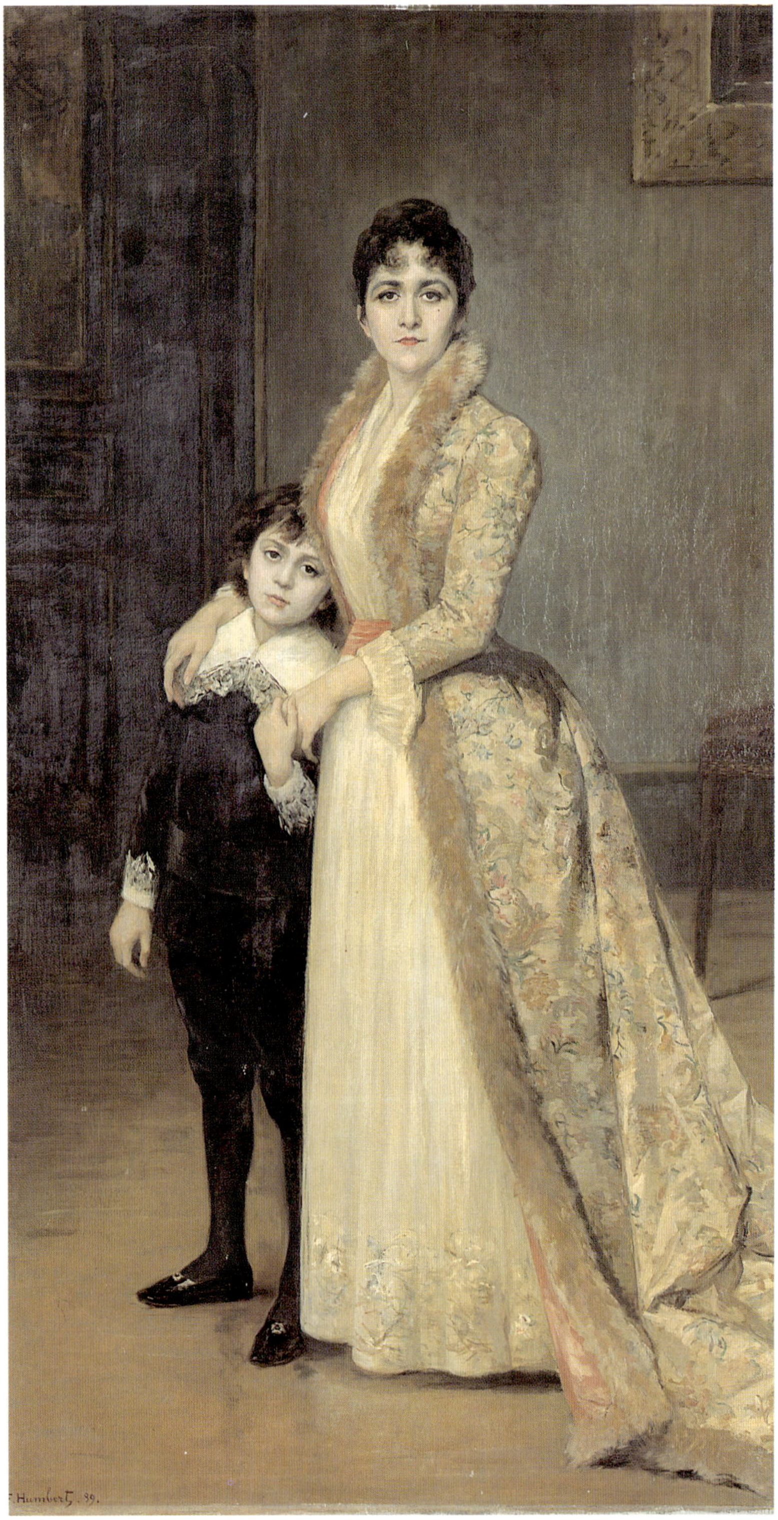

Ferdinand Humbert,
Baroness Gourgaud and her son, *1889.*
Musée d'Orsay, Paris.

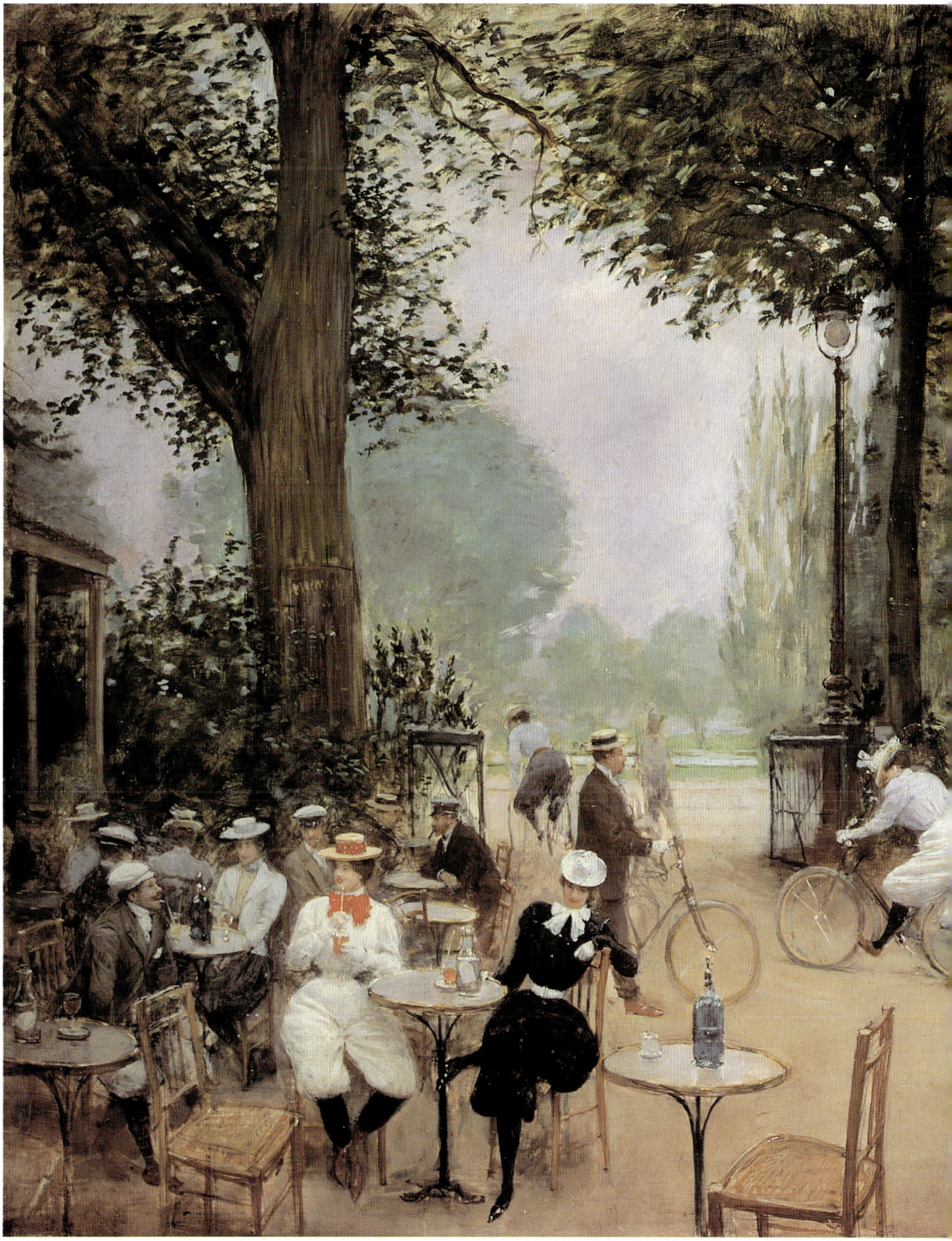

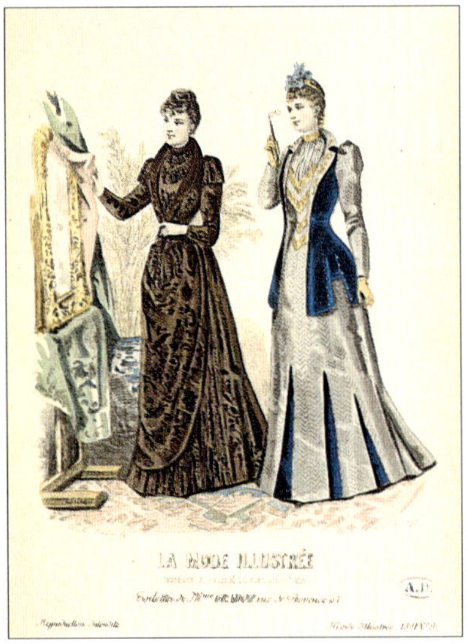

Henri Fantin-Latour, Portrait of Sonia, *1890. National Gallery of Art, Chester Dale Collection, Washington (facing page).*

La Mode illustrée: *dress in bronze brocade with a small pattern and mid-season dress, March 1891 (left).*

La Mode illustrée: *Mademoiselle Boitte's hats, October 1891 (right).*

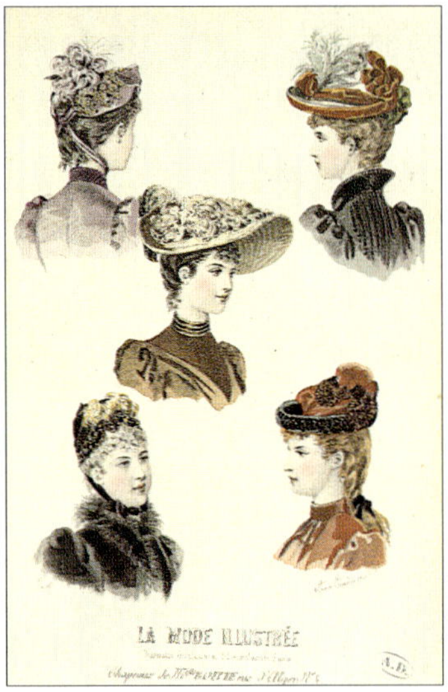

The new and inescapable accessory, lasting to 1900, was the boa. *L'Art et la mode* of 31 January 1891 listed the names of all types of boas in a double page of illustrations with captions. They range from the 'first boa' to the 'British boa' which is worn when skating, by way of 'honest boas perfectly resembling those which are not'. *The Portrait of Sonia* by Fantin-Latour (1890, Washington DC, National Gallery of Art, Chester Dale Collection) might very well illustrate the latter, just as an undated letter of Degas to Mme Dietz-Monin illustrates, if not the dishonest boa, then at least the destructive boa or the boa which sows discord:

> Let us drop the subject of the portrait, I beg you. I was so surprised by your letter, proposing that I reduce it to a boa and a hat, that I shall not reply to you. I thought that Auguste or M. Groult, to whom I had spoken of your latest idea and my absolute disinclination to accede to it, had informed you of this.
>
> Should I say that I regret having started something in my own way, only to have it entirely transformed in yours? That would not be very polite, but all the same...But, dear Madam, I cannot say any more without making you aware of how hurt I am.
>
> Leaving aside my unhappy art, please accept my best regards.[2]

The years 1892–6 were a period of excess. Sleeves were inflated to the point where they became, in 1895, veritable hot-air balloons. The silhouette in fashion prints is so stylized that it resembles a kind of hour-glass: sleeves a metre wide, tiny waist, bell skirt flared into a corolla, occupying a space as wide as that across the shoulders. The outfit is as conspicuously cumbersome as the crinoline, but with a radically different balance (or rather imbalance). The stance of the figure has changed completely: a decisive, striking woman has made her appearance.

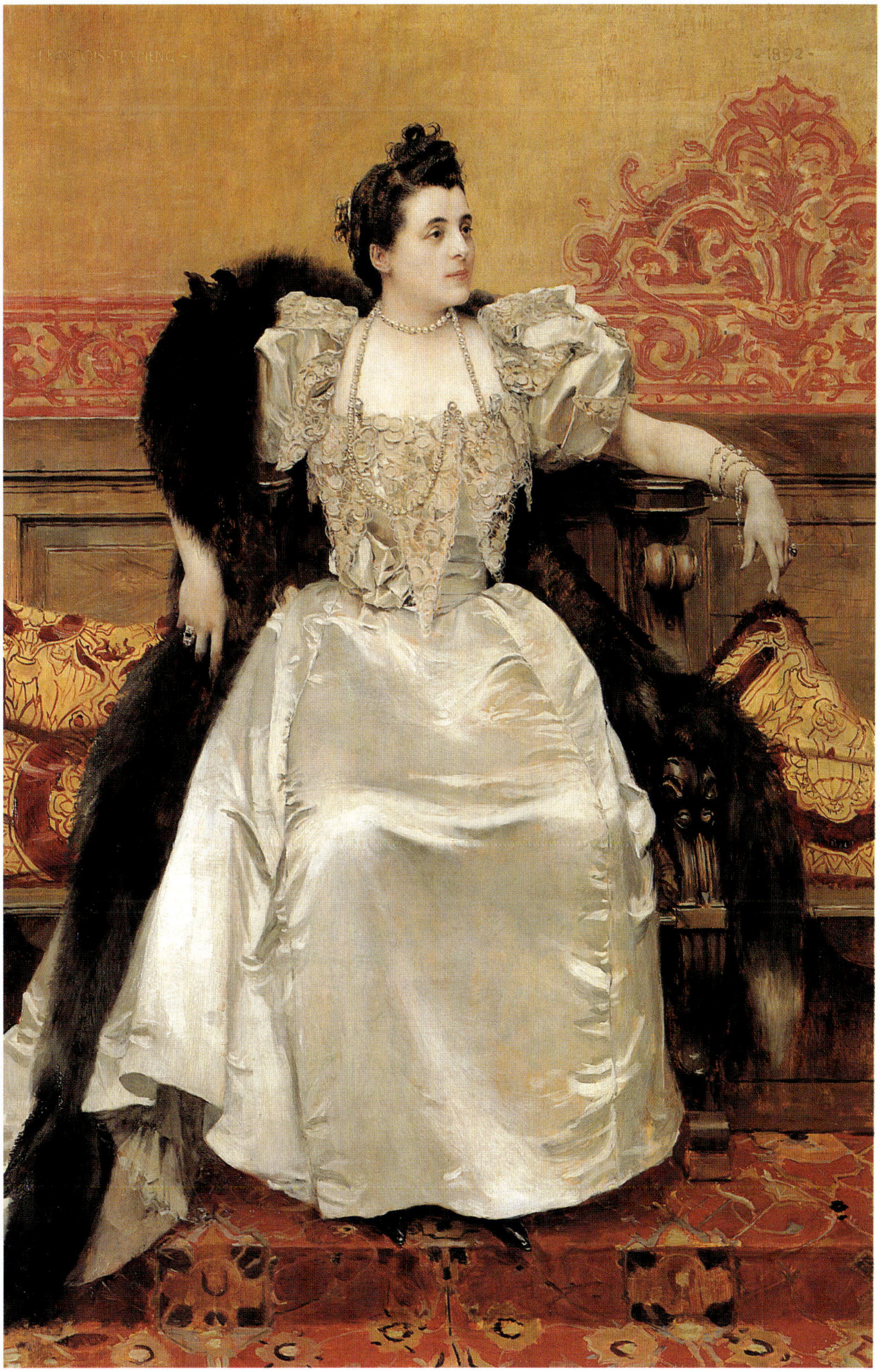

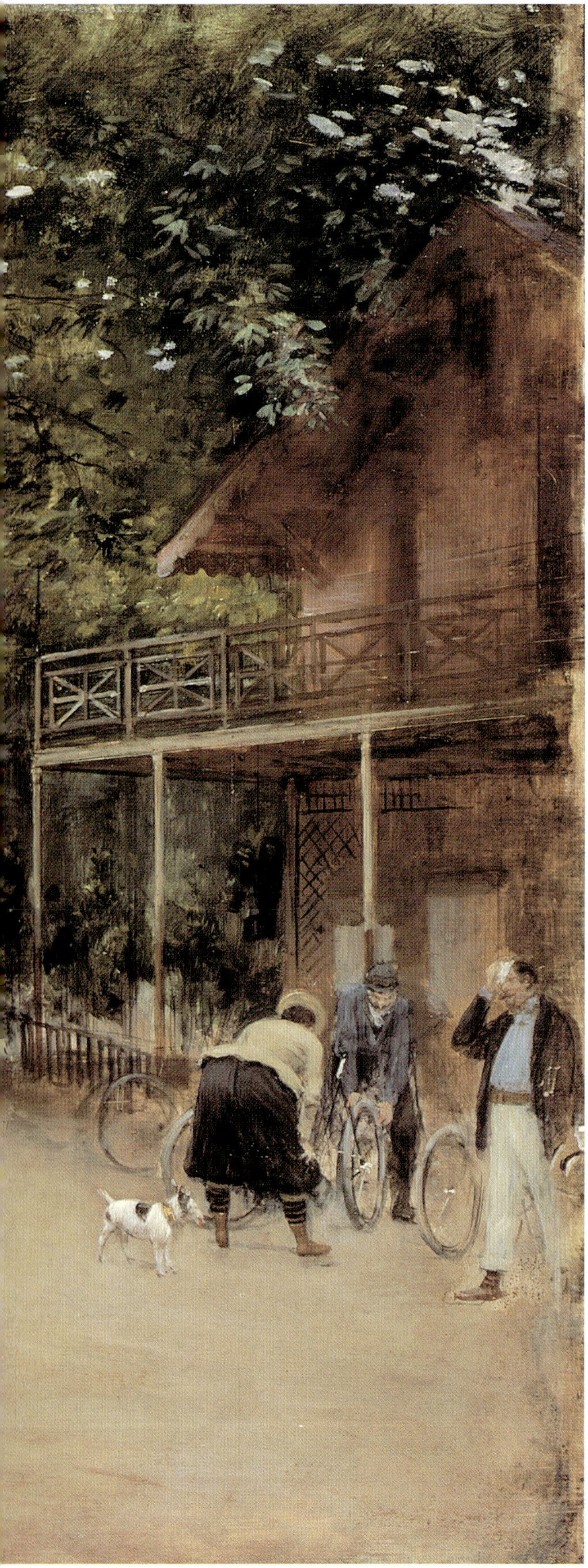

Jean Béraud,
The Chalet du cycle
in the Bois de Boulogne, *c. 1900.*
Musée Carnavalet, Paris.

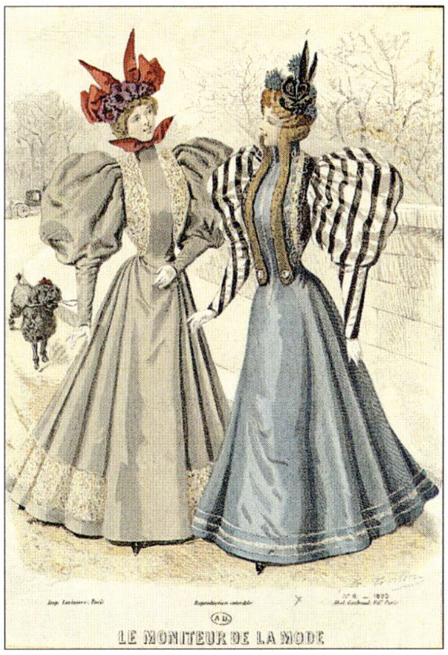

François Flameng, Madame Gaston Menier, *1892. Musée du Petits Palais, Paris (facing page).*

Le Moniteur de la mode: *town fashions, 1895 (left).*

La Revue de la mode: *town fashions, 1892 (right).*

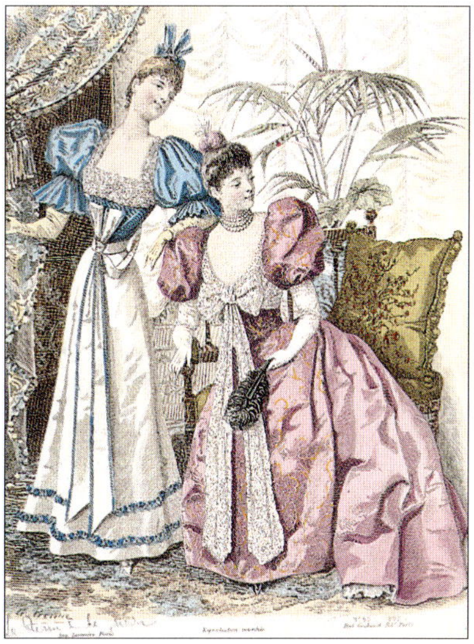

Even if social pressures were still very constricting, women's status was evolving towards greater freedom and responsibility. The Belle Epoque was the period when women gained access to secondary education, the right to divorce, to professional life and participation in sport. There was a great vogue for cycling, shown by Béraud in *Le Chalet du cycle in the Bois de Boulogne* (c.1900, Paris, Musée Carnavalet).

Fashion reflected these changes. Pantaloons, which had provoked such a scandal when Miss Angela Bloomer wore them for the first time in 1850, reappeared in the outfit of velocipede riders, though in the very modest form of wide, baggy trousers. Reactions were again very violent, but to no avail: this time the trousers won the day, their comfort and rationality earning them unanimous support among young women. Men confined themselves to noting this state of affairs and expressing their astonishment. For example, Mallarmé, who had been asked: 'Which do you prefer, male trousers or the skirt, from the threefold viewpoint of beauty, hygiene and correctness?' replied: 'Confronted by your question, as by those straddlers of steel, I am no more than a passer-by who takes cover. But if their motive is to show their legs, I should prefer the dazzlement to come (melting, piercing me with its darts) from a raised skirt, that feminine vestige, and not from mannish trousers.'[3]

Another sign of the transfer of male garments to the female wardrobe was the emergence of the *costume-tailleur*. Originated by an Englishman, Redfern, it comprised a long skirt, a jacket and a long-sleeved blouse. The jacket was inspired by the men's garment, with the same collar, the same straight sleeves with turned-up cuffs and the same material. Little by little, this new outfit was widely adopted, both by the first working women and by the elegant creatures for whom to order their clothes from an English tailor was the latest thing.

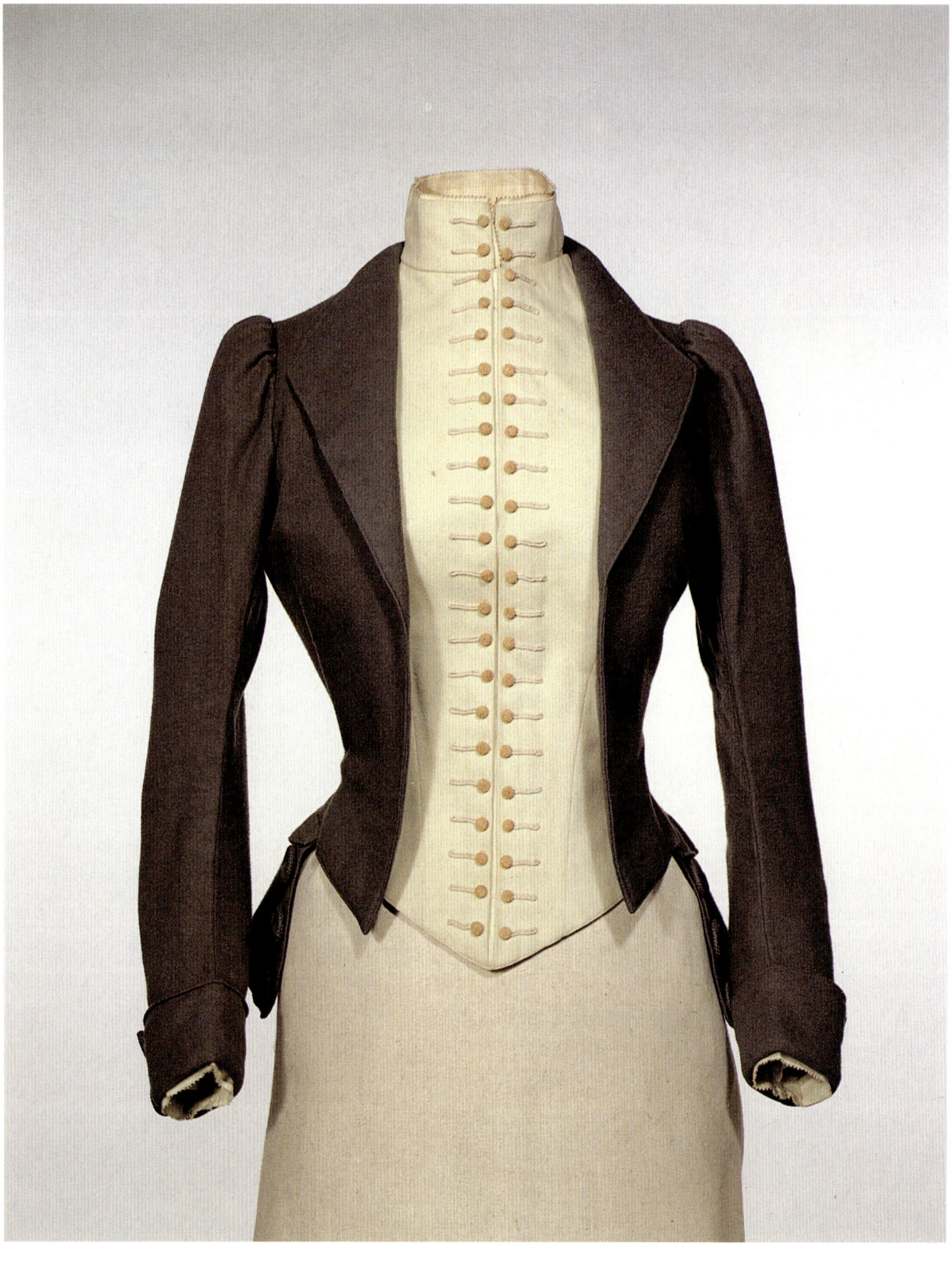

Tailored jacket, signed Rouff, c.1890. Musée de la Mode et du Costume, Paris.

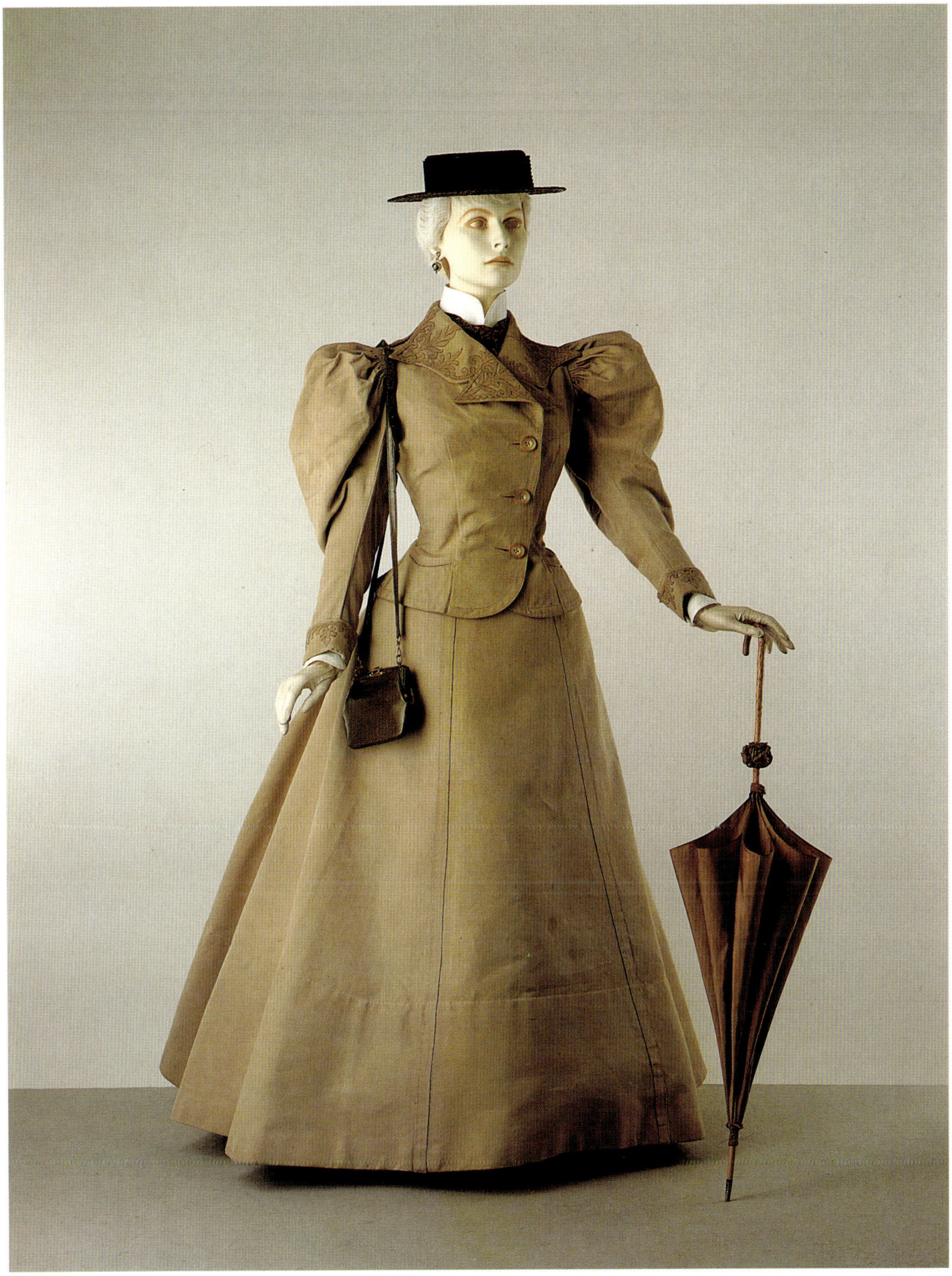

Tailored cotton jacket, signed Jacques Doucet, c.1895. The Victoria and Albert Museum, London.

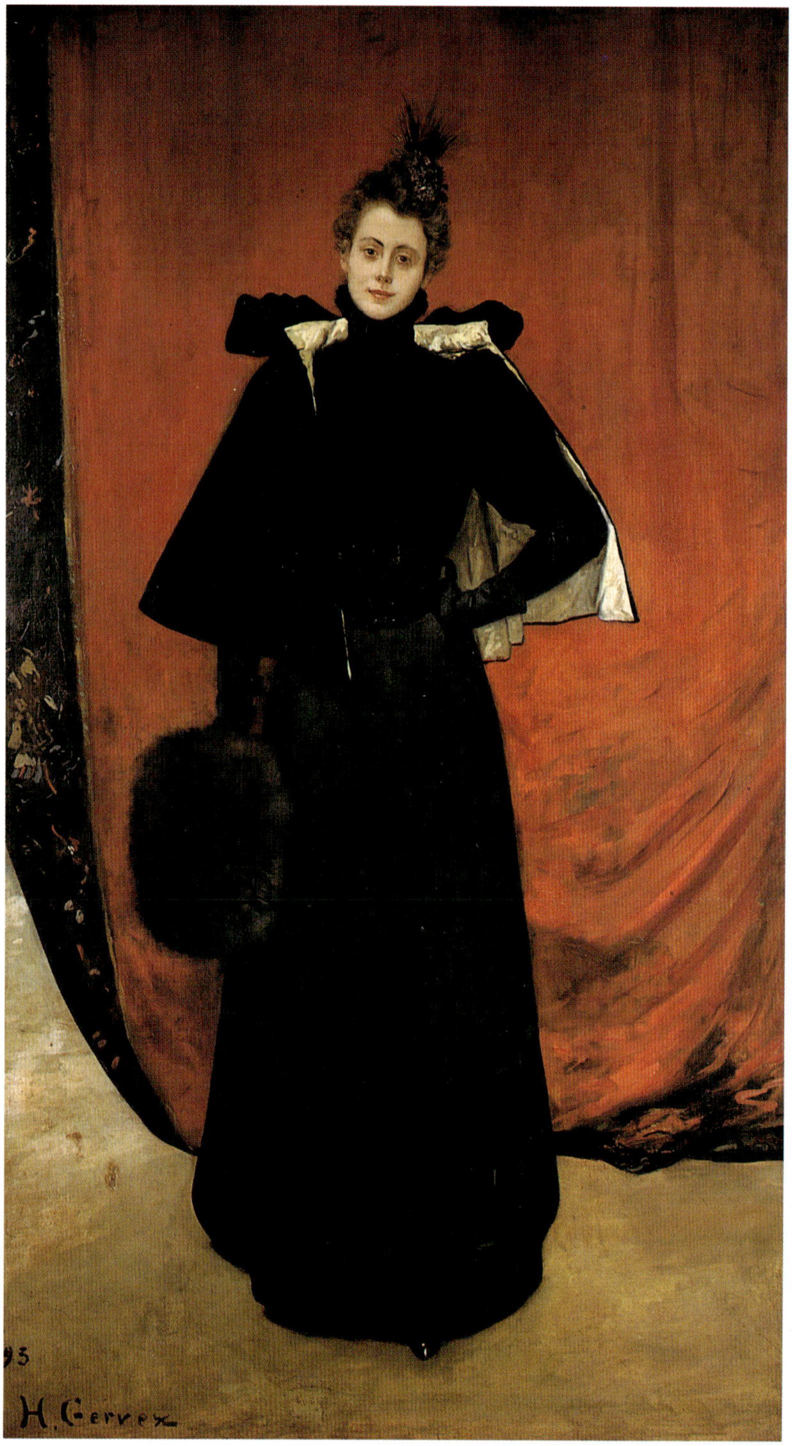

Henri Gervex, Portrait of Madame Gervex, *1890.*
Musée des Beaux-Arts, Chambéry.

'Bodice-jackets' had wide lapels, pointed or flounced, or superimposed collars. The corsages of dresses were made, as before, of yokes, but the use of superimposed 'berthas' (often of lace or point lace) increased, like that of collarettes and 'epaulettes' (flounced material covering the shoulder). In fact, anything that could overload the bust was adopted. To contain this amplitude, coats and jackets took on the form of capes: *collets*, *pèlerines* and *mantes* were different kinds of cape. Fur remained a favourite trimming for such garments. Gervex, in portraying his *Woman leaving the theatre* (1890, Chambéry, Musée des Beaux Arts), evokes the grace of the little *collet* - like a butterfly that has settled on the shoulders. Fabrics and colours remained those of the preceding years, brocades and moirés becoming more and more popular. Hats looked somewhat extravagant, with plumes projecting from the top of the head, or with 'antenna' ornaments, scrolls, little wings or bows adorning flat hats.

In 1896–7 sleeves reverted to being small balloons or little flounces forming epaulettes. The skirt also grew narrower, with a floating hem and a small train. At last a new, supple silhouette, accentuating the curve of the back and a prominent bosom, prefigured the twentieth century. With Art Nouveau, a new style came into being, in which the outline was shaped by nothing except a corset, and then by the body itself (when Poiret, influenced by the Russian ballet, launched the *style sultane* in 1911). Designers' inspiration was freed from the historical references which had been a dominant characteristic of fashion in the nineteenth century, and had been no less influential in the fine arts. Indeed, a gaze turned permanently towards the past, though sometimes tinged with exoticism, was at the heart of the whole sartorial creation of the period, when fashion seems to have been entirely indifferent to contemporary cultural or political events.

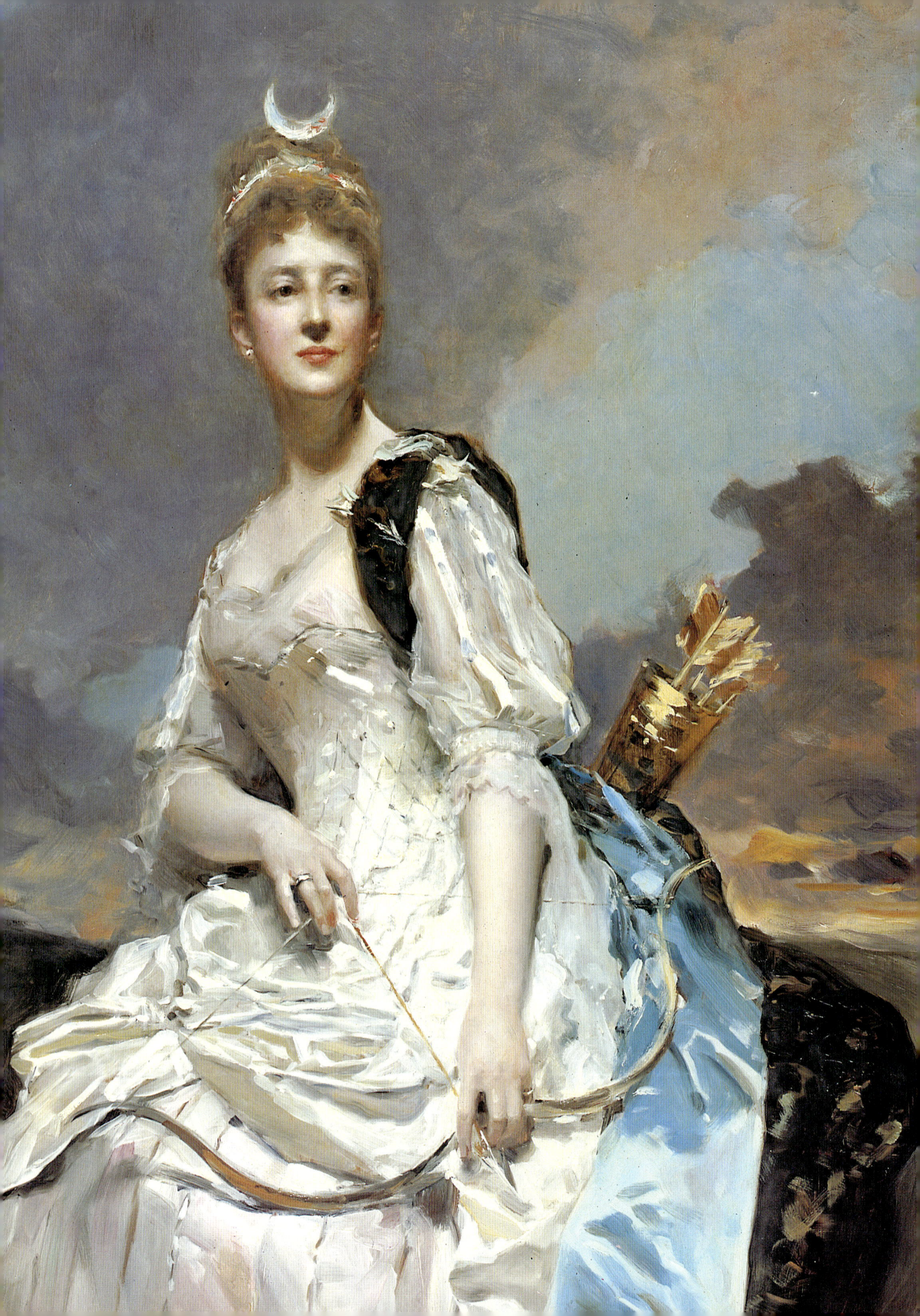

Chapter Three

Historicism and Exoticism

Raimundo de Madrazo y Garreta,
The Marquise D'Hervey Saint-Denys as Diana, *1888 (detail).*
Musée D'Orsay, Paris.

Historicism

Bals masqués and fancy-dress balls

The nineteenth century inherited an infatuation with fancy dress from the *ancien régime*. The July Monarchy revived the Shrovetide Carnival, and after 1833 most Paris theatres opened their doors for a season of masked balls.[1] This institution continued in the second half of the century; in addition, costume balls were held by the court and by society women.

There are many accounts of these festivities: *Le Journal des demoiselles* of 1854 describes the Tuileries ball where the empress 'in a Grecian costume of dazzling beauty' and a 'Polish queen' rubbed shoulders with numerous Louis XV and Hebrew costumes.[2] Later, in 1862:

> The empress wore a gown of red satin with an overskirt of black velvet, covered in diamonds. Princesse Mathilde, dressed as a noble lady from the Medici era, was literally covered in the beautiful emeralds we know so well, while Princesse Clothilde wore powdered hair and a robe of red brocade... Mme la Comtesse de Castiglione was disguised as Salammbo ...and Mme la comtesse de Brignont as a Bacchante...[3]

The author of the article in *L'Artiste* earnestly pursues a debate which had been provoked by the costume of Mme de Castiglione, judged by some to be 'from the time of Augustus' and by others to be 'an archaeological costume worn by the Carthaginian Queen Salammbo' or, again, Etruscan: 'However, my hypothesis – and historians will agree it is the most likely – is that Mme de Castiglione was a Roman lady from the age of Commodus or Heliogabalus, a time when people liked to mingle Roman and oriental elements in their costumes.'[4] As we see, the archaeological enthusiasm of such experts knew no bounds. The Comtesse can be seen dressed as an Etrurian queen, an eighteenth-century *marquise* and as the Hermit of Passy, in a series of watercolour photographs kept at the Château de Compiègne. Indeed, this curiously narcissistic person transfigured herself more and more frequently in such likenesses, most of which were intended for the eyes of Napoleon III.

Flaubert's heroine (Salammbo) likewise found herself reincarnated in many society ladies intoxicated with exoticism. As was only proper, queens and famous courtesans of former centuries were also favourite models. The Marquise d'Hervey Saint-Denys, for example, chose a costume of Diana and had herself immortalized by the Spanish artist Madrazo y Garreta, dressed in pseudo-seventeenth-century attire and flourishing the huntress's quiver and arrows. In her hair she wears a crescent inlaid with diamonds, a fashionable adornment which is to be seen in a number of portraits, such as that of *Madame Stern* by Carolus-Duran (Paris, Musée du Petit Palais), or the *Portrait of the Comtesse Aymery de la Rochefoucauld* by Chaplin (Paris, private collection).

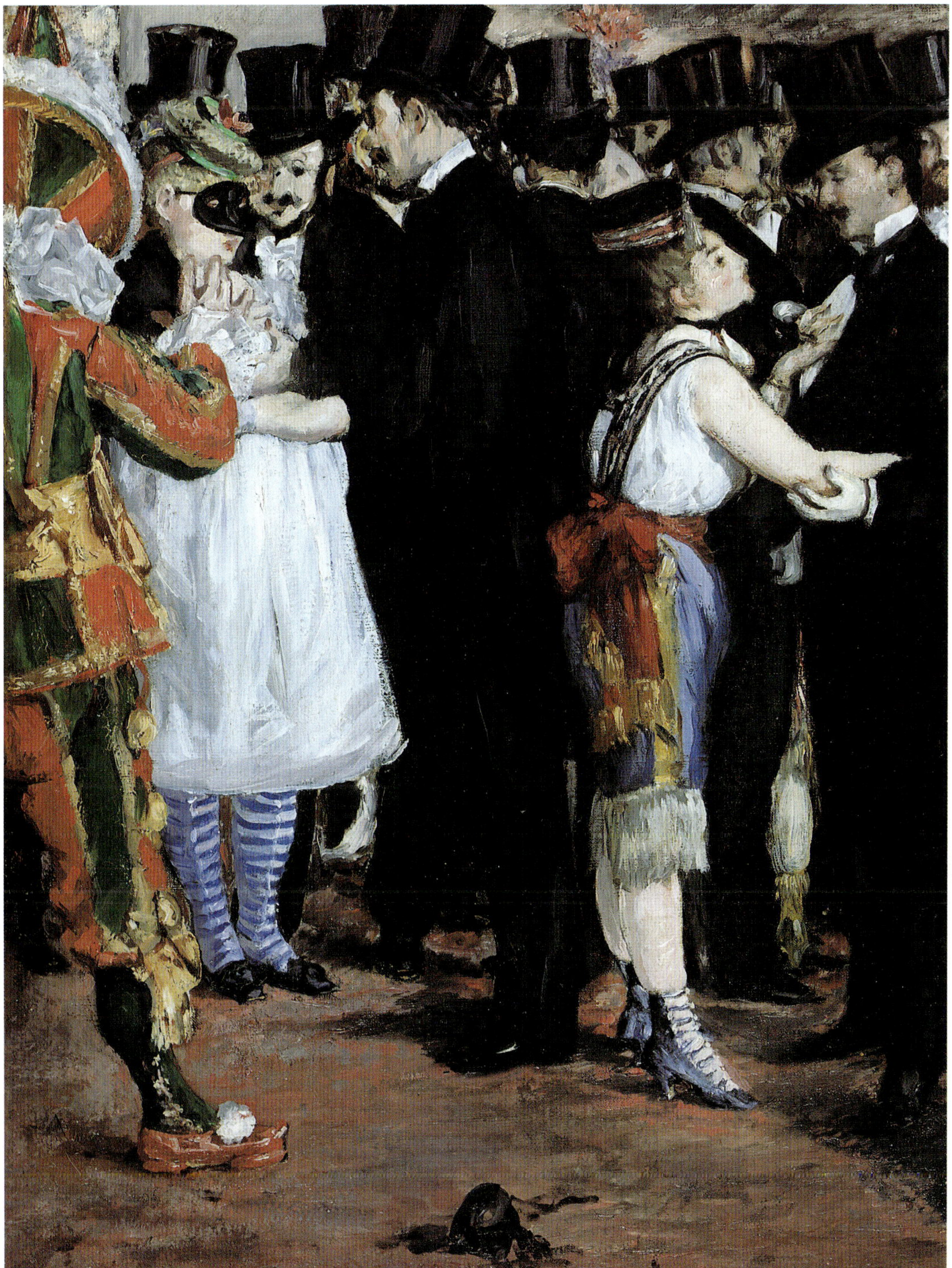

Edouard Manet, Masked Ball at the Opera, *1872–1873 (detail). National Gallery of Art, Washington.*

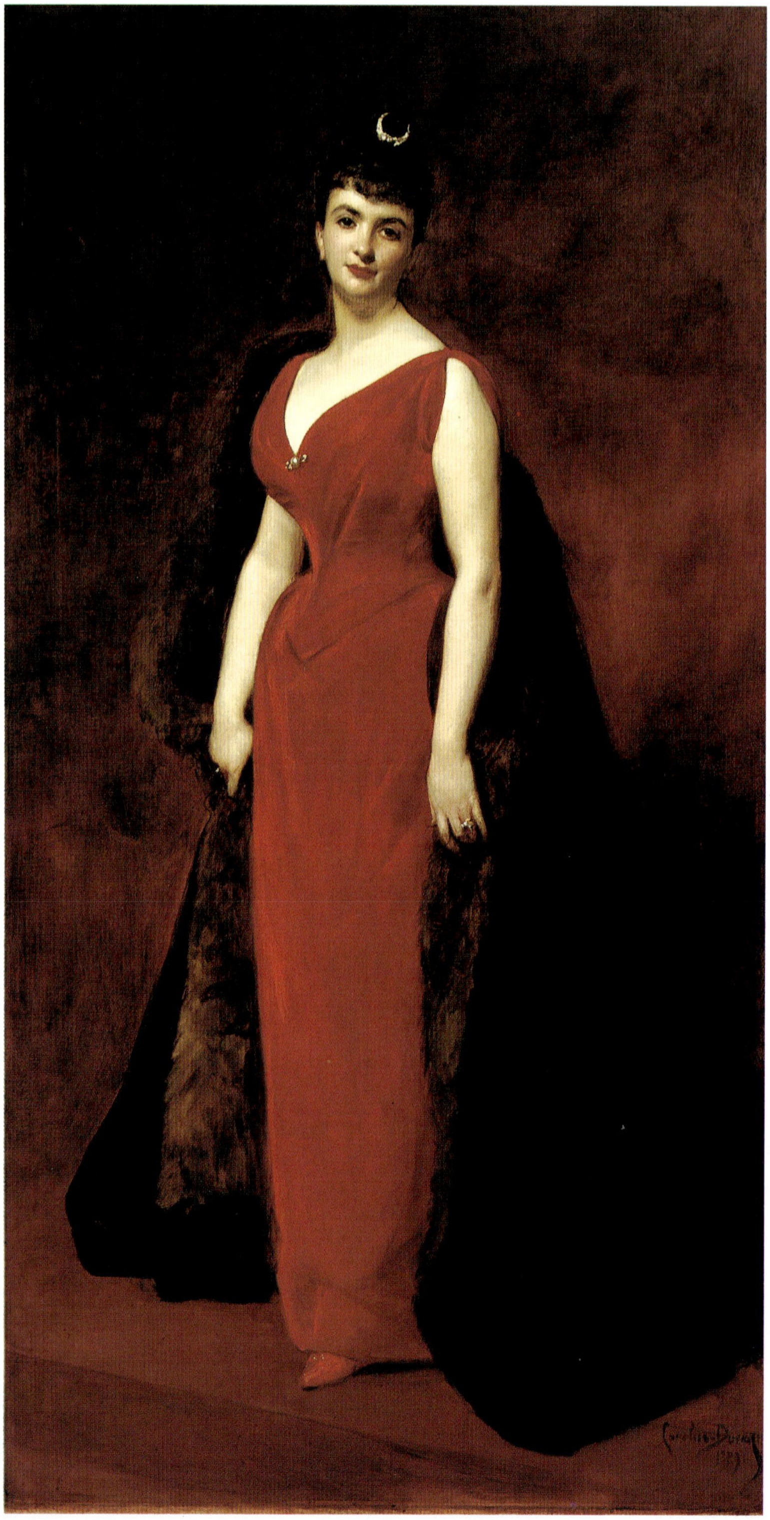

Carolus-Duran,
Madame Stern, *1889.*
Musée du Petit Palais, Paris.

Raimundo de Madrazo y Garreta, The Marquise d'Hervey Saint-Denys as Diana, 1888.
Musée d'Orsay, Paris (facing page).

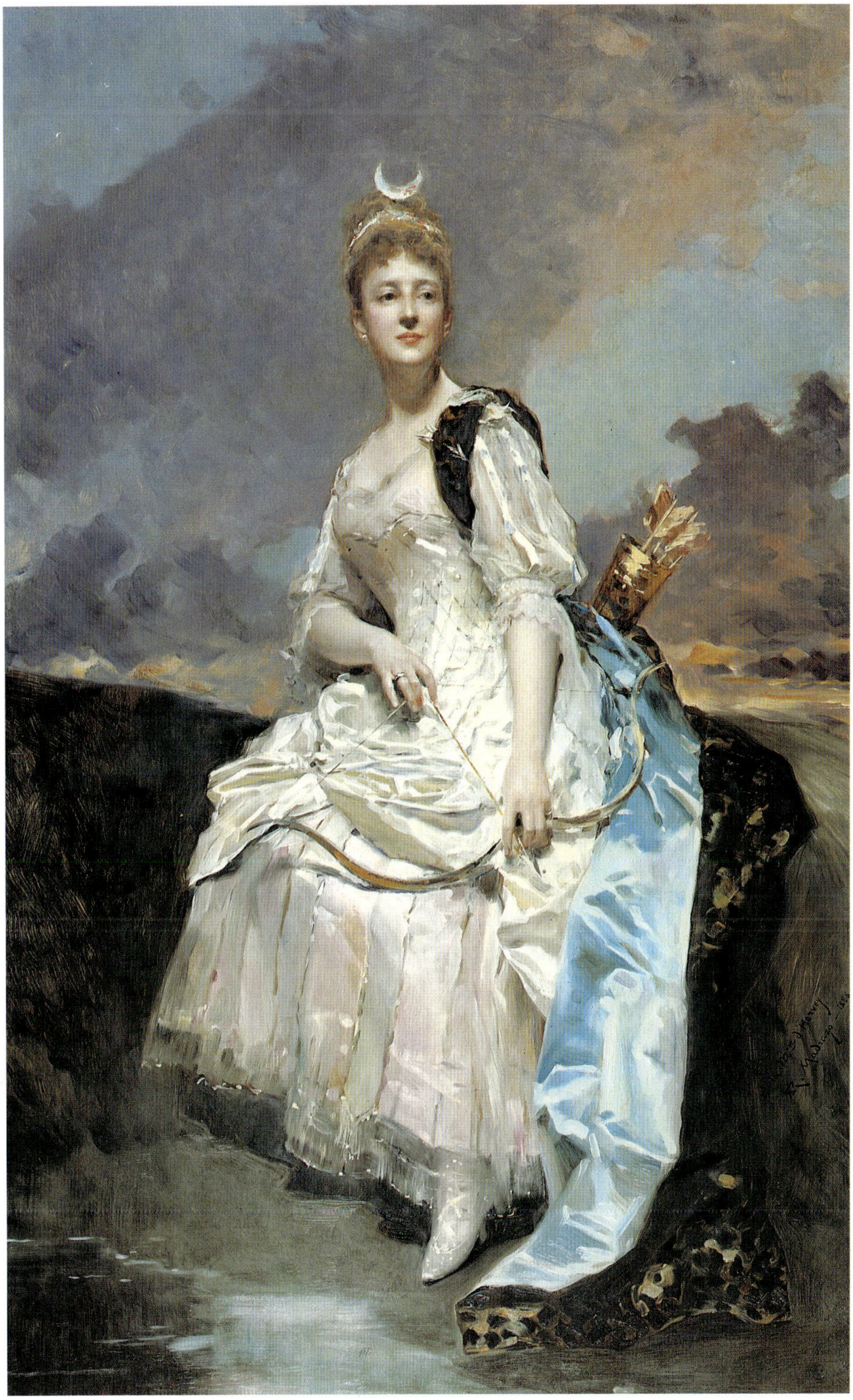

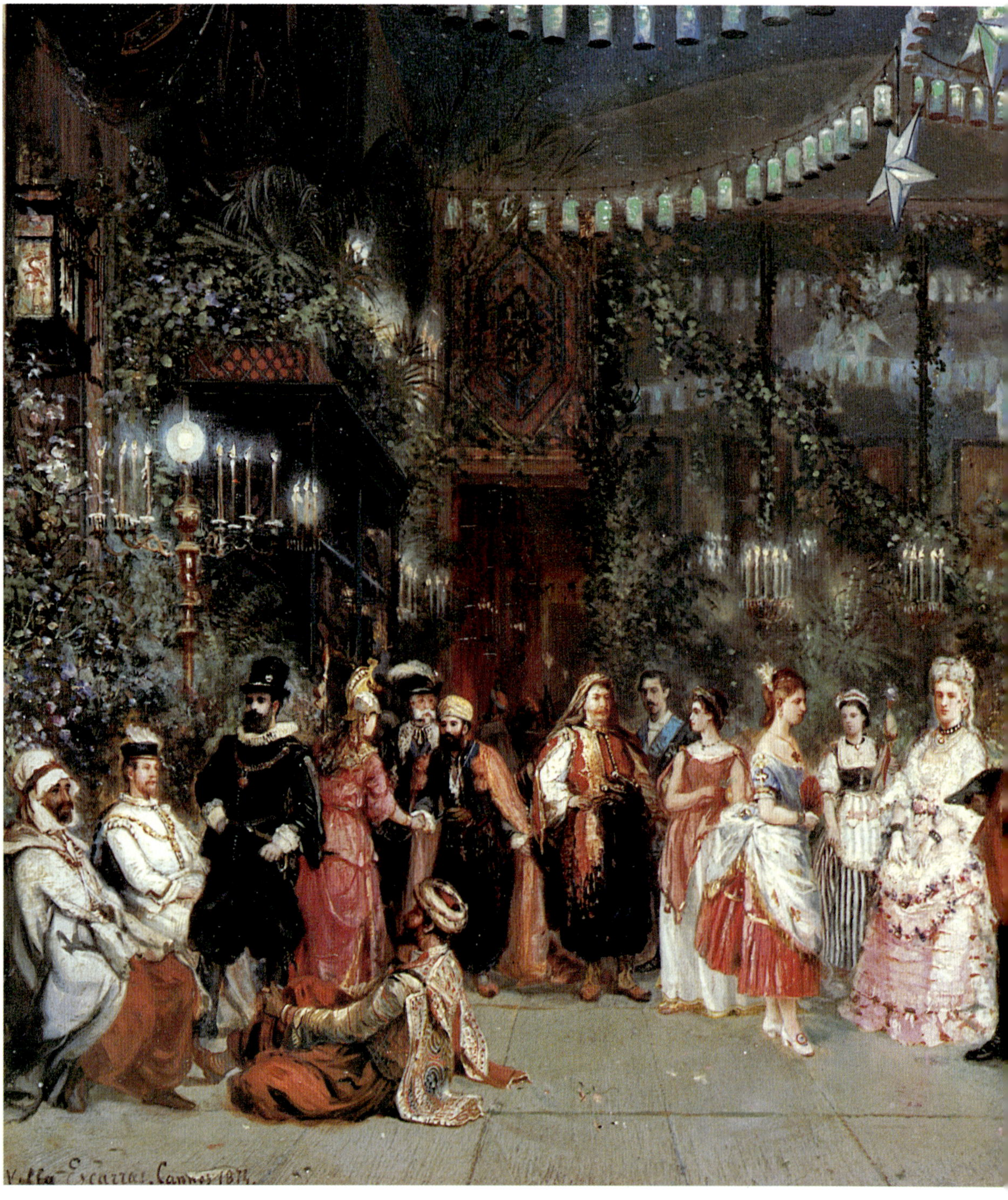

Pierre Van Elven, Baron Lycklama's fancy-dress ball, *1874. Musée de la Castre, Cannes.*

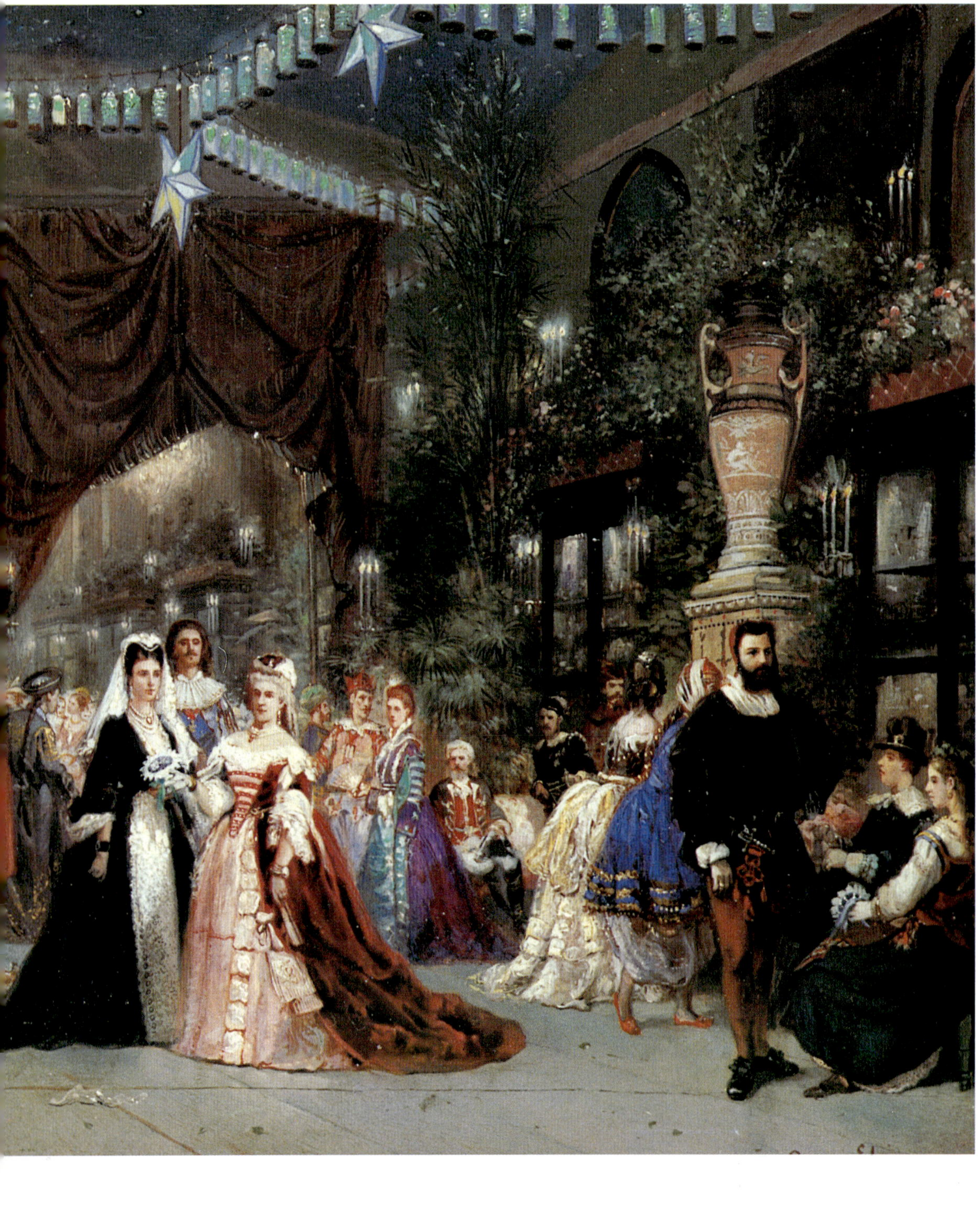

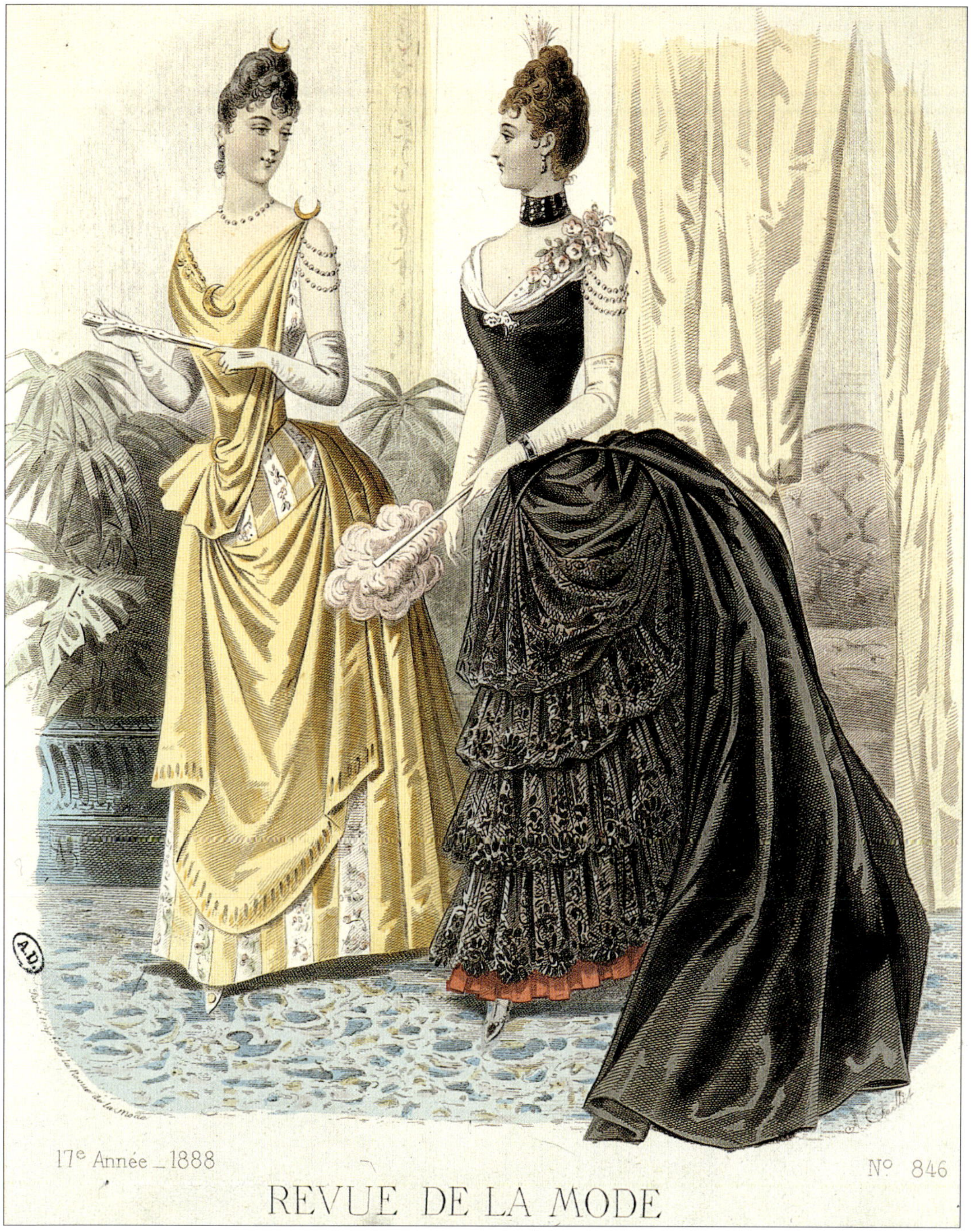

La Revue de la mode: *ball-gowns, 1888.*
Le Moniteur de la mode: *fancy-dress costumes, supplement to the second issue of January 1863 (facing page).*

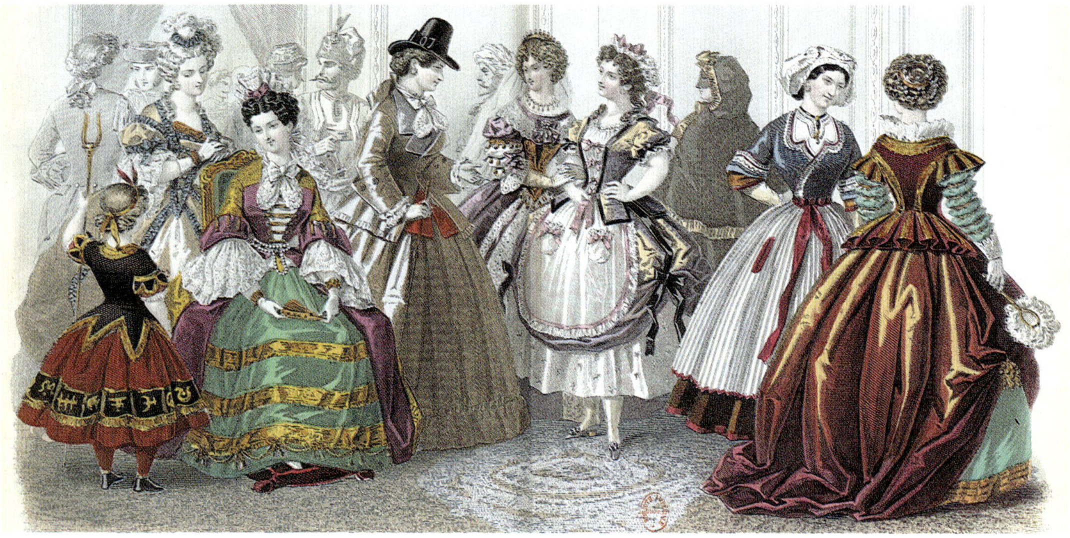

The inspiration for these costumes was often taken from fashion publications which, apart from illustrated reports on past balls, also published pattern plates, such as *Les Filles de l'empire céleste* (Paris, 1850) showing oriental-style outfits, or extracts from the book by César Vecellio, *Costumes anciens et modernes* (1590), republished in 1859 by Firmin-Didot.

In the nineteenth century, people were passionately interested in the history of dress. The century of the Enlightenment had laid the foundation for precise historical research, but it only produced solid results in the following century. Collections abounded: in 1852, Paul Lacroix published *Les Costumes historiques de la France d'après les mouvements les plus authentiques, statues, bas reliefs*...This ten-volume work took its inspiration from famous works of art and from a very old collection of watercolours, *Le Recueil Gaignières* from the sixteenth century, kept in the Cabinet des Estampes at the Bibliothèque Nationale. This source was used later by Augustin Challamel for *La France et les français a travers les siècles* (published in four volumes in 1884). Two other works had a similar resonance: *Le Costume historique* by Racinet (six volumes, 1888), made up of large colour plates mingling history and exoticism, and the older *Galerie des modes et des costumes français* (400 colour plates, published in 1778–88), which was highly prized. This documentation was used by couturiers, but also by history painters, for whom historical accuracy was becoming an unavoidable necessity.

The Press made such data easily accessible by publishing separate booklets and lithographs. For example, *La Mode artistique* of 1873 offered its readers, for 48 francs, the ninety-six plates of 'historical French modes and costumes, drawn and engraved by the Pauquet brothers after the best artists of each epoch and the most authentic

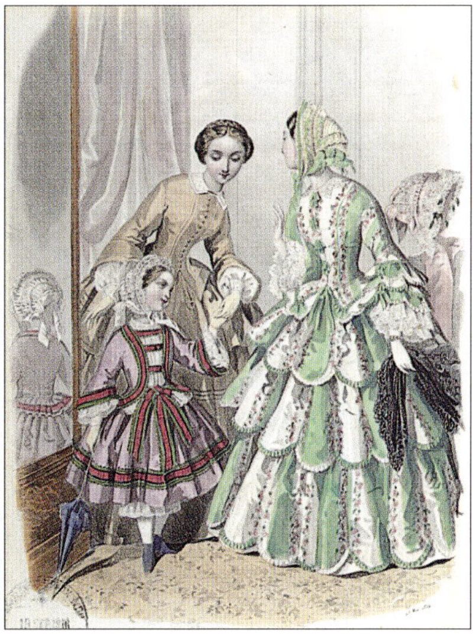

Le Magasin des demoiselles, *25 May 1854 (left).*

Le Magasin des demoiselles, *25 May 1854 (right).*

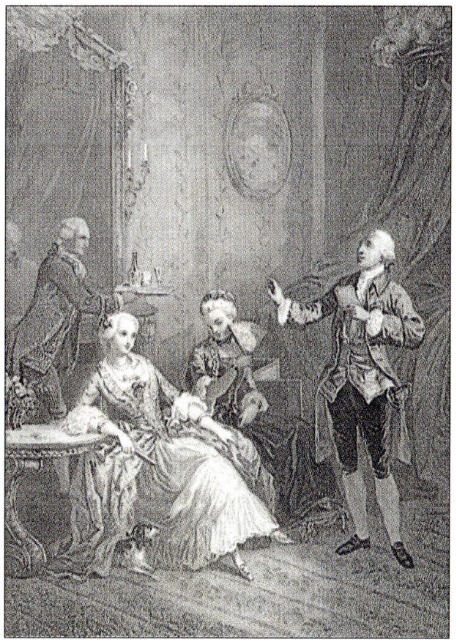

documents'. Rejecting an over-literal use of these patterns for fancy dress, the publicity notice claims that

> the great lady, as well as the couturière, could derive much profit [from the plates] by creating novelties mingling the fancies of one century with those of the previous one, and matching the whole to the taste of today which, we should be aware, is especially fond of reminiscences of times past.

This desire, satisfied by fancy dress, to escape from the present in time and space, was also expressed in everyday fashion. Not the least paradoxical aspect of this fashion is that it was both modern (in that it was the source and product of a fast-expanding industry) and historicist, in its desperate attempt to resurrect the aristocratic past. In a similar paradox it was middle class – or was in the process of becoming middle class, since ready-made clothing was spreading fashion throughout society – yet was also highly élitist. Everywhere, we come across an astonishing, even touching nostalgia. Articles and reports lamented the blessed times before the Revolution, when 'etiquette decided everything, governing fashion without interference'.[5] At Saint-Cloud the Princesse de Metternich held pastoral festivities where women's faces were made up and powdered white in a style inspired by the paintings of Watteau and Lancret.[6] Collections of costumes also demonstrate the frequent use of eighteenth-century dress, transformed and adapted to nineteenth-century idiom.

Couturiers at the museum

Patterns were taken from museums, and sometimes from portrait galleries in country houses.[7] Maxime, in *La Curée*, goes to the Louvre looking for hairstyles for her mother-in-

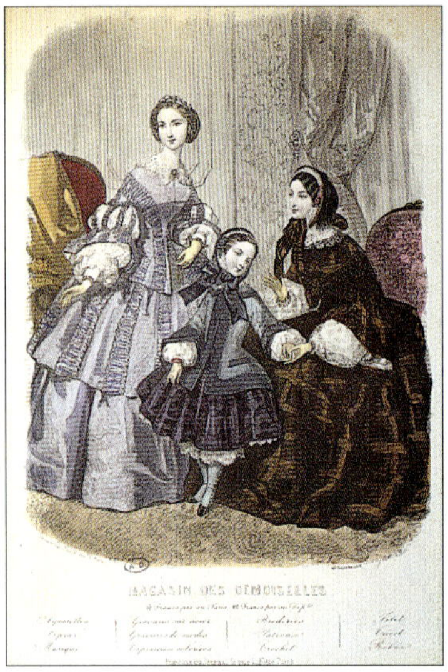

Le Magasin des demoiselles, *25 November 1856* *(left)*.

Harper's Bazar, *1872* *(right)*.

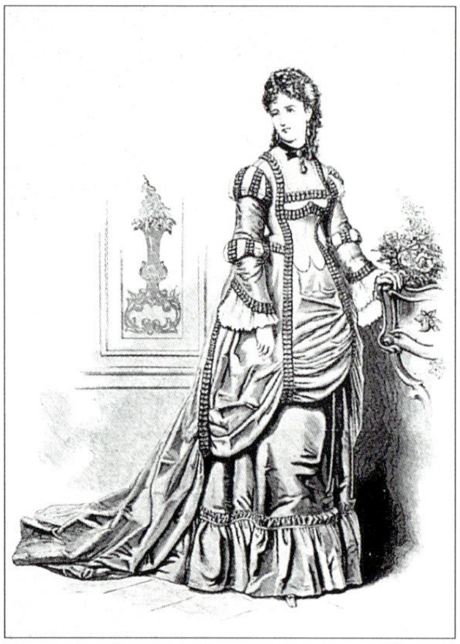

law; jewellers frequent the Musée Campana, while couturières 'study the beauties of Louis XIII, Louis XIV and Louis XV, in search of ideas for sleeves, *décolletés* and collars. 'Collars are worn very large. They are given all kinds of historical names recalling the reigns of Louis XIII and Louis XIV, Cinq-Mars, Anne of Austria, Mancini, etc. All these fancies are copied from portraits of the time.'[8] Couturières make much of their erudition in their publicity: 'Mme X...consulting the last century from the cool fans of Watteau to the aristocratic paintings of Largillière, makes dresses that would have drawn admiring glances at the Trianon.'[9] Accounts of such fashions are innumerable. If they are to be believed, an army of couturières ferreted among the galleries of the Louvre in search of Louis XIII hats or Madame Dubarry corsages. Unfortunately, no direct correlation has been established between an old painting and a nineteenth-century dress, for several reasons: very little research has been done on historicism in fashion, and the content of costume collections is, after all, limited; finally, the couturières' own interpretations cannot be ignored.

These historical details provided the 'novelties' of each season; they caused a stir and then went out of date, just as they had done when they first appeared, only to re-surface amid the same furore a few years later. Thus 'Louis XV shoes' were already out of fashion in 1853, but this did not prevent them from re-appearing intermittently up to 1900.

Some artists were given special attention: van Dyck, Rubens, Watteau, Largillière, Vigée Lebrun. The portraits of Marie de' Médicis[11] by Rubens, and especially those of Hélène Fourment, are mentioned very frequently. Rubens had been an example throughout Europe since the eighteenth century. A novella by Théophile Gautier, *La Toison d'or*, may have been inspired by him. Its hero, Tiburce, in love with the

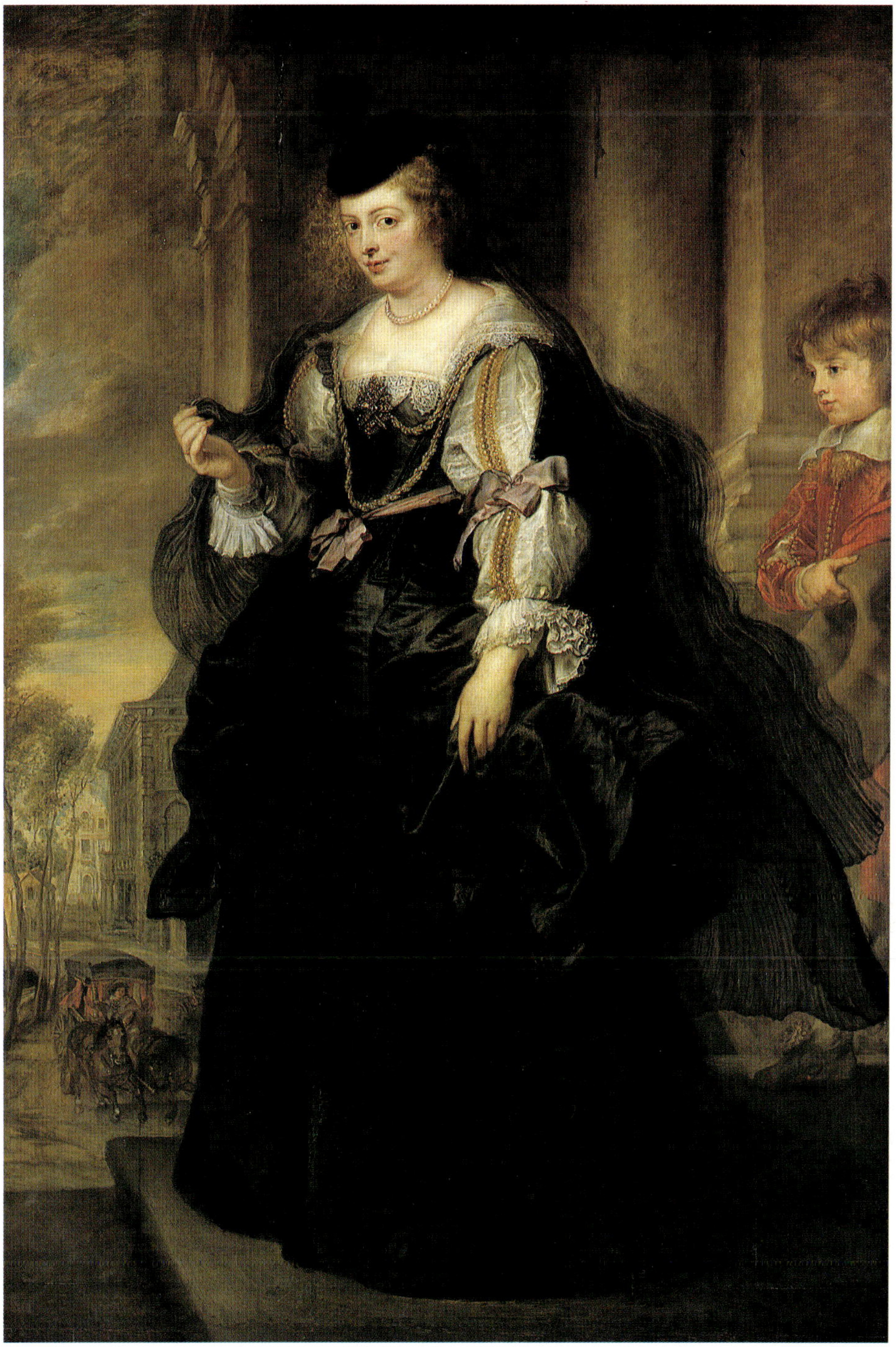

Peter Paul Rubens, Hélène Fourment in a carriage, *c.1631. Musée du Louvre, Paris.*
Antoine Watteau, L'Enseigne de Gersaint, *1720 (detail),*
Palais de Charlottenbourg, Berlin (facing page).

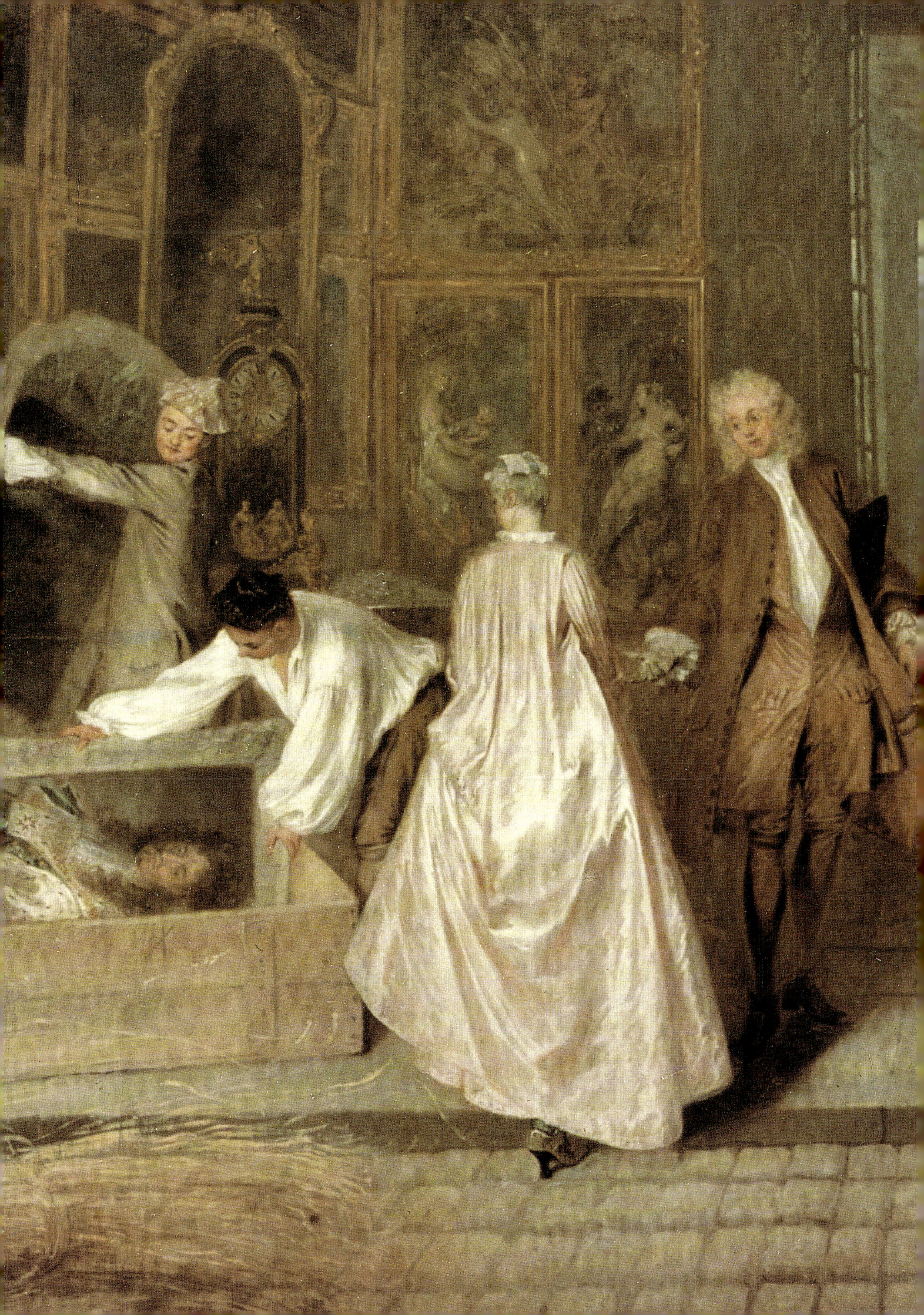

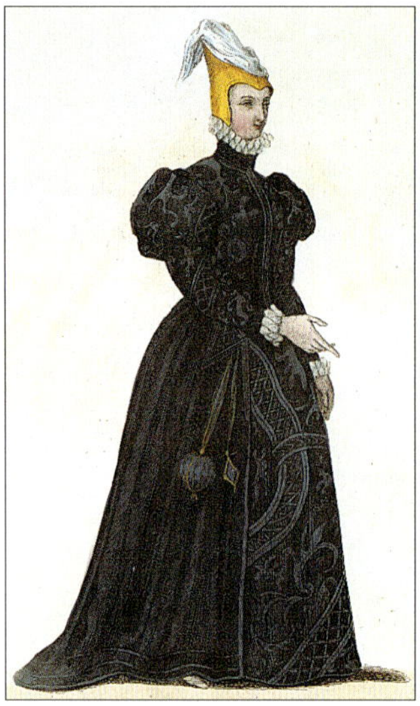

Paul Lacroix,
French costumes from
their origin to our day:
Louise Labé, vol. II,
1834–1839
(left).

La Mode illustrée,
black ensemble in
neo-Mary Stuart style, 1871
(right).

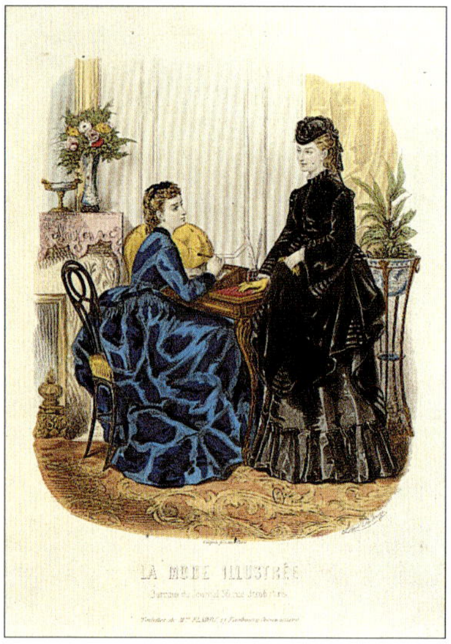

Magdalene in the *Descent from the Cross*, makes the girl he loves wear the dress in the painting, telling her,

> by way of explanation, that he was very fond of sixteenth-century costume... No doubt you have witnessed those extraordinary theatre performances known as *tableaux vivants*. The most beautiful actresses are chosen, then dressed and posed in such a way as to reproduce a well-known painting: Tiburce had just created a masterpiece in this genre. You could have sworn it was a piece cut from a canvas by Rubens.[12]

The 'Rubens dress' inspired by the *Portrait of the artist's wife* (Lisbon, Gulbenkian Foundation) had already been much in vogue in the eighteenth century, especially in England. The portrait, at that time attributed to van Dyck, was used as reference material for costume balls and for portraits in the neo-seventeenth-century style. It was considered good form to have oneself painted in a costume, pose or background in the manner of van Dyck, which guaranteed an aura of nobility, dignity and timelessness.

This sartorial interest in Rubens persisted in the following century. Théophile Gautier, in unison with the couturières, expressed his wonderment at the portrait of Hélène Fourment, shown in the Salon Carré at the Louvre: 'one cannot tell what the dress is made of – of nothing, of a little oil rubbed on the canvas – but never was any queen more richly attired; these seemingly haphazard brushstrokes shimmer and glisten like satin'.[13] The choice of satin, which adorned all women at the time, cannot have been pure coincidence.

Watteau, too, was enthusiastically rediscovered, thanks to the Goncourt brothers in particular. The 'Watteau dress', taken from *L'Enseigne de Gersaint*, 1720, from now

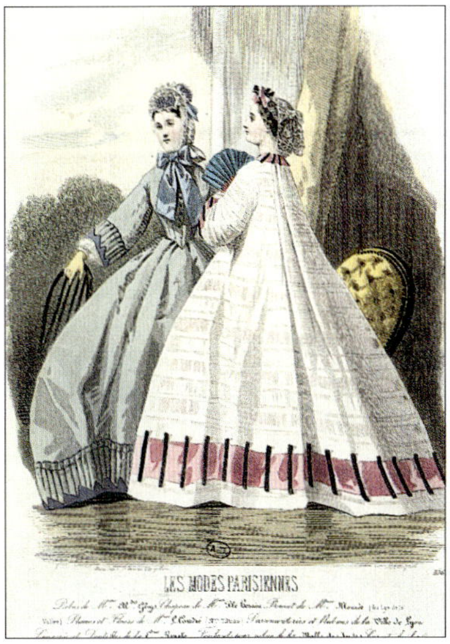

Les Modes parisiennes, *pleated négligé in the style of Watteau, 8 August 1863 (left).*

La Galerie des modes, *woman dressed in Polish style, 1778 (right).*

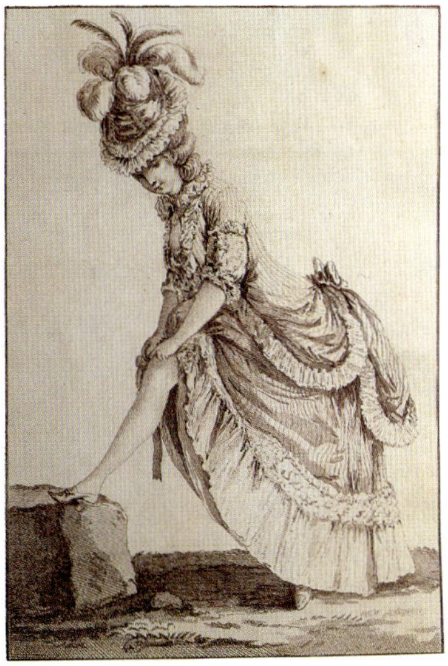

on meant a floating dress *à la française*. It was characterized by one or more flat pleats starting from the neckline at the back and widening down to the skirt. The nineteenth century took over these floating folds for indoor dresses (the only ones which were allowed to follow the figure at all closely), but also for jackets and coats.[14] Once again, 'Watteau' became a generic term referring to a neo-eighteenth-century style, and this artist's works inspired many a piece of frippery, from the 'pierrot collar' to painted fans and parasols.[15]

In some cases subjects would break free of their portrait painter and become models in themselves. Mary Stuart was taken as a pattern for fashion and her hat (which was certainly not worn only by her), the *chapeau Marie Stuart*, a small flat bonnet with a point above the forehead, was a leitmotif of nineteenth-century fashion.

The fashion press established a very close relationship between fashion and culture. While it transported its women readers into the past with its sartorial fantasises, historical accounts were used to 'support' such escapism. Thus, the Mary Stuart style in fashion prints was accompanied by long extracts from her biography, and passages on 'the eighteenth-century woman' by the Goncourts were illustrated with neo-Pompadour dresses...[16]

Versailles resuscitated

In describing the historicism of fashion in the second half of the nineteenth century, it is impossible to avoid mention of the eighteenth. The crinoline, which resurrected the hoop petticoat, is undoubtedly its most obvious symbol. However, no element of clothing, whether neckline, sleeves or various forms of ornament, was overlooked: there were pagoda sleeves, Fontanges bows, Louis XV waistcoats, dresses *à la Watteau*, and so on. This Pompadour style, which extended as far forward as the Louis XVI style, was matched by a rediscovery of the same period in literature (the Goncourt brothers in particular, as we have just seen) and art (the predilection for Boucher, Fragonard, Moreau the Younger, the revival of the Boulle style, etc.). Another source of the style was Empress Eugénie's professed admiration for Marie-Antoinette, her identification with the last queen of France. One of the first portraits of her painted by Winterhalter is *Empress Eugénie in eighteenth-century costume* (1854, New York, Metropolitan Museum of Art). She poses in front of a natural scene, in an acid-yellow taffeta dress embellished with black bows, blue ribbons, strings of pearls, fringes and tassels. Her hair, powdered white, is decorated with ribbons and a spray of feathers. In this way she seems to be unwittingly illustrating a sardonic comment of the Goncourts': 'Marie-Antoinette at Mabille'.[17]

At a ball in February 1866 she again dressed as Marie-Antoinette, this time in a dress copied from a portrait of that queen by Vigée-Lebrun (1787, Versailles, Musée National du Château). Critics have often noted a similarity to eighteenth-century painting in Winterhalter; but here the presentation of the sitter in strict profile, standing out very clearly against the background, also recalls the silhouette, which flattens volume and dehumanizes the model.

Eighteenth-century costume portraits were much in vogue and were appreciated far beyond the court of Napoleon III. Tissot painted genre scenes with girls in the late eighteenth-century dress which met with great success in Paris, then in London (*Bad News*, 1872 Cardiff, National Museum of Wales; *La Lecture*, 1872, location unknown). Similarly, a number of painters successful at the time but now forgotten, J. Worms, E. Toudouze, C. Chaplin and A. Axilette, appropriated these historical evocations and produced paintings in fancy dress, as if the Salon were about to be transformed into a masked ball.

The admiration of the 'Spaniard' (Empress Eugénie) for the 'Austrian' (Marie-Antoinette) gave rise to the invention, in 1854–5, of the Marie-Antoinette fichu (a small shawl), decorated with two lace flounces, which is said to have inspired a *bon mot* of Manet: 'On entering the house of Mme Viot [a famous *modiste*], who was leaning against the mantlepiece wearing a Marie-Antoinette fichu and an arrangement of lace which set off the whiteness of her hair: "Sapristi, Madame," he exclaimed, "That's a handsome way to go to the scaffold."'[18]

In the 1870s, bodices appeared with basques extended by a polonaise. The open dress *à la polonaise* had come into being in 1772–4. It was characterized by three rounded flaps bunched up on the skirt; these were supposed to symbolize the partition of the former kingdom of Augustus III. *Monsieur and Madame Sisley*, the double portrait by Renoir (1868, Cologne, Wallraf-Richartz-Museum), shows Madame Sisley in a double polonaise on a striped skirt: the first in white material hooked to the waist,

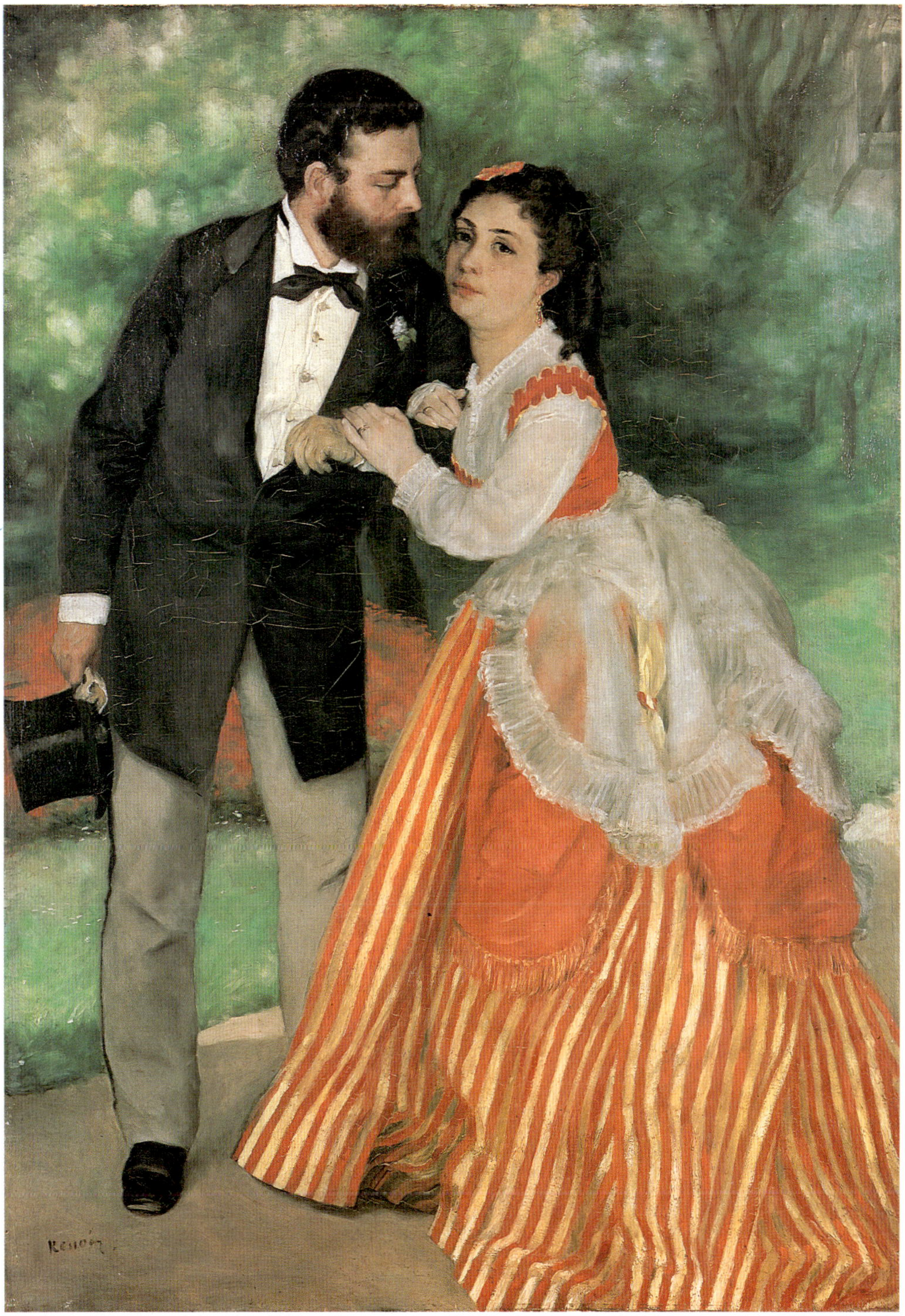

Pierre Auguste Renoir, Monsieur and Madame Sisley, *1868. Wallraf-Richartz Museum, Cologne.*

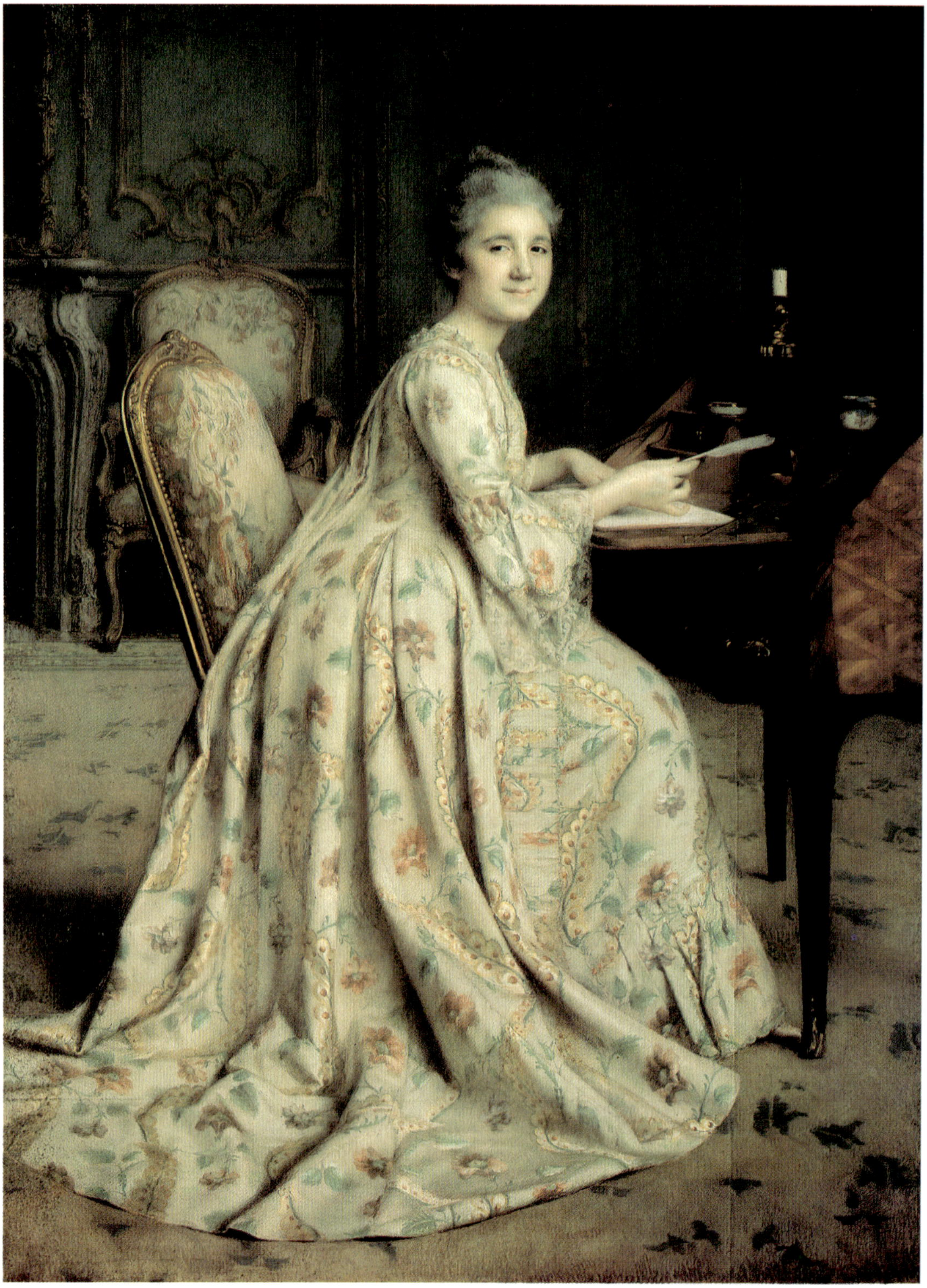

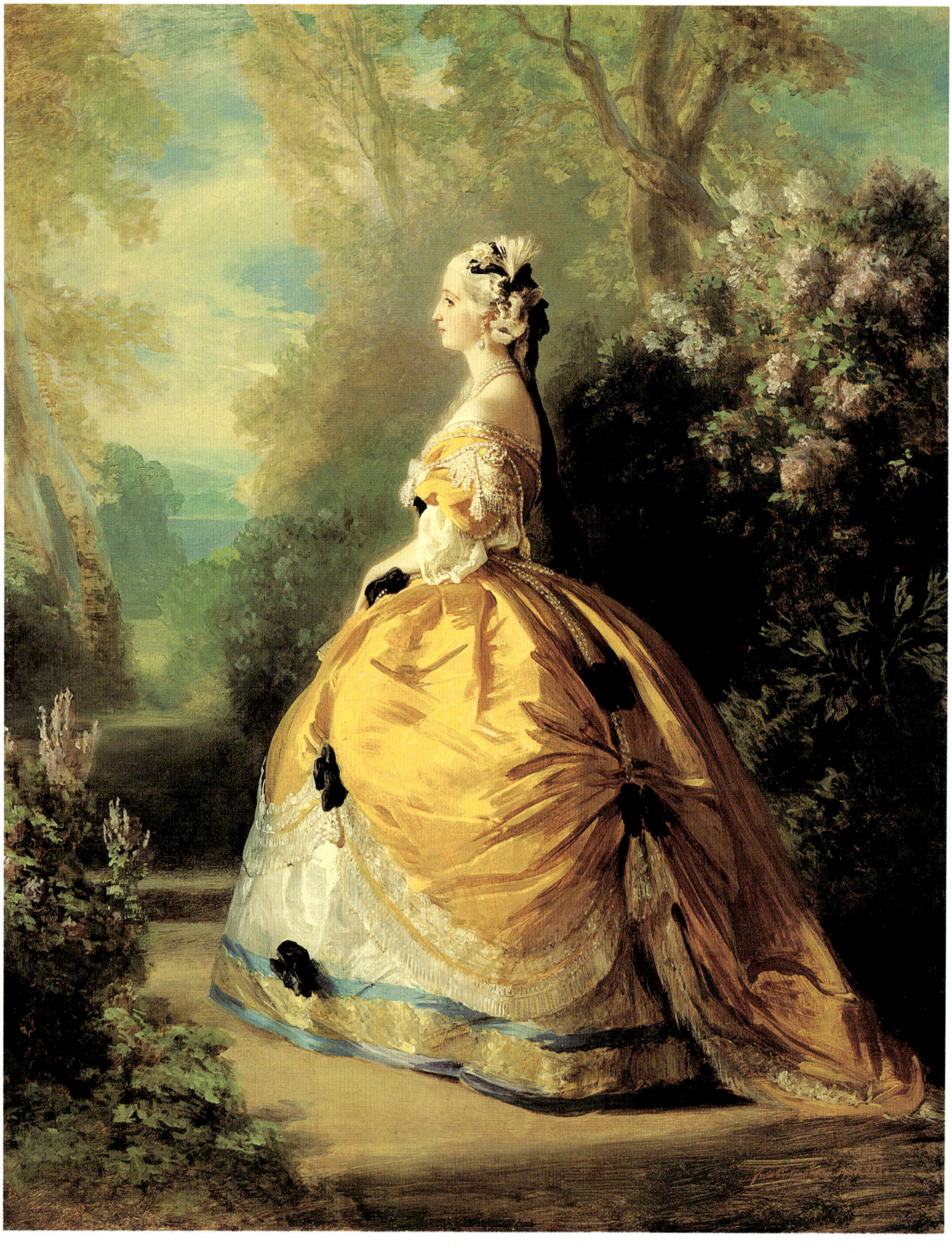

Franz-Xaver Winterhalter, The Empress Eugénie in 18th-century costume, 1854.
The Metropolitan Museum of Art, New York.
Alexis Axilette, Madame Dubois-Mouchet, *no date. Musée des Beaux-Arts, Angers (facing page).*

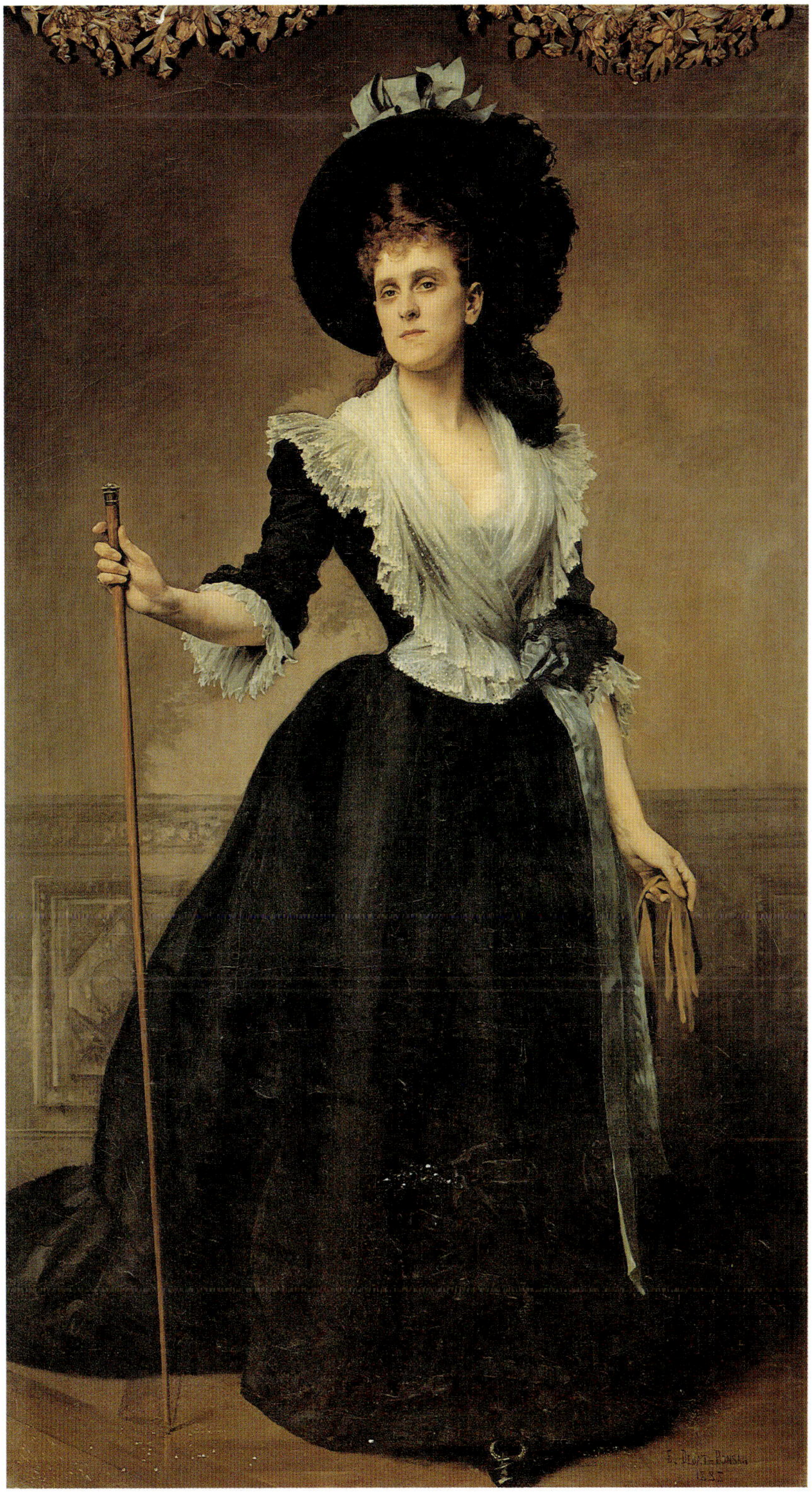

Edouard Debat-Ponsan,
Countess Edmond de Récopé, *1888.*
Musée du Petit Palais, Paris.

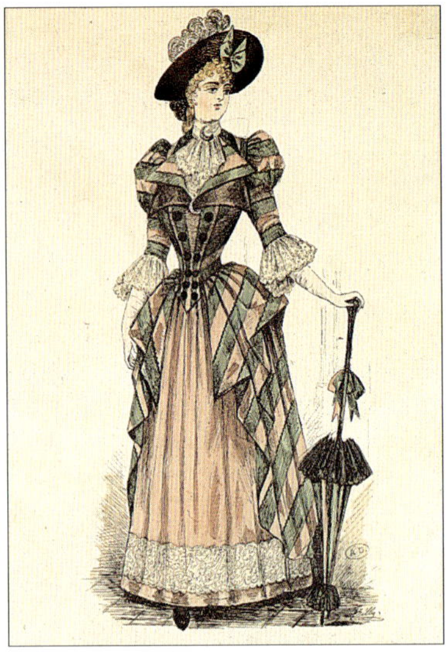

L'Art et la mode: *spring outfit in neo-Louis XVI style, 1889 (left).*

Neo-Directoire dress, 1887–1888. The Victoria and Albert Museum, London (right).

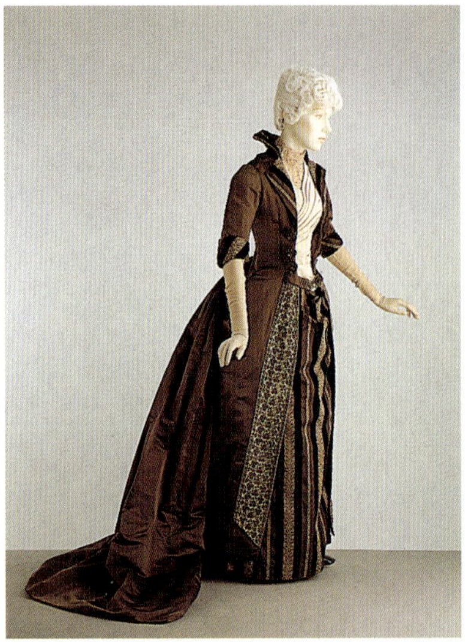

the second, which is red, forming part of the bodice. Throughout the Third Republic the polonaise was also adapted to coats and mantelets, until women finally tired of it.

The eighteenth century was a source not only of patterns but of fabrics. In the *Portrait of Madame Moitessier* by Ingres (1856, London, National Gallery), the dress, sprinkled with bouquets, can be compared to that in the *Portrait of Madame de Pompadour* by Quentin de la Tour (pastel, Paris, Musée du Louvre, Département des Arts Graphiques), or that of the *Marquise d'Aiguirandes* by Drouais (1759, Cleveland, Cleveland Museum of Art). Brocaded, flowery materials remained much in favour until the end of the century.

In fact, allusions to the eighteenth century never ceased to be made. In the 1890s they mainly took the forms of a neo-Louis XVI and a neo-Directoire style. At that time 'Louis XVI-style gowns', 'Merveilleuse hats' and 'Directoire belts and suits' were in vogue. In the 1890s, the Comtesse Edmond Récopé, in her portrait by Debat-Ponsan (1888, Paris, Musée du Petit Palais), wore a Worth costume comparable to that in the *Portrait of Madame Molé-Raymond* by Vigée-Lebrun (1787, Paris, Musée du Louvre). The large hat is inspired by the *chapeau Montgolfier* (hot-air balloon hat); the cane, here an accessory of the painter's, the Charlotte Corday fichu (a fashion accessory which appeared in 1859) and the pose itself seem perfectly to illustrate d'Uzanne's comment: 'Some of our fashions are no more than simple copies of paintings by masters. A fashion for fashions is emerging.'[19] At first sight, the portrait of the comtesse seems to be that of a woman in costume; then, if we consult fashion prints, we note that fashion in these years very often took the form of a literal quotation of the Louis XVI style. This ambiguity leads us to suspect that at that time historical fancy-dress was becoming the sole motive force in fashion creation.

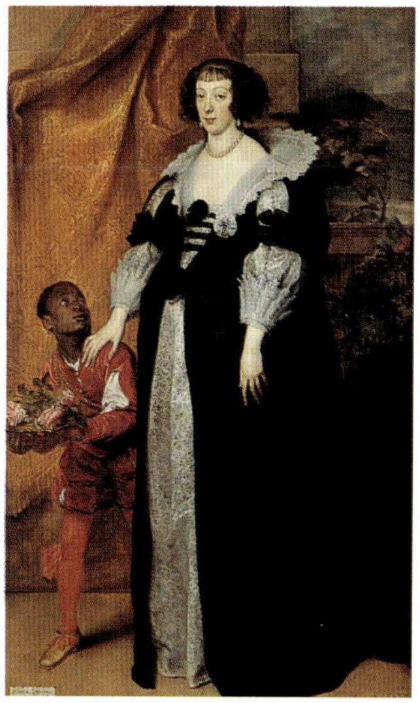

Anthony Van Dyck, Henriette de Lorraine, *1634. The Iveagh Bequest, Kenwood (left).*

Dress for a reception in neo-17th-century style, signed Worth, c.1895. The Brooklyn Museum, gift of the Princesse Viggo, New York (right).

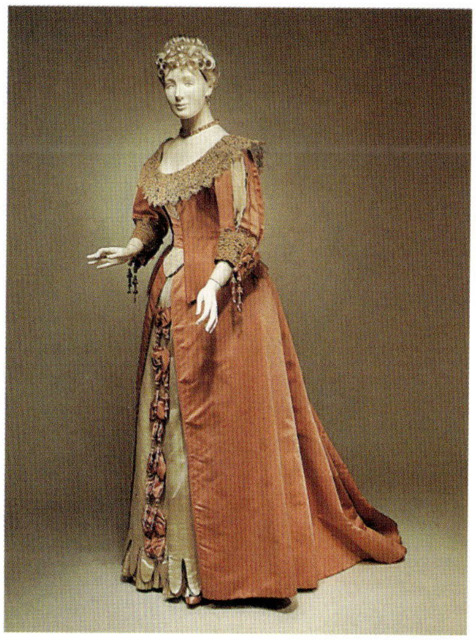

A 'fashion for fashions' did indeed establish itself with the Second Empire, for in contrast to the first half of the nineteenth century when allusions followed each other in a clear sequence, from the ancient style to the troubadour style, there was now a telescoping of sources which mingled all centuries together.

Allusions to the eighteenth century were coupled to references to the seventeenth, simultaneously and with equal weight. The nineteenth century also saw a flourishing of cloak-and-dagger novels (Alexandre Dumas), and the rediscovery of the Le Nain brothers (by Champfleury) and of Velázquez. 'Musketeer collars' *à la Mazarin*, 'Anne of Austria sleeves', 'Medici collarettes', 'Sévigné dresses' and 'half-length sleeves *à la Montespan*' preoccupied fashion no less than the 'Marie-Antoinette fichu'. These terms referred essentially to square-cut or raised collars spreading like fans behind the head, lace cuffs and sleeves flared at the elbow.

The dress worn by Mrs William Astor in her portrait by Carolus-Duran (1890, New York, Metropolitan Museum of Art) is a creation by Worth. It shows a combination of various seventeenth-century elements: the lace collar and the two triangular openings in the skirt and the bodice over a lighter material may come from the portrait of *Henriette de Lorraine* by van Dyck (1634, London, Iveagh Bequest, Kenwood), but the puffed lace sleeves, the notched shape of the collar and the turned-down neckline, are much closer to the *Portrait of Béatrice de Cuzanne* by the same painter. An undated work attributed to Monet, *Young woman* (Berlin, private collection), shows a woman with averted face in a similar position to *Camille in a green dress.* She is wearing a dress with 'musketeer' collar and puff sleeves, and a small seventeenth-century hunting hat.

Nor is the neo-sixteenth century forgotten, as is shown by the race-course

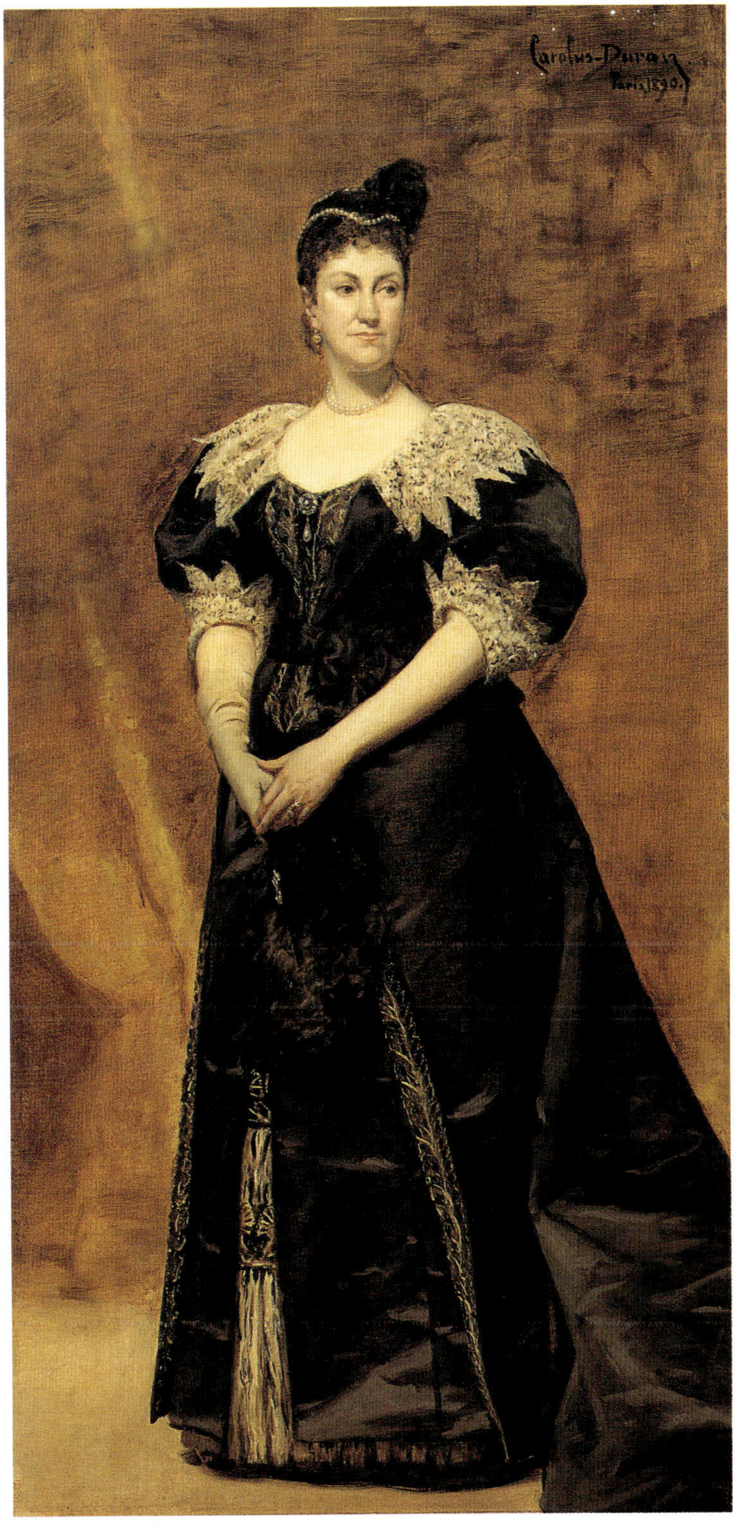

Carolus-Duran,
Mrs William Astor, *1890.*
The Metropolitan
Museum of Art,
New York.

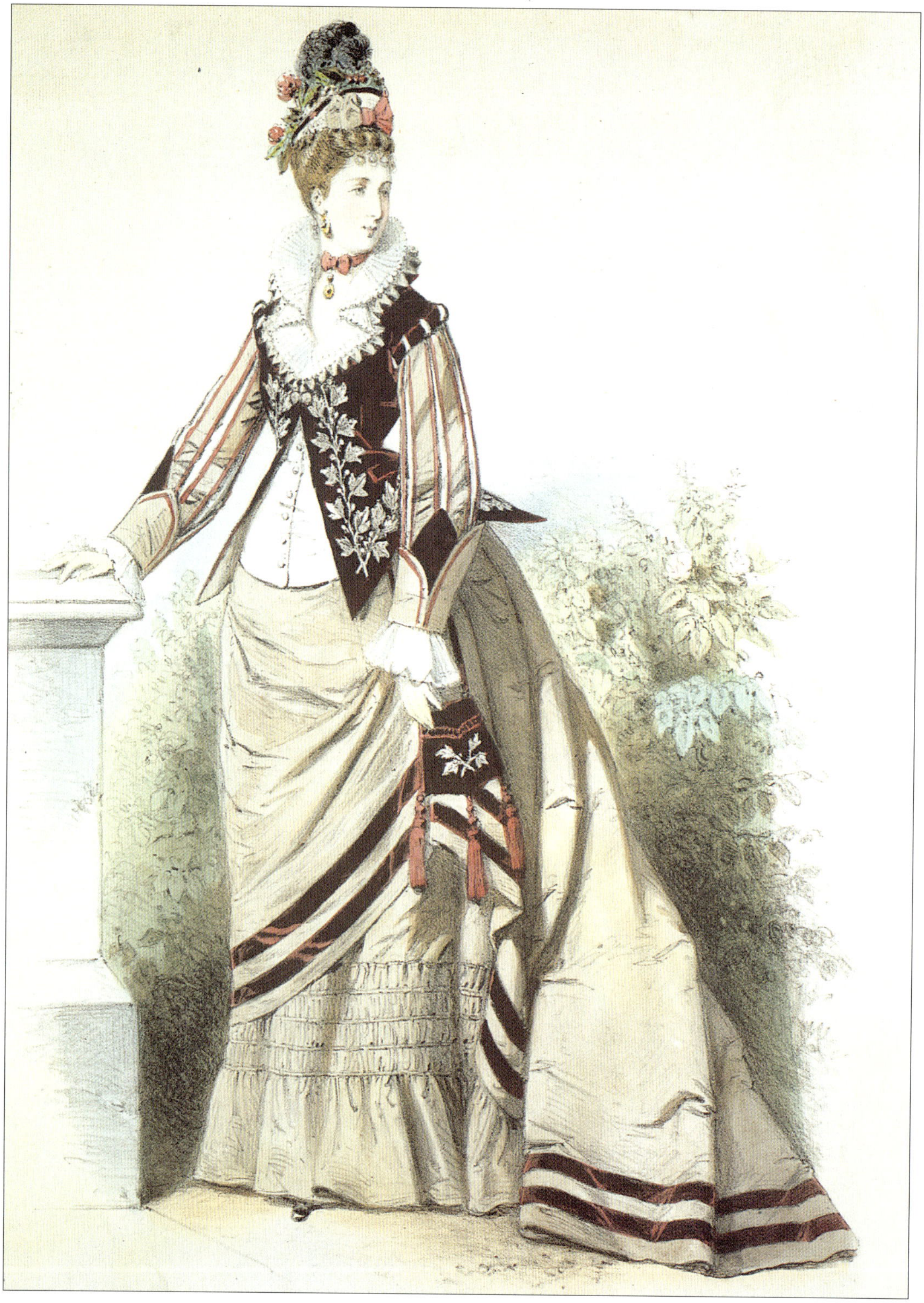

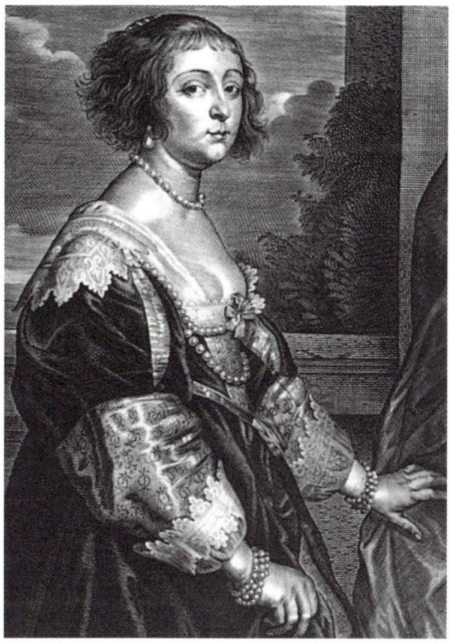

La Mode artistique, outfit for the races, 1874 (facing page).

Engraving after Anthony Van Dyck, Béatrice de Cusance, *no date (left).*

Peter Paul Rubens, Rubens, his wife Hélène Fourment and their son Peter Paul *(detail), 1639. The Metropolitan Museum of Art, New York (right).*

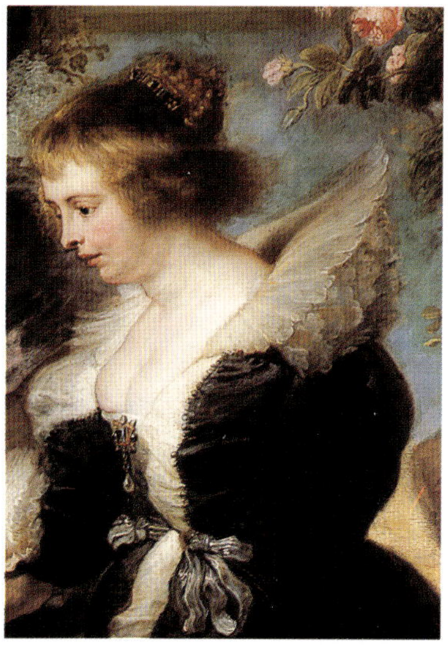

costume in a print in *La Mode artistique* (1874), or by Worth's adoption of slashed sleeves. We saw earlier the influence of the Mary Stuart style, referring to a hat or sleeves 'gathered in puffs from top to bottom, and closed'.[20] 'Henri II ruffs' and 'Charles IX hats' were other neo-sixteenth-century accessories. At the end of the century these borrowings become more and more common. We read in *L'Art de la mode* in 1881, for example: 'For three years fashion has been a loyal subject, switching from the Henri II style to the manner of Watteau, from the court of the royal palaces to the Trianon.'

Eclecticism

The mixing of allusions in architecture, which gave rise in the same period to a neo-Gothic church (Ste Clothilde) and a neo-Renaissance library (Ste Geneviève), is paralleled in fashion from the 1870s by the juxtaposing of dresses inspired by the sixteenth, seventeenth and eighteenth centuries. Thus, it is not uncommon to find a neo-sixteenth century gown and a neo-eighteenth century robe side-by-side in the same engraving. Eclecticism also brought about a coexistence of different styles in the same dress, just as the Opéra Garnier associated features from Renaissance and Baroque art with elements proper to the nineteenth century. The robe of Madame Feydeau, in her portrait by Carolus-Duran (1878, Lille, Musée des Beaux-Arts) adopts the same approach: over a modern framework (the bustle) neo-sixteenth, neo-seventeenth and neo-eighteenth century styles intermingle in a creation which is, finally, an original and characteristic product of the nineteenth century.

Nineteenth-century fashion drew its inspiration from the past but, in most cases, transformed and adapted it. In this it was very close to fashion of the 1980s, which also

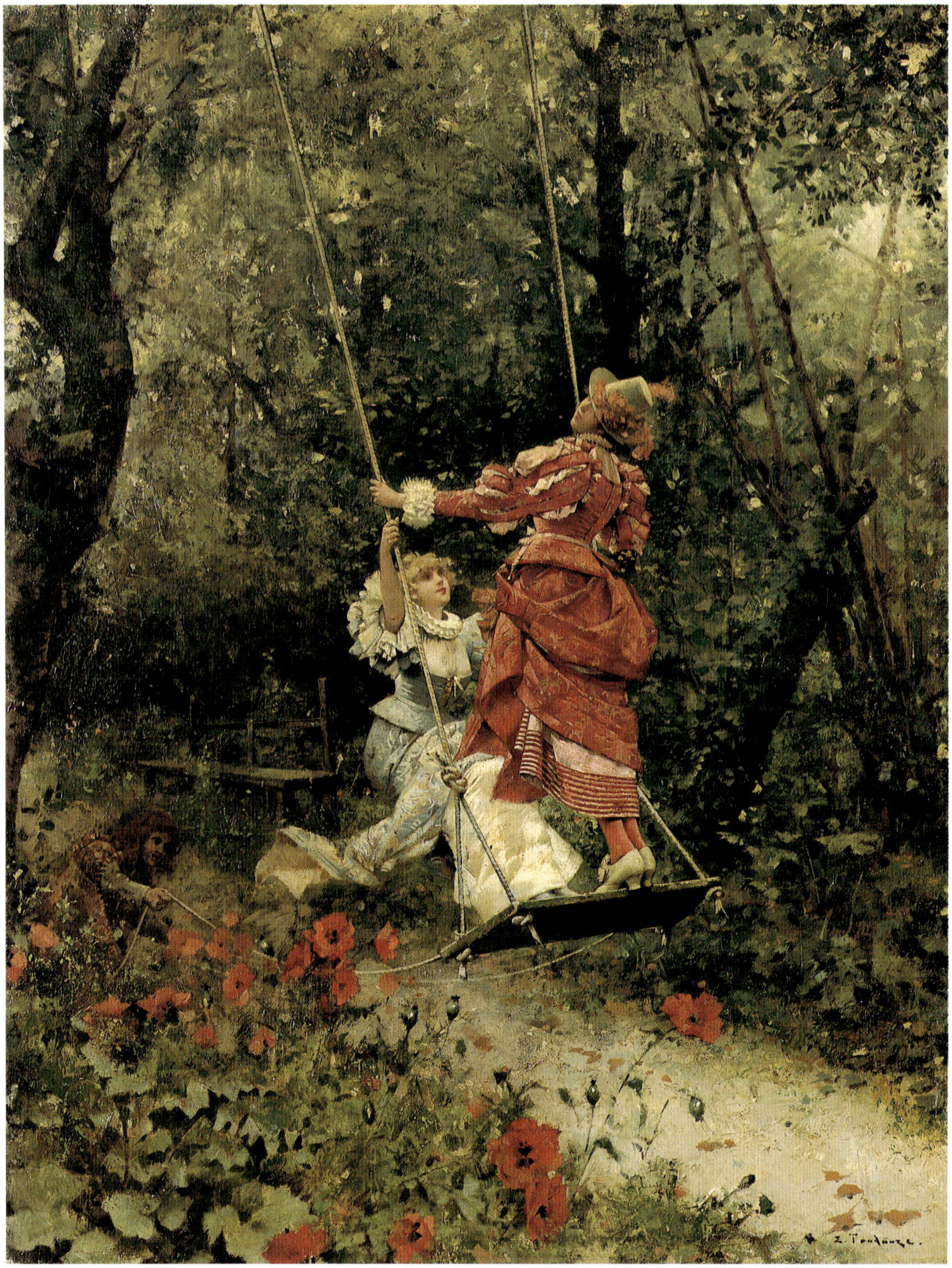

Edouard Toudouze, The Swing, *no date. Musée des Beaux-Arts, La Rochelle.*

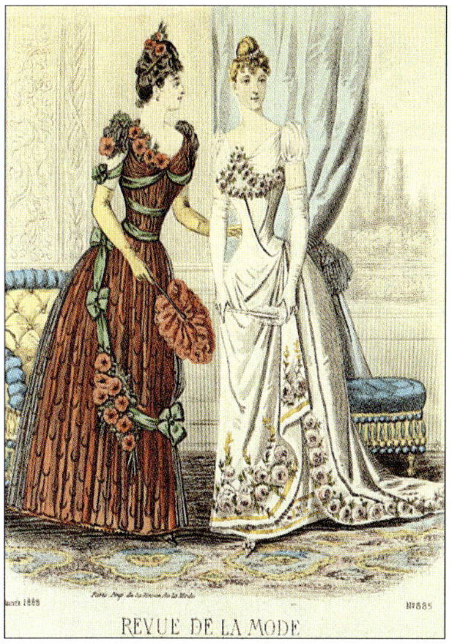

La Revue de la Mode, *neo-Empire ball-gowns, 1888 (left).*

La Mode illustrée, *neo-18th-century dress and neo-17th-century dress, 1871 (right).*

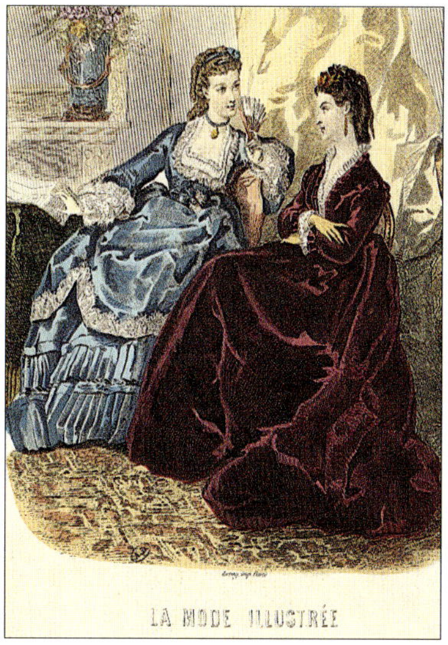

made extensive use of historical references. The revival of the neo-Empire line at the end of the nineteenth century illustrates the way in which an epoch inevitably adapts and borrows from the past. A print in the *Revue de la mode* in 1888 shows, on the right, a dress inspired by the high-waisted gowns of an earlier time; it has the same small balloon sleeves, the light drape on the bosom, the white hues and the pursuit of feminine grace in the use of garlands and pink flowers. Yet it is worn with a long corset and a bustle – a total contradiction. To realize this we need only compare it to the flowing robes in the portraits of *Christine Boyer* by Gros (Paris, Musée du Louvre) and of *Madame Récamier* by François Gérard (1805, Paris, Musée Carnavalet).

Very often, too, fashion's historicism went no further than terminology. As we saw in the case of colours, this was a time when people liked giving things obscure names. In themselves, these signified nothing,[21] or were a pretext for poetic creations, like the 'Hubert-Robert hat', 'a crown of flowers or foliage placed on a strip of plain or ruffled velvet',[22] or the creations of Madame Virot, which outdid the dreams of young girls:

> The Valkyrie hat in gold straw, a pointed skull-cap surmounted by white wings and with muslin drapery fixed in the form of cabbage-bows by rings of jet. Then the ravishing Greuze [named after the painter] in Italian straw and point lace, decorated with a graceful Charlotte Corday knot of cream ribbon with pink, green and mauve check.[23]

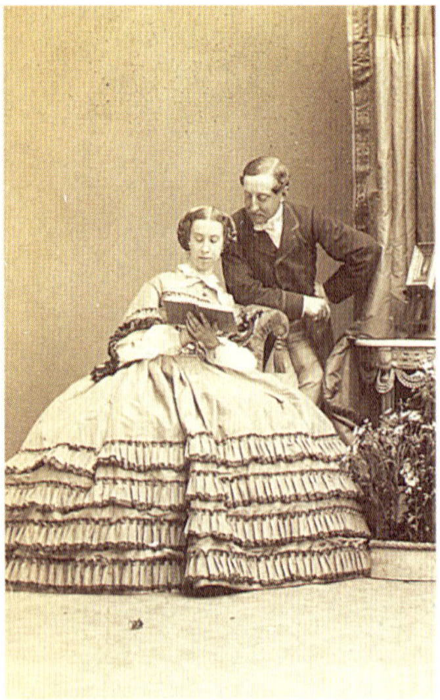

Disdéri,
The Baron and Baroness de Walmont, *1861.*
Musée d'Orsay, Paris (left and right).

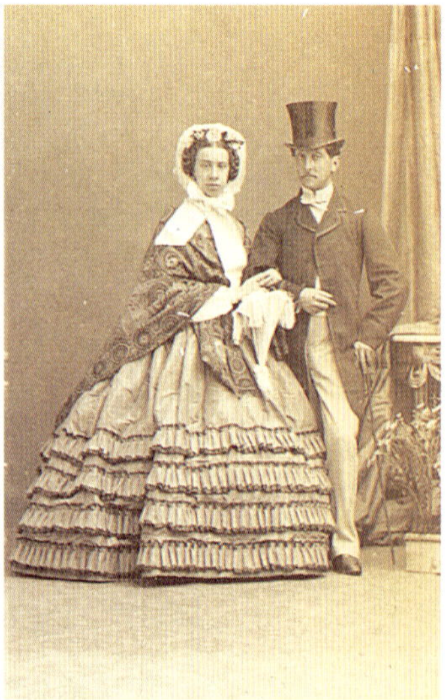

Exoticism

Although exoticism left its mark on fashion in the nineteenth century, its influence was much less deep than that of historicism. Its effects were confined largely to the fantasy element and to accessories.

It was in the form of accessories that it first entered French fashion in the first half of the nineteenth century. The campaigns of Napoleon stimulated imports of cashmere shawls, brought into fashion by the 'return from Egypt' style. Throughout the first half of the century and up to about 1870, the cashmere shawl was an indispensable accessory, which was soon copied by French manufacturers with the aim of reducing if not stopping the imports. Nevertheless, imports of shawls and then of ready-made oriental garments continued, becoming more diverse as the century advanced. These two types of clothing, the shawl and the ready-made garment (jackets, coats) were the main items in the exotic wardrobe.

To these we should add some fabric motifs, such as Persian flowers, hieroglyphs and Chinese characters, and decorative and trimming motifs such as the 'Balkan braid' decorating dolmans, 'hussar' and 'Zouave' jackets, or pompon tassels and bells for 'El Kebir coats' and 'Turkish jackets'.

As happened with historicism, an exoticism of terminology grew up. During 1858 large open sleeves were successively called 'Greek', 'Persian' and 'Chinese'. In 1863, *La Mode illustrée* offered a 'Spanish burnous' in tartan material. The names were chosen for their poetic resonance – 'a dress in corn-yellow alpaca from Turkey'[24] – or out of patriotism. Contemporary events, especially wars, left an untroubled, frivolous trace in fashion. In the *Journal des dames* of January 1855, for example, Mme Fanny Richomme theorizes as follows:

> The dress of coarse Asian fabric reminds us that while our soldiers are fighting in the Crimea, French industry is showing its sympathy for their efforts by highlighting their success. All the fabrics of the day bear glorious names. *Bomarsunaine*, *Sylistrienne*, *gros d'Alma*, *Eupatorienne* and Crimean velvet glisten and shimmer, or hang in soft folds; I would go further and say that the *Sévastopolienne* proudly spread before us tells us with trembling voice: 'Do not sell the pelt of the bear before the bear lies dead.'[25]

In 1859, at the time of the French intervention in Italy, we hear of 'Magenta' or 'Solferino' woollen velvet fabrics, then of 'Garibaldi shirts'. The French campaigns in Algeria, Tunisia and Morocco were no less fertile in nomenclature.

The rise of exoticism was the result of several factors: military conquests and the creation of protectorates; archaeological and cultural discoveries; and the reverberations of the Expositions Universelles (1855, 1867, 1878 and 1889 in Paris), which brought the public directly into contact with foreign products for the first time: Chinese and Japanese silks and kimonos were sold at the exhibition of 1878. Quite apart from these major events, commercial exchanges were increasing, many shops selling antiques or exotic objects were opened and the big stores set up oriental departments. Although references are mixed and are not always easy to disentangle, exotic terms in fashion had three principle sources: Spain, the East and Japan.

Spain

Spain had been made fashionable by the Romantics. Travel writings by Dumas, Mérimée and Gautier sent a wave of 'tourism' to this distant country, or at least spread book-knowledge about it. The detailed descriptions of dress to be found in Alexandre Dumas's *Le Voyage de Paris à Cadix* or Théophile Gautier's *Le Voyage en Espagne* give a clear idea of typical costume. The interest in the country was accompanied by a rediscovery of Goya and Velázquez, thanks largely to Louis-Philippe's *Galerie espagnole*. Finally, the Spanish origins of Empress Eugénie, born at Montijo, were not without influence on the French in the Second Empire.

Hispanic-style garments were the mantilla, a black lace veil originating in a Spanish ceremonial garment, and its derivative, the mantelet or manteletta, a women's short cape. Both survived until 1900. The bolero, a small open waistcoat worn by matadors, appeared in the years 1855-60. The *Portrait of Mademoiselle L.L.* by Tissot, also entitled *Young woman in a red jacket* (1844, Paris, Musée d'Orsay), gives emblematic expression to this garment. It is also seen in the work of Courbet, in the *Portrait of*

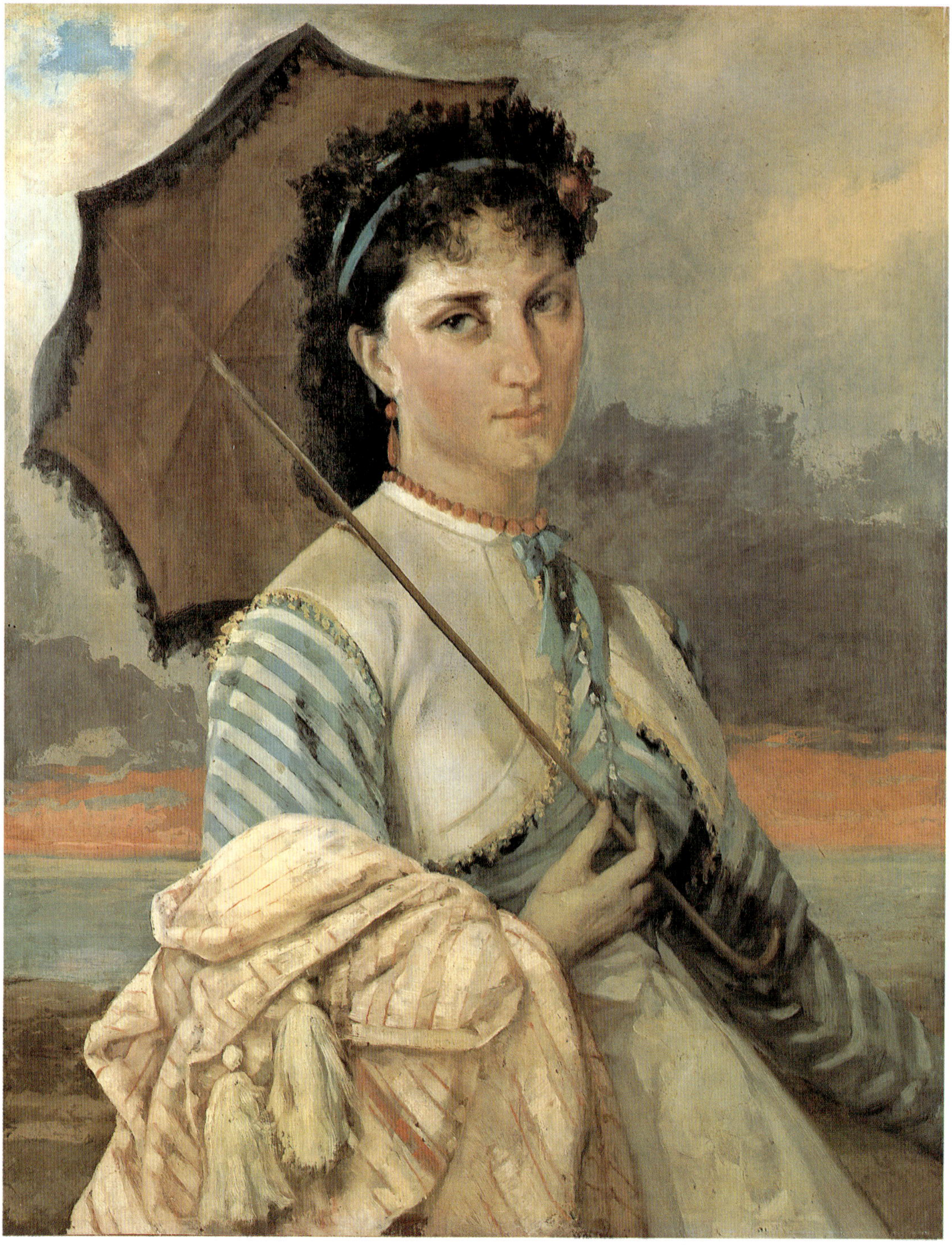

Gustave Courbet, Mademoiselle Aubé or The Lady with a parasol, *1865. Art Gallery, Glasgow.*

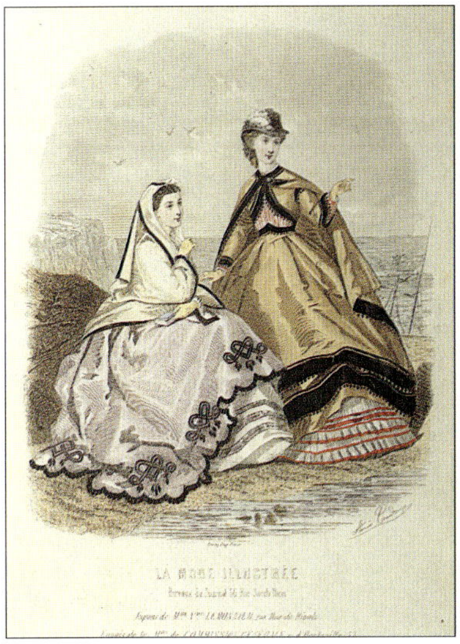

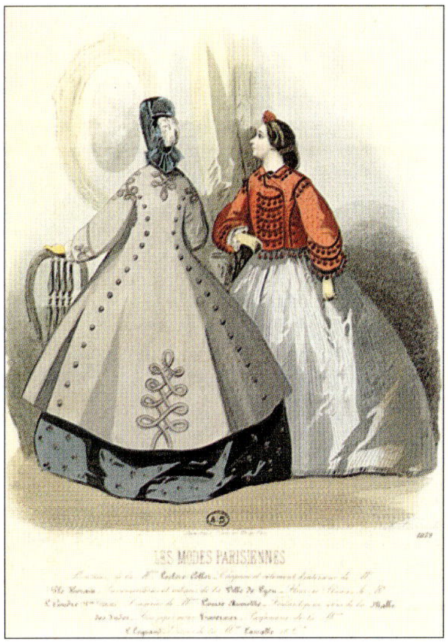

La Mode illustrée, *bathing costumes, 1864 (left).*

Les Modes parisiennes, *indoor outfit and town outfit, 31 October 1863 (right).*

Mademoiselle Aubé (1865, Glasgow Art Gallery). The sitter is in three-quarter view, half-length, with the beach at Trouville in the background. The setting is not without significance: exotic garments, more than anything, were needed by those wishing to appear chic at the seaside or on holiday in the country.

Mademoiselle Aubé's costume is of calculated elegance: a blue-and-orange striped bodice with plain skirt and sleeveless bolero, a striped shawl decorated with tassels and trimming, gloves, parasol. The ensemble derives mainly from the Orient, and is an example of the telescoping of sources, the bolero being called the 'Spanish jacket', the 'Figaro jacket', or the 'Zouave jacket', depending on the year and the writer concerned.

In general, anything decorated with passementerie, lace, hairnet or black stones was likely to be interpreted as of Spanish origin. Thus, Marguerite d'Aincourt speaks of the 'Spanish dress strewn with jet, covered with fine blonde-lace – a most decorous dress in its sombre richness'.[26] However, even if we include in it the 'Vélázquez' (a black lace talma, or long cloak) and the fanciful sleeves *à la castillane* or *andalouses* referred to from time to time, the Spanish influence was, finally, rather superficial.

Painting is misleading on this point, since the nineteenth century produced many portraits of women in Spanish-style dress. They are either portraits of Spanish dancers or singers, following a tradition inherited from the eighteenth century (Courbet, *Signora Adela Guerrero*; Winterhalter, *Adelina Patti;* Manet, *Lola de Valence*; Sargent, *La Carmencita*, etc.), or paintings of women in costume (Manet, *Young woman in a Spanish costume* and *Victorine in matadore costume*; Henri Regnault, *The Comtesse de Barck in Spanish dress*). In the latter case, the costumes are exceptional outfits which have little to do with fashion, but much to do with fancy-dress fantasy. Artists adored the costume of Majo (Théophile Gautier even had one made for him by a Spanish

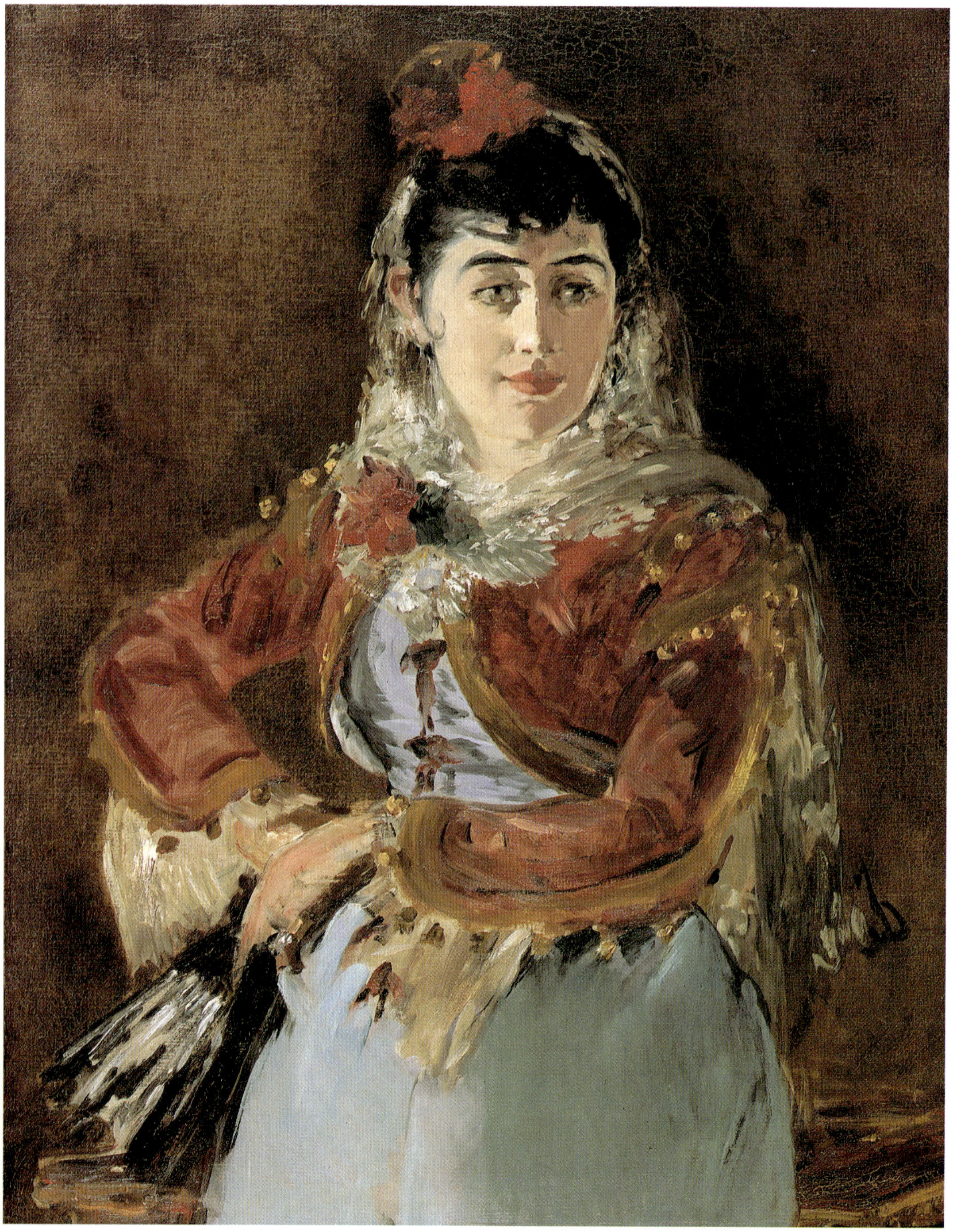

Edouard Manet, Emilie Ambre in the role of Carmen, *1879–1880. Philadelphia Museum of Art, Philadelphia.*
John Singer Sargent, La Carmencita, *1890. Musée d'Orsay, Paris (facing page).*

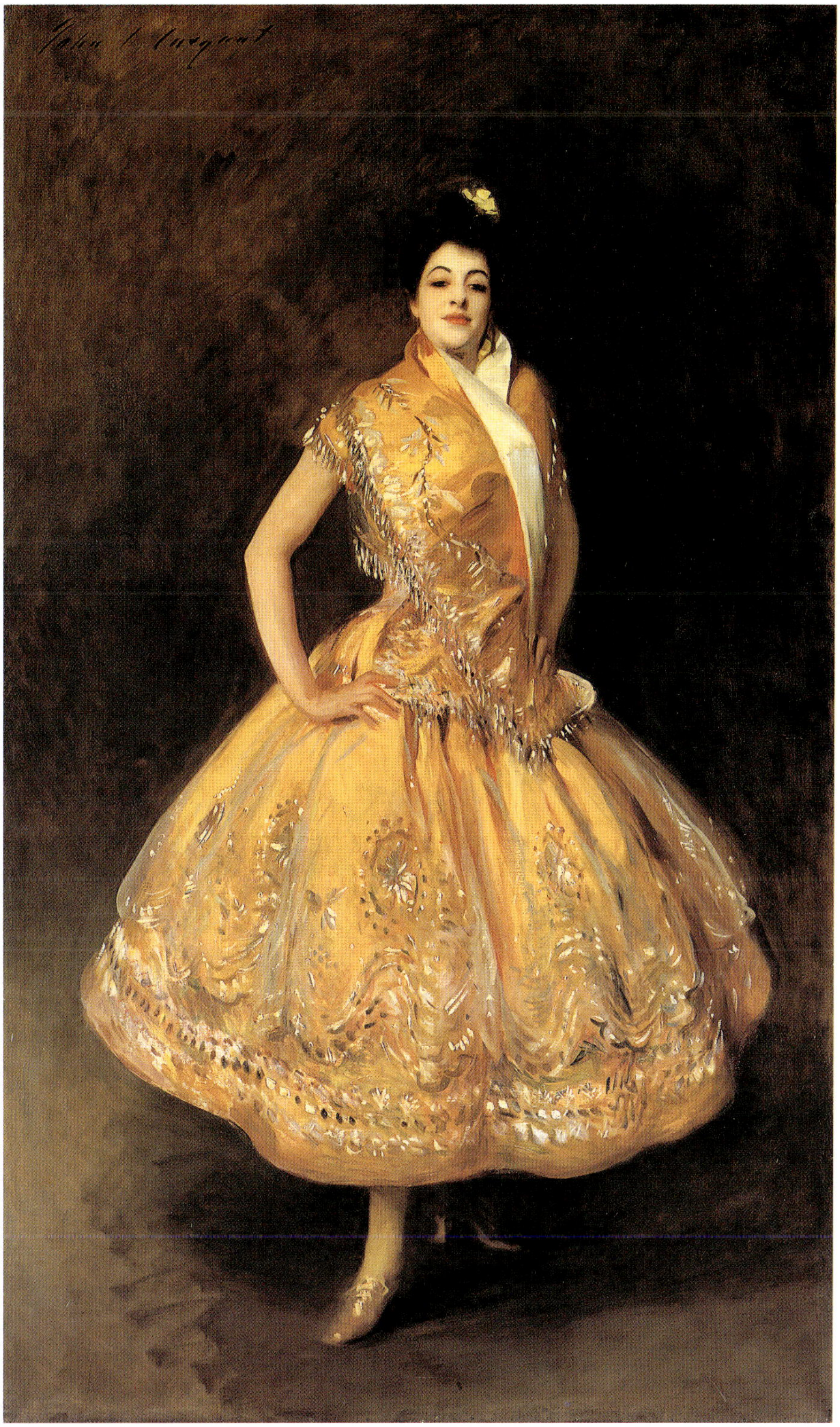

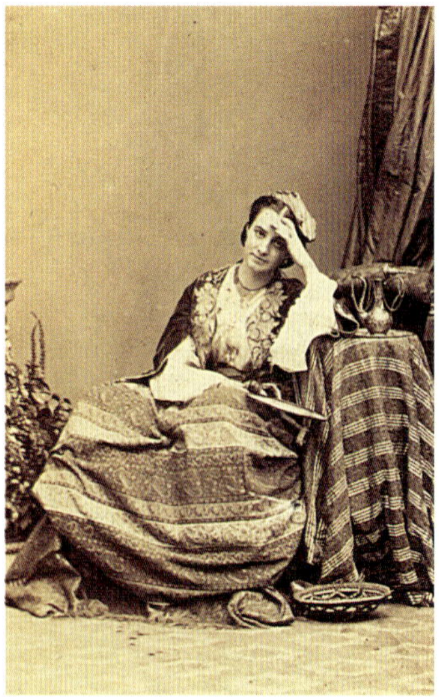

Disdéri,
Countess Ferri-Gisani, *1862.*
Musée d'Orsay, Paris
(left and right).

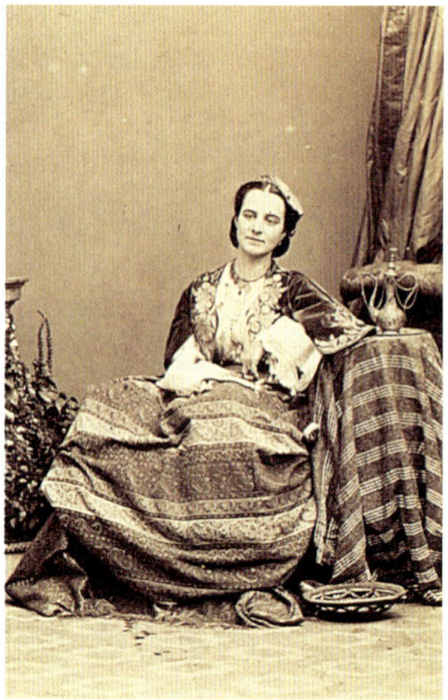

tailor); moreover, for artists to adorn their models with such costumes was normal practice in studio compositions, inherited from history painting. The same phenomenon is observed in portraits of women in oriental dress. If Mme Stora had herself painted by Renoir in Algerian costume – *L'Algérienne* (1870, The Fine Arts Museum of San Francisco) – this was not unconnected to the profession of her husband, an antiques dealer selling Arabian curios on the boulevard des Italiens. When Manet depicted Nina de Callias dressed à *l'algérienne* (1873–4, Paris, Musée d'Orsay) he chose the eccentric attire she liked to wear when receiving friends at her brilliant salon for writers and artists. As for the Marquise de Laubespin, in 1876 she asked the orientalist Charles Landelle to portray her in Egyptian costume, following a journey to Egypt she had made some years earlier.

Exoticism, which only affected fashion through fancy dress, was far more important for painting, where it influenced both the Impressionists and the academic painters. Artists enlisted the help of antiquarians or tailors to provide them with models. Or else they 'adapted' garments, in the manner of Jules Worms, a specialist in genre scenes in the eighteenth-century or Spanish style. The Musée de la Mode et du Costume, in the Palais Galliéra, owns the skirt used by the artist for his painting *Une vocation*, in 1881. Isolated from the painting, the skirt is no more than a conventional flounced garment of 1856, decorated with a motif of rose bouquets.[27]

The Orient

The Orient had played an important role since the eighteenth century, when *turqueries* were much in vogue and very numerous, influencing creations such as the *robe à la sultane*. Then, as we have seen, Egypt attracted increasing interest, from the Egyptian

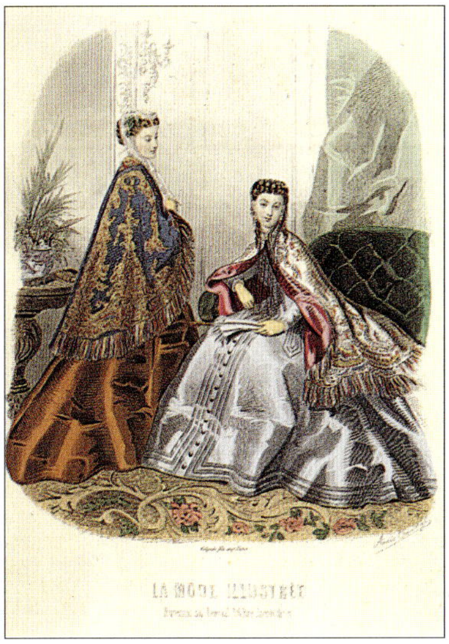

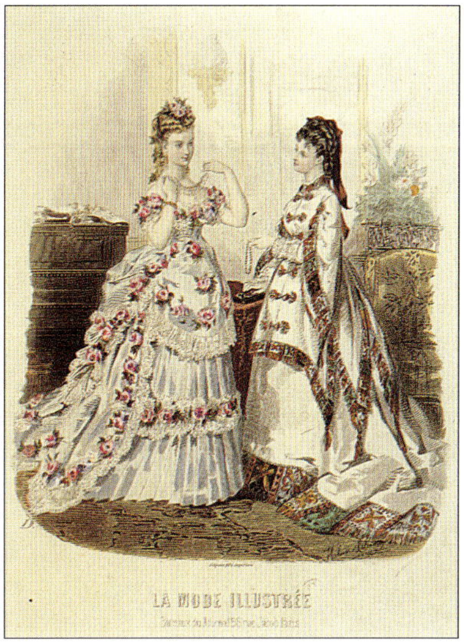

La Mode illustrée, *hooded cloak and ball-gown, 15 March 1868 (left).*

La Mode illustrée, *1872 (right).*

campaigns to the opening of the Suez Canal. In the second half of the nineteenth century exoticism turned its interest to North Africa, where recent conquests had facilitated new contacts (Alexandre Dumas, *Le Veloce*, *Le Voyage de Cadix à Tunis*; Delacroix, *Carnets de voyage*, a travel journal of his diplomatic mission to the Emperor of Morocco in 1831).

In the years 1854–5 orientalism left its imprint on clothing. 'No doubt we shall be wearing oriental dress for the next few months, as there is no shop which does not spread arabesques and palms before us.'[28] Fabric manufacturers created motifs inspired by the 'war in the East' (Arabic symbols, Persian designs), and jewellers made bracelets decorated with crescents. Women could buy a mangaïa or Tunisian shawl with stripes in two colours, or a burnous. The Algerian burnous, a kind of large cape decorated with trimming, was one of the few exotic elements that was fully absorbed into fashion. It was an imported item and was worn as such on the way to a ball, with surprising success, until the end of the 1870s.

Japan

Japan opened its doors to the West and signed the first commercial treaties in 1855. Several shops selling curios, kimonos, tea and Japanese engravings opened in Paris during these years: Samuel Bing in the rue de Provence; Chez Desoye, rue de Rivoli, where artists came in search of kimonos or prints; La Porte Chinoise, rue Vivienne; Au Céleste Empire, rue Saint-Marc, and others. The first large Japanese collections were brought together through the influence of such connoisseurs as Théodore Duret, Cernuschi, Emile Guimet, Burty and the Goncourts.

Japanese art had considerable reverberations in painting and decoration, but a very

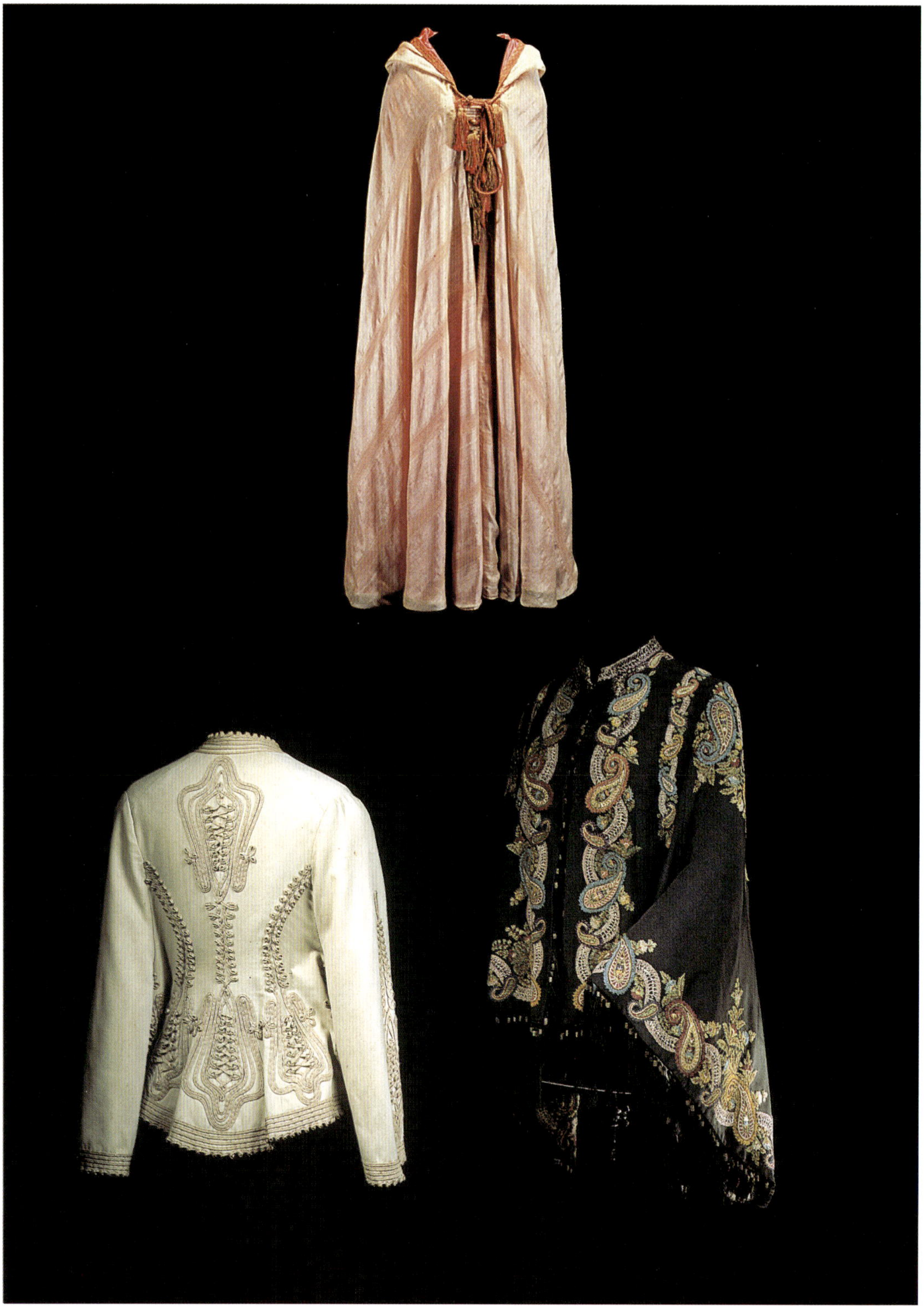

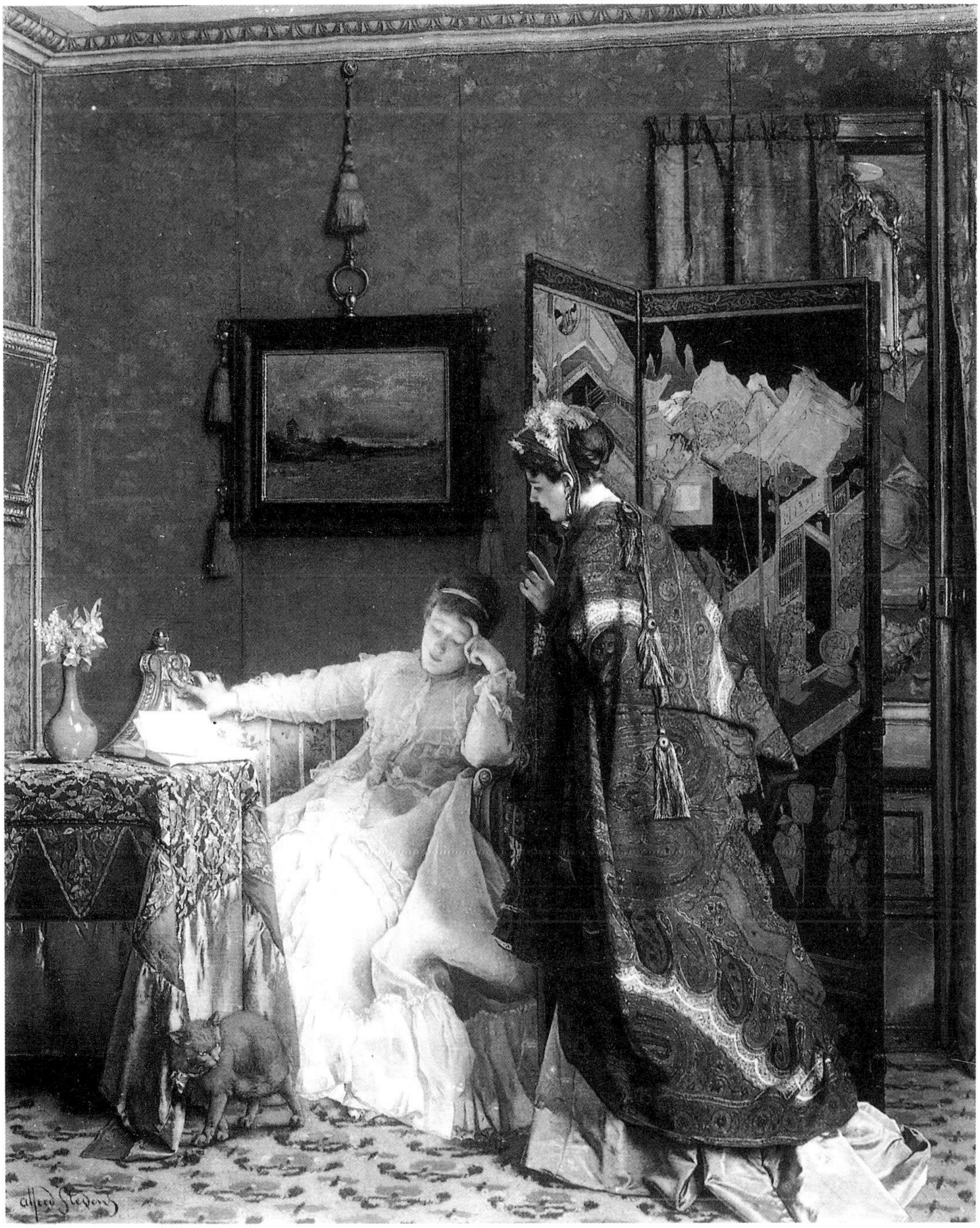

Alfred Stevens, The visit, *no date. Mme Cardon's Collection, Brussels.*
Hooded cloak, called burnous, in ivory silk gauze, probably made in North Africa, 1850–1870.
Union française des arts du costume, Paris (facing page, above).
Dolman in beige woollen cloth, 1871–1872. Musée de la Mode et du Costume, Paris (facing page, below left).
Cashmere evening cloak (burnous), 1870. Musée de la Mode et du Costume, Paris (facing page, below right).

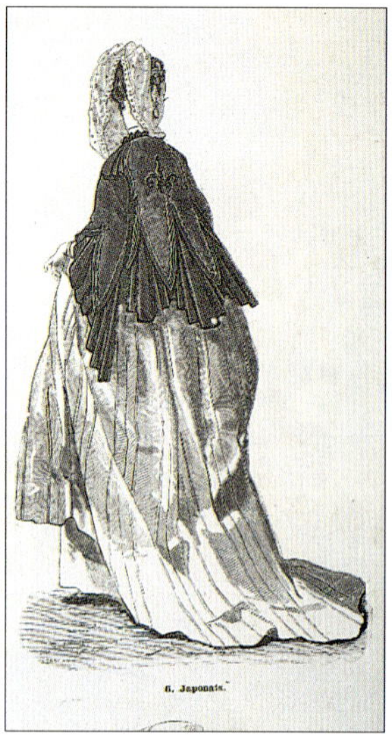

New Summer fashions for the summer of 1868 by the designer Robert Frères, 85 rue de Richelieu, Paris, *detail: 'Japonais'* (*left*).

Le Journal des demoiselles: *Collection of ready-made cloaks, 'Le Japonais', October 1887* (*right*).

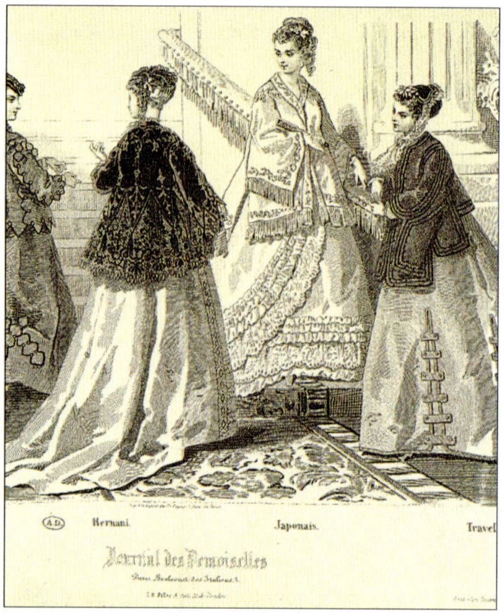

limited impact on fashion. The main connection which has been established is the kimono worn as a peignoir,[29] together with ready-made garments such as the 'Japanese manteletta', which took over the kimono's shawl collar and wide sleeves with square flaps. Glistening fabrics in the Chinese or Japanese style enliven the costume collections (two such costumes, which belonged to the Princesse Mathilde, can be admired in the Château de Compiègne).

Prompted by the American artist Whistler, who was well versed in Japanese fashions and produced many works evoking Japan (*La Princesse du Pays de la Porcelaine*, 1863–4, Washington DC, Freer Gallery of Art, is the most famous), portraits of Parisian women in Japanese dress are very numerous: Tissot (*La Japonaise*, 1864, Dijon, Musée de Beaux Arts), Monet (*La Japonaise: Portrait of Camille*, 1868, Boston, Museum of Fine Arts), Stevens (*La Parisienne Japonaise*, 1872, Liège, Musée de Beaux-Arts). Although these artists were fascinated by the brightly spangled dresses, they used them only anecdotally, in the same way as they introduced fans or folding screens, to pander to the public taste for orientalism. Whistler's interest in things Japanese went deeper. Dissatisfied with contemporary fashion, he even designed a wholly original dress inspired by Japan for a portrait of Mrs Leyland (New York, Frick Collection). In the 1900s Klimt followed a similar path in his portrait of Emilie Flöge.

In France it was not until much later that the Japanese influence had its full effect, with the Nabis and, especially, *The Peignoir* by Bonnard (Paris, Musée d'Orsay). Here, in the material striped in ochre and yellow, rendered matt by the use of paint containing glue, Bonnard achieved an extraordinarily exact likeness of precious Japanese fabrics. He also revived the sinuous outline of the human body – a seemingly abstract form devoid of volume – found in Japanese prints. One might wonder if the 'S-

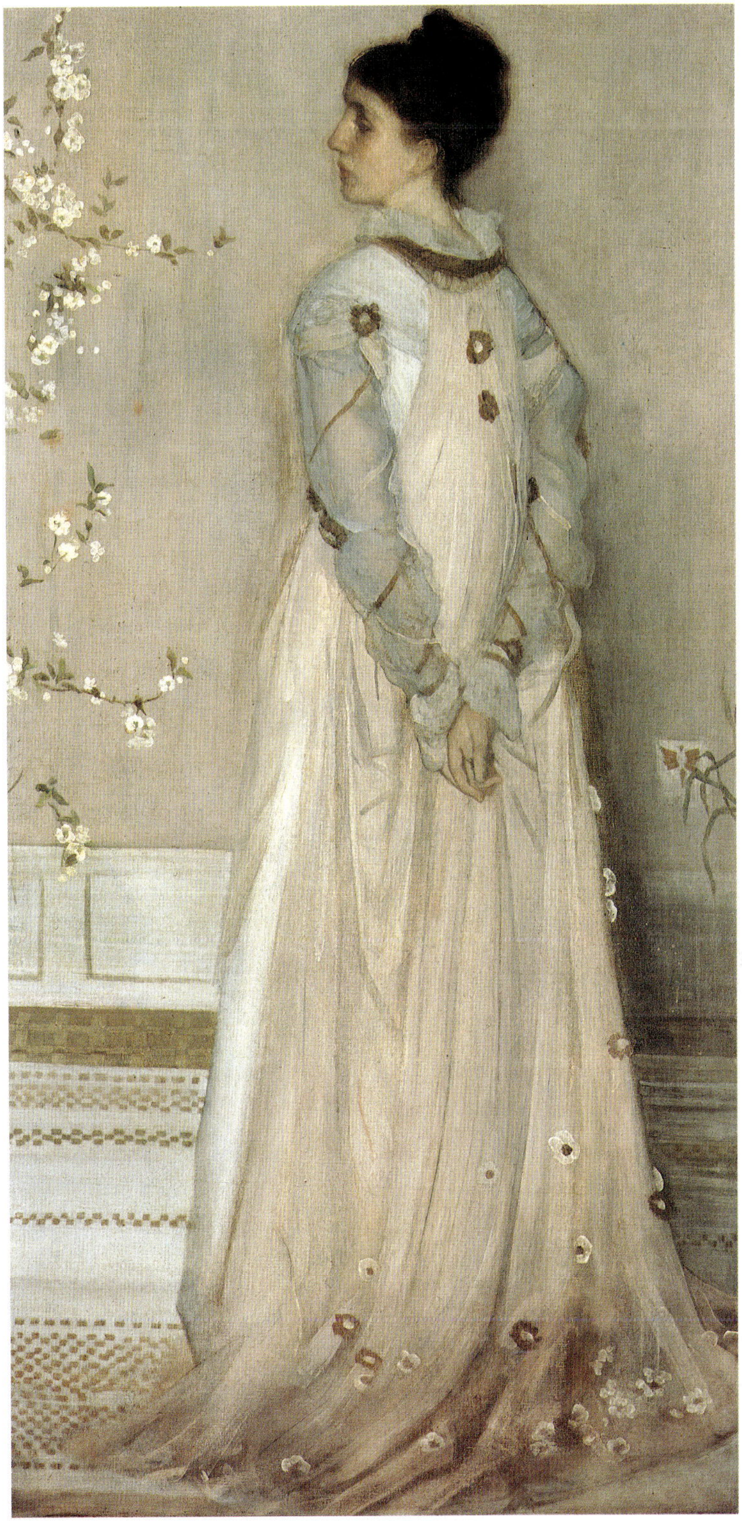

James Abbott McNeill Whistler, Mrs Fredrick R. Leyland, *1872–1873. Frick Collection, New York.*

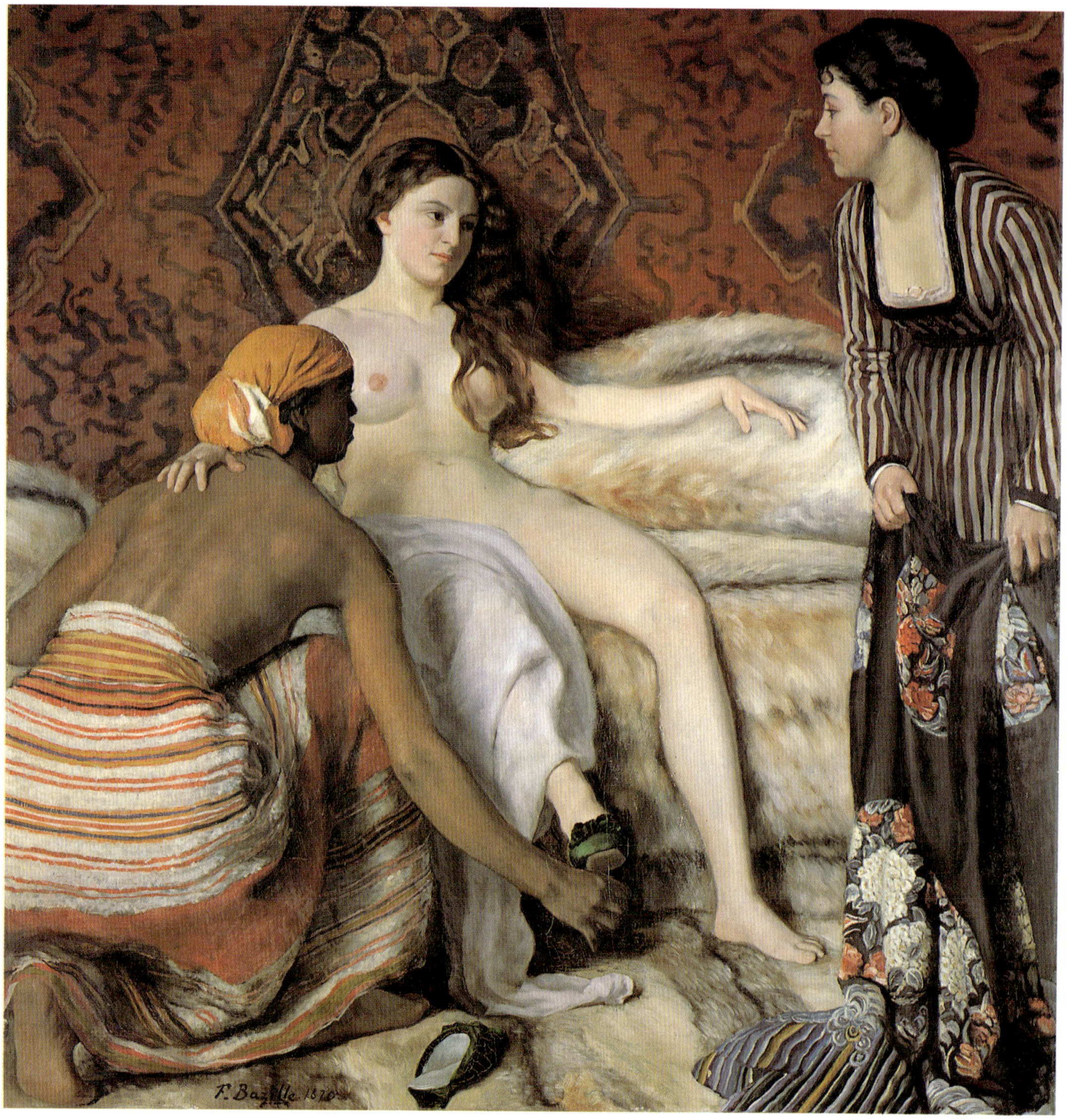

Frédéric Bazille, La Toilette, *1870. Musée Fabre, Montpellier.*
Gustav Klimt, Emilie Flöge, *1902, oil on canvas. Historisches Museum der Stadt, Vienna (facing page, left).*
Pierre Bonnard, The Peignoir, *1892. Musée d'Orsay, Paris (facing page, right).*

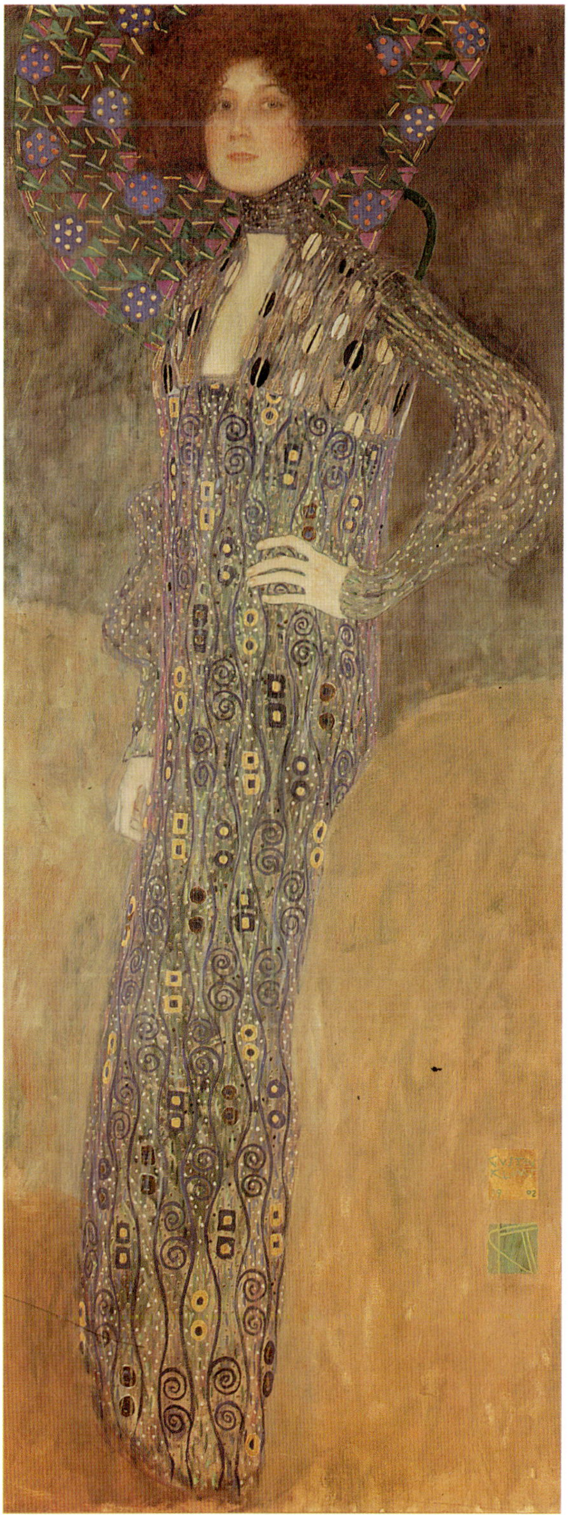

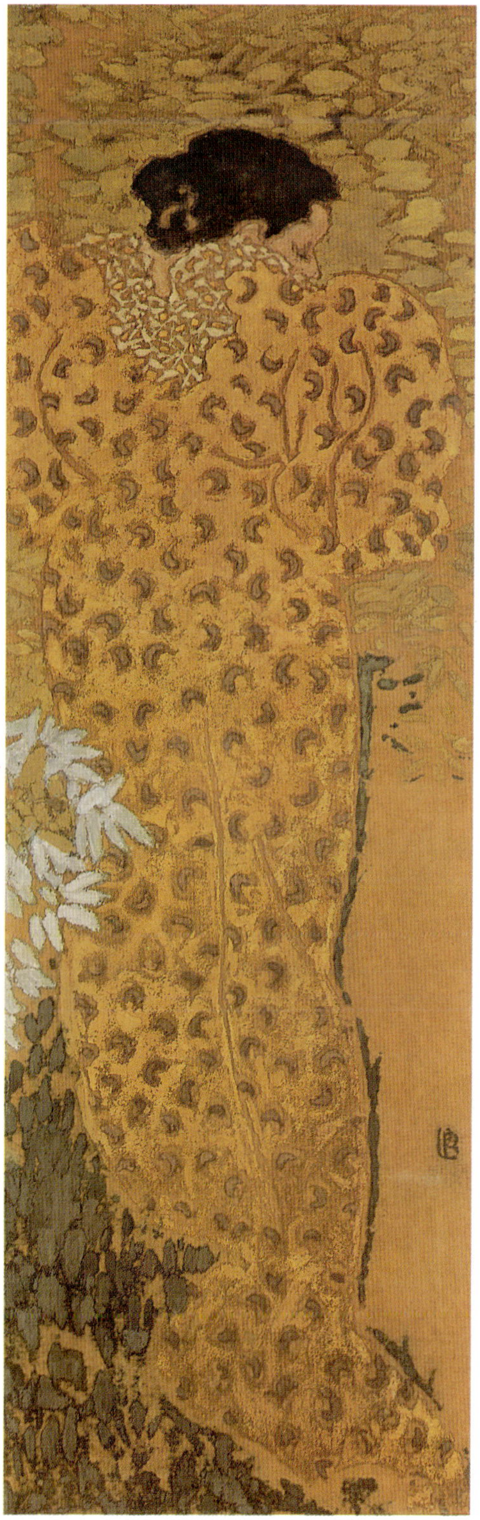

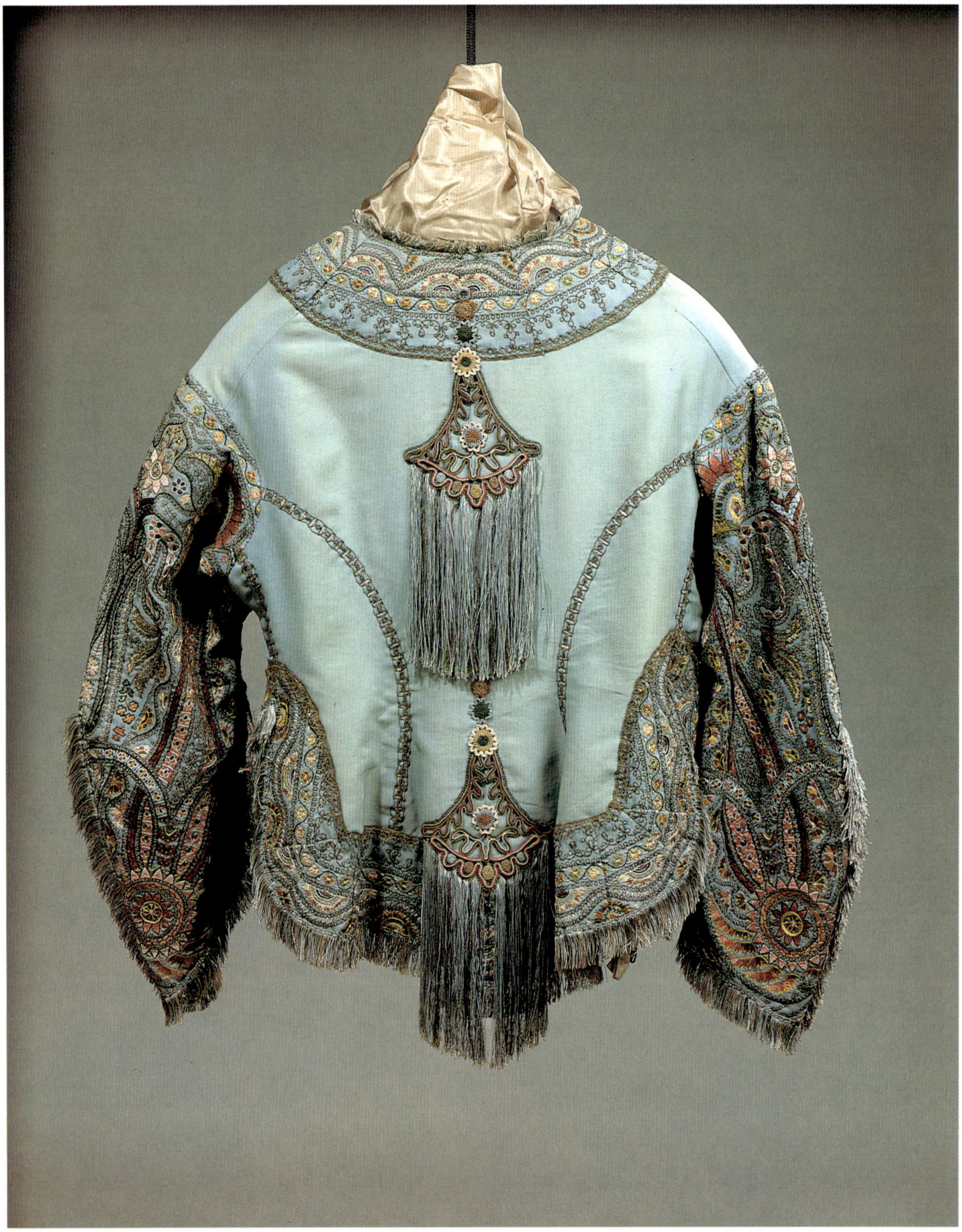

Princess Mathilde's Chinese-style visiting dress, back view, no date.
Musée du Second Empire, Château de Compiègne.

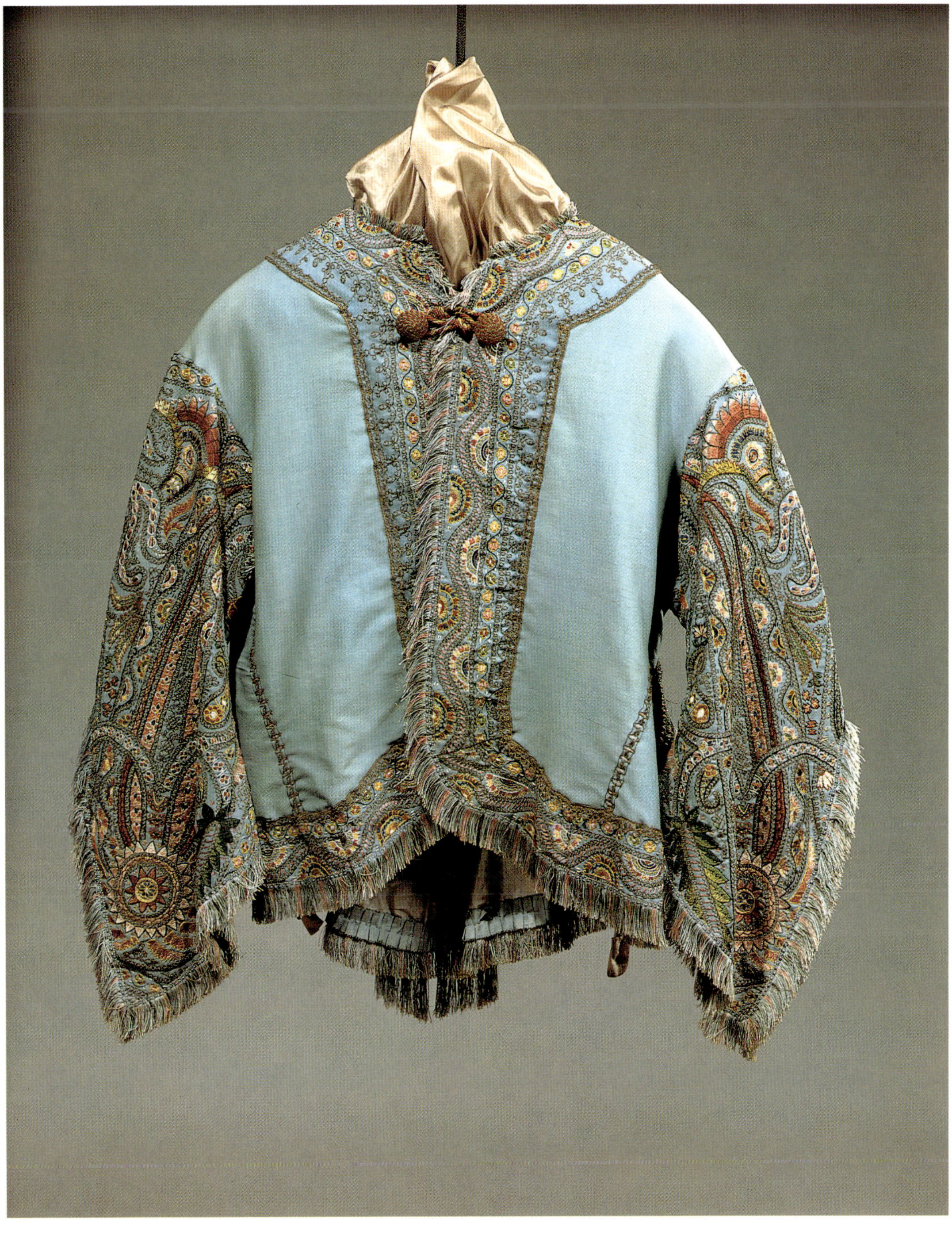

Princess Mathilde's Chinese-style visiting dress, front view, no date, Musée du Second Empire, Château de Compiègne.

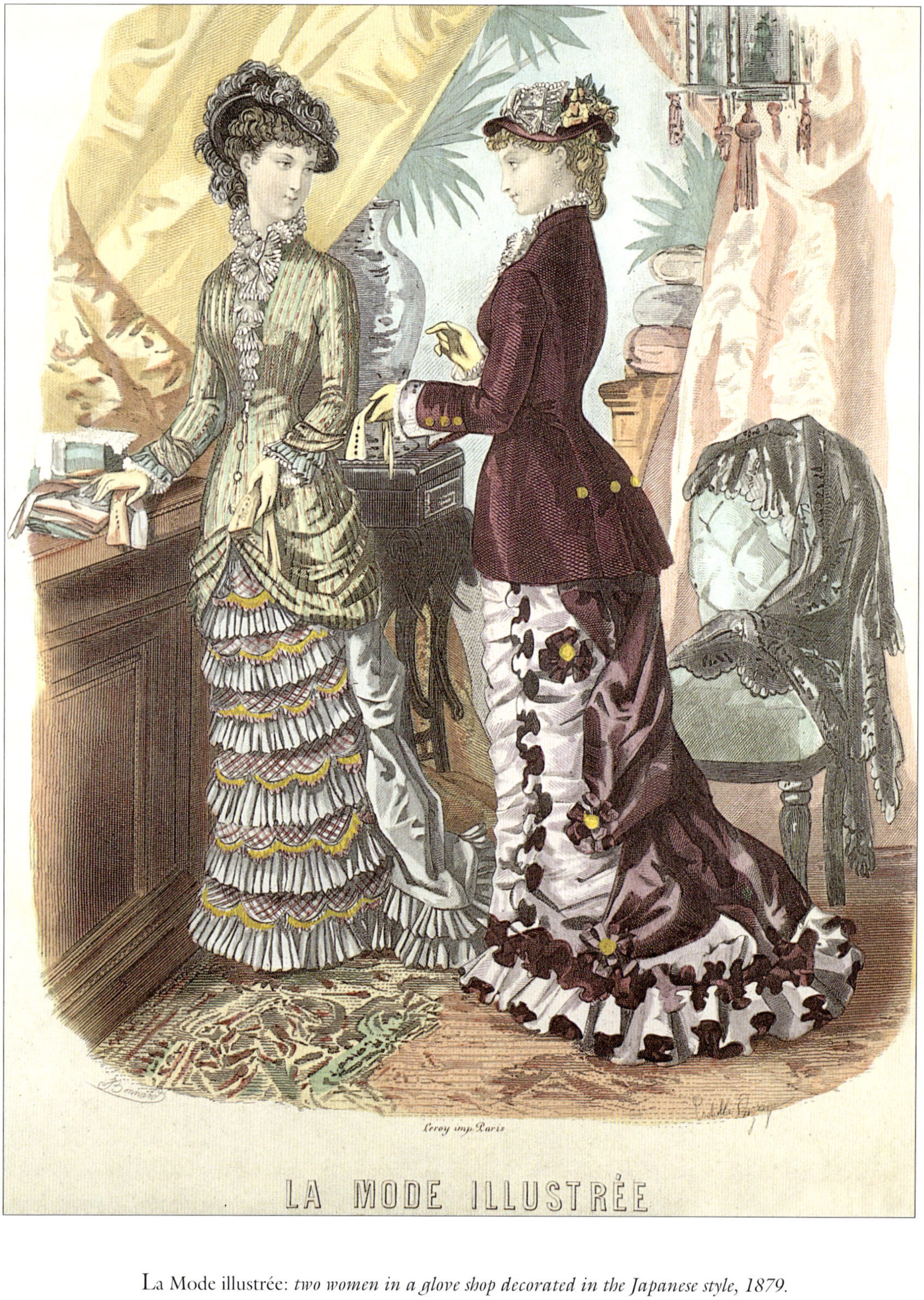

La Mode illustrée: *two women in a glove shop decorated in the Japanese style, 1879.*

line' of Art Nouveau is anything other than this same search for a floating, swaying silhouette. In this way Japonism finally set its stamp on fashion at the end of the century, not so much through the adoption of sartorial details, but less directly and more deeply, in terms of volume and line.

In comparing the manifestations of historicism and exoticism in fashion and painting, we notice that they do not follow strictly parallel paths. While art criticism was lamenting the decline of history painting, fashion was absorbing historical references more and more deeply. Exoticism and orientalism found a unanimous response among painters, whereas their influence on fashion was far more superficial. However, despite these apparent contradictions, it can be seen that fashion did play a role in the evolution of painting, and especially history painting. Indeed, although the latter still featured just as prominently at the Salon, it was being transformed into a costumed genre scene, a potted archaeological reconstruction of past centuries (whether antiquity, the Renaissance or the eighteenth century), a vehicle no longer for conveying ideals but for picturesque anecdotes. As these scenes were much like those to be found in costume balls, couturières and painters studied history paintings as source material for their own works. Critics discussed the historical accuracy of costumes in the paintings of Gérôme or Baudry as earnestly as the fashion press debated the fancy dress worn at society balls. It is as if history had been emptied of its moral significance so that it could be absorbed into everyday life.

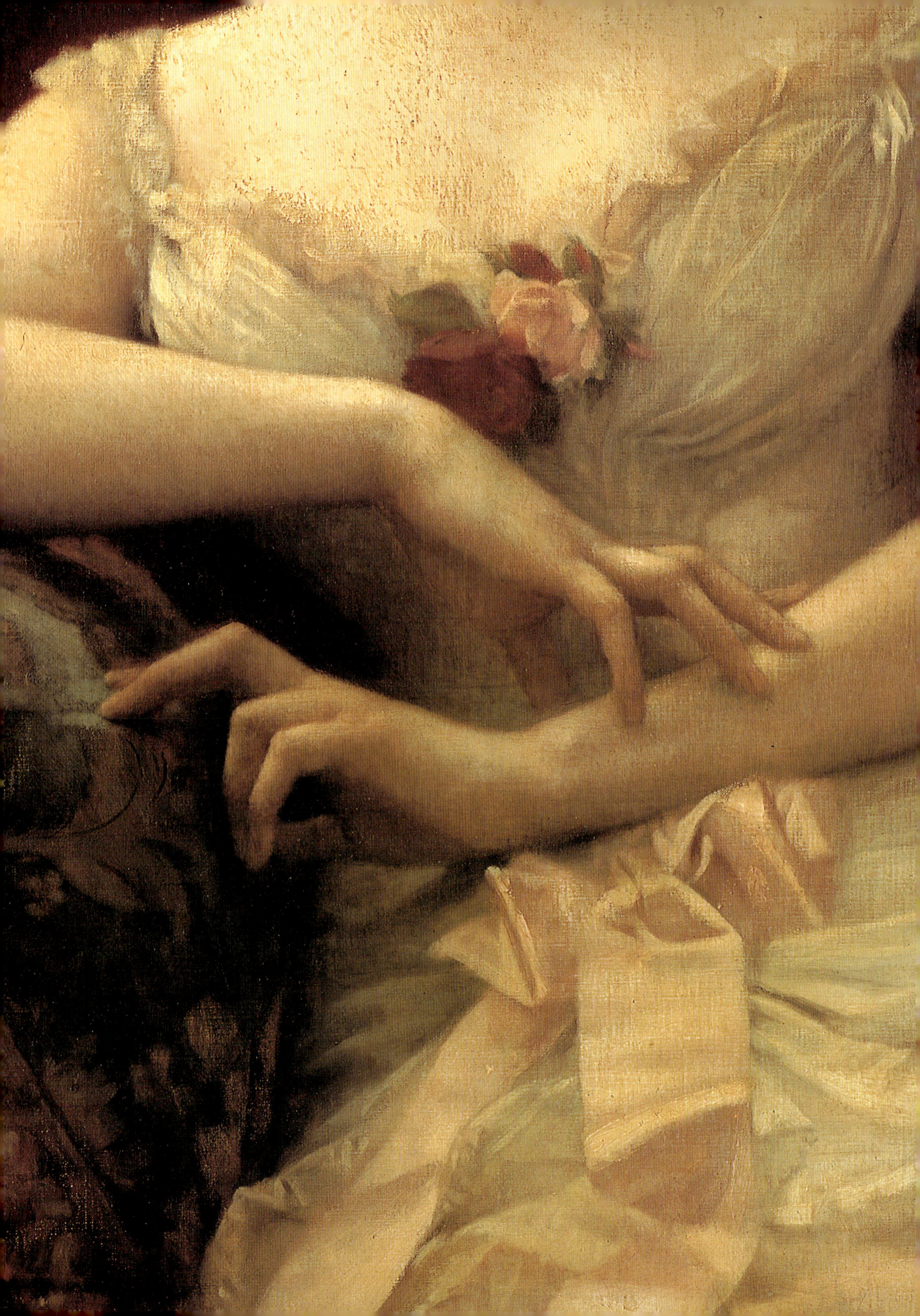

Chapter Four

Art and Fashion

Alexandre Cabanel,
Madame Edouard Hérve, *1884 (detail).*
Musée du Petit Palais, Paris.

Fashion – the woman's muse

An artistic discipline

In the nineteenth century, new links were formed between art and fashion. These two spheres of consumption, now enlarged to include the middle classes, became closely interconnected. In connection with historicism we have already seen the major role played by old paintings in fashion. Worth even confessed, without false modesty, that he 'drew his inspiration regarding antiquity from Gérome and Alma-Tadema, his idea of the Renaissance from Tissot, and his vision of the *parisienne* from Stevens'.[1] The couturier, therefore, left no source of inspiration untapped; works from the past (mainly by Rubens and van Dyck) were supplemented by contemporary references. A fashion journal invited couturiers to take their inspiration from a 'pretty Venetian patrician' from the sixteenth century painted by Alexandre Cabanel:

> the velvet robe has wide sleeves lined with pink satin over clinging under-sleeves of white muslin gathered into puffs. The bodice has a round waistline, a square-cut *décolleté*, and is closed at the front by narrow ribbons. The red velvet hat with raised brim is garnished with pearl motifs.
>
> This type of dress would be delightful if modernized, and we shall certainly see the hat adorning some elegant parisienne.[2]

If such a dress existed, we can be sure that it had been removed far from the sixteenth century by the filter of the couturier and the painter. Even art critics expressed the desire that paintings should inspire the fashions of tomorrow. For example, William Bürger (Théophile Thoré), discussing a painting by Whistler inspired by Japan, *La Princesse du Pays de la Porcelaine*, commented in 1865:

> I should like fashion to take its cue from her costume. Perhaps it will be seen at a court ball this winter, when the princess from the lands of porcelain will have a great success in a pearl-grey dress with a floral design, a saffron cloak, a bouquet of tropical flowers, a poppy-red waistband, with a fan of paradise feathers in her right hand.'[3]

Here, the language of criticism is exactly that of the fashion journalist. Conversely, fashion creations were drawn into the realm of art criticism, since Worth could say: 'I am a great artist; I have Delacroix's sense of colour and I *compose*. A *toilette* is as good as a painting.' In the same context the couturier also compares his supremacy to that of Ingres, mischievously bringing together the two most violent antagonists in the history of art. It was often said that Worth revolutionized the status of the couturier. Certainly, through his pride and his genius, he did much to enhance the prestige of his profession. Meanwhile, fashion was gaining increased recognition in the public mind through the influence of the Press. The comparison with Delacroix had even been made on behalf

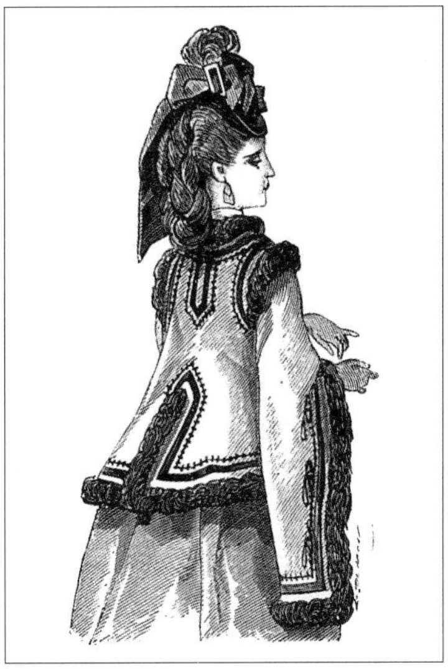

Charles Blanc, L'Art dans la parure et dans le vêtement: *dolman, page-boy sleeves 1875 (left).*

Charles Blanc, L'Art dans la parure et dans le vêtement: *Medici collar, 1875 (right).*

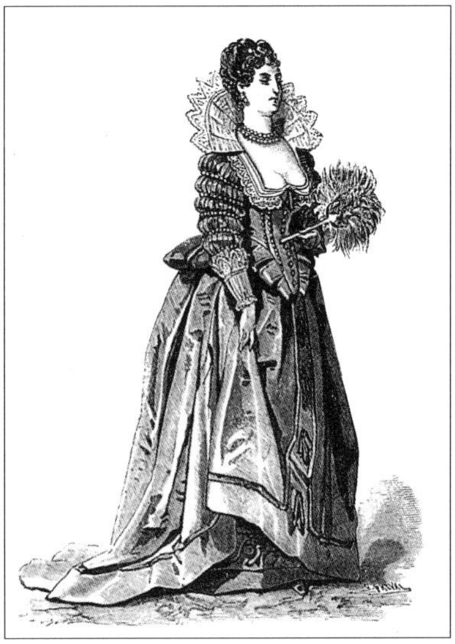

of a tailor in 1857.[4] In this way a very close correlation between art and dress was established in this period. The expression 'the art of dressing' was taken in the literal sense, and everything conspired to make fashion an artistic activity. The material and social importance of fashion to women has been mentioned; it was also given a role in the realm of the mind.

The elevation of women through fashion was not the work of some reactionary thinker. On the contrary, it was an idea that found much favour in modernist discourse, and notably in Baudelaire. In his *Notes sur Paris* (1887), Taine tells us that: 'A true *toilette* is worth as much as a poem.' According to Octave Uzanne: 'Dress for women is the first of arts, the one that contains all the others. It is her offensive armour, her harmonious palette.'[5] Aphorisms abounded. The society lady brought up in the familiar, artistic milieu of museums was 'privileged'. The others, those ignorant of the codes of etiquette, had to serve an apprenticeship in this new artistic discipline.[6]

In 1875 Charles Blanc, an influential figure in the world of fine arts who was both a critic and co-founder of *La Gazette des beaux-arts*, published *L'Art dans la parure et dans le vêtement*. This work, intended for both couturiers and women, offered at the same time a history of costume, practical advice and aesthetic theories. Coming from such an eminent and respected figure, it deserves our attention. It was in fact a pendant, written for women, of a manual which had had considerable resonance among artists (Seurat, in particular): *La grammaire des arts et du dessin*, which had come out eight years before. In *L'Art dans la parure et dans le vêtement*, Blanc applies to women, or rather to their dress, the same kind of grid as an artist uses in 'squaring-up' a canvas, so that he can discuss fashion in terms of the same basic laws and principles that he had set out for art in his *Grammaire*. According to him, the art of dressing was governed by the expressive power of line (a theory he had taken over from Humbert de Superville), by the law of the simultaneous contrast of colours (taken from Chevreul[7]) and by the unity and harmony of a *toilette* with the soul.[8] For example, the tilt of a hat decisively affects the figure's expression,[9] and 'the artist may, at his discretion, reinforce or soften, inflame or pacify, the natural colours of the person he wants to embellish, by means of extraneous colours that he introduces into her attire'.[10]

Just as Baudelaire had done, Blanc highlights the links between fashion and the manners of a society, between mode and morals. He warns women against 'dissonant apparel', analysing the idiom of costume in relation to the historical and social conditions which produced it.

His contemporary garment, the bustle, designed to be 'seen in profile', moved him to write as follows:

> the profile is the silhouette of a person who ignores us, who passes, who is in flight from us. Dress has become an image of the rapid movement which is taking hold of the world and is carrying off even the guardians of the domestic hearth. We can still see them today, now dressed and buttoned up like boys, now festooned with braid like army officers, walking on high heels that impel them forward; we see them quicken their pace, cleaving the air and accelerating life as they devour space and are devoured by it in their turn.[11]

This is a surprising text from many points of view. Though giving expression to a somewhat nebulous morality, as here, it nevertheless prefigures some profoundly innovative artistic themes. A woman in a Monet painting will illustrate Charles Blanc's study of the transformation of a complexion under a mauve-lined sunshade,[12] and the Duchesse de Guermantes, wearing dresses 'endowed with meaning', will be the prolonged echo of Proustian ideas which antedate Proust: 'Before a woman has put on the dress she wishes to wear, even before she has foreseen its cut and ordered its style, she has already betrayed something of her fleeting thoughts and her mood, simply by her choice of the material, which has caught her eye and laid bare her preferences.'[13]

But if this text modernizes the terminology relating to fashion idiom and colours (and it seems addressed no less to those who create fashion than to the portrait painters who depict it), it also adopts some existing leitmotifs of the women's press. On the subject of the hat, that 'indicator of morals' dear to the deportment manuals, we read: 'It is permissible to dream in a sky-blue hat, but to cry in a pink hat is not allowed.'[14] On the necessary study of the art of the past: 'A woman who wishes to do all she can in order to please should...consult the portraits painted by the most famous artists in that genre, Rubens, van Dyck, Velázquez, Reynolds, Lawrence, Gérard and Ingres'.[15] Not forgetting, later in the text, the inevitable reference to *Le Chapeau de paille* by Rubens, used more than once in the Press.

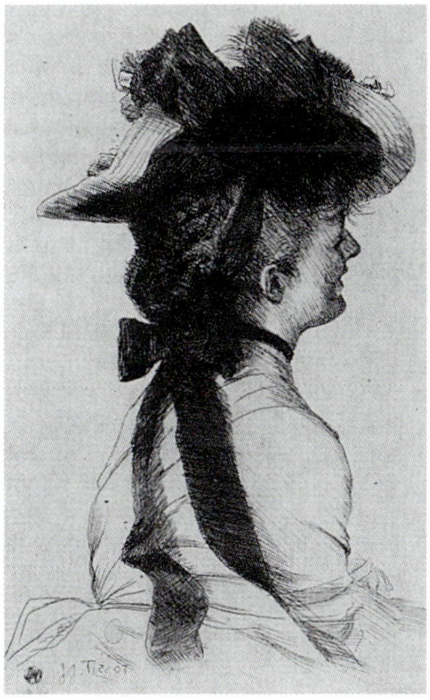

James Tissot,
The Rubens hat, *1875.*
Bibliothèque Nationale, Paris (left).

Peter Paul Rubens,
Portrait of Suzanne Fourment *or* Le Chapeau de paille, *c.1625.*
The National Gallery, London (right).

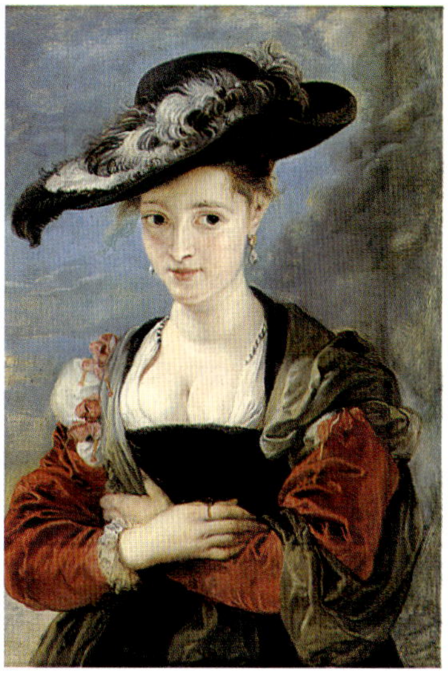

This reference to the importance of an artistic culture undoubtedly comes naturally to a man who was primarily an art critic. Of course, an approach which involves extracting the quintessence of elegance from a model from the past remains very abstract. Nevertheless, as we have seen, such advice was constantly being given. One might ask whether this insistence on the origins of fashion in painting was not an attempt to find new reference points, now that neither the court nor etiquette could provide guidance. Were Rubens, Worth and Carolus-Duran the new directors of fashion? And did couturiers, who may be supposed not to have spent all their time making faithful copies at the Louvre, need to claim a knowledge of art in order to be credible?

Leaving aside Charles Blanc, we may wonder why, for example, the journal *L'Art de la mode*, which addressed itself 'solely to women of high society', advised its readers to 'spend one day each month in the studio of a real painter: Baudry, Cabanel, Carolus Duran, Madrazo', in order to 'have within yourself a feeling for colour, and also for line'.[16] All these painters, highly fashionable and extremely expensive, were inaccessible to the average middle-class woman. To take lessons in fashion from exalted persons - was that not to reinvent an élitist manner of dressing?

To return to Charles Blanc, I suggest that we find in his work a nostalgia for a harmony between social class and appearance, especially in his analysis of the growth of luxury in the Second Empire, which 'corrupted morals, to the point where it became difficult to pick out a well-bred women simply from her style of dress'.[17] His analysis of fashion reveals, in fact, the same ambiguity as does the man himself. Both a liberal and a progressive, and very close to his brother Louis Blanc, a militant socialist, he was nevertheless faithful to the theories of Quatremère de Quincy, believing in the primacy

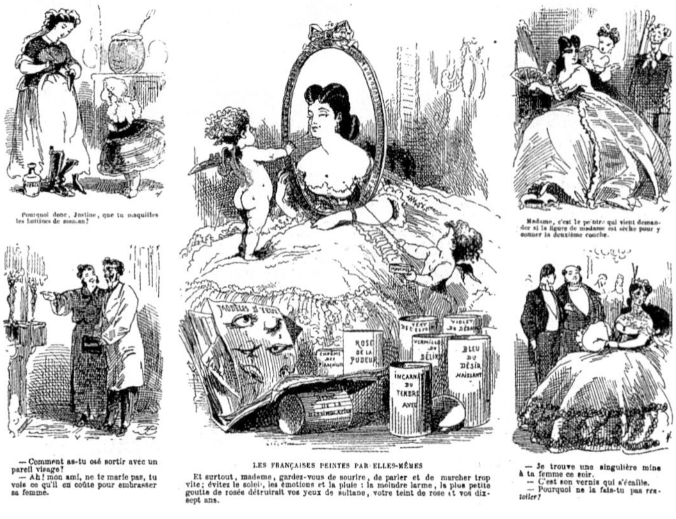

La Vie parisienne, *Make-up in families, French women painted by themselves'*, *1864.*

of history painting and in the spirituality of art. For this reason he is sometimes classified among the modernist set, and sometimes among its opponents. Rather than weighing up the traditionalist and progressive elements in his book, our concern is, firstly, to note the artistic status he accorded to the couturier and to fashion,[18] which is surprising in a man preoccupied with the hierarchy of genres; and, secondly, to examine its educational function. Just as art criticism in the nineteenth century undertook to teach the public the basic stylistic principles of art appreciation, his aim was to inculcate the basic tenets of an education in fashion. For Charles Blanc the essential thing was to serve the cause of progress and to support democracy by instruction.

Make-up or 'the art of painting oneself'

The issue of make-up crystallized the movement which was tending to turn woman into an artist. This is seen clearly in the two finest eulogies of fashion: *De La Mode*, by ThéophileGautier, published in 1858, and *L'Eloge du maquillage* by Baudelaire, first published in 1863.

These two texts, which seem to go far beyond the concerns of women, were at the heart of a fierce debate carried on in the Press. The society journal *La Vie parisienne* of 1864, for example, quotes a passage from *L'Eloge du maquillage*, introducing it as follows: 'the question of make-up is far from having been resolved. In an article on modern life by Charles Baudelaire in *Le Figaro*, we find this eloquent passage intended to deal a rude blow to the adversaries of this somewhat shameful fashion.'[19] Despite the bantering tone, to set up Baudelaire as the spokesman of perfumers and make-up men deflates our academic image of the poet rather surprisingly. Baudelaire found the term *maquillage* (make-up) vulgar, preferring to call it 'face painting'. In 1881, *L'Art de la mode* spoke of 'the art of drawing upon oneself in pastels'. In 1858, Gautier eulogized 'the art of painting oneself' with face powder:

> Just as skilled painters harmonize flesh tints and drapery with light glazes, so women whiten their skin, which would look icy beside moire, lace and satin...With this fine powder they impart to their epidermis the mica effect of marble...Perhaps even a vague shiver of modesty induces women to place on their shoulders, breasts and arms this light veil of white dust which attenuates their nudity by depriving them of the warm, provocative colours of life. In this way their form takes on something statuesque; it is spiritualized and purified.[20]

This delicate praise meets the detractors of make-up on their own ground. To those who accused it of being an instrument of depravity, Gautier demonstrates that it forms part of an artistic pursuit of beauty. Make-up, like fashion, of which it is an extension, conceals and runs counter to nature, moving away from life and towards the ideal. It was precisely this last aspect which fascinated Baudelaire and which he developed in his text, going further than Gautier. Feminine make-up, which he sees as an example of tribal dress, is a means of disguising and beautifying nature. If nature is the seat of all vices, 'virtue...is artificial, supernatural, since, at all times and among all nations, gods and prophets have been needed to teach virtue to bestialized humanity.'[21] Just as the teaching of virtue enables man to attain the good, the practice of make-up – and more generally of fashion – enables women to attain the beautiful. It gives them a means of creating a 'supernatural' beauty.

> Fashion should be considered as a symptom of the aspiration of the human mind towards the ideal, which floats above the earthly coarseness and uncleanness accumulated by natural life, as a sublime distortion of nature, or rather as an ever-renewed attempt to reform nature.

In this notion of beauty as a cultural product, Baudelaire flatly contradicts the theory of imitation. We shall see how he uses the concept of modernity to arrive at a definition of art.

'A woman is quite within her rights, and she is even performing a kind of duty, in striving to appear magical and supernatural...as an idol, she must gild herself to be adored.'[22] A woman only exists by turning herself literally into a work of art. Her sole weapon in this attempt is fashion.

The question of make-up was posed, as we have seen, in the terms of a truly aesthetic debate. Treated neither as a sensationalist issue nor as a subject of moral controversy, it enriched the discourse of art criticsim and became a new factor in painting: critics were often to challenge painters to render 'an artificial complexion', 'powdered, velvety flesh' or 'make-up for the theatre and for the bedroom'.[23]

The writers' muse

Fashion and literature

In the nineteenth century woman was entrusted, as we have seen, with a kind of artistic mission to be accomplished by means of her clothing. Can fashion therefore be seen as a new Muse?

Intellectuals had had to take fashion seriously as an important social factor in the late eighteenth century. It was rediscovered in the nineteenth. In 1830, Balzac attempted to define fashion, producing a number of texts: *Traité de la vie élégante*, *Physiologie de la toilette*, and *Des modes à la mode*. Acutely aware of the symbolic importance of dress, he planned to compile a *vestigomanie* – a catalogue of sartorial meanings.

As fashion's prestige grew in the second half of the nineteenth century, it began to exert a fascination on writers. Zola wrote *Au Bonheur de dames* and Degas proposed to the publisher Charpentier that the book be published with real samples of fashion items glued to its pages instead of illustrations. Baudelaire studied the paintings and engravings of Watteau, Saint-Aubin and Moreau the Younger (as did the Goncourt brothers for their study of *La Femme au VIIIe siècle* of 1862), apparently with the idea of writing a history of fashion. Baudelaire was enchanted by the collection of engravings by Pierre la Mésangère sent to him by Poulet-Malassi, which traced fashions from the Revolution to the Consulate.

Many famous writers contributed to the fashion press, which was not compartmentalized in the way it is today. Its contents were made up of reports on elegant society and on cultural life (theatres, the Salons and the Expositions Universelles), practical advice, history, literary articles and essays. And if the feminine press was enriched by art criticism, journals devoted to the fine arts reported on fashion. In 1851 *La Mode poétique* and *Les Muses de la mode* were founded with the aim of writing on fashion in verse, though both were short-lived. More interesting was the experience of Mallarmé. In 1874 the poet founded a review, *La Dernière Mode*, the aim of which he defined (in the eighth and last issue) as: 'To study fashion as an art.' In the issue of 20 December 1874, he began with a bow to this new queen:

> What's this? From her royal dais, made of fabrics from all centuries, from those worn by Queen Semiramis to those contrived by the genius of Worth or Pingat, Fashion, parting the curtains, suddenly reveals herself to us, metamorphosed, living, bearing the future...

In his journal he published many writers - Banville, Daudet, des Essarts – but

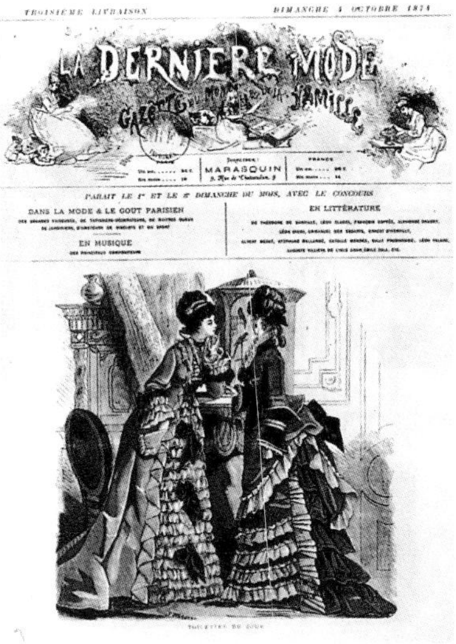

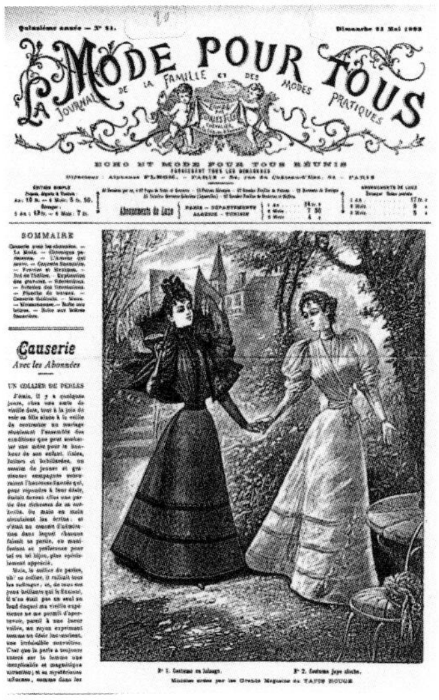

La Dernière Mode, *cover of 4 October 1874 (left).*

La Mode pour tous, *town fashions, cover of 21 May 1893 (right).*

wrote all the headings himself: 'The gazette of fashion', 'Correspondences', 'Paris chronicle', under such pseudonyms as 'Marguerite de Ponty', 'Miss Satin', 'Head Waiter at Brébant's', 'A Creole Lady', 'A Lady of the Manor from Brittany', 'Zizy, the Good Mulatto Woman from Surat', 'The Negress Olympe', 'An Ancestor', or even 'A reader from Alsace'. After the eighth issue, having run out of money, he handed over the journal to the Baronne de Lomaria, who had already been involved in various fashion reviews.[24]

In *Mallarmé et la mode*, Jean-Pierre Lecercle shows that the poet made himself into a real journalist with a style like that of his colleagues, all poetic elements being excluded (although humour and fantasy were present). Did this demonstrate fashion's inability to act as a Muse? Mallarmé sums up his frivolous excursion as follows:

> When hard up, and on one occasion when I bought some ruinous boats, I've had to do a few jobs, solid work but nothing more (*Dieux Antiques* and *Mots Anglais*), which it would not be polite to discuss. Apart from them, my concessions to necessity, as to pleasure, have been infrequent. At one time, however, despairing of the despotic book on Myself I had begun, and after peddling a few articles here and there, I tried, on my own account, to edit a journal, *La Dernière Mode*, on dress, jewellery, furniture and even theatre and dinner menus; and its eight or ten issues, when I have brushed off the dust, are still able to plunge me into long reveries.

Art in the fashion press

As we have said, all the women's journals included articles of art criticism, the tenor of which usually reflected the academic taste of the nineteenth century. However, there

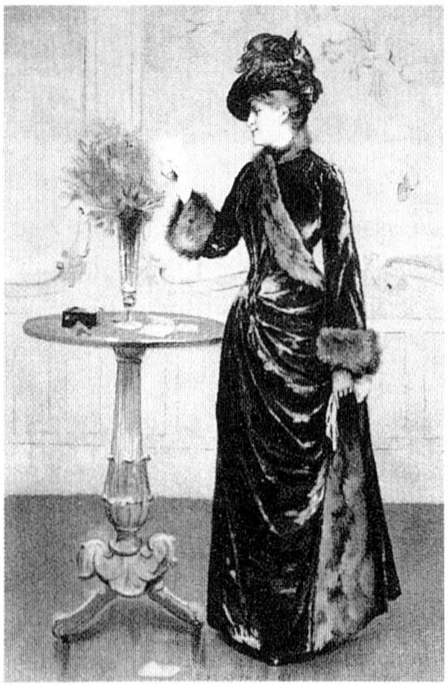

La Revue illustrée, *Jean-Paul Sinibaldi, 'Coat from chez Félix', 1886 (left).*

L'Art de la Mode, *two women in a museum, 1882 (right).*

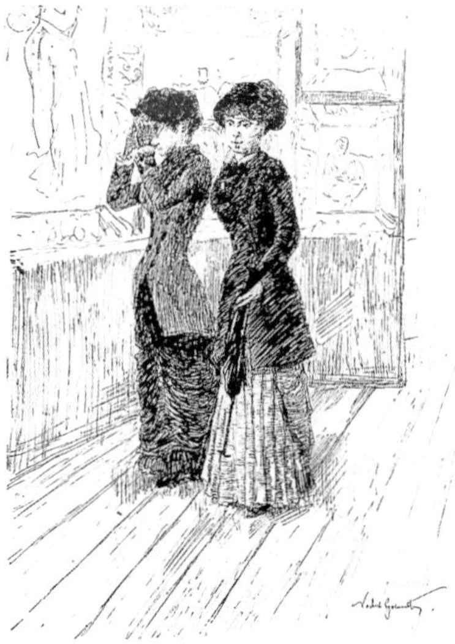

were a few more modern society journals such as *La Vie parisienne* and *L'Art de la mode* which, while not going so far as to support Impressionism, denounced the facile conventionalism of the art that was generally admired. But some journalists took the links between art and fashion further. *L'Art de la mode*, in particular, reproduced a colour lithograph by Stevens, Madrazo or Renoir, or an engraving by Goeneutte or Leloir, in each issue.

In a society column in 1881 we find this very interesting contribution, which seems avant-garde even today:

> The most noteworthy innovations in feminine dress are paintings on satin, muslin or faille. In them the artist's paintbrush contributes to women's attire, heightening it in a picturesque way. You can imagine the attraction and the value of a dress with decoration signed by Madrazo, Madeleine Lemaire, Chaplin or de Nittis. These are truly dresses that deserve to be framed, and no daughter of Eve can do without their fantasies. The Baronne de Poilly, who has just moved into her villa at Trouville, much to the satisfaction of the élite circle she presides over each year, recently wore one of these artistic dresses, which caused a sensation in the supremely elegant surroundings in which it appeared.[25]

In *La Revue illustrée*, Sinibaldi and Béraud were also active collaborators, providing illustrations of exclusive designs created for the review. For example, Sinibaldi painted a young woman in a coat 'from the house of Félix'. This painting was indistinguishable from the elegant genre scenes shown at the Salon, so that some confusion arose between the artistic productions of these painters and work commissioned from them by journals – a confusion denounced by these same journals,

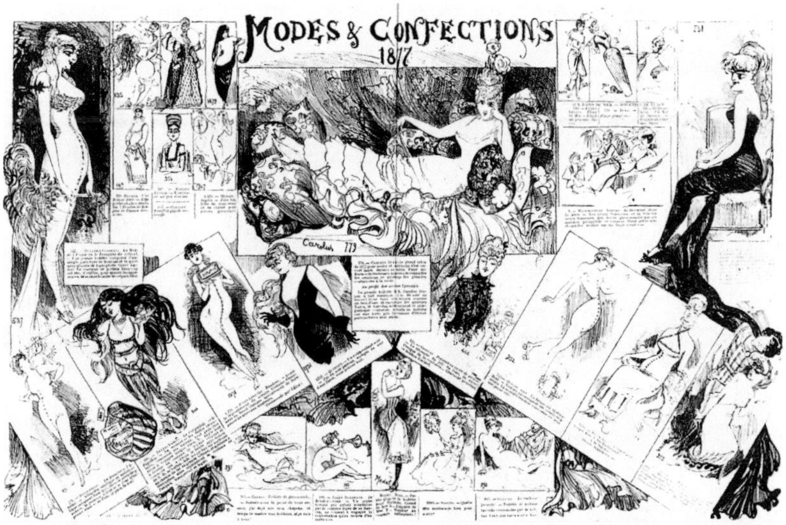

La Vie parisienne: *'At a picture exhibition, Designer fashions and ready-made clothes for the year 1877'.*

which often carried caricatures of painters turning into sellers of novelties: 'Maison Carolus-Duran ... new lines in velvet, lace and fans' (*L'Eclipse*, 'Le Salon comique' by Hadol, 9 June 1872). 'Maison Jean Béraud, mannequin with moving head for couturières. Fabrics guaranteed to be of good complexion' (*La Vie parisienne*, 'La Boite aux aquarelles, le Bazar de la rue Sèze', 16 February 1884). This satirical presentation of the Salon as a vast novelty shop naturally raises questions about the importance of contemporary dress in painting.

Fashion and society art

The Salon – where fashion is created

In the nineteenth century no portrait painter could escape the subject of fashion. Early in the century the status of portrait painting rose sharply. The state commissioned numerous official portraits in the guise of public images. The middle classes, having aquired sufficient status to have their portraits painted, threw themselves on this ancient aristocratic privilege with gusto. An enormous demand for personalization emerged. 'The public is passionately in love with its own image.'[26] The bourgeois, eager to be immortalized, went to Disdéri for a portrait photograph or, if he had the money, to a painter.

> Henriette. Oh, Father, just look at this pretty portrait! How graceful and soft and colourful it is! What lovely velvet, such lifelike fur! That's just how I'd like to be painted.
>
> M. Perrichon. Not at all bad, my dear child. It's a Chaplin. Now if your husband hadn't got involved in that foolish speculation ... he could have treated you to it.[27]

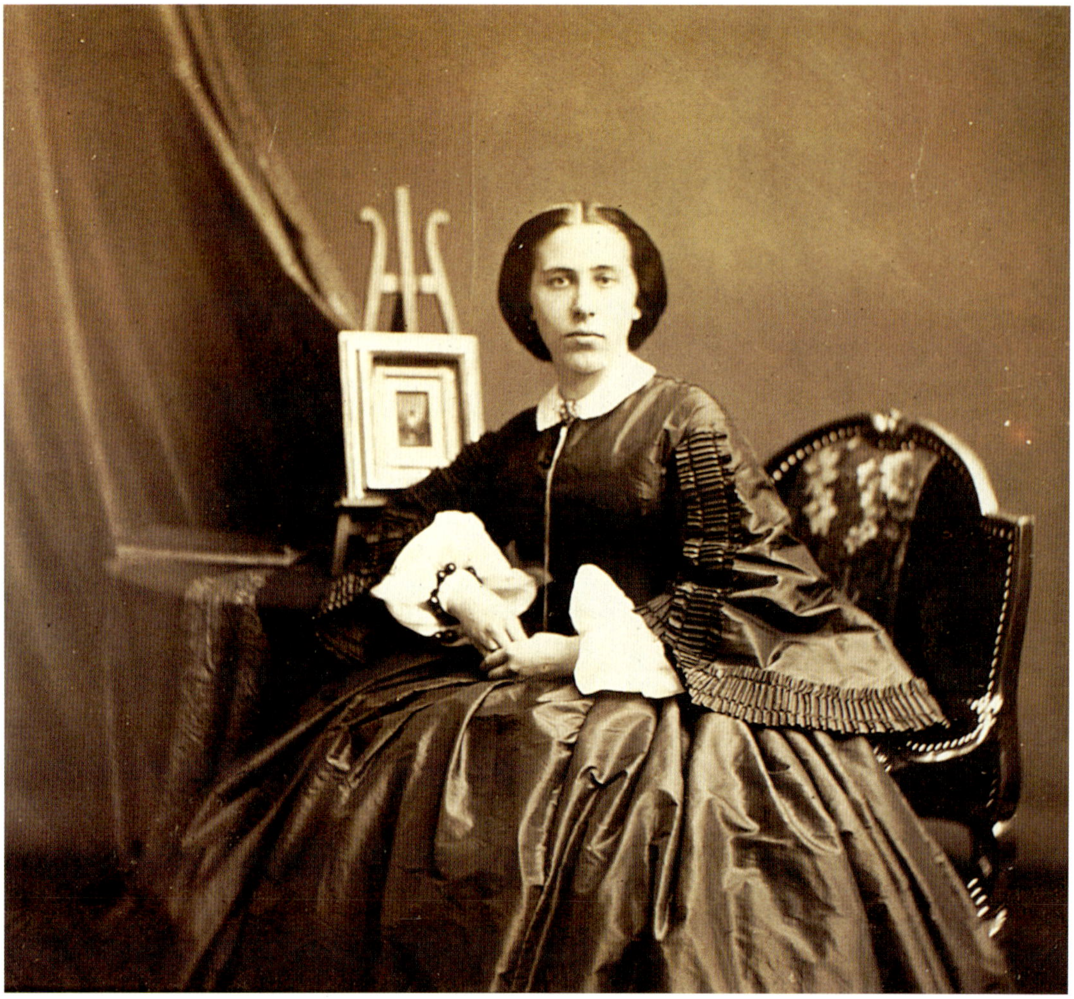

Disdéri, Baroness d'Heutze, *1860.*

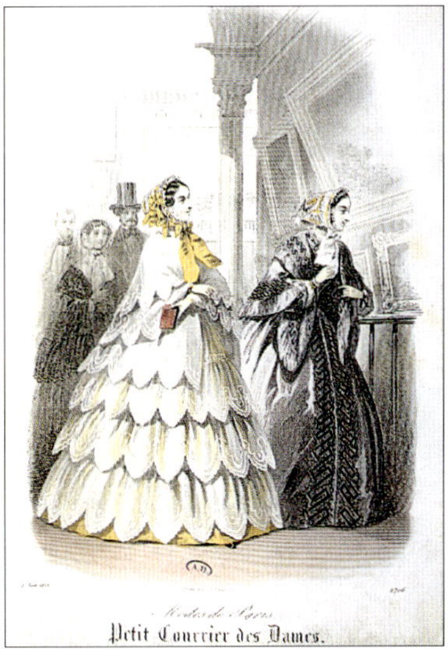

Le Petit Courrier des dames, *two women at the Salon, 4 June 1853 (left).*

Bertall, La Comedie de notre temps, *'When I tell you that it is a dress from Worth, it is because I recognize the style', Vol. II (right).*

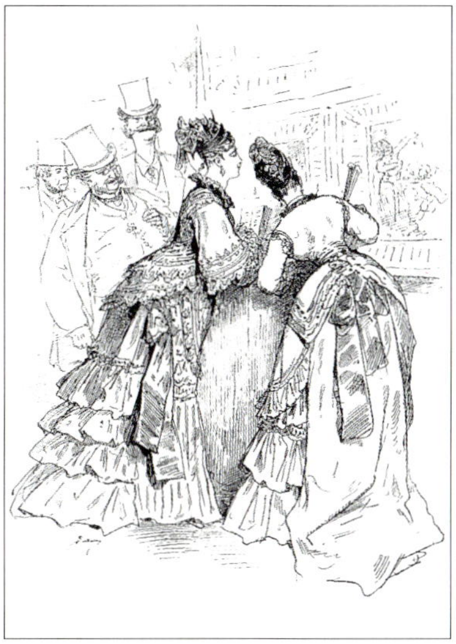

This narcissism provided a livelihood for many a painter. One commentator complained:

> This flood of portraits rises every year and threatens to inundate the Salon. The explanation is simple: apart from people who want their portraits painted there is hardly anyone left who buys paintings.[28]

The career of an artist in the nineteenth century passed through the Salon which, with the Expositions Universelles, was the only means of gaining public recognition. But the Salon was also a highly fashionable place to be seen. Mothers took their marriageable daughters there; elegant women showed off their latest *toilette*. 'Nothing but coaches and *toilettes* all round the Palace of Industry.'[29] A watercolour by C. Guys shows two well-dressed women at the 'Art exhibition', and, conversely, fashion prints showed a model at the Salon, catalogue in hand.

Attending the Salon was just like going to a social gathering.[30] One of the amusements was to identify the sitters in the portraits, who were indicated only by their initials in the catalogue. One can imagine the public's interest in the dresses worn by the sitters, as they played these snobbish games. A society woman knew full well that, more than her face, which after all was known to everyone, it was her dress that would arouse excitement and comment. 'There is one thing women prefer even to being beautiful, and that is to be well dressed.'[31] Above all, one had to avoid being painted in a dress with last year's look. And a dress which aroused notice earned excellent publicity for the couturier. At that time when advertising was making a timid appearance in the Press, mention by critics was more effective. They wrote at length on the dresses (this was also a means of enabling the reader to identify them, since the catalogue was not illustrated), and gave as much attention to the finish of a dress as to its psychological effect.

The portrait painter as subordinate

For the sitter, the portrait was a true social consecration. This, in turn, placed heavy constraints on the painter. Victor Cherbaliez, in his *Salon de 1876*, wrote an essay on the painful situation of the portraitist: 'Among the most assiduous and busiest visitors to the Salon are those who are agonizing over who is to paint their portrait…The portrait painter's lot is a hard one, since it requires much study and talent, as well as troublesome subservience.'[32]

The first aspect of this subservience was the sitter's physical appearance, which the painter could not choose and which inevitably attracted critisism: 'Is that really me? At any rate, you do not show me to advantage. All right, if you insist, I do look a little like that, but I did not think I was so far from the ideal. You could have done better by me.'[33]

A rather surprising and symptomatic feature of the debate, to us, is the association of the ideal with a physical quality. This takes us back to the text by Baudelaire in which the bourgeois, that 'hyperborean brute', that 'eternal spectacle-wearing Eskimo', is made to ask: 'What imagination does it take to paint a portrait? To paint my soul, which is so visible, so clear, so well-known? I pose, and it is I, the sitter, who do most of the work. I am the artist's real supplier. All by myself, I provide his subject matter.'[34]

This gives rise to a first misunderstanding between artist and sitter: the bourgeois is convinced that the only skill needed by the portrait painter is that of a good copyist; but at the same time he expects to be transfigured, idealized, as if the depiction of his soul – and an ideal soul at that – would emerge spontaneously from the pores in his skin.

A second, no less formidable subservience made itself felt when the sitters

> took it into their heads that they resembled a portrait of someone else…Before long, a stout lady would go to see M. Marchand and tell him: 'Sir, you have at the Salon a portrait of Mme la Baronne d'A, which I found charming. It has something of the delicacy of line, the exquisite elegance you displayed in that graceful ceiling painting in which you were pleased to show Psyche sitting on a cloud amid zephyrs and lifting her head to receive the trembling kisses of Love. I don't ask you to paint me as Psyche; but I would like to look like the Baronne d'A. Like her, I'll have a rose in my hair and my fingers shall be entwined.' The same day a repulsive brunette will say to M. Baudry…'You'll dress me in blue like Mlle D., and I wish to look as striking and elusive as she.'[35]

For the artist, the choice of dress was a more difficult task than it seems at first sight. The meticulous, almost obsessive attention paid by Ingres to the clothes of his sitters is well known. It was, incidentally, this interest in dress that enabled Dr Hans Naef, a specialist in Ingres portraits, to re-date several works, thanks to the collaboration of Madeleine Delpierre, curator of the Musée de la Mode et du Costume. The painter's correspondence shows how exacting he could sometimes be. He writes to Mme Moitessier:

> You are, of course, very beautiful in yourself, and on mature reflexion I have abandoned the idea of a full soirée hairstyle. This will make the portrait more tasteful, as I fear that such hair would be distract attention from the head. Even the jewellery on your breast is too old-fashioned, and I beg you to replace it with a gold cameo.[36]

We know that during the seven years spent on this portrait the choice of dress was a delicate issue, much discussed and often revised. After Ingres, painters were prepared to spend much time on the choice of dress, even taking a certain pleasure in such questions. Degas assiduously frequented the studios of modistes. Antonin Proust reports of Degas: 'He spent a whole day in rapture before the materials unrolled by Mme Derot. The next day it was the hats of a famous *modiste*, Mme Virot, that fired his enthusiasm. He wanted to compose a *toilette* for Jeanne [Mlle Demarsy].'[38] Carolus-Duran was just as concerned about his sitter's dress, 'deciding the colour and cut in advance. He went to the couturier's to manage the trying-on session'.[38]

Bonnat left behind the reputation of being extremely demanding with regard to his clients' dress: 'When you have thought well about what you are about to do,' a journalist advised a young woman who wanted to have her portrait painted by Bonnat, 'order a "portrait-by-Bonnat" dress; there are special models.'[39]

A painter as well-known and respected as Bonnat could take the liberty of imposing 'Bonnat dresses' on a clientèle chosen by himself. By contrast, a painter making his début at the Salon would seek to paint an eminent sitter who, by the very fact of commissioning him, did much to ensure his success. This was not achieved without pains, endured this time by the painter, who had to bow to the whims of his client. The Spanish dancer, La Carmencita, only agreed to pose for John Singer Sargent after receiving three thousand dollars in jewels.

Worth, supplier by appointment

Worth was undoubtedly the most important 'supplier' to portrait painters. From Winterhalter to Carolus-Duran, from Bonnat to Debat-Ponsan and even to Renoir and Manet, his dresses are found everywhere.[40]

In Renoir's case, the portrait in question is *Madame Charpentier and her children* (1878, New York, Metropolitan Museum of Art). And it is clear that it was Mme Charpentier who imposed her choice of dress on the painter. Robida reports:

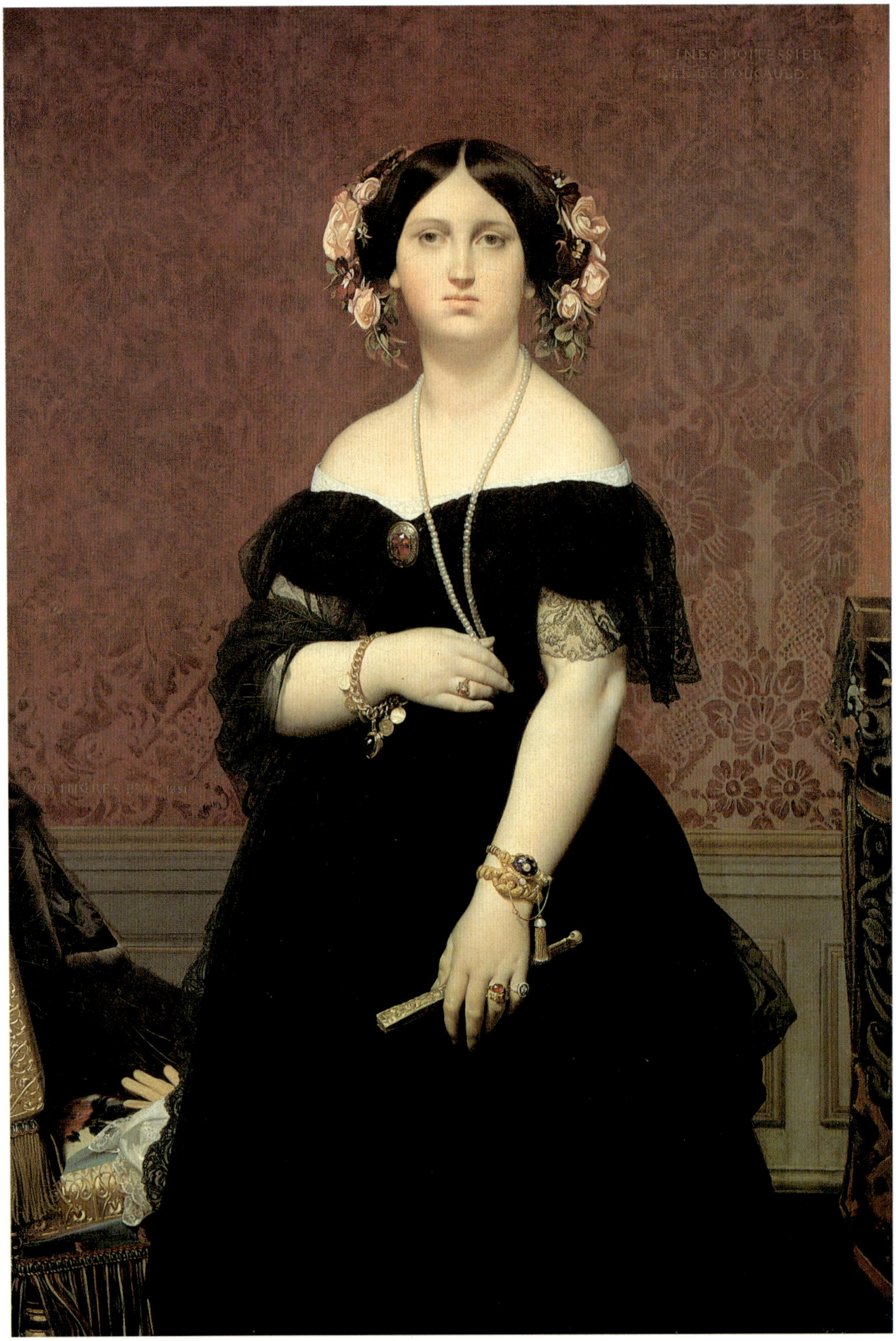

Jean-Auguste-Dominique Ingres, Portrait of Madame Moitessier, *1851.*
National Gallery of Art, Washington.

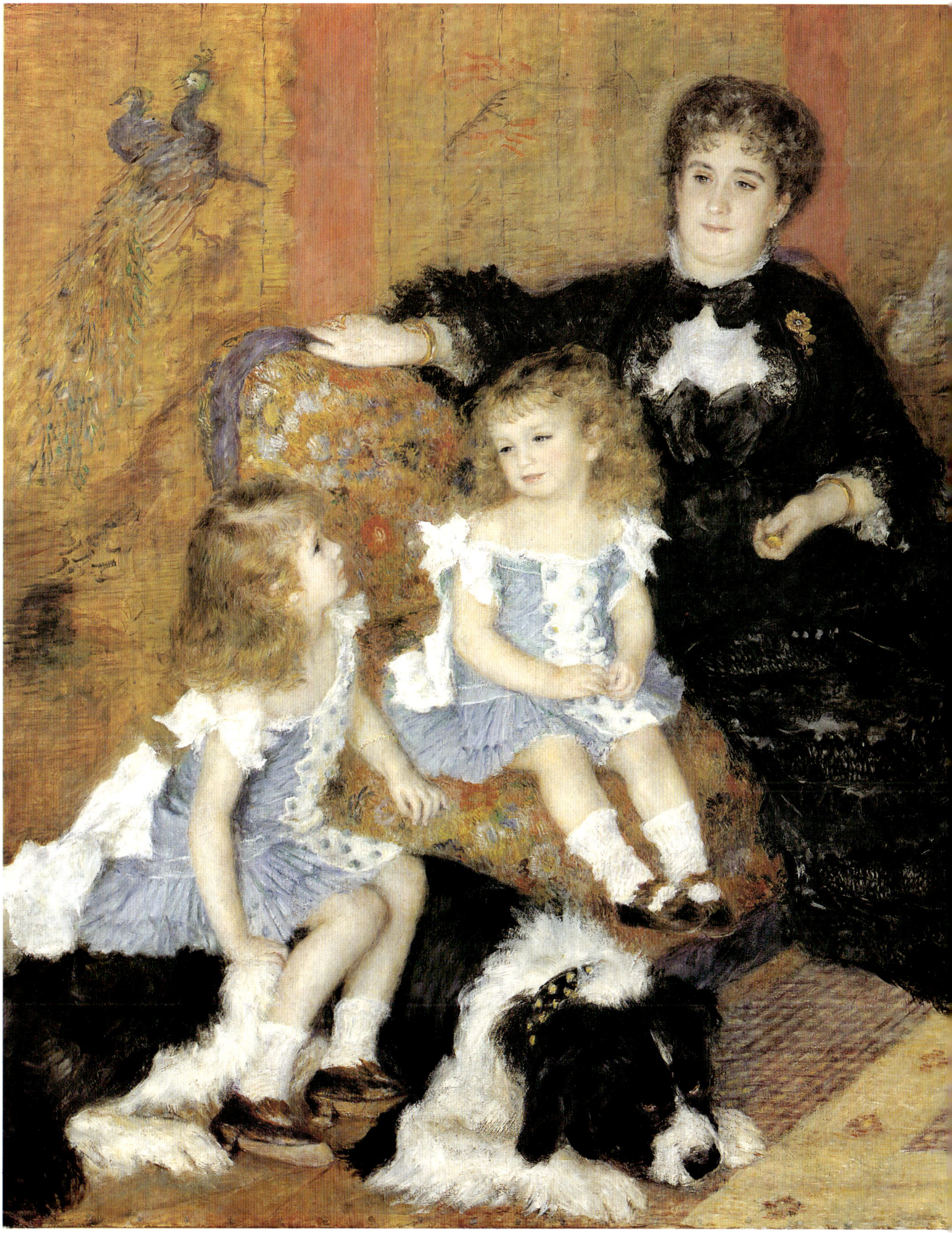

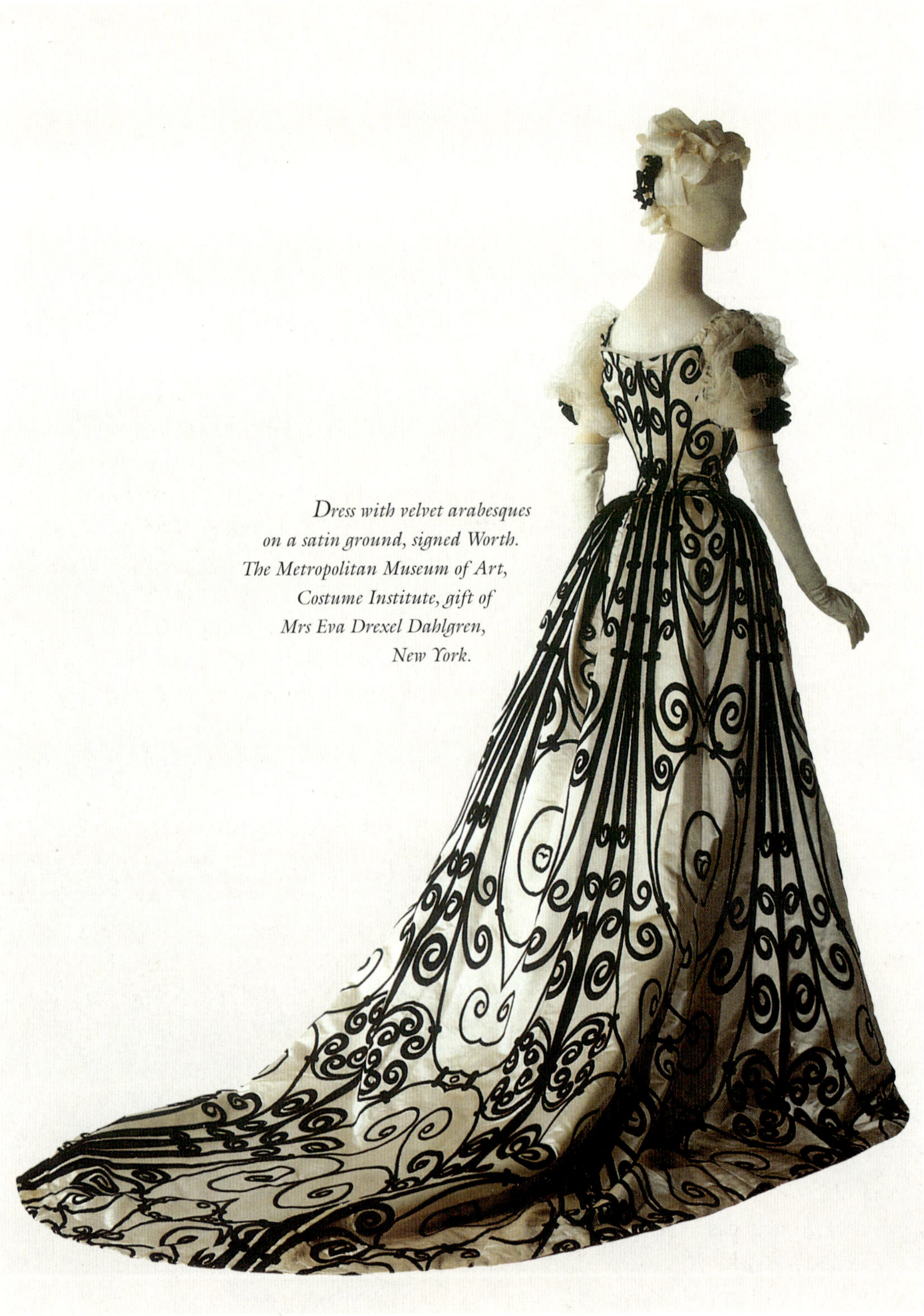

Dress with velvet arabesques on a satin ground, signed Worth. The Metropolitan Museum of Art, Costume Institute, gift of Mrs Eva Drexel Dahlgren, New York.

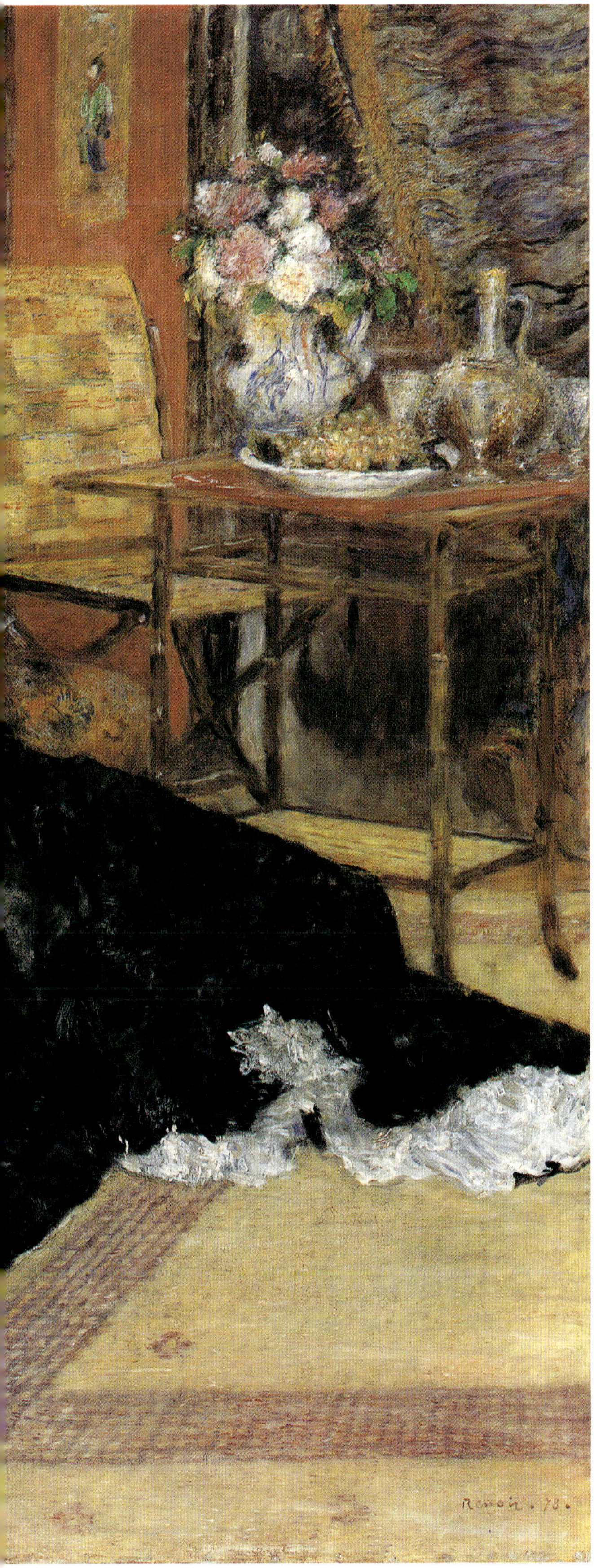

Pierre Auguste Renoir,
Madame Charpentier and her children, *1878.*
The Metropolitan Museum of Art, New York.

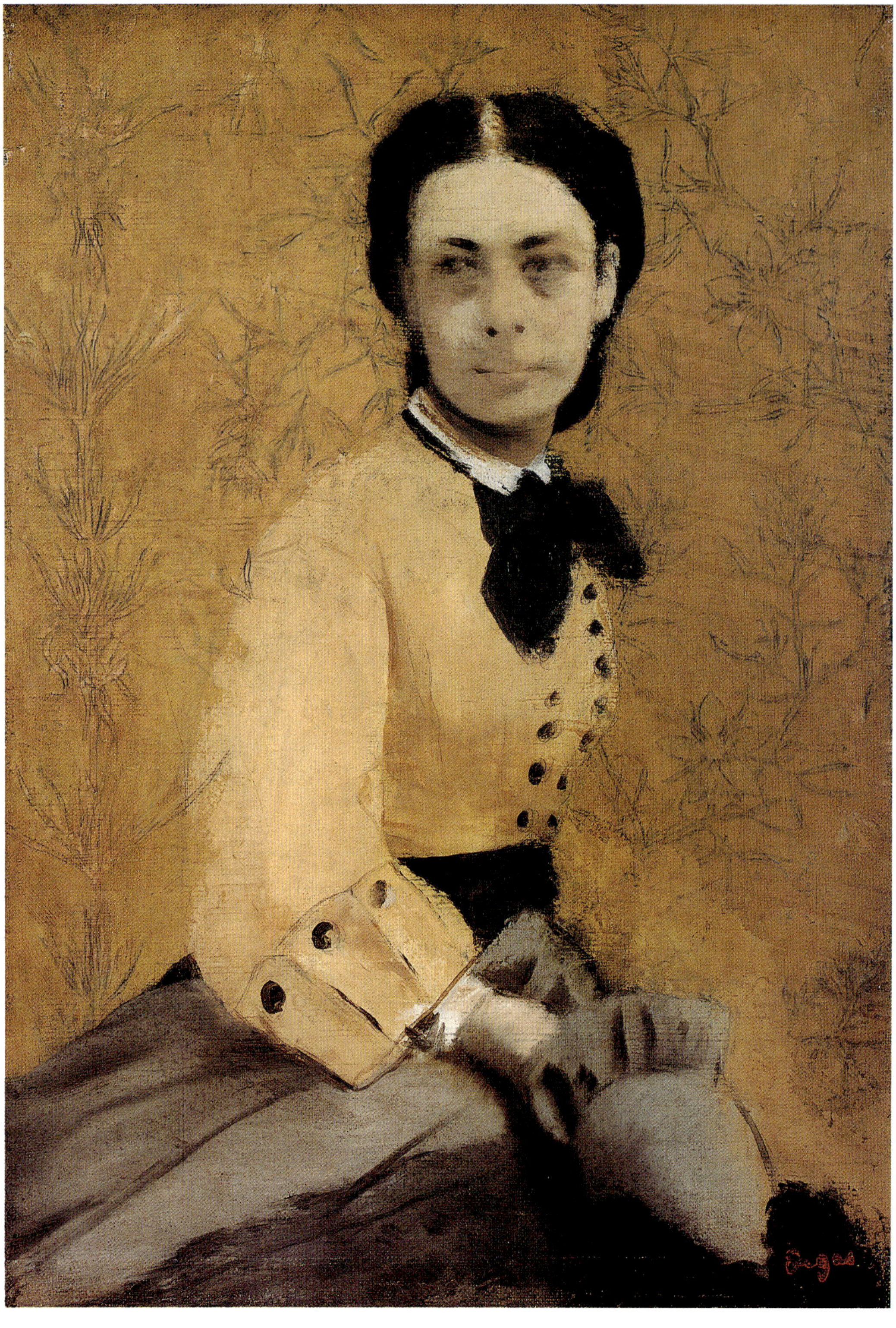

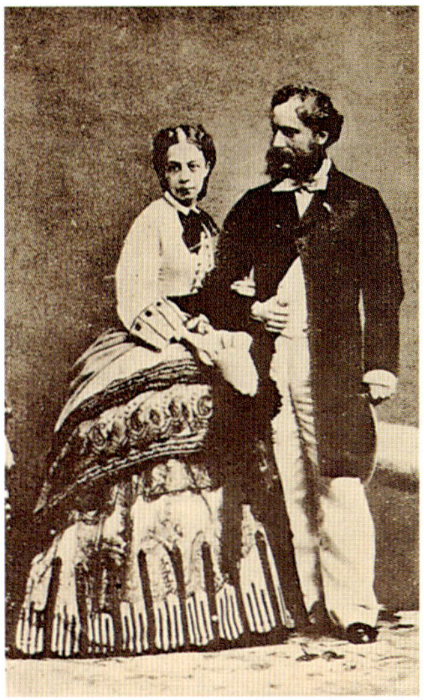

Edgar Degas, Portrait of Princesse Pauline de Metternich, *c.1861. The National Gallery, London (facing page).*

Disdéri, The Prince and Princesse de Metternich, *1860 (left).*

Disdéri, Madame Ferran, 1861. Musée d'Orsay, Paris. (right).

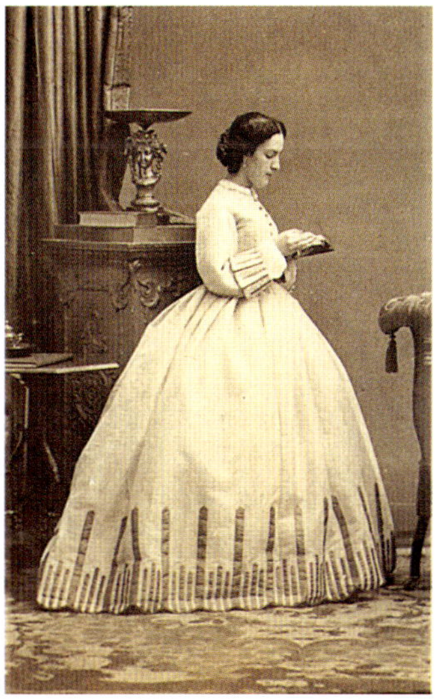

> In it my grandmother is sitting in her little Japanese salon wearing a long black dress by Worth, who had also been couturier to her mother. The dark dress is brightened only by the *guimpe* on her corsage, the light cuffs and some gems, while there is a lace dust ruffle under the spreading train.[41]

Worth dresses were very expensive, and Manet talks with touching pride of the fur-lined coat worn by Méry Laurent in his portrait *Autumn* (1881, Nancy, Musée des Beaux-Arts):

> She has had a pelisse made for her by Worth. Ah, what a pelisse, my friend, fawn with an old-gold lining. I was stupefied...When I left Méry Laurent I told her: "When that fur is worn out, you'll leave it to me, won't you?" She promised. It will make a splendid background to some things I am dreaming of.[42]

This enigmatic last phrase makes us wonder what Manet may have been planning in conection with fashion. It reveals, at least, his desire to own a fashionable wardrobe to serve as a working tool. It was a tradition for academic painters to try to acquire a studio stock of costumes and accessories. This is quite clear in the case of Tissot, Stevens (who is said to have obtained his dresses from the Princesse de Metternich)[43] and Toulmouche, who interspersed their work with a small number of fetish dresses, sometimes slightly modified (a peignoir, a visiting dress for Tissot; a yellow dress covered in striped muslin, a dress with ribbons and a negligé for Stevens; an indoor dress with a fur border for Toulmouche). These model dresses, constantly re-used, seemed to correspond most closely to the artists' ideals of beauty and elegance.

Worth's presence within art production is due both to the quasi-monopolistic position he held in luxury couture, and to the legitimate desire of sitters to be seen by their contemporaries, and posterity, in their best finery. And the most lavish finery at that time was the ball-gown.

The ball-gown: modest or immodest?

In looking at society portraits, one is struck by the overwhelming predominance of ball-gowns. Zola himself had noted: 'Portraits often give the rather amusing impression of a soirée where all the guests are hooked to the walls observing a discreet silence.'[44]

All these women in evening dress are shown against a plain, neutral background, or else against a natural scene of the kind conventional in neo-eighteenth century art, and especially in Winterhalter.

The portrait had its conventional poses: standing or seated, with her hands delicately crossed, the woman does nothing. Sometimes a curtain (echo of the state portrait) or a staircase (Carolus-Duran, *Madame la Marquise Anforti*, Musée de Cambrai) adds a theatrical quality to the portrayal, as if the woman, who does nothing except pose, needed a surfeit of stage sets to tell us: admire me as I am, as the work of art I have become.

In a parallel situation, the same concerns were aired in relation to the proper way to enter a ballroom:

> One makes one's *entrée*, as the familiar expression has it. This is generally a rather trying moment. All eyes are fixed on the new arrivals; their names are whispered, their bustles given a glance which is perhaps well-meaning, perhaps... One needs to be a girl long accustomed to society, or else to have innate assurance, to pass this test without discomfort or embarrassment. There's no advice I can give here, my young friends, except to be at all times what you should always be, timid and modest.[45]

When a woman is seated, the skirt billowing out in the foreground is a pretext for demonstrating an artist's skill in the rendering of fabrics. The crinoline, 'that pedestal of beauty', is sometimes turned into 'whipped cream', for in the treatment of fabrics the cliché was always at hand. Winterhalter adored vaporous tulle, enveloping his sitters almost systematically in its white cloud. This was in keeping, of course, with the fashion for white imposed on the court by Empress Eugénie, and with the popularity of tulle, an ornament applied to ball dresses throughout the Second Empire. Mallarmé explains the reason for this infatuation: 'I would define the tradition obeyed, more or less, by all ball-dresses, as follows: they should make make the wearer appear light, vaporous, aerial, wafted along by that higher form of walking that is called dance – a divinity appearing in a cloud'.[46]

Satin, following Ingres, seems to have been a focus of rivalry among painters, as if rendering its brilliance and shimmer were a kind of test that every portrait painter had to pass. Painters excelled at contrasting satin and fur (Cabanel, *The Comtesse*

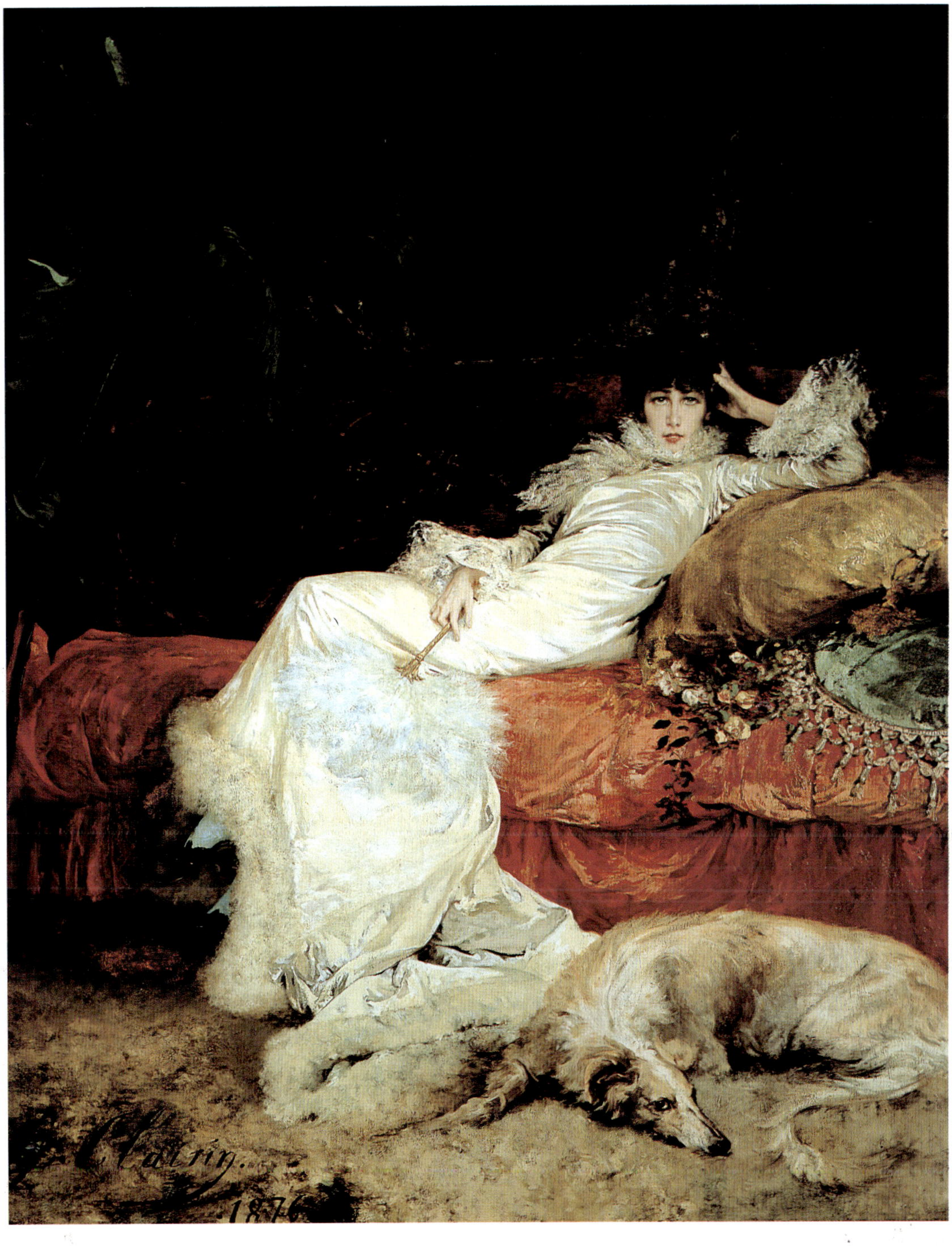

Georges Clairin, Sarah Bernhardt, *1876. Musée du Petit Palais, Paris.*

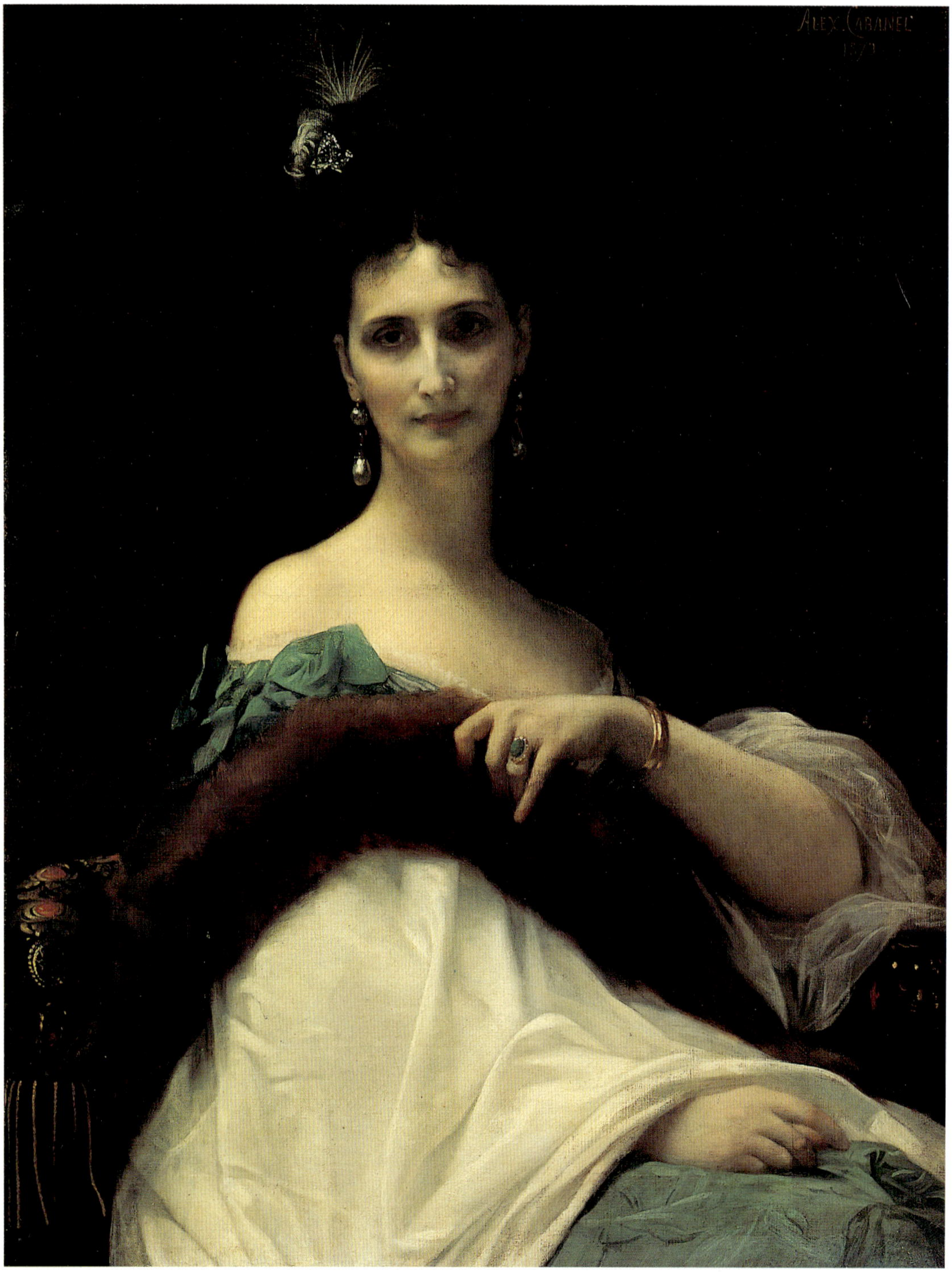

Alexandre Cabanel, The Comtesse de Keller, *1873. Musée d'Orsay, Paris.*
Léon Bonnat, Madame Pasca, *1874. Musée d'Orsay, Paris (facing page).*

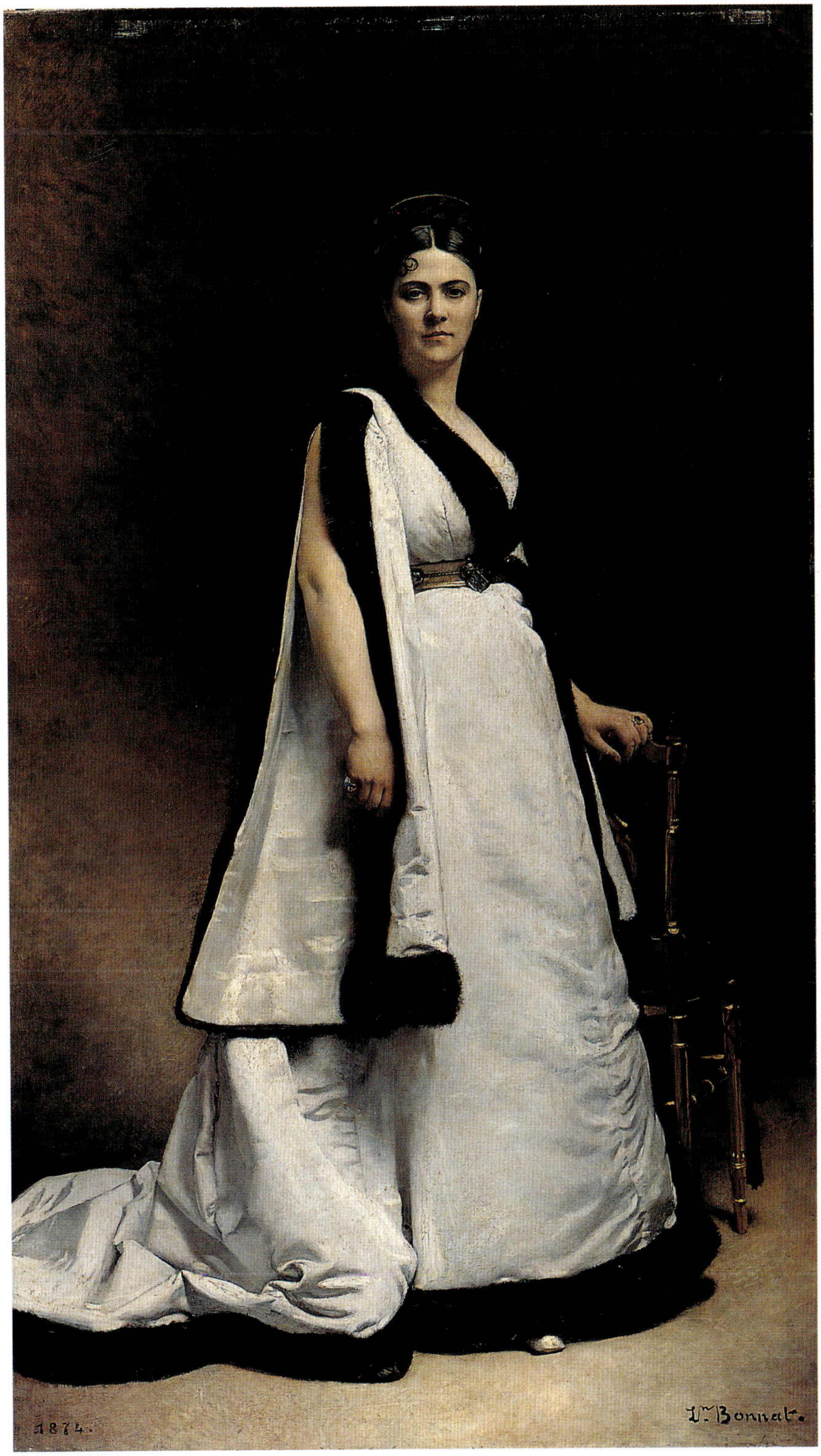

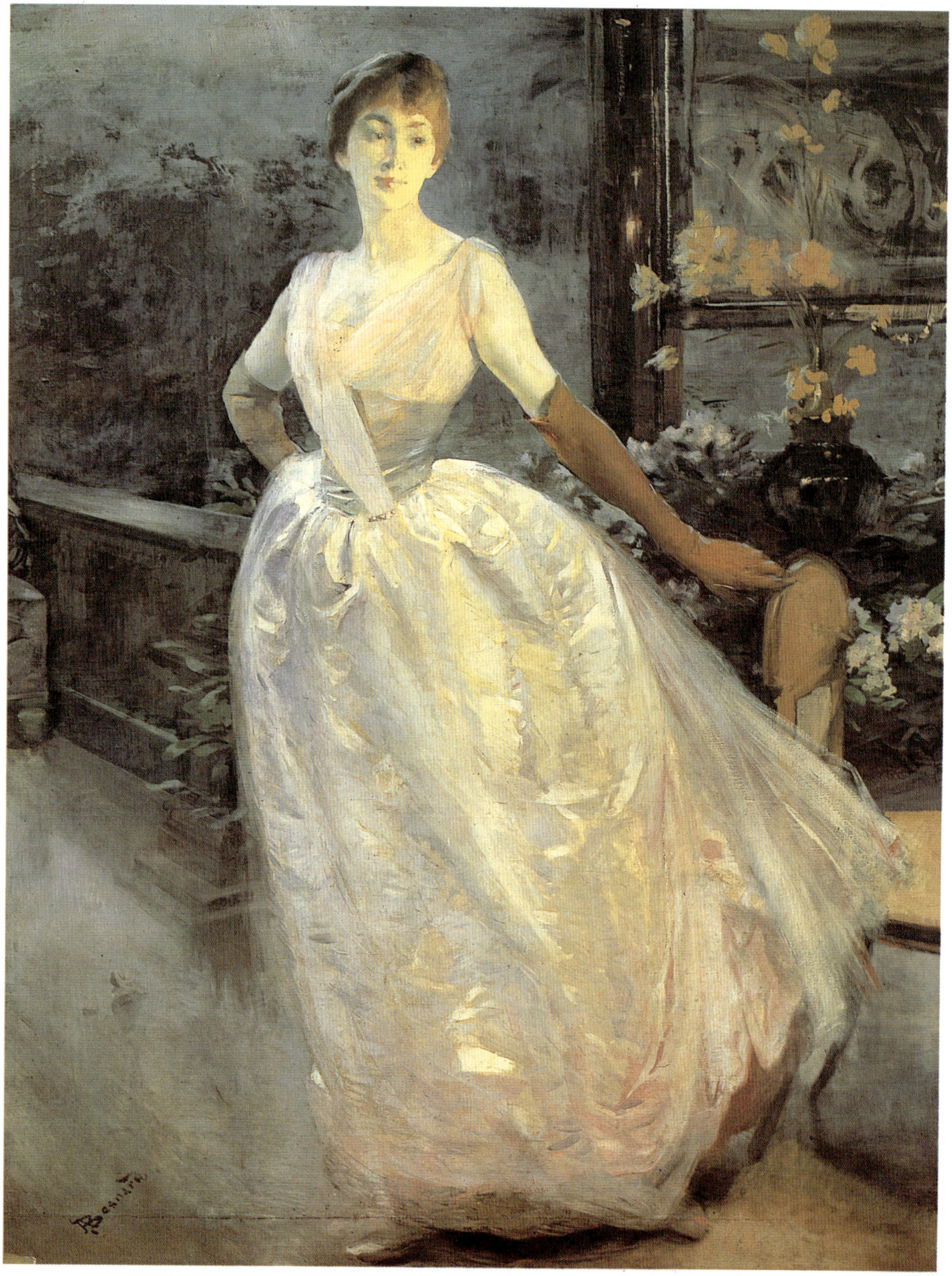

Albert Besnard, Madame Roger Jourdain, *c.1886. Musée d'Orsay, Paris.*

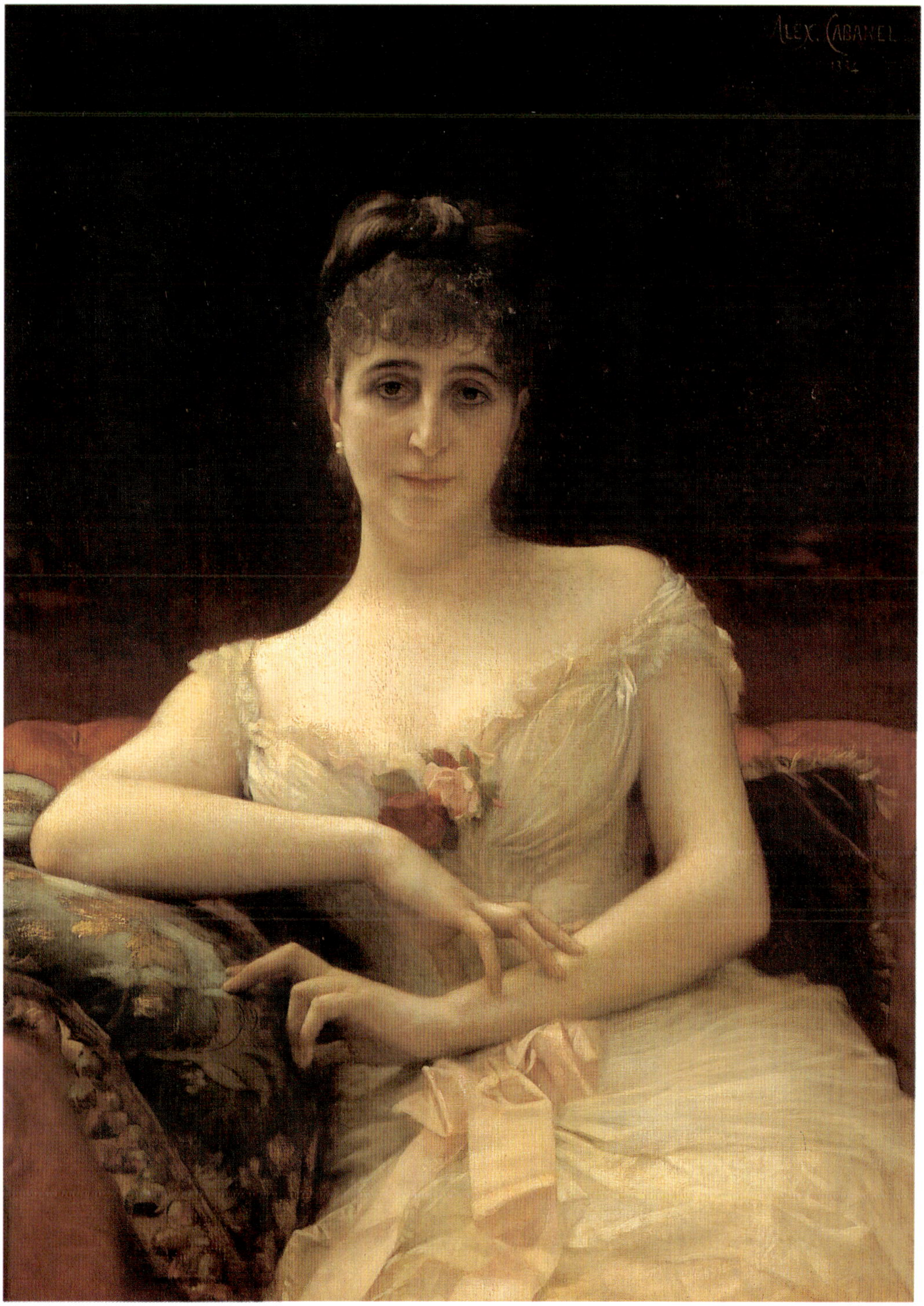

Alexandre Cabanel, Madame Edouard Hervé, *1884. Musée du Petit Palais, Paris.*

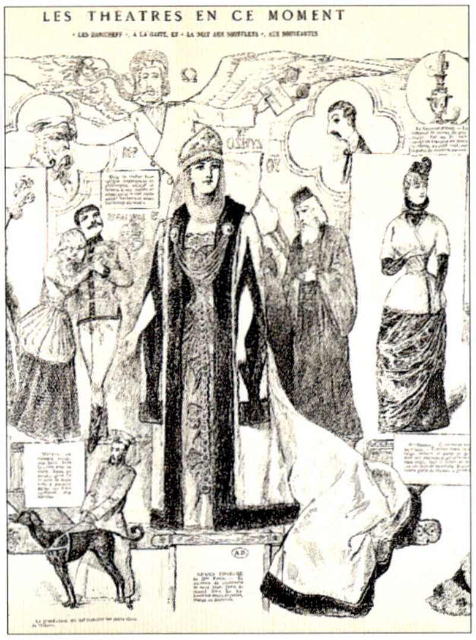

L'Art et la mode, *'Theatres of the present day', detail, 11 October 1884 (left).*

La Revue de la mode, *1884 (right).*

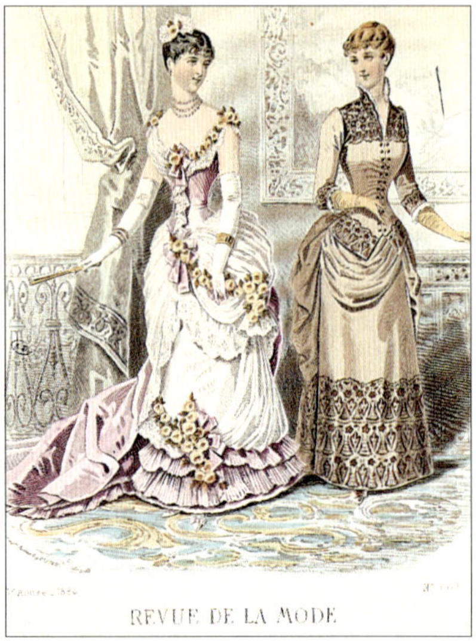

de Keller, 1873, Paris, Musée d'Orsay; Bonnat, *Madame Pasca*, 1874, Paris, Musée Orsay; Clairin, *Sarah Bernhardt*, 1876, Paris, Petit Palais). When the vogue for velvet equalled that for satin about 1889, it was rendered with the same brilliance.

Alain Daguerre de Hureaux explains the emergence of these *'trompe l'oeil* dresses'[47] by the fact that Ingres's techniques had been taken over by hack painters. Ingres, in 'his almost wearisome attention to the rendering of details, with a finesse of observation sometimes verging on the tenuous', sought to express 'the mode of life of the middle class, which is one of display; for it, appearance takes the place of substance and cannot be imagined in isolation from its elaborate sartorial framework, which finally becomes, as it were, internalised.'[48] By applying the same pictorial treatment to the face and to the accessories, painters registered the woman's status as an object. The second-generation painters probably did not understand their master's motives. They copied Ingres because he was the model most recognized and admired, and perhaps, too, because his attention to luxury recalled the state portrait of preceding centuries.

There is, at first sight, a certain paradox in having one's portrait painted in a ball-gown. In a society overburdened with propriety and morality, why expose oneself in such a way to the gaze of any bystander?

This tendency of fashion highlights a further characteristic of academic art in the nineteenth century. The artist may go as far as he likes in evoking an eroticized universe. As long as he respects a certain number of codes, he will scandalise neither the jury nor the public. 'Cabanel knows how to give ladies "a distinguished air". However low-cut their *décolletés* may be, they do not thereby cease to be modest; for he transforms women's bodies into dreams.'[49] In that 'morbidly elegant' century, a proud,

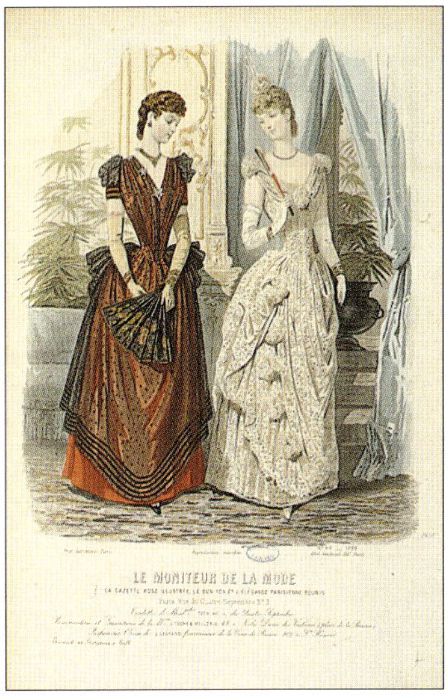

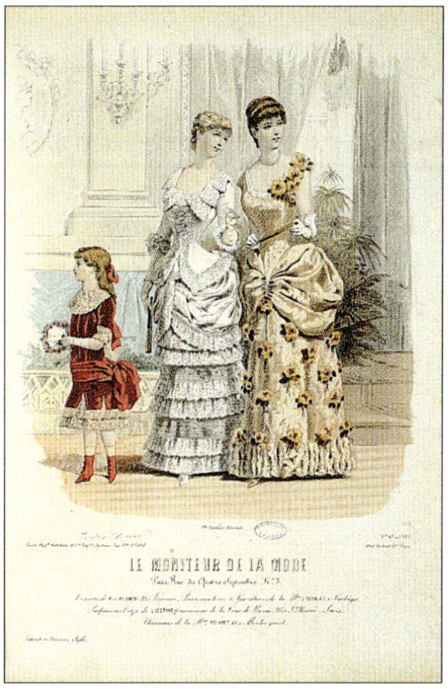

Le Moniteur de la mode, *1888 (left)*.

Le Moniteur de la mode, *1882 (right)*.

arrogant bearing concealed all the devices of seduction, channelled all desires. In the same way, painters used classical or biblical subterfuges in order to show licentious scenes which, without such pretexts, would have shocked and offended respectable society.

In the guides to etiquette, the relative 'debauchery' entailed by the ball-gown was justified as follows:

> When evening comes one dresses exclusively for one's own society. One no longer needs to fear having one's conduct misinterpreted by the mob, and people of our circle know how to judge us. One is allowed to show a certain disregard for opinion…a benevolent elegance prevents judgements from ever being final or brutal.[50]

The same hypocrisy is reflected in painting. In reviews of the Salon, beauty is always linked to distinction. We could not be further from Baudelaire's dictum: 'Beauty is always bizarre.' Jules Claretie points out the ambiguous use of language with regard to a portrait by Dubufé of a woman whose dress is 'most admirably *décolleté*': 'She is very alluring and, one might say, very distinguished.'[51] Earlier, writing of a portrait by Cabanel, he refers to a 'figure both arrogant and charming, with a haughty face…and a provocatively majestic air'.[52] Because Manet rejected conventions and refused to idealise

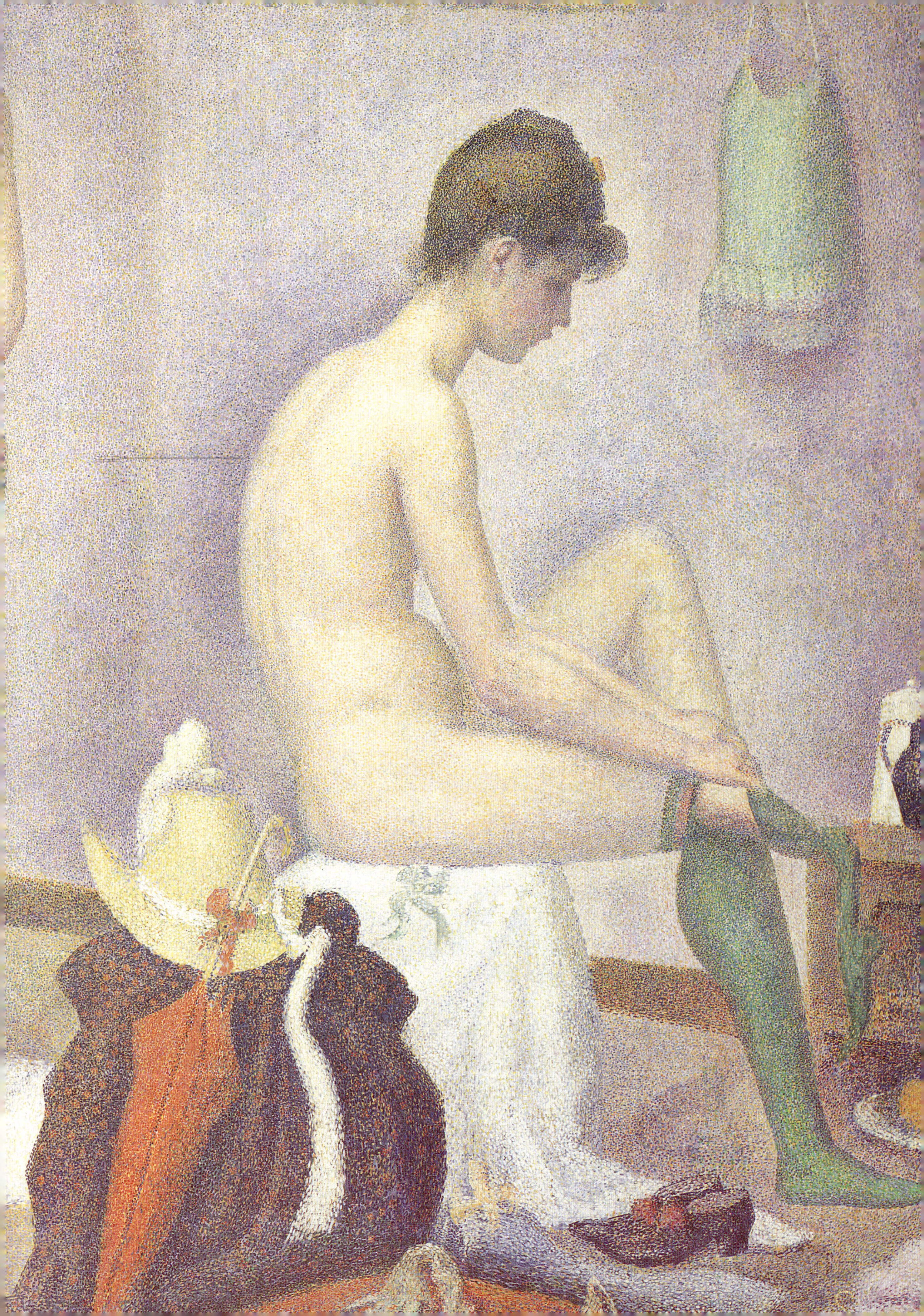

Chapter Five

Fashion and Modernity

Georges Seurat, Les Poseuses, *1886–1887 (detail).*
The Barnes Foundation, Merion.

Pleas for contemporary dress

Unlike clothing in our day, nineteenth-century dress was an architecture superimposed on the body, hiding it to a great extent and modifying it profoundly. Characterized by an accumulation of ornaments (the *style tapissier*) and bulging successively from hips, buttocks and bust, its effect was to disguise the human form. Clothing, like a shell, was completely separate; it 'has its own dignity and elegance, which do not depend absolutely and solely on the body it covers. What is above can have a different grace to what is below'.[1]

The real body, constrained and deformed by the corset, fattened by an excess of food, was an unknown and incongruous object. Théophile Gautier sums up the paradox:

> Clothing in modern times has become a kind of second skin...to the extent that the real shape of the body has been completely forgotten. Anyone who has some acquaintance with painters and happens to enter a studio when a model is posing, has a half-unconscious feeling of surprise mingled with disgust at the sight of this unknown creature, the male or female amphibian posing on the table.[2]

Such an effect is conveyed by *The Artist's Studio* by Courbet (1855, Paris, Musée d'Orsay) where a very large group of clothed men and women make the two nude models seem strange and out of place, and by *The Bathers* (1853, Montpellier, Musée Fabre), where the painter takes pleasure in accentuating the deformity of flesh.[3]

Fashion redefines the nude

This horror of the body raises the question as to how to define the nude.

According to Théophile Gautier, the artist must combine the model in front of him with the ideal pattern from antiquity. For him, that ideal cannot be called into questioned. Zola, by contrast, clearly denounces the trap into which this hybrid manner of composition leads the artist:

> Our civilisation has so little respect for the body that it seems inclined to make it more ugly...This is why painters, not daring to portray the vulgarity of their models, make them into statues instead of women. Some of them pillage antiquity; others invent transparent tones, nuances. If there is any painting which runs counter to nature, it is certainly the one which depicts our contemporary Venuses.[4]

And such Venuses were legion. There was, perhaps, never such a love for the nude as in that society whose extreme reticence warned its members not to expose a piece of male underwear to the eyes of a young girl for fear of frightening her, or made a young man blush at the sight of an ankle.[5] However, the nudes at the Salon were 'made up'.

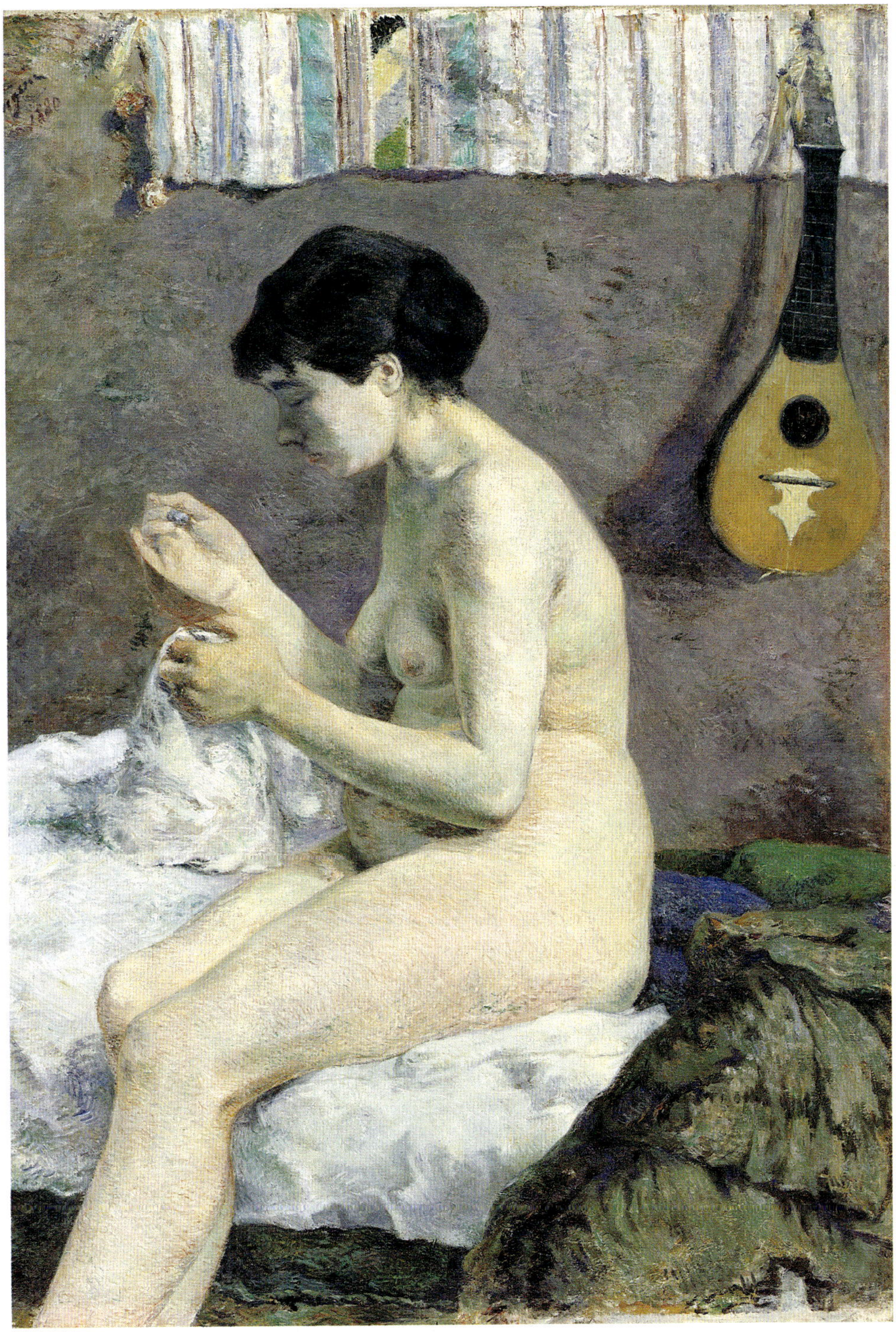

Paul Gauguin, Study of a Nude *or* Suzanne sewing, 1880. *Ny Carlsberg Glyptotek, Copenhagen.*

'If M. Manet had at least borrowed M. Cabanel's powder puff and had dusted the cheeks and breasts of Olympia, the girl would have been presentable.'[6] Proudhon, Zola and Huysmans, among others, pilloried these mythological nudes - 'hairdresser's dummies', 'soft octopus flesh' - which were giving victory to a school which 'if we are not careful, will become quite simply the most absolute negation of art!'[7] In the search for the realistic, modern nude, dress had an emblematic value. It gave the nude its temporal quality and its truth. The discarded clothes state clearly: this woman has just undressed; she has not materialized from Olympus or from the pages of the Bible.

Thus, Courbet's bather is an ordinary middle-class woman accompanied by her servant, about to take a dip; at least, that is the fiction Courbet wants us to see. When Manet took up the same subject in *Déjeuner sur l'herbe* (1863, Paris, Musée d'Orsay), what are the men's clothes and the superb still life composed by the model's cast-off garments, if not an emblem of a new art? Manet is poking fun at a relic of mythological and classical painting. Either the woman is naked or she is not. If she is naked, she is a courtesan, *Olympia* thus being the reply to the *Déjeuner sur l'herbe*. In this way, garments crystallize the element of scandal. When Degas suggested to the academic Gervex that he should show the underwear the woman has taken off at the foot of the bed in his painting *Rolla*, his intention was far from innocent. The painting was removed from the exhibition because of its immorality.

In earlier painting, clothing had been proper in an outdoor setting, while the nude was confined to the boudoir and the studio. The visible proclamation of the new aesthetic regarding the clothed and the unclothed is to be found in Seurat's *Les Poseuses* (1886-7, Merion, Barnes Foundation). The three girls have undressed and are posing, quite unequivocally nude, for the painter. Their clothes and accessories are seen behind them in *La Grande Jatte*, a painting within a painting, in which the women dressed in the latest fashion could be the outward, everyday doubles of these same nudes (the clothing dates them to the present, out on a Sunday stroll at a time when the strapontin was in fashion). To combine the two in this way was to renew the classical tradition of the nude study while subordinating it to the presentation of a large fresco of contemporary life.

'The satin corset is perhaps the nude of our time',[8] Manet had declared to a journalist apropos his painting *In front of the mirror* (1876–7, New York, Guggenheim Museum). We have arrived at the paradoxical situation where a partly-nude woman has far more power and reality than the academic nude.

Depictions of women in their underclothes disappeared from the art scene in the Second Empire. Only caricaturists and isolated artists such as Guys and Courbet still touched on this theme. For a long time it was a taboo subject in the Press, and licentious illustrations only reappeared prolifically with *La Vie parisienne*. A strip cartoon published in *Le Rire* in 1895 and entitled 'The New Temptation of St

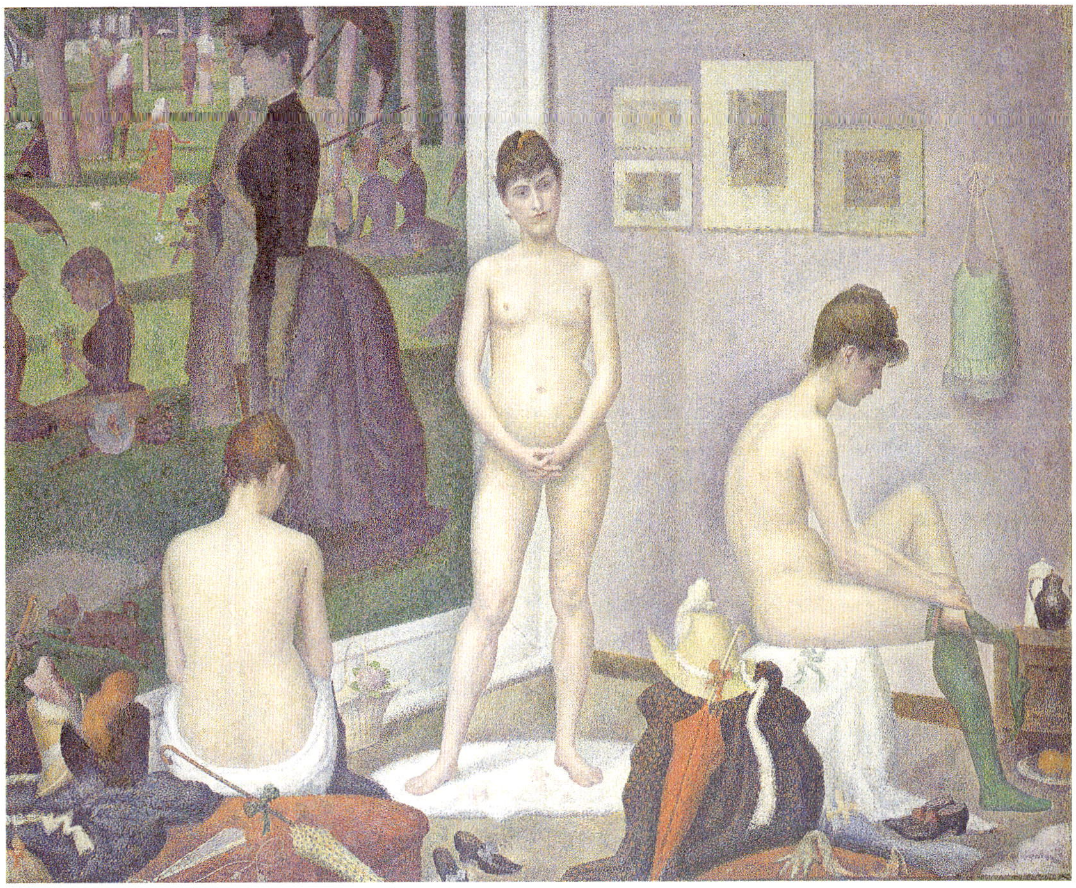

Georges Seurat, Les Poseuses, *1886–1887. The Barnes Foundation, Merion.*

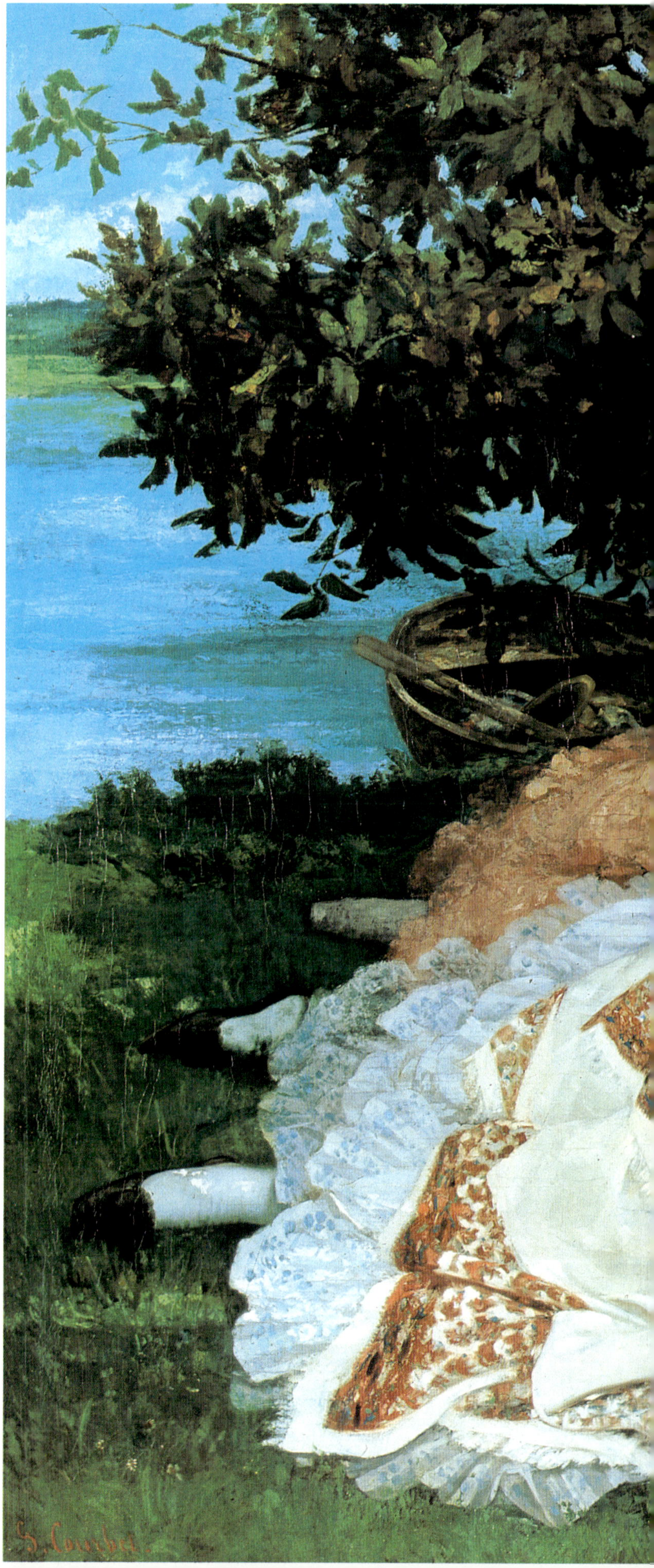

Gustave Courbet,
Les Demoiselles des bords de la Seine, *1856.*
Musée du Petit Palais, Paris.

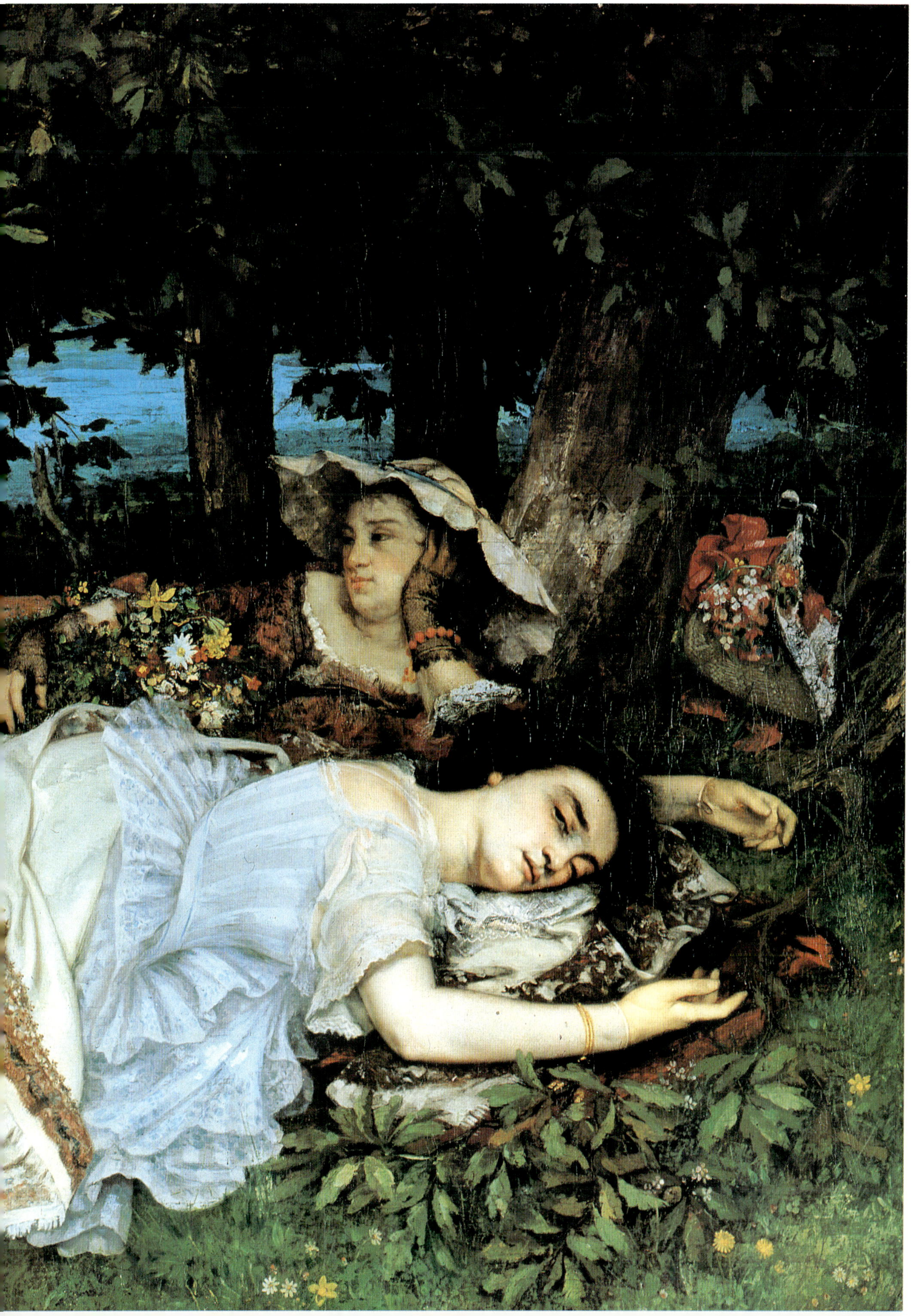

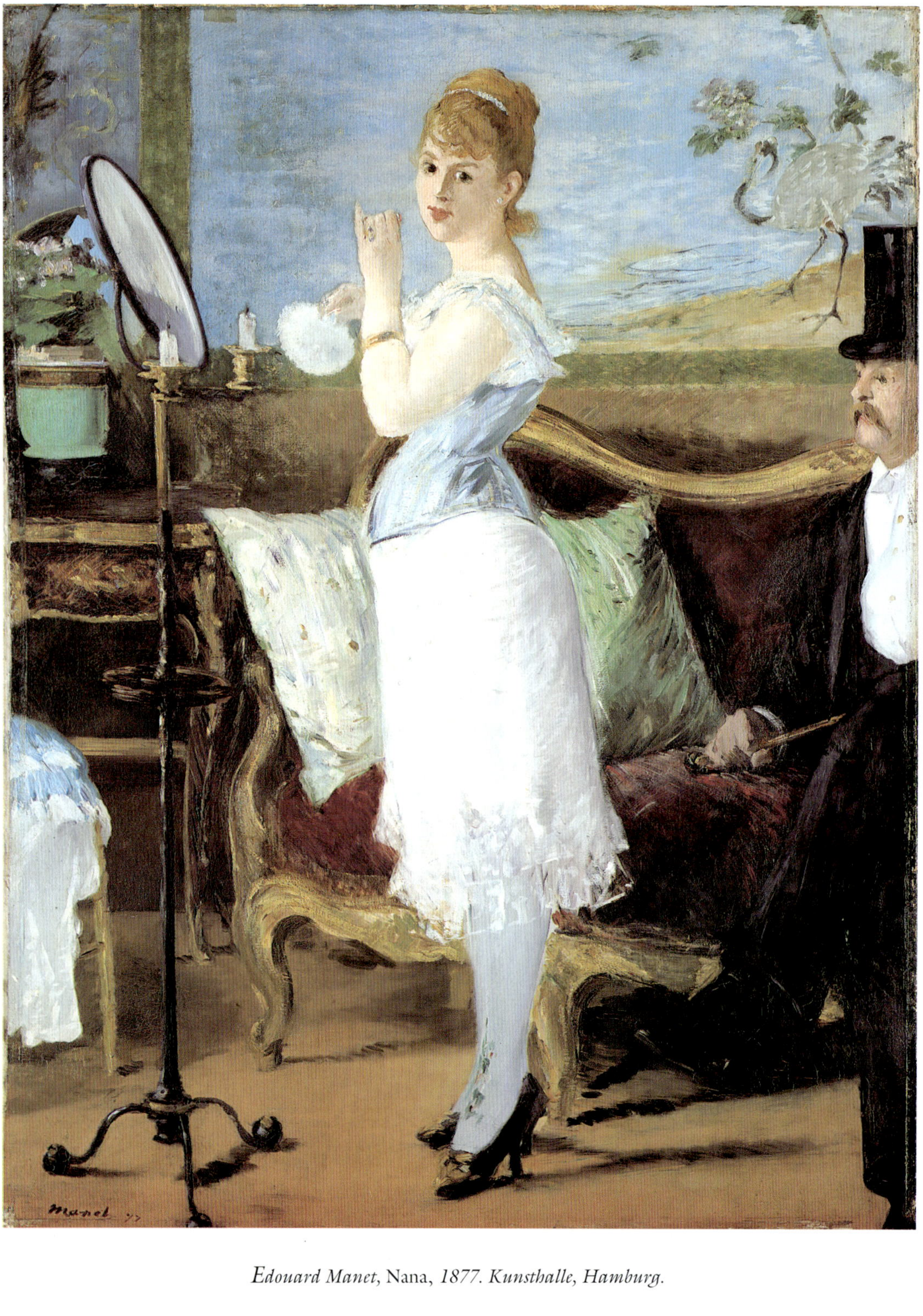

Edouard Manet, Nana, *1877. Kunsthalle, Hamburg.*

Anthony' shows the monk completely unmoved before a nude woman, becoming progressively more interested as she puts on her clothes, and totally delighted when she appears, like Nana in the painting by Manet, in her corset and petticoats.[9]

Twenty years before *Nana*, Courbet had provoked the same kind of scandal with his *Demoiselles au bord de la Seine* (1857, Paris, Musée du Petit Palais). In compiling a kind of anthology of Parisian leisure activities, he had painted two girls stretched out on the grass, one of them half-undressed. 'This bundle of fabrics', as Maxime Du Camp had disdainfully called it – in reality a subtle description of the different materials of the petticoats, corset and shawl of the girl in the foreground – was taken as a frightful provocation. For Courbet's contemporaries, the fact that she had kept her gloves on was the last straw. The incongruous presence of the gloves emphasizes that she is midway between being dressed and undressed, symbolising the immorality of women.

Mythological costume or modern dress?

The nineteenth century inherited the dispute between the ancients and the moderns. In the previous century, modern dress had already been considered undignified, dispelling the quality of eternity that was sought in a painting. Roger de Piles, in his *Cours de peinture par principes*, had raised the question of the legitimacy of contemporary dress as opposed to mythological costume:

> Nowadays, sitters in most portraits are dressed in a somewhat bizarre fashion...Those in favour of such dress argue that, since fashion is very changeable in France, portraits appear ridiculous six years after they are painted... Others, however, maintain that fashion is essential to portraits, since it contributes not only to the depiction of the person but to that of the time...If I might attempt to adjudicate between the two parties, it seems true to me that it is far more difficult to extract something beneficial to a painting from fashionable clothes than it is to dress portraits agreeably when one is free to use whatever one finds suitable. I believe, too, that fashionable clothes might sometimes be used for family portraits, while costume of some virtue, some dignity, or of some pagan divinity, should be used at other times.

The debate was renewed at the end of the eighteenth century, and again in connection with the question of realism. Costume was now invoked as a fundamental element in defining this tendency:

> It appears that our dress,' [wrote Champfleury] 'is not a costume...What artists call costume, that is to say, a thousand knick-knacks (feathers, beauty-spots, plumes, and so on), may amuse frivolous minds for a moment; but the serious representation of present-day people, with round hats, black suits, polished shoes or peasants' clogs, is far more interesting.[10]

Part of the famous plea for the black suit extolled by Baudelaire and Gautier, following Balzac's example, goes as follows:

> As for the suit, the dress of the modern hero... studios and society are still full of people who would like to poeticize Anthony with a Grecian cloak or a parti-coloured costume.
>
> And yet, has it not its own beauty and native charm, that victimized suit? Is it not the necessary attire for our sickly time, which wears a symbol of perpetual mourning on its black, skinny shoulders?... For the heroes of the Iliad reach only to your ankle, Oh Vautrin, Rastignac and Birotteau – and you, Oh Fontanarès, who dared not tell the public of the sorrows you bore beneath the funereal, contorted dress coat we all have to wear.[11]

More than twenty years later, Baudelaire's wish to see men painted in their modern suits still persisted. Théophile Gautier took up the plea again in 1858: 'Modern dress prevents them [sculptors and painters], so they tell us, from producing masterpieces. To listen to them, it's the fault of black suits, paletots and crinolines that they are not Titians, van Dycks or Velázquezes.'[12] Artists who are too ready to decry the ugliness of modern dress, and to lament the passing of embroidery, furbelows and togas, those pretexts for 'bulging muscles', do not realize, Gautier argues, that their antique model is incompatible with this dress: Antinous would be ridiculous in a black suit, since the black suit is appropriate to stoutness and muscular indolence. Inhibited by a 'misunderstood antiquity',[13] such artists were pastiching a defunct concept of the nude.

In the nineteenth century, fashion shook the academic edifice to its foundations by calling into question the study of the nude as a basic artistic exercise. The challenge the century set for itself was to extract beauty from modern dress and to present fashion as a new field for artistic research. After Baudelaire, everyone stressed how anachronistic it was to depict a man in ancient dress and to paint him 'in the manner of' this or that school. According to Zola,

> the painter is nearly always anxious to imitate a school. He wants to paint like Rubens, Rembrandt, Raphael or Velasquez. His head is full of an ideal linked to the past. He tries with all his might to lie, instead of attempting to give a faithful representation of the person in front of him.[14]

The historical truth demanded by Zola should be accompanied by physical truth, for 'apart from the need which artists feel to assimilate the style of a painter from the past, their only concern is to please the sitter'.[15] But now, physical and psychological truth were also required by a new art which was not encumbered by the convention of idealisation. Dubufe who, it seems, pleased his sitters very much, since he made them

all pretty and, consequently, all identical, was condemned by critics, even by the most conservative ones such as Edmond About, for his facile style, which combined chic with affectation. He was certainly not alone in this, and in face of the flood of bland portraits the primacy of character was reaffirmed. Clothing was seen to play a part in defining an individual, since the choice of dress reflected deep motives located outside the dictates of society. 'Gesture, grimace, dress, even decor – everything must help to show "a character".'[16]

These portraits revealed the general attitudes, the common choices symptomatic of a society. Critics, realising the importance of dress as context, insisted that it was a necessary condition of the truth of a portrait: 'What we need,' Duranty explained, 'is the special note of the modern individual in his costume and in the midst of his social habits.'[17]

Among critics, Baudelaire was the first to draw attention to the fact that clothing, apart from 'placing' each individual in society, gave insight into that society, into

> the morals and aesthetics of the time. The idea a man has of beauty is reflected in his whole manner of dressing; it crumples or starches his suit, makes his gestures rounded or pointed, and even subtly infiltrates his facial features. The man finishes up resembling that which he would like to be.[18]

The artist's task, therefore, was to reconstruct a society's idea of beauty from these costumes and to transcribe it. 'It is much easier to declare that everything about the costume of a period is absolutely ugly than to try to extract the mysterious beauty which may be contained in it, no matter how minimal or evanescent it may be.'[19]

'The painter of modern life'

Baudelaire went much further than his contemporaries, who had seen in fashion only a means of access to modern subjects, enabling them to escape from pastiche. He made fashion the starting point of a new ideal and the basis of his aesthetic of modernity.

This was not the case with Théophile Gautier, who was otherwise quite close to Baudelaire. Gautier did not question the classical ideal. He wanted to show only that fashion gives access to the eternal and universal beauty of antiquity in a far more appropriate way than imitation. The example he chose to conclude his eulogy of women's hairstyles illustrates his argument well: 'If the Venus of Milo recovered her arms and if a society lady were kind enough to lend her her corsage, she could go to a *soirée* with her hair just as it is. What a tribute to the fashion of our time!'[20]

After the Salon of 1846 Baudelaire had asserted not only that beauty is ancient and eternal, but that it includes a dichotomy. 'All beauties contain...something eternal and also something transitory – the absolute and the particular.'[21] In his essay on the Salon of 1859 he took his 'rational and historical theory of beauty' further: 'Beauty is

made up of an eternal, invariable element which is exceedingly difficult to define, and a relative, circumstantial element which is, if you will, alternately and simultaneously, the time, fashion, morals, passion.'[22]

In this way Baudelaire continues to juxtapose antithetical concepts – eternal and temporal, invariable and occasional – to express the duality of beauty, a fusion of the abstract and the contingent. In defining the transient, particular element of each epoch, which forms the other half of beauty, he associates collective factors – the time, morals – with individual ones – passion – while fashion has a share in each. Later in the essay he combines all these factors under the heading of modernity: 'Modernity is the transitory, fugitive, contingent half of art, the other half being the eternal and immutable.' Fashion is therefore one of the manifestations of modernity. And 'in order that "modernity" may be worthy to become antiquity, the mysterious beauty involuntarily imparted to it by human life must be extracted from it'.[23]

If modernity is to gain access to the eternal and immutable level (antiquity), the artist must draw from it something hidden which, in fashion, is 'the taste for the ideal'. (It has been noted that it was especially clothing which, for Baudelaire, contained this 'mysterious beauty'). Fashion is bound up with modernity but at the same time, being 'the symptom of the taste for the ideal', it draws us towards the eternal. Baudelaire used fashion to define his aesthetic of modernity because it illustrates the duality of modern beauty.

'In reality,' Gérald Froidevaux explains, 'fashion is a synonym for modern beauty: it is not just one half of it, but both at once. It is the equivalent of modernity, which creates and dismantles beauty in an incessant process.'[24] Fashion, as the modern expression of the ideal, appears to the painter as a new means of attaining modern beauty and thereby creating 'modern art'.

Baudelaire's choice of Constantin Guys to illustrate his definition of a modern painter is puzzling. Why a water-colour painter and not a painter in oils? Was he trying to avoid controversy by failing to mention either Daumier, Courbet or Manet? Did he find all the qualities he sought combined in Guys, whereas they were found only dispersed in the painters he admired? He praised Guys's curiosity and childlike genius, his sharp eye allied to quickness of hand. 'Having set himself the task of seeking and explaining beauty in "modernity", M. Guys likes to show women embellished with every kind of artificial finery, no matter to which order of society they belong.'[25]

From the tart to the society lady, Guys chose those whose aim was to project an appearance, and in them Baudelaire found his own cultural idols of fashion. But what attracted the poet most of all was that all the artist's different sketches of the crowd have a quality which transcends representation. Constantin Guys was able to give his silhouettes and their attitudes a look of eternity; he elevated them to the status of historic figures.

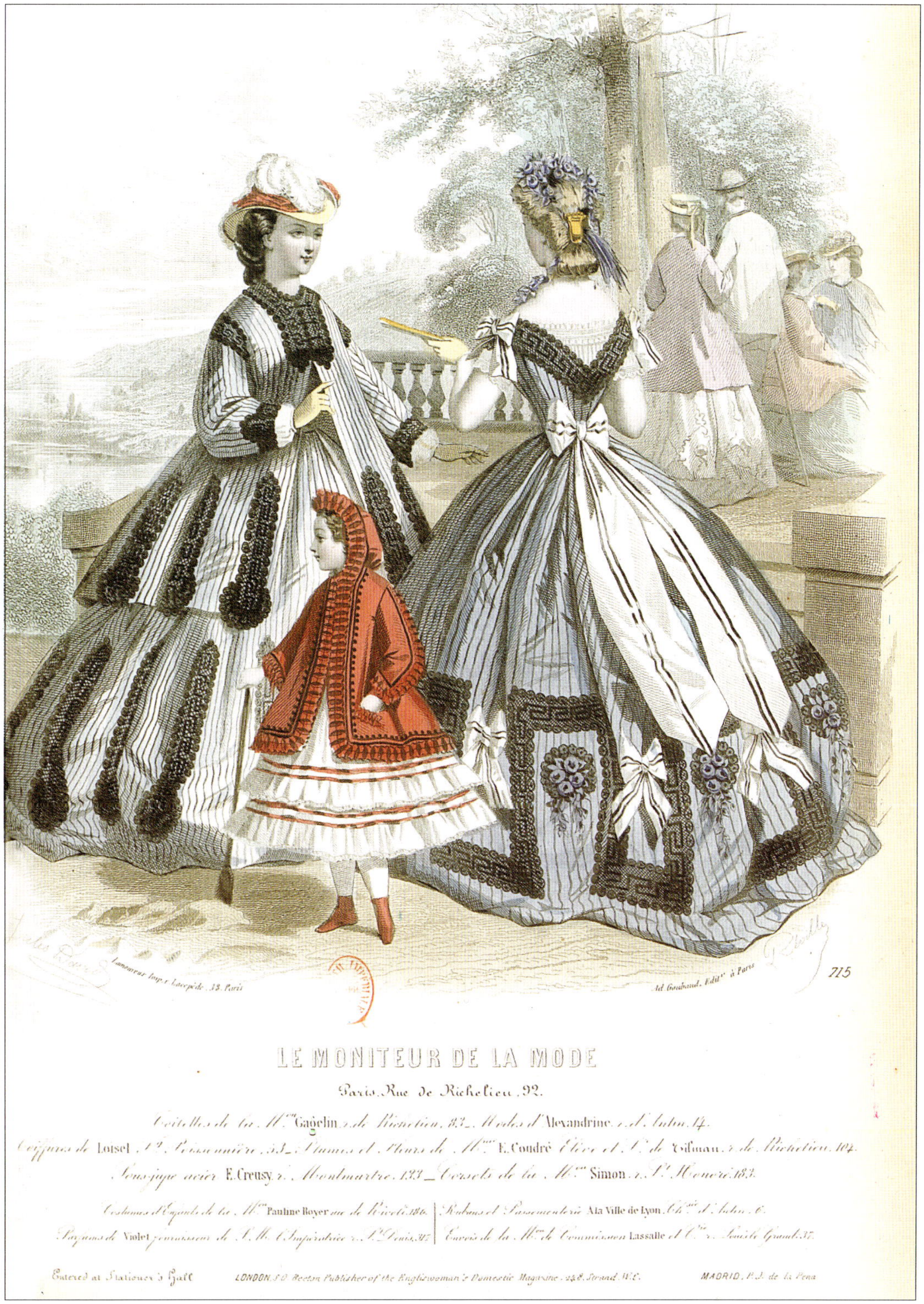
715
LE MONITEUR DE LA MODE
Paris, Rue de Richelieu, 92.
Gagelin
Alexandrine
Coiffures de Loisel
E. Coudré
Sous-jupe acier E. Creusy r. Montmartre. 133 _ Corsets de la Mon Simon r. St. Honoré. 183.
Pauline Boyer
A la Ville de Lyon
Parfums de Violet
Lassalle
Entered at Stationer's Hall
LONDON, S.O. Beeton Publisher of the Englishwoman's Domestic Magazine. 248, Strand. W.C.
MADRID, P.J. de la Pena

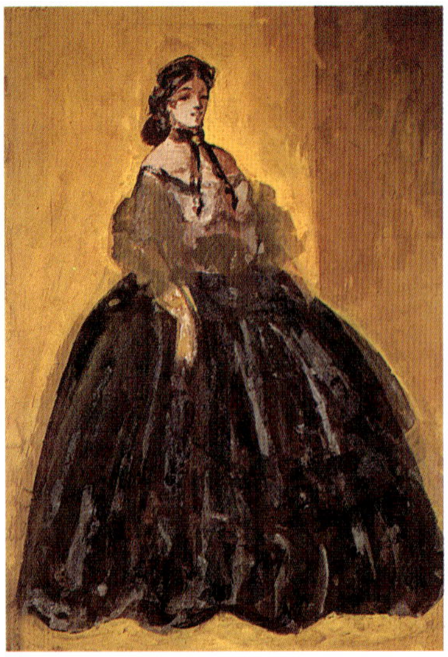

Le Moniteur de la mode, *fashions for taking the waters and for full-dress occasions, September 1863 (previous page).*

Constantin Guys, Woman in a crinoline, no date. *Musée du Petit Palais, Paris (left).*

Constantin Guys, Two women in flounced dresses, *no date. Musée Carnavalet, Paris (right).*

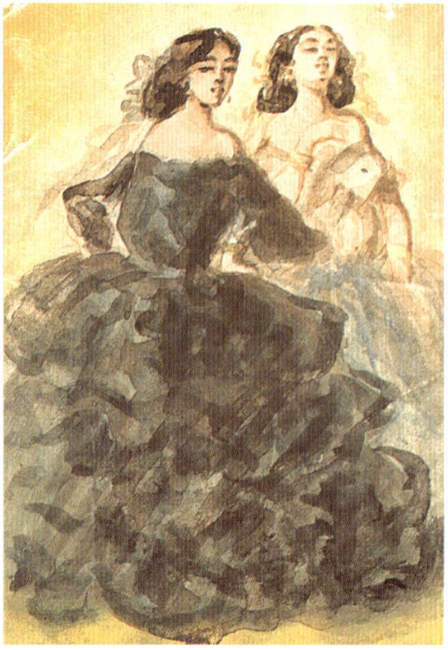

THE ROLE OF FASHION PRINTS

Fashion for all

Charles Baudelaire's reflections on the Salon of 1846 discussed above were inspired by a magazine, the *Journal des dames et des modes.* This periodical, founded in 1797 and edited by Pierre La Mésangère, was the most famous and widely-read fashion journal of the early nineteenth century in France. Its prints, which fascinated the poet, were signed by such talented engravers as Vernet, Lanté and Gavarini. The journal was one of the first illustrated fashion periodicals.

Fashion prints had been published in the seventeenth century, but at that time they were distributed singly or in collections. The Cabinet des modes of 1785 and the Journal de la mode et du goût of 1790 were innovative in that they included fashion prints. Earlier, in 1677, *Le mercure galant* had published the first illustrated fashion reports, but it used drawings with captions (sometimes giving the addresses of suppliers - a major novelty).

Fashion prints were only distributed widely after 1830, thanks to the rapid growth of the women's press, which continued until the Franco-Prussian war of 1870, when the number of journals published amounted to eighty, and was supplemented by the first illustrated catalogues of the great stores and by more and more specialized journals for professionals - tailors, couturiers and *modistes.* The readership reached in this way was extraordinarily wide: each class of society had its journal.

The imagery of fashion was created, therefore, in the Second Empire, and it is interesting to note the quality of the art directly associated with it. Following La Mésangère's example, editors commissioned artists such as Jules David, a lithographic

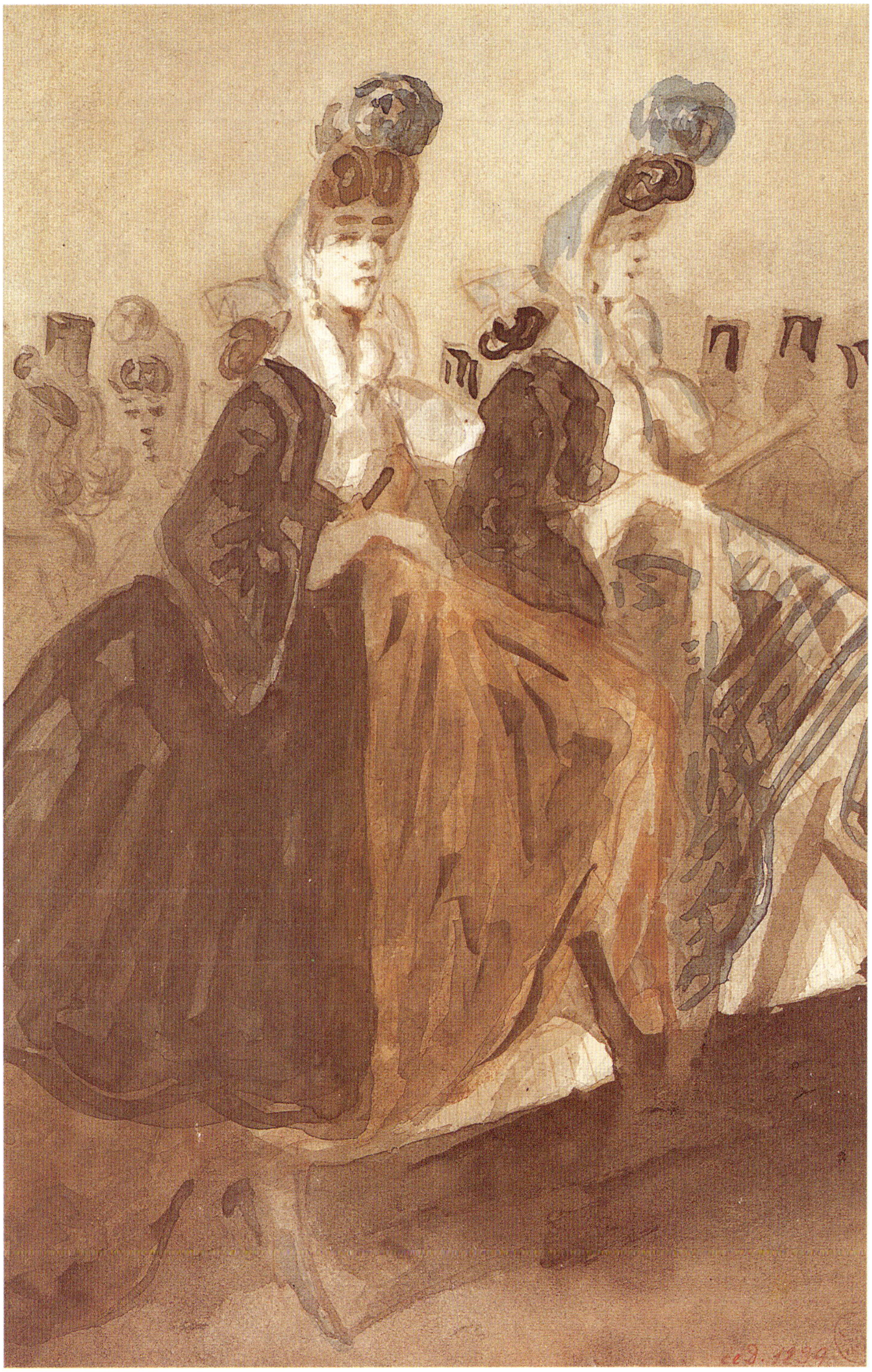

Constantin Guys, Ladies of the night walking out *or* Two women wearing blue feathers, *no date.*
Musée Carnavalet, Paris.

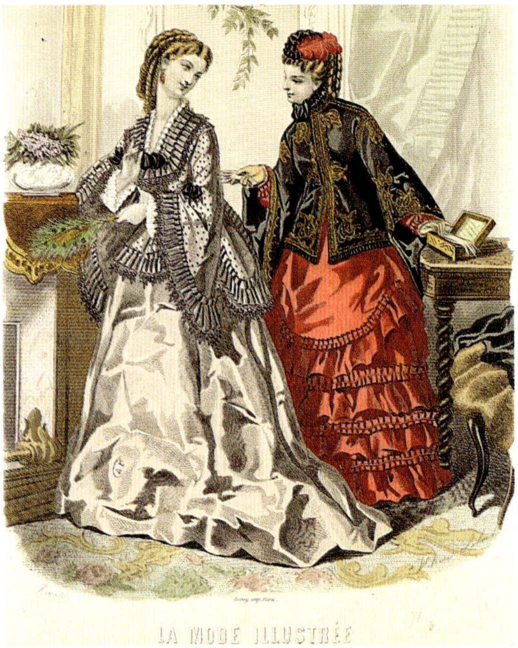

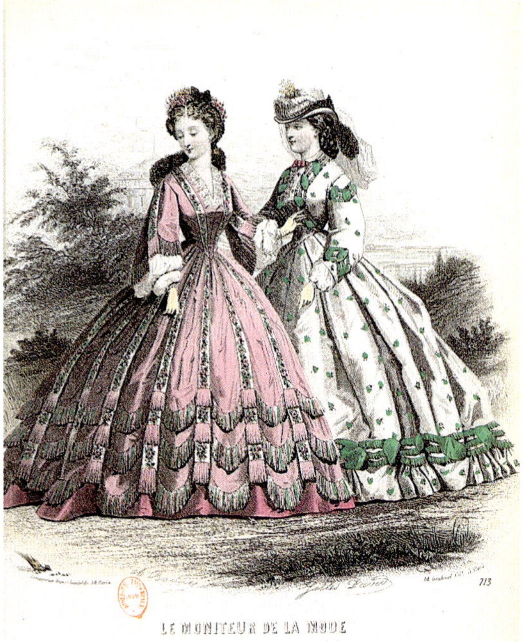

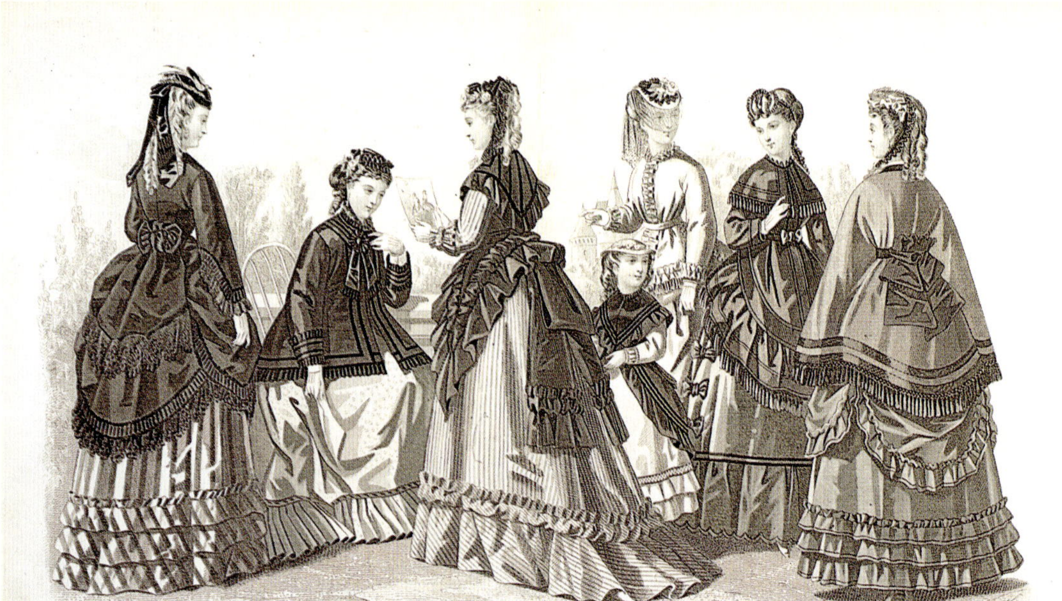

La Mode illustrée, *1871 (above left).*
Le Moniteur de la mode, *fashions for the country and for a dinner party, August 1863 (above right).*
Le Follet: *'Coats and ready-made clothes from the Grands Magasins du Coin de Rue, 8 Rue Montesquieu, summer season 1869'. Bibliothèque des Arts décoratifs, Paris (below).*

draughtsman and a pupil of Pierre Duval Le Camus (1790–1854), who was himself a pupil of David, and F.C. Compte-Calix, a painter of genre scenes and portraits who exhibited at the Salon, as well as the Colin sisters, Héloïse, Anaïs, Laure and Isabelle, daughters of the lithographic painter Alexandre-Marie Colin, a friend of Delacroix, Géricault, Gavarini, Gautier and Musset. Very soon the sisiters were exhibiting at the Salon and contributing to fashion journals. Héloïse, Anaïs and Laure all married painters: Jean-Baptiste Leloir, Gabriel-Auguste Toudouze and Gustave Noël, and continued their careers in fashion. The two elder sisters were the better known, often working together. Their married names, Héloïse Leloir and Anaïs Toudouze, occur very frequently in almost all the periodicals of their time.

The print was always made using a watercolour as a model. Its design went through four stages: the draughtsman produced sketches of a garment at a fashion house or in a novelty shop, painted the final watercolour and then passed it to the engraver who reproduced it exactly. In the printer's workshop the engraving was then painted by four women (one for each colour) to produce the final coloured print.

Stereotyped silhouettes were created in the initial watercolour, and the postures hardly changed after that. These were stylized women, brunette or blonde, dressed differently in each plate. Until 1855 they were often seated, but with the growth of the crinoline they stood up to give the widest possible view of their skirts. When the interest of the garment shifted to the back after 1870, they were frequently seen from the back or in profile.

They often went in pairs. Sometimes there were as many as nine of them, for example when showing a large store's range for the new season. Logic played no part in this, and a woman in a walking outfit was often seen in a garden side-by-side with a woman in a ball gown. Despite these conventions dictated by the need to give the fullest possible definition of a garment, the background was progressively enriched. Whereas in the preceding centuries the figures had been always isolated on a blank page, in the nineteenth they were put into context. Women were shown at home, in a rich, carefully-arranged interior where mirrors, portraits and carvings evoked the ancien régime. Very often they were seen in a public garden or the park of their château, when staying in the country during the summer and autumn. As the century advanced more of the backgrounds were outdoors and the activities became increasingly varied. Seaside scenes are shown from about 1858-60, railways around 1865. Women are seen in hunting outfits, on their outings in town or setting off on a journey. Engravings tend increasingly to resemble genre scenes, and we can count five stereotyped sketches: the promenade, the theatre, the outing in town, the visit to the Salon and to a lady friend.

At this point it is tempting to draw parallels with the subject matter of Manet and the Impressionists: *La musique aux Tuileries* or *The Railway* by Manet; *Women in a garden* by Monet; *La Lecture* by Berthe Morisot; Renoir, etc. In *La musique aux*

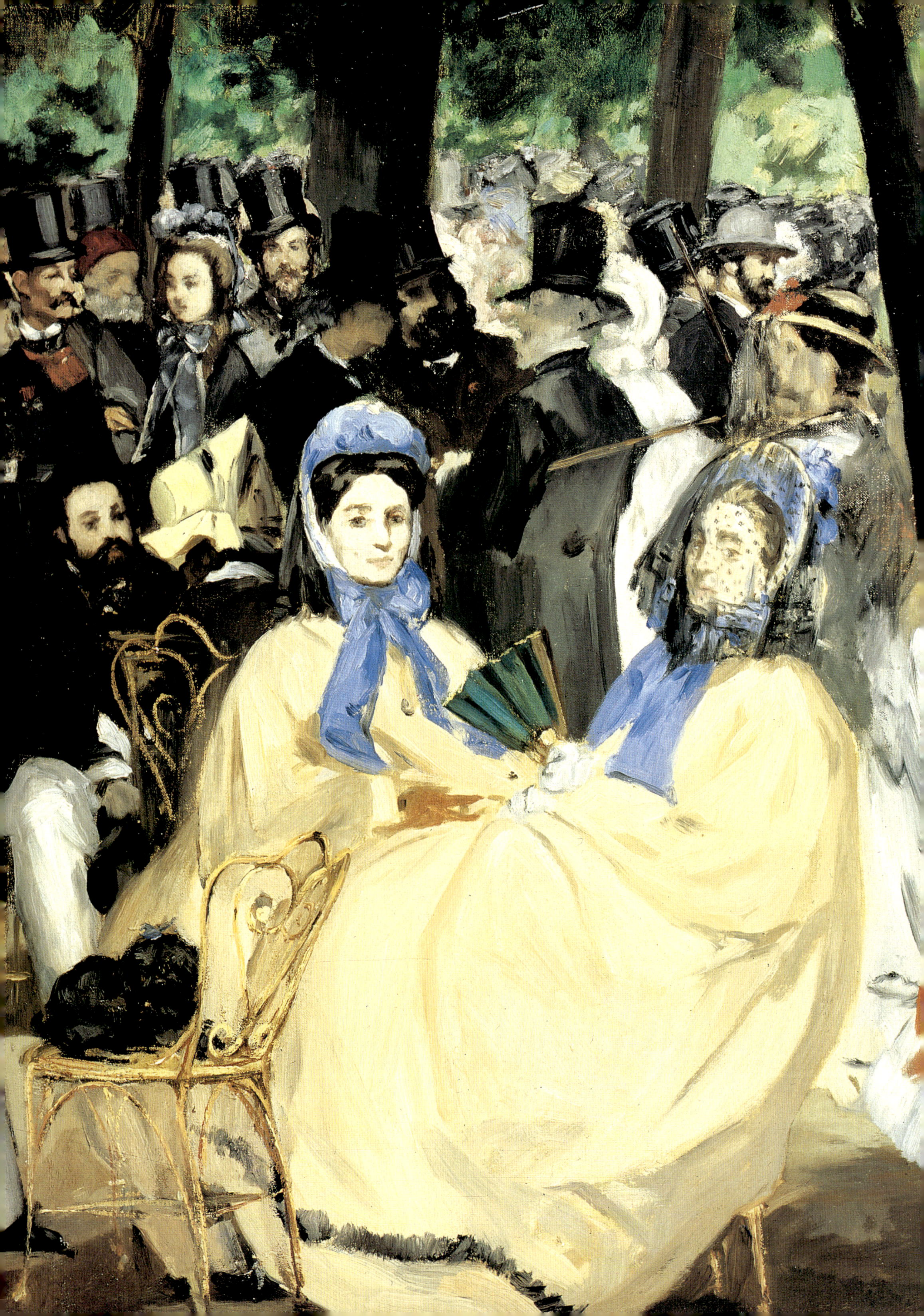

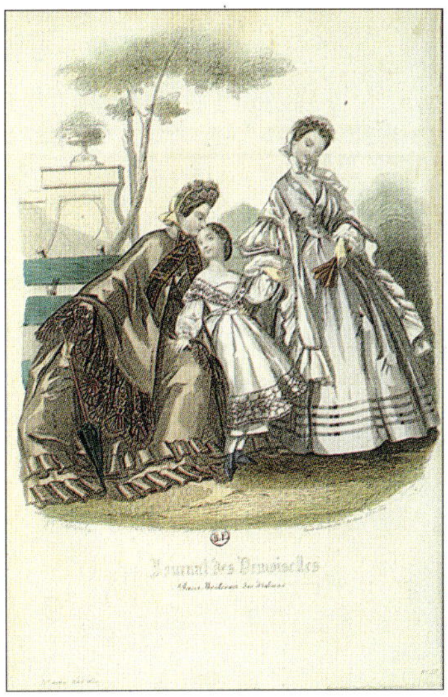

Edouard Manet,
La Musique aux Tuileries,
1862. The National Gallery, London. (facing page).

Le Journal des demoiselles,
August 1862 (left).

Le Magasin des demoiselles,
May 1864 (right).

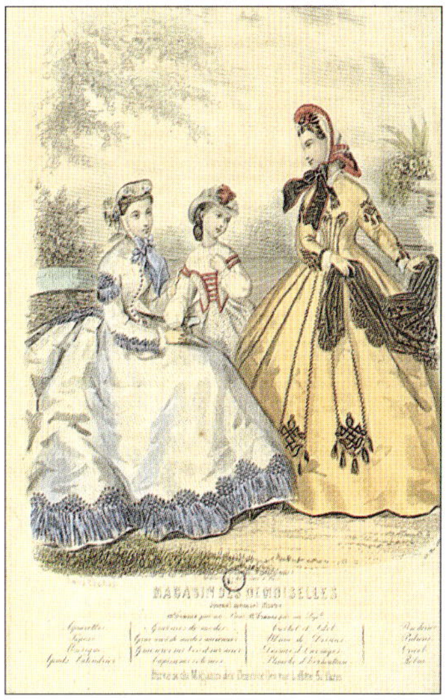

Tuileries, the group of two women sitting on the left, which attracts the eye in order to guide it towards the crowd, is reminiscent of a fashion plate, especially through the attention given to the town costumes and the 'artificial' arrangement of the two women. As in a print, they are in three-quarter view, one of them not even having room for her legs. And as in a print, the depiction of park chairs is the main indication of the location of the scene and gives it the quality of modernity.

Winterhalter, in *The Empress Eugénie and her court*, shows an assembly of women in ball-gowns at a meeting of sorts. As in a print, there is a discrepancy of style between the evening dress and the natural background sketch, which looks more like a theatre set. Is this pure coincidence – or is an unconscious influence at work? It has been proved in some cases that the influence was direct.

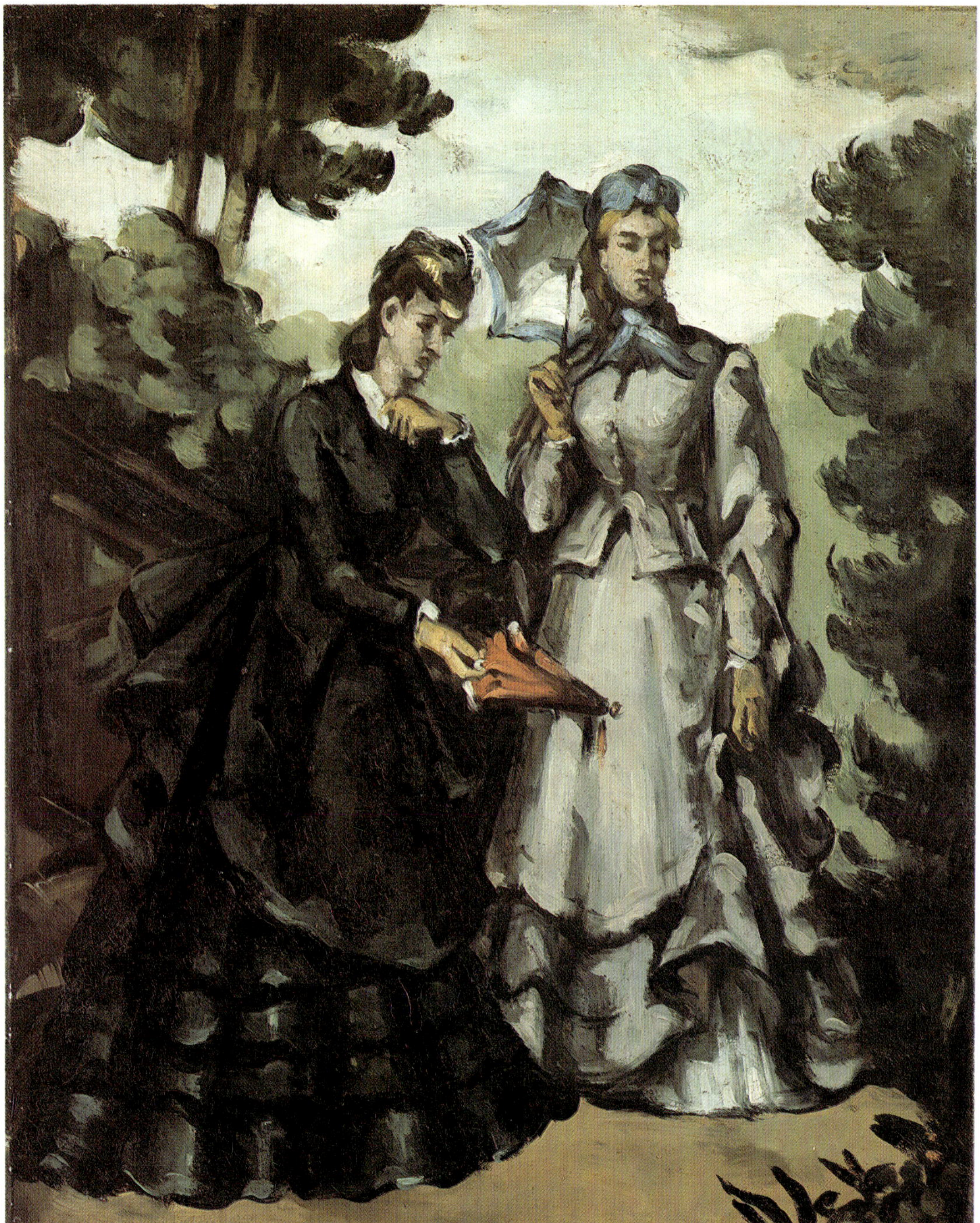

Paul Cézanne, La Promenade, *c.1871. Private Collection, New York.*

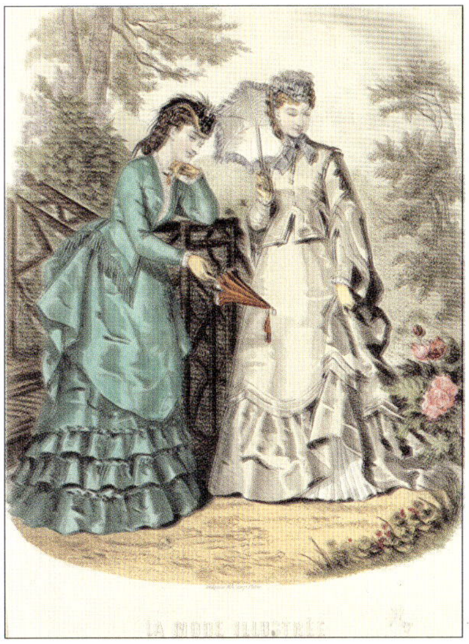

La Mode illustrée, *1871 (left).*

Paul Cézanne, La Conversation, *c.1871. Galerie Bernheim-Jeune, Paris (right).*

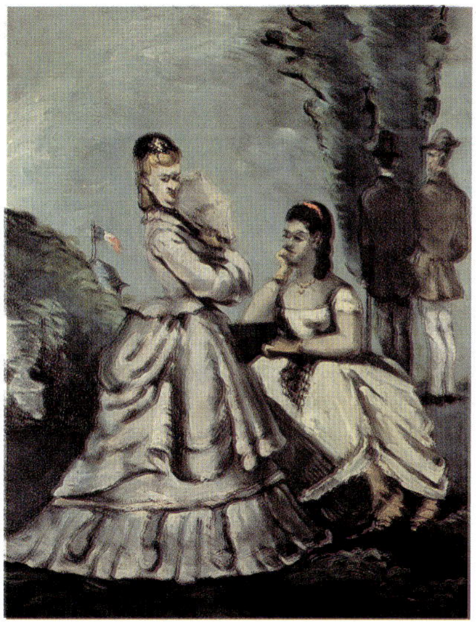

The influence of fashion prints on painters

The journals could not fail to catch the attention of painters. Like the rest of the Press, they were new collections of images which could not be ignored. If painters made use of photographs (Degas reproducing a photograph of the Princesse de Metternich or Tissot one of his mistress, Kathleen Newton), one can imagine that, in the same way, they used these prints as a source of information. Ambroise Vollard confirms that this was the case with Cézanne: 'At certain moments of exasperation with the perversity of things, Cezanne would fall back on the pictures in the *Magasin pittoresque*, of which he had several volumes at his house, or even his sister's fashion journals.'[26]

Since that was written John Rewald has discovered two issues of *La mode Illustrée* from 1871, 'La promenade' and 'La conversation', and the corresponding fashion plates. Cézanne was not in the least interested in details of clothing, and reproduced the two silhouettes in his tough, masculine style, stripping them of all prettiness and affectation. He conveys their statuesque quality, and the artificiality of the scene. In *La Conversation*, he includes two men seen from the back as a pendant to the two women, each group ignoring the other in the isolation of their sex. Another oil painting, *Interior*, juxtaposes a woman in a ball dress to another in town costume with a red paletot, and a little girl. Unlike the print, Cézanne places them against a dark background, which imparts a disturbing quality to the scene and is in startling contrast to the engraving.

Mark Roskill, in his article 'Early Impressionism and the fashion print', traces influences on the work of Monet. In *Le déjeuner sur l'herbe* (1865–6), the female figures, seen from the back, appear as in a fashion print (especially in the fragment in the Musée d'Orsay). In *Women in a garden* (1866), fashion conventions are still more

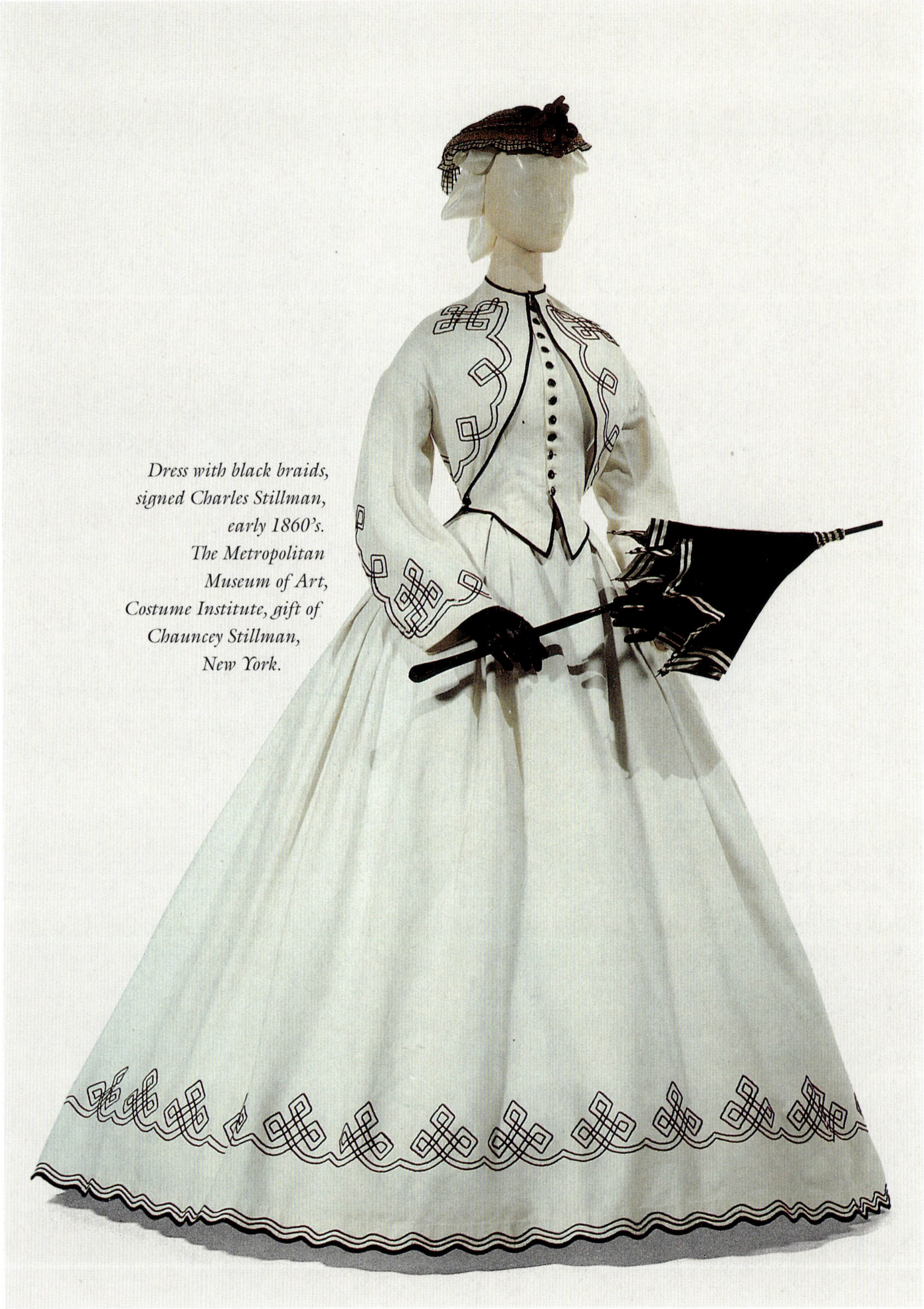

Dress with black braids, signed Charles Stillman, early 1860's. The Metropolitan Museum of Art, Costume Institute, gift of Chauncey Stillman, New York.

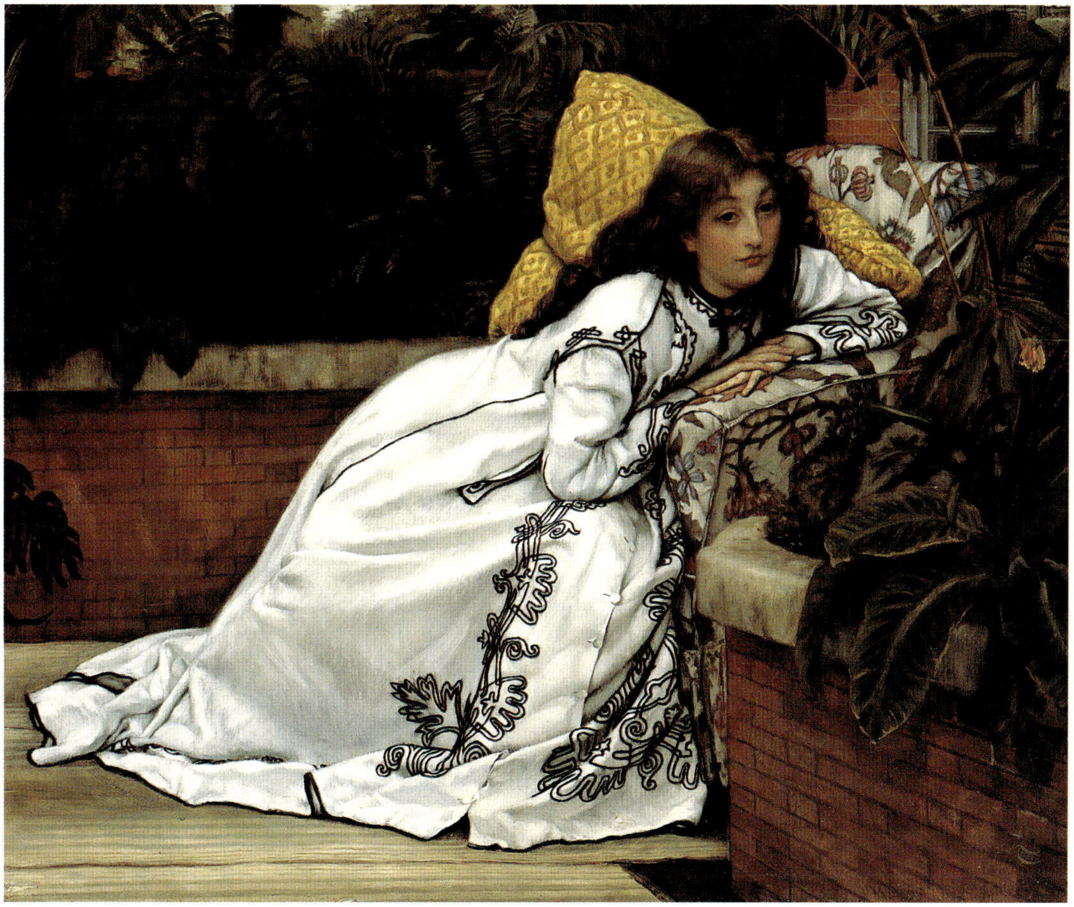

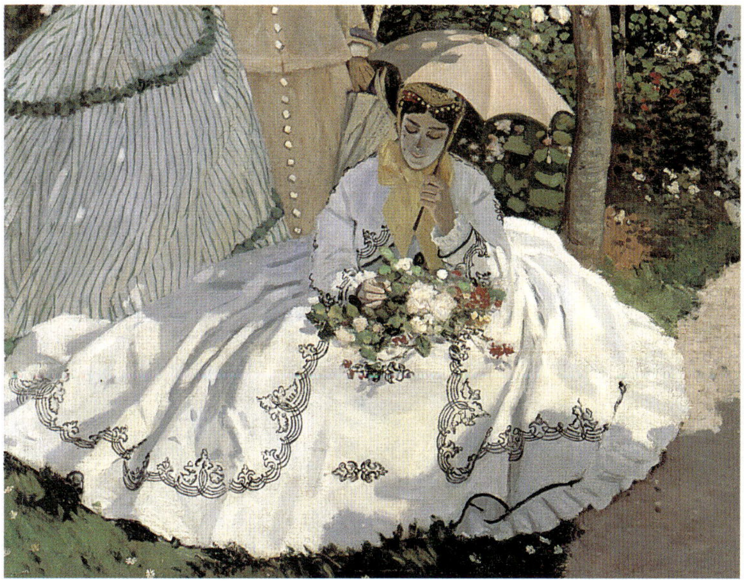

James Tissot, Young girl in an armchair (The Convalescent), *1870. Art Gallery of Ontario, Toronto (above).*

Claude Monet, Women in a garden, *1866 (detail). Musée d'Orsay, Paris (left).*

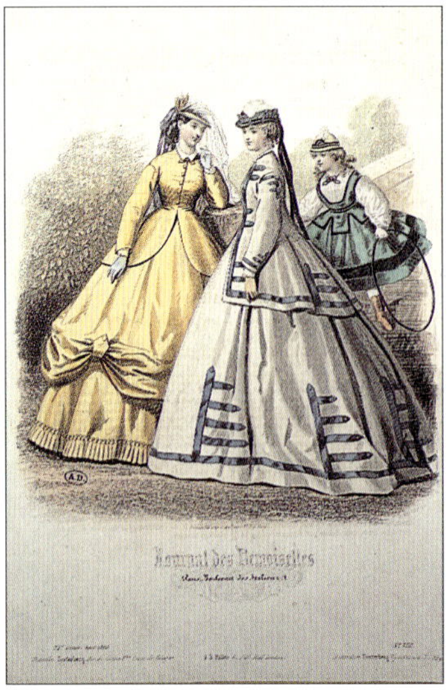

Le Journal des demoiselles, *August 1865 (left).*

La Mode illustrée, *1861 (right).*

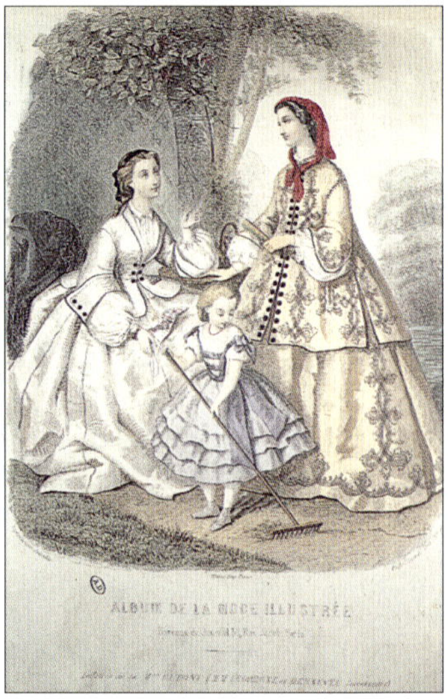

visible in the stiffness of the artificial poses adopted to allow the dresses to spread to their full amplitude, without interfering with each other but without allowing the four women to engage in conversation. Finally, it may have been prints which suggested to Monet that he should use the same model, Camille, wearing a different dress each time.

Valerie Steele argues that Boudin might have induced his pupil to find inspiration in reviews of female fashion.[27] Boudin certainly made skilful use of the fashionable aspect of the beach at Trouville, realising that he had discovered a rich new seam. He paints his female figures according to the conventions of the fashion print; he even places them, one seated, another from the back, another in profile, as if a single person were rotating to show us all sides of a dress. The Annenberg Collection (New York, Metropolitan Museum of Art) owns a sketch, *The Princesse de Metternich on the beach*, which looks more like a fashion illustration than a portrait: she is in profile in a very elegant seaside dress. Here Boudin shows the same rapid, brilliant, agile style that is found in Watteau's sketches. As Tissot and Degas were also to do, he seeks to capture the 'harmonious whole' – a correspondence between dress, gesture, angle of head and pose. In this way he comes close to being a painter of modern life, in one of its aspects as defined by Baudelaire.

Prints give examples of new poses. In his article Mark Roskill compares *Camille in green dress* by Monet (1866, Bremen, Kunsthalle) to a plate from the *Monde élégant* of February 1866. The print shows two women and a little girl. One of the women is in three-quarter rear view, her face in profile turned to the right, her left hand playing with the string of her hat. The likeness to the pose of Camille is very striking. Théophile Thoré has shown that this painting was intended to replace *Déjeuner sur l'herbe*, which had not been finished in time for the Salon of 1866. Monet is said to

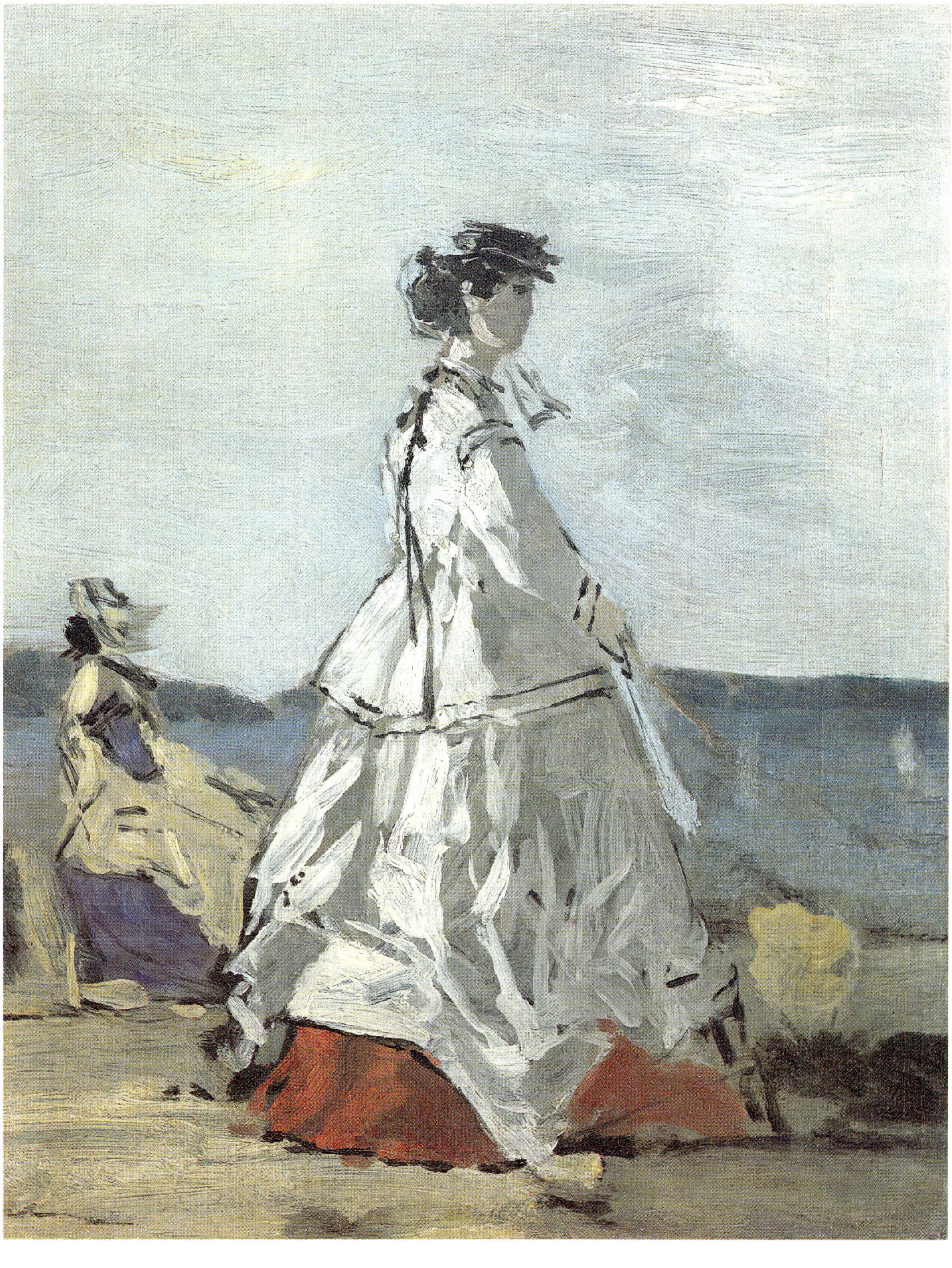

Eugène Boudin, The Princesse de Metternich on the beach, *c.1865–1867.*
The Metropolitan Museum of Art, New York.

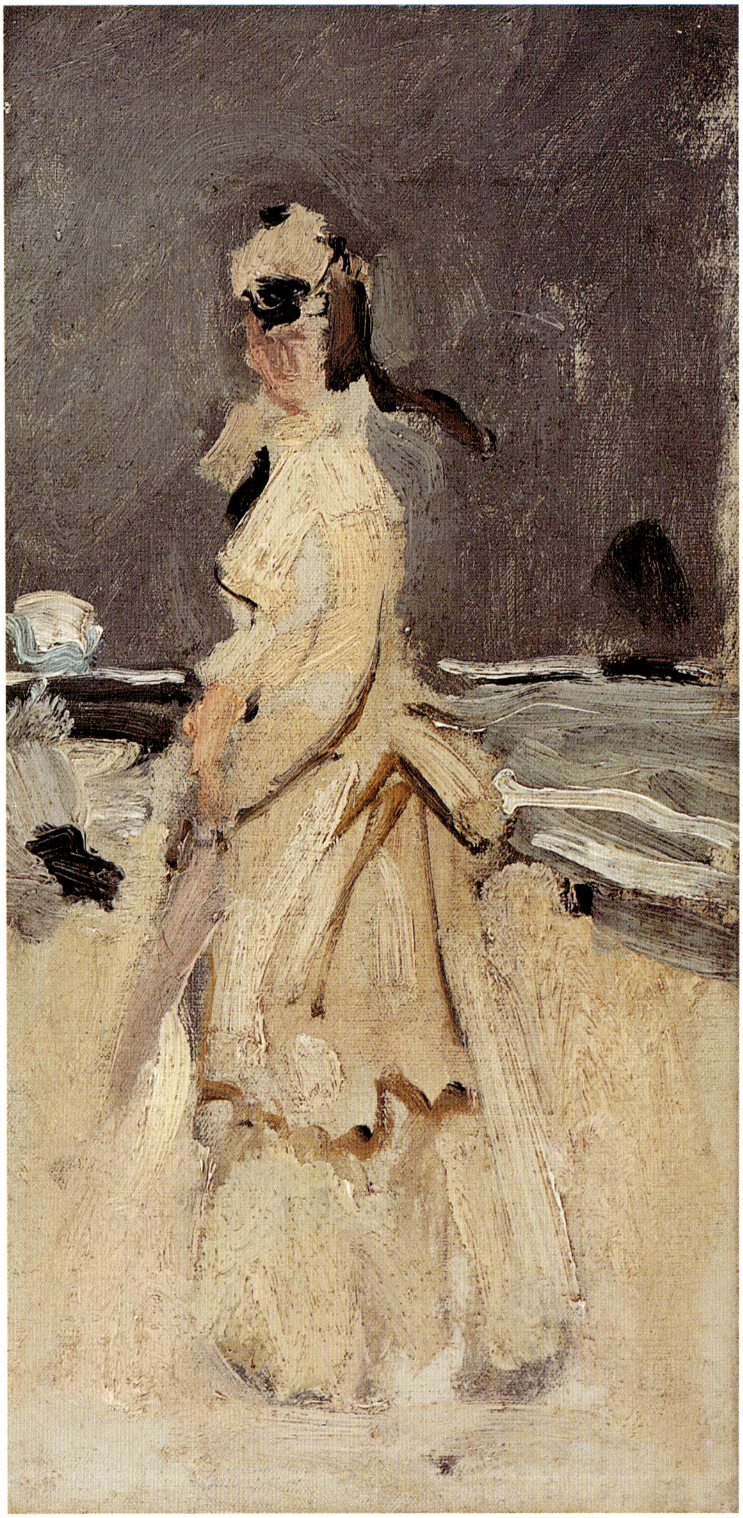

Claude Monet, Camille on the beach, *c.1870–1872. Musée Marmottan, Paris.*

Aristide Maillol, Woman with a parasol, *c.1895. Musée d'Orsay, Paris (facing page).*

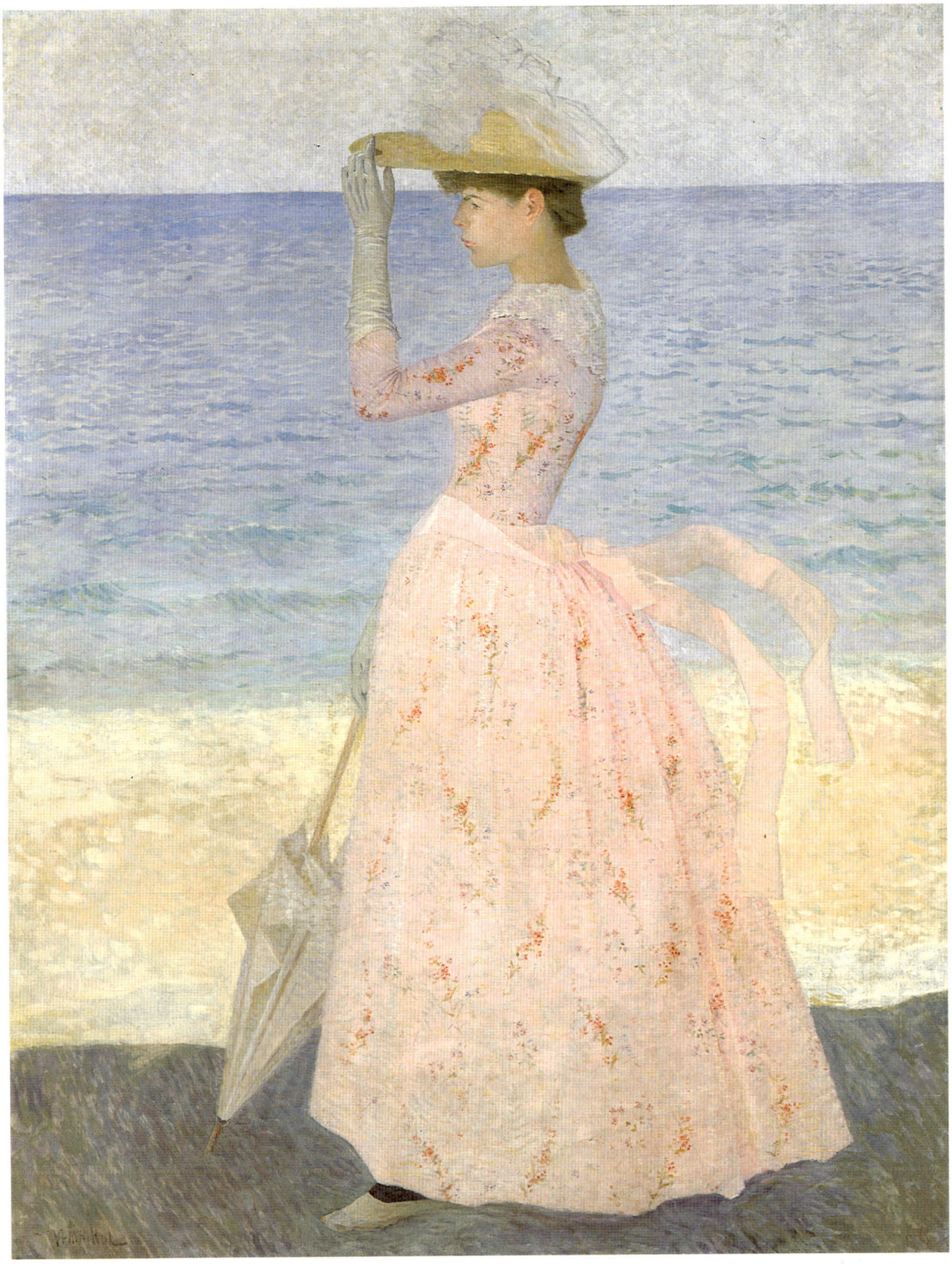

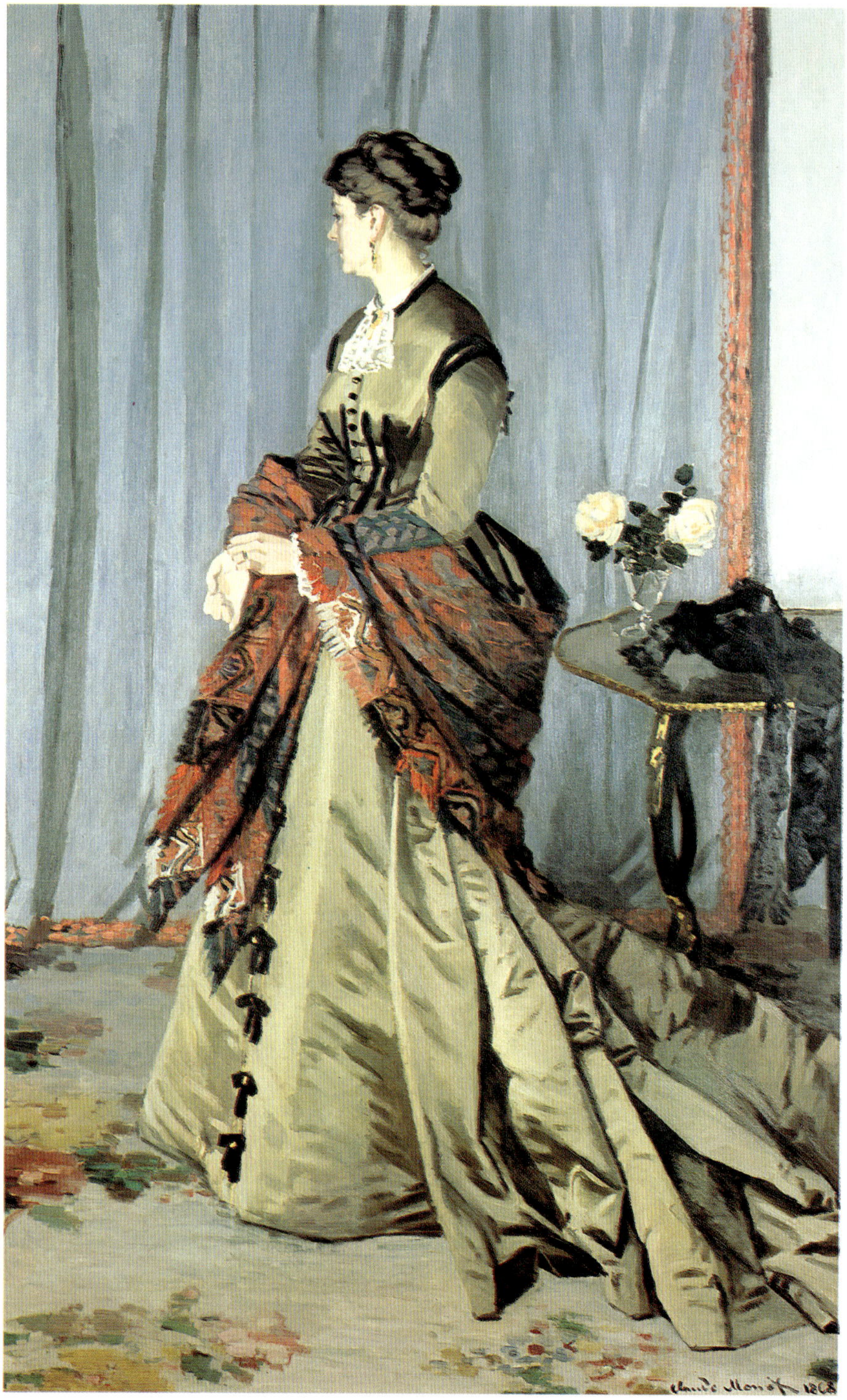

Claude Monet, Madame Gaudibert, *1868. Musée d'Orsay, Paris.*

have completed the portrait in four days, and a letter to Bazille indicates that he had very probably hired Camille's dress for the occasion.[28] As can be seen from his use of a very unusual pose for a portrait, Monet was concentrating on the dress, especially the shimmer of the striped skirt. The effect of the stripes has a mysterious power; in a kind of low-angle shot the eye is guided from the train to the jacket and the face. This earned the painting both its success and the criticism that the dress eclipsed the face and the personality of the sitter:

> A dress is no more a painting than a correctly-written sentence is a book. One can do a bit of dressmaking and yet still have everything to learn. What does the dress matter to me if I can't imagine a well-modelled body inside it, or even the trite outline of the mannequin, if the head is not a head and the hand is not even a paw.[29]

Two years later, the *Portrait of Madame Gaudibert* (1868, Paris, Musée d'Orsay) earned the same disapproval. This painting had been commissioned by a rich merchant from Le Havre. Monet was in a more than precarious financial situation at the time, and *Women in a garden* had been rejected for the Salon of 1866. It may have been the combination of all these factors – a critical situation, the wish to please his client, fear of another setback – which induced the artist to paint a portrait of a dress quite close in design to the *Camille* which had been accepted for the Salon of 1866. The model is seen in receding profile and no expression – even less than on Camille's face – can be seen. Monet has borrowed from the fashionable portrait all the elements of the setting - carpet, curtain, pedestal table, cashmere shawl – which contribute to the impression of bourgeois well-being. But at the same time he escapes the genre by his rapid brushwork and the averted face of Mme Gaudibert. She denies us access to her soul, and is absorbed into the colourful shapes of her clothing and the background. It is no longer a portrait but a painting. The merchant F. Martin wrote to Eugène Boudin:

> One can't deny that the fellow has had the audacity to produce an original painting and that the pursuit of truth has been his primary aim. But as for the execution, it's downright vulgar, and neither the delicacy of the flesh nor the subtlety of the type has been respected. It's a painting, but it is not a portrait.[30]

It has often been said that Tissot was inspired by fashion prints in his two portraits for the Salon of 1864: *Two Sisters* (Paris, Musée d'Orsay) and *Mademoiselle L.L.*, also called *Young woman in a red jacket* (Paris, Musée d'Orsay). In the first, the inspiration came from the combination of a young woman and a little girl in a neat white dress in a park, and in the second, from the freedom of the pose. There is, indeed, a certain boldness in the girl in the latter work, sitting nonchalantly on the corner of a table, staring at the beholder without bothering to look modest and timid in the way

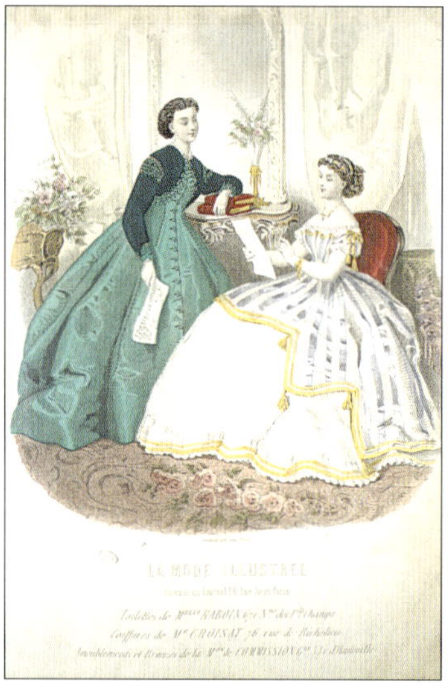

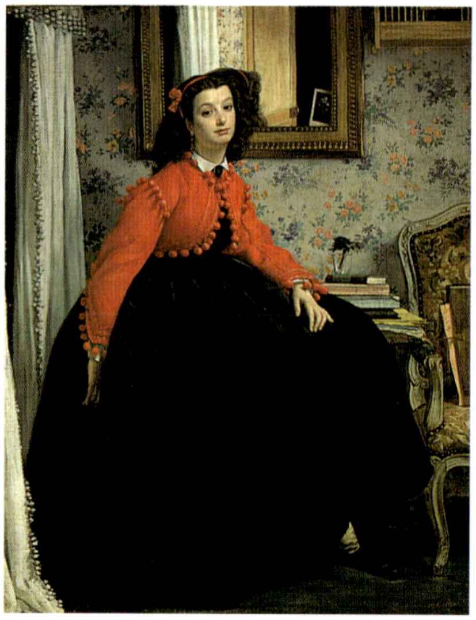

La Mode illustrée: *indoor fashions and ball -gown, 1866 (left).*

James Tissot, Young woman in a red jacket, *1864. Musée d'Orsay, Paris (right).*

La Mode illustrée, *1866 (facing page,left).*

Pierre August Renoir, Madame Monet on a sofa, *1872–1874. Foundation Calouste Gulbenkian, Lisbon (facing page, right).*

recommended by the etiquette manuals. An echo of this is found in a plate in *La Mode illustrée* (1866), where a girl dressed in the same bolero over a princess dress is leaning on her elbows on a chest of drawers with a mirror, with the same head position and a similar pose. One wonders (the print being of later date) whether its author was not inspired by Tissot; in that case there would be a very plausible two-way influence between artists and fashion prints, since illustrators are sure to have visited the Salon.

Another print in *La Mode illustrée*, dated the same year, shows a woman in a blue peignoir decorated with a paisley pattern, reclining on a couch. In 1872–4 *Madame Monet on a sofa* by Renoir (Lisbon, Gulbenkian Foundation) is in the same pose, but laterally inverted, on a white sofa, with the same type of indoor dress with paisley designs. Instead of a book, Mme Monet is reading a newspaper, and her left arm is similarly lying across the armrest. The impressionistic treatment of the dress does, it is true, clearly distinguish the painting from the print, but this does not reduce the importance attached to the dress. Contrary to what might be expected, the Impressionist dress is never neglected and is always very legible.

These three examples show how the fashion print was able to instil novelty and freedom into the portrait. But it was a two-edged weapon, and its negative effects are seen in the work of such painters as Stevens, Giraud and Toulmouche (the latter, we should recall, was linked to Monet through having married one of his cousins; enjoying immense success, he was the young painter's artistic tutor when he arrived in Paris, advising him to study under Gleyre). These painters, far from renewing their art, became bogged down in an extremely detailed description of the world of women. Their sole aim in their paintings seems to have been to give a brilliant and sentimental transcription of women in their finery, taking over the conventions of fashion prints to a

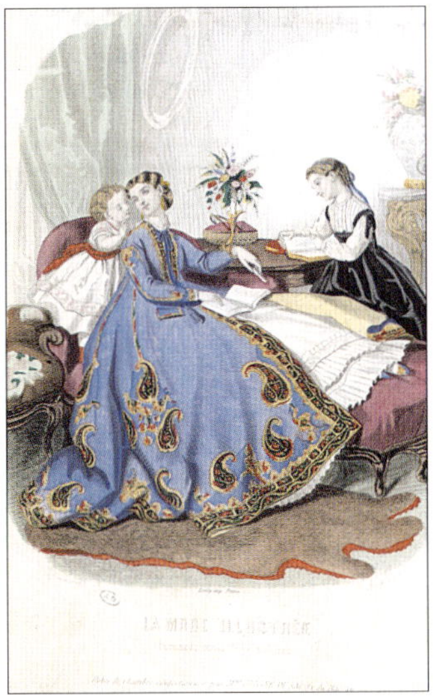

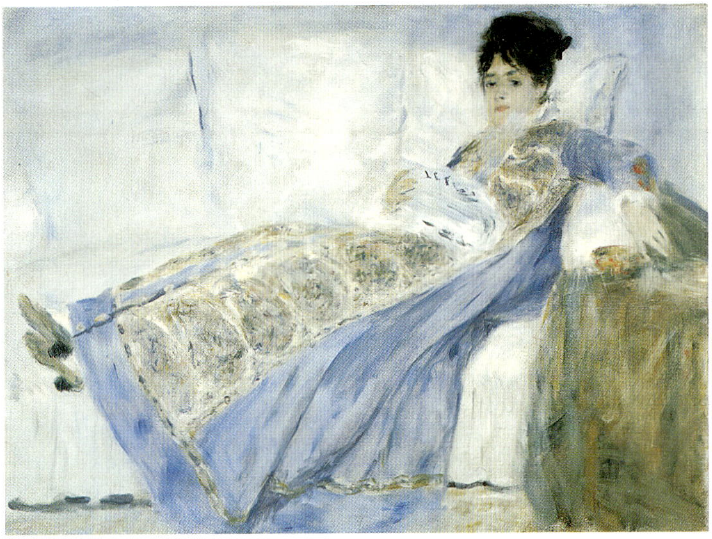

significant degree. In *The visit* or *Two friends*, Stevens adds a standing woman in town clothes to a seated woman in indoor dress in a horizontal plane without depth. The psychological relation between the two women hardly exists; all that matters is luxury, coquetry, appearance. Toulmouche and de Jonghe do likewise, and also illustrate another subject dear to the women's press: the education of children.

The theme of the seasons, dealt with by artists like Stevens, Tissot or Abbéma, is another example of fashion's grip on painting. The influence of Japanese prints, in which a season is represented by a woman against a natural background in a vertical format, has been rightly stressed. However, in the West this theme had hitherto been depicted either by mythological figures or by human activities (work in the fields, rustic games). But to associate a season with a woman's dress was unique to the language of fashion. Perhaps such a combination had special significance at that time in the nineteenth century.

Idealized genre scenes were very popular with the public. Zola denounced the mediocrity of these pictures, which he already called 'fashion prints', but they delighted visitors at the Salon: 'If your painting is as flat as a coloured engraving in the Magasin des demoiselles, and if your figures look like cardboard dummies dressed by Worth, your success will know no bounds.'[31] In such works the public saw a demonstration of artistic skill combined with easy, understandable subjects less boring than history paintings, which allowed them to daydream. Some critics such as Thoré-Bürger were taken in by them, seeing these genre scenes as continuing an ancient tradition and brilliantly resurrecting the art of Metsu and the Dutch tradition. Even Théophile Gautier saw the work of Alfred Stevens as 'the poem of the society woman'.[32]

This admiration shows how widely aesthetic judgement fluctuates with time.

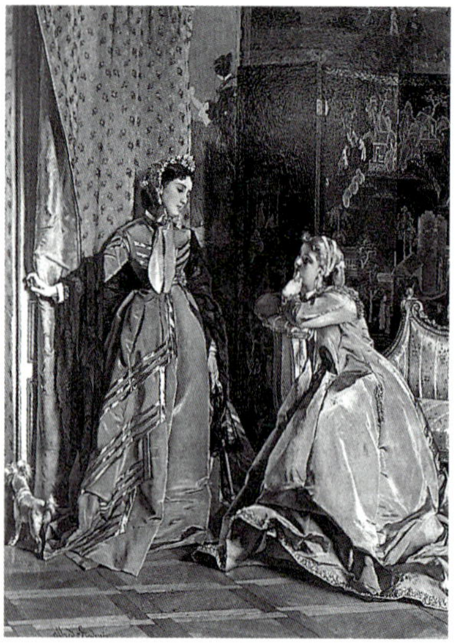

Alfred Stevens, Two Friends, *Exposition Universelle, 1867. Present location unknown (left).*

Raimundo de Madrazo y Garreta, The Morning Visit, *no date. Sterling and Francine Clark Insitute, Williamstown, Massachusetts (right).*

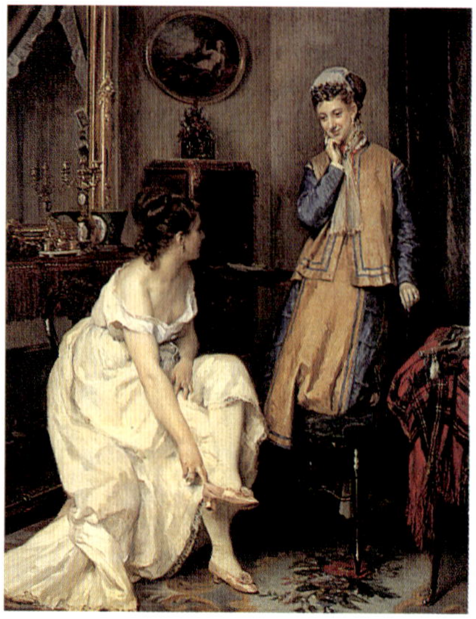

Painters definitively classed as hacks today seemed 'modern' to their contemporaries; for example, Carolus-Duran, or Gervex, who was called the 'leader of the modern school'. Between the art that was officially and publicly recognized at the time, which might be called 'society art', and the work of the innovative painters who were rejected and outlawed, there were not the clear boundaries we like to draw today. The ambiguous influence of fashion prints is one illustration of this. The cliché of the *parisienne* is another.

In search of the parisienne

As if spellbound by the idealization of the contemporary woman, painters sought to capture the essence of this ideal in portraits of the *Parisienne.* First sketched in the first half of the century by the pens of Balzac (*Les Parisiens comme ils sont,* 1830–48) and Taxile Delord (*La Physiologie de la Parisienne*, 1841) and the pencil of Gavarni, she had emerged as a dominant literary figure. But her nature had never been clearly defined.

We should not believe that her nature was simply a matter of geography. According to *La Physiologie de la Parisienne*, many *parisiennes* were born in the provinces. She did not come from any particular class – she was 'everywhere and nowhere. You find her in the faubourg Saint-Germain, on the chaussée d'Antin, in the faubourg Saint-Honoré and even on the place Bréda'.[33] She might be a *modiste* or a society woman; what makes her stand out first of all is her sophisticated, resplendent dress: 'Take away the Parisian woman's ankle-boots of satin and polish, her silk scarf, her gloves, her fans and her thousand jewels, and you will see what is left. A woman.'[34]

Her clothes and accessories were not only her nature but her weapons, for *parisiennes* were all equally seductive to the gaping bystander: 'Parisian women are the sultanas of the West. They pass before the admirer's gaze, nimble, light, flighty and radiant, like houris in Mohamet's heaven.'[35]

But clothes alone did not make the *parisienne.* Her whole being radiated a charm which she deployed like an idol – but she was an active idol fully aware of her powers. She has 'every voluptuous grace, every virtuous charm – but hers is the virtue that come after the fall. She is the French Magdalene.'[36]

In 1874 Renoir painted a portrait, *La Parisienne* (Cardiff, National Museum of Wales) which was shown at the first exhibition of the Impressionists. Jean Prouvaire describes it as follows:

> You hardly glimpse the tip of her ankle-boot, like a little black mouse. Her hat, almost over her ear, is daringly coquettish. Her dress is too closed. Nothing more irritating than shut doors. Is this picture a portrait? One fears that it is. The face, bizarrely old but also puerile, smiles a false smile. Yet the whole has something naive about it. You'd say that this little person was being chaste on purpose. The dress, very well painted, is a heavenly blue.[37]

Half-angel, half-demon, child and adult, her ambiguity makes her all the more seductive. The model, Mme Henriot, was a young actress, and this choice of subject was no accident. At the Salon the same year, the painter Ernest-Ange Duez (1843–96) also showed a *parisienne* with the title *Splendour.* Approaching the subject from a moralising angle, he composed a diptych, *Splendour* and *Misery,* in which the jaunty *parisienne* with her little poodle is contrasted to a woman who has sunk into poverty. The *parisienne* is seen in profile, emphasising her bustle just as in Renoir; she is also wearing a hat, but her costume as a whole is much more aggressive, especially her striped bodice. Lacking the ambiguity and subtlety which made up the whole charm of the Renoir portrait, the painting seems like an social indictment. Nevertheless, it had a big success and earned critical accolades, including that of Zola, who undoubtedly saw literary themes in this description of decadence. The painter was awarded third prize.

At the Salon of 1882 Manet exhibited – in addition to his *Bar at the Folies-Bergère* – a portrait, *Jeanne* or *Spring,* intended to form part of a series of four paintings on the theme of the seasons commissioned by Antonin Proust. *Autumn,* a portrait of Méry Laurent, was also a part of this project, which was interrupted by the artist's death. We have already noted that the association of a woman with a season was much in vogue. In 1869 and 1876 Stevens had painted *Spring* and *Autumn* for King Leopold II of the Belgians, two women seen full-length in kakemono format. In 1877 Tissot entitled one of his portraits of Kathleen Newton *October.* Louise Abbéma chose Mlles Bartet, Samary, Sarah Bernhardt and Reichemberg to represent the *Four Seasons* at the Salon.

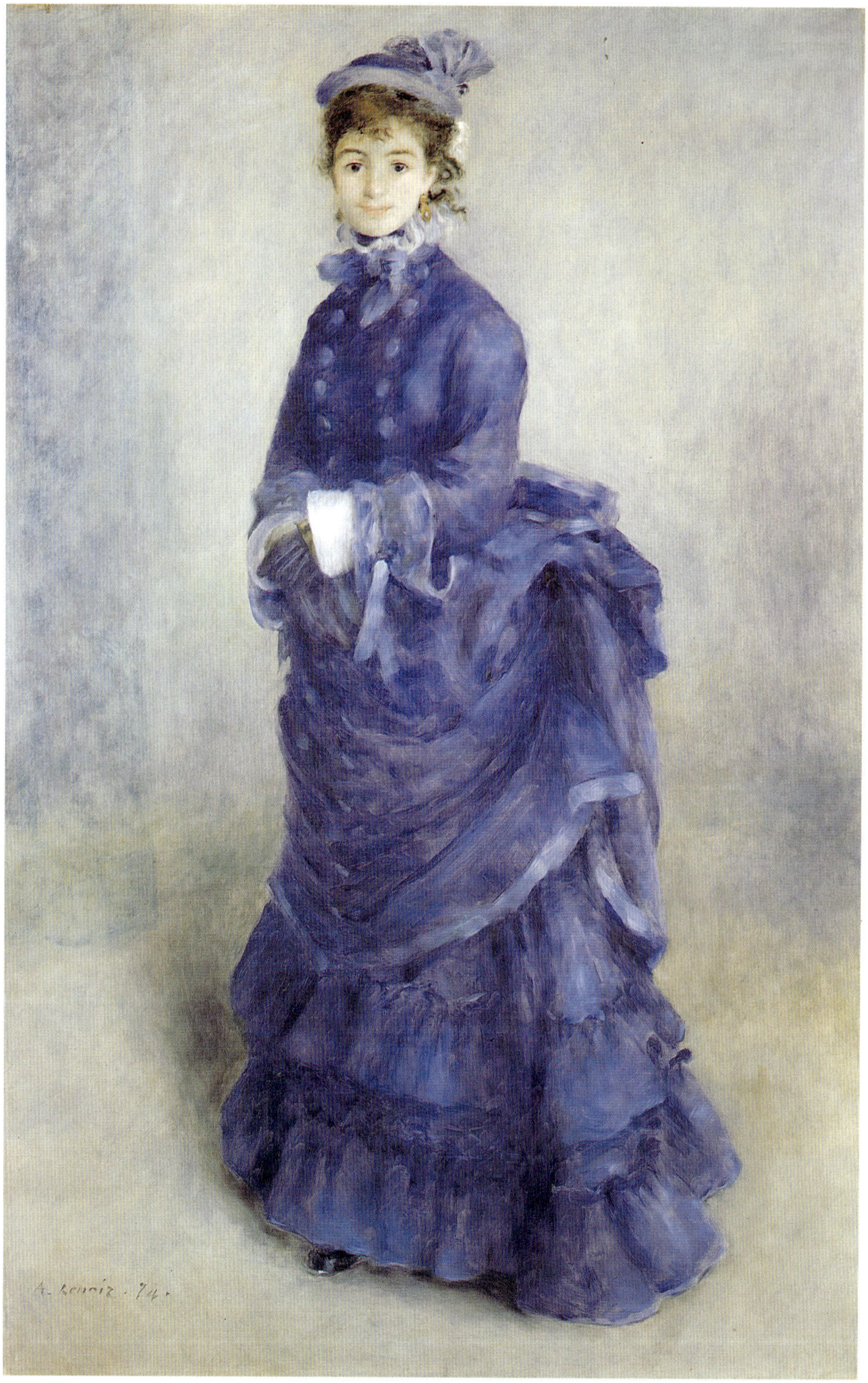
A. Renoir . 74 .

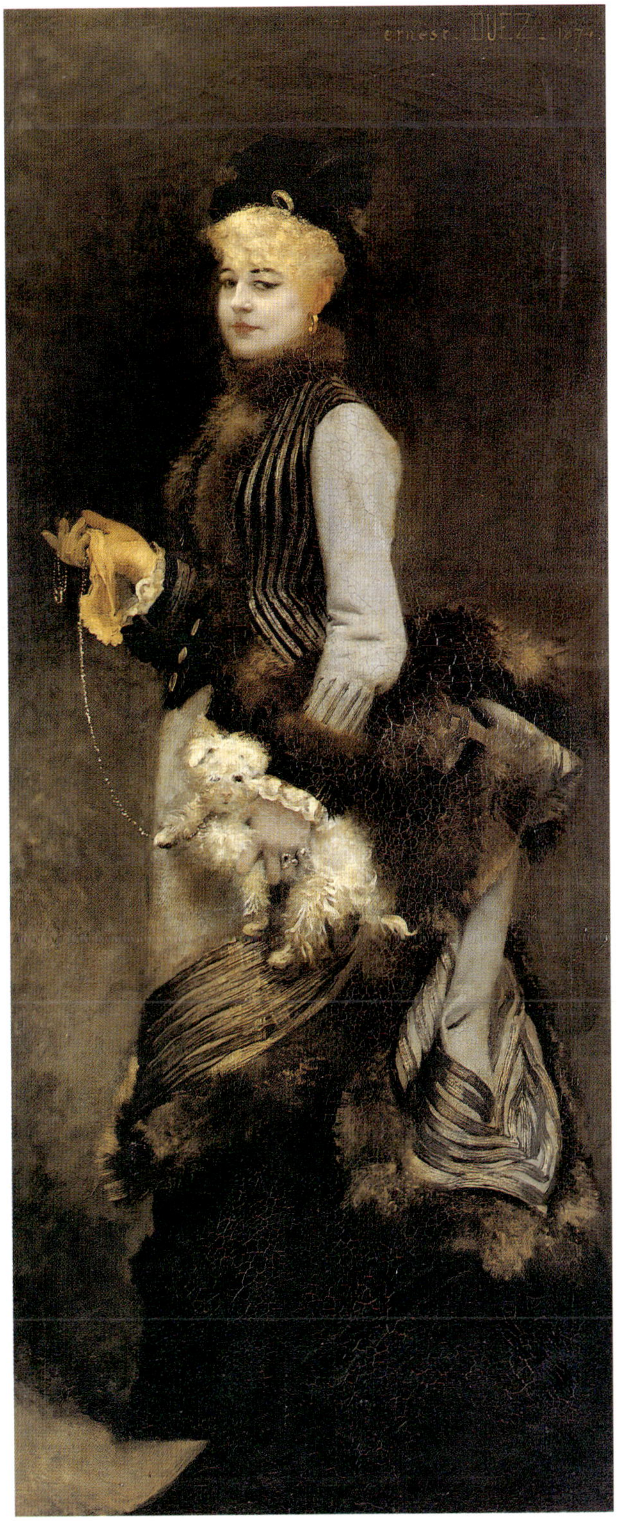

Ernest-Ange Duez,
Splendour, *1874. Musée des Arts décoratifs, Paris.*

Pierre Auguste Renoir,
La Parisienne, *1874.*
National Museum of Wales, Cardiff (facing page).

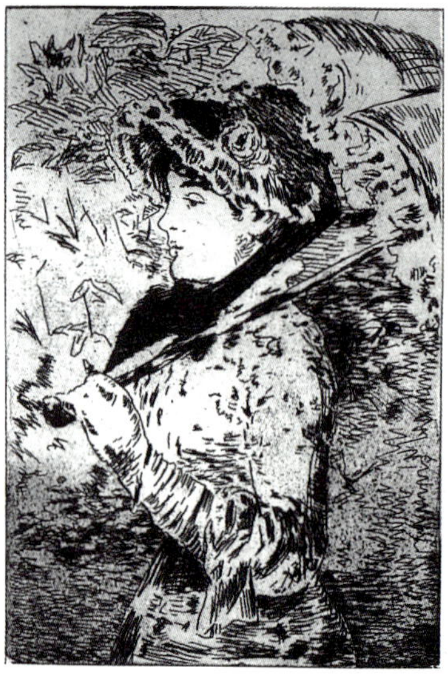

Edouard Manet,
Jeanne *or* Spring, *1882*
(left).

L'Art et la mode:
'Sa majesté la Parisienne',
facsimile by Desjardin after
Alfred Stevens, 1880.
(right).

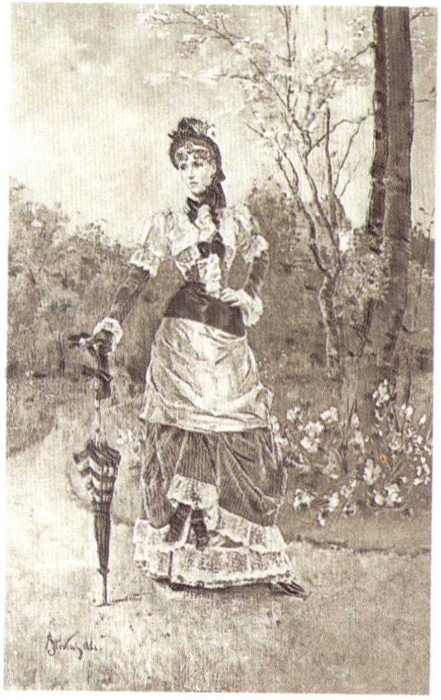

Manet showed a young actress, Jeanne Demarsy, posing in a posing in a floral dress and a flowery hat, with a sunshade in her hand.

> He is trying to express a value familiar to him, the elegance of a fashionable young woman. But in taking this elegance to its extreme, he is seeking the factor within 'the latest fashion' which decisively affects his art. The idea of fashion is inseparable from a new form of portrait...'The latest fashion, you see,' Manet once said, 'is absolutely necessary for a painter. It's what matters most'.[38]

When Jacques-Emile Blanche expressed his surprise at the difference between Manet's interpretation and the insipid dress and sunshade he found lying in the studio, Manet insisted: 'Isn't it just right? Isn't it silky, rich, completely elegant?'[39] Manet had succeeded in capturing on his canvas the mysterious, impalpable essence of the *parisienne.* His contemporaries made no mistake. For once the approval was unanimous:

> The nice little pink face under the powder, the snub nose, the pretty eyes sheltered under the poke bonnet, the whole image of the smart *parisienne* walking in a garden under a transparent parasol – it's simply exquisite.[40]
>
> She has brown hair and a snub nose, her red lips give away her sensuality while her brown eyes shaded by long lashes denote her indifference. As a soldier carries his rifle, so she shoulders her grey parasol ...This woman is a *parisienne* of today.[41]

The physical type defined here is almost a cliché: the pretty snub-nosed face is found in all portraits of the *parisienne.* A year later, Charles Giron also showed a

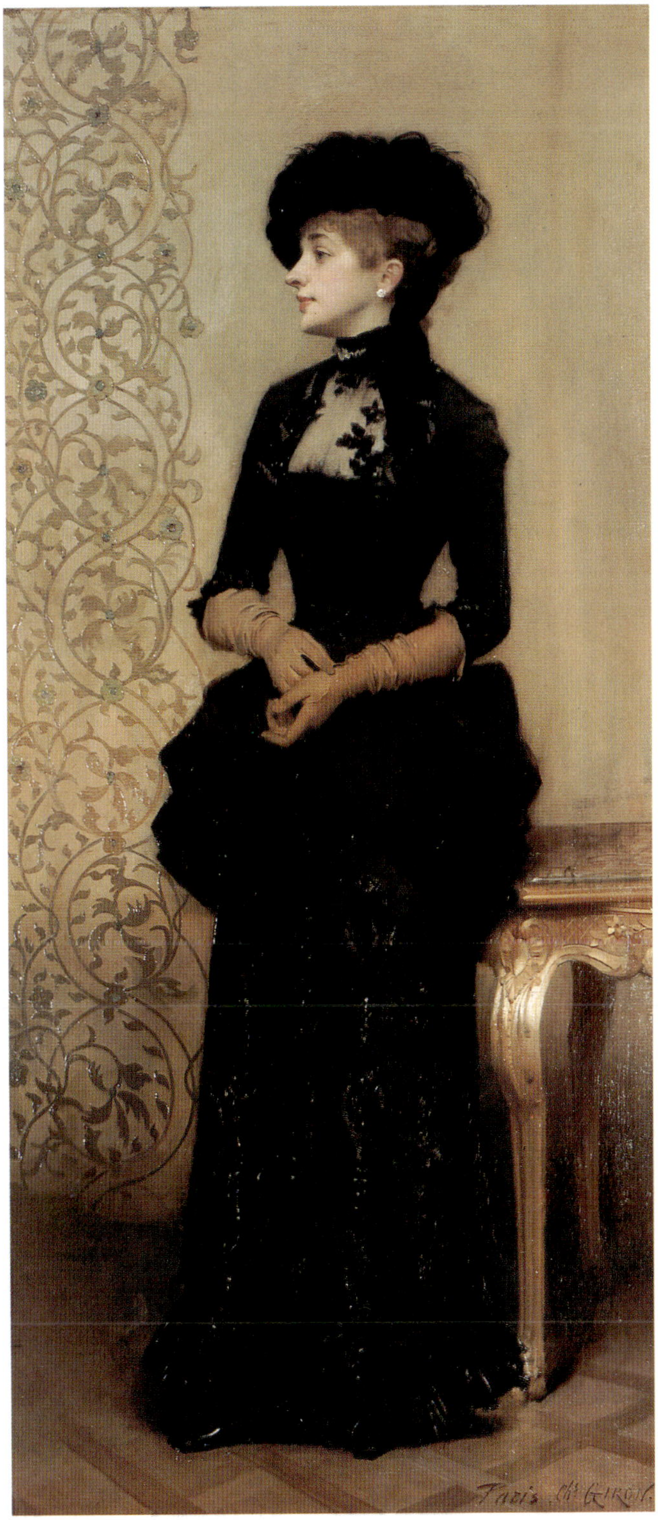

Charles Giron,
La Parisienne, *1883. Musée du Petit Palais, Paris.*

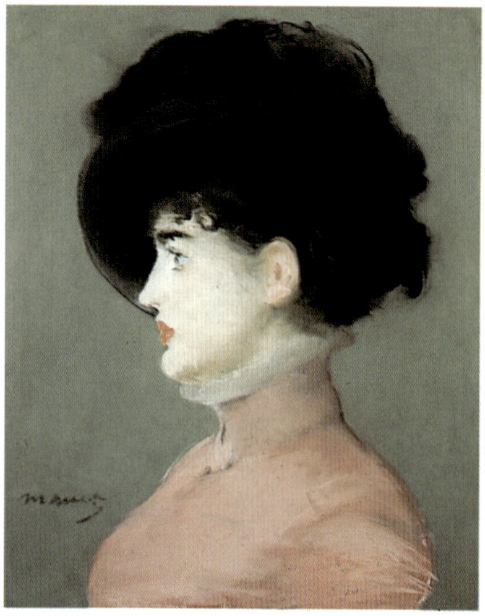

Edouard Manet,
La Viennoise. Portrait of Irma Brunner, *c.1880. Musée d'Orsay, Paris (left).*

La Revue de la mode, *hats, 1882 (right).*

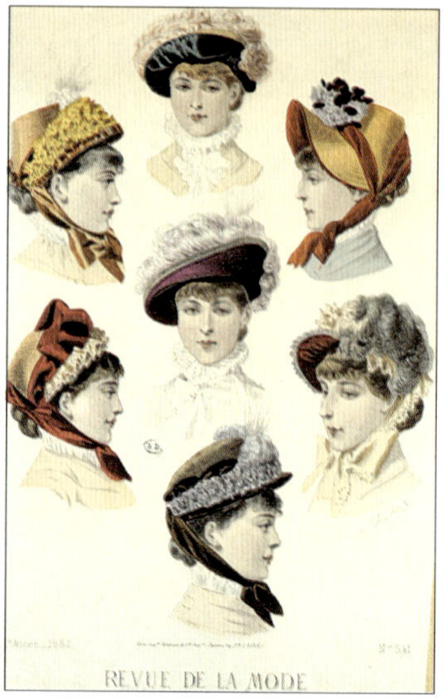

Parisienne at the Salon (1883, Paris, Musée du Petit Palais): she has the same lively, pert face with raised eyebrows, small nose and determined mouth. This physical type, alert and diminutive (the stout figure of the Second Empire is a thing of the past) expresses what unites all these women, from the actress to the *cocotte* and the society lady: impudence, flightiness, a certain frivolity.

Accessories as emblems

To the physical type is added a second cliché: the *parisienne's* accessories. They are carefully selected and are not used at random. They are indispensable, and no painter can omit them, always giving them the same meaning, so that they become true attributes. Suede gloves and muff are obligatory in winter. The hat is tilted coquettishly over one ear (Renoir and Giron, *La Parisienne*; Manet, *La Lecture de l'illustré* and *Irma Brunner*). The ankle boot is half-revealed, either advancing surreptitiously from under the skirt (Renoir, Giron), or visible beneath a bunched skirt (Tissot, *October*, Montreal, Musée des Beaux-Arts; Béraud, *Parisienne*, Place de la Concorde, Paris, Musée Carnavalet). For 'a *parisienne* is recognized everywhere by her footwear'.[42]

The gesture of lifting her skirt becomes almost mythical: it discloses a dainty foot, a delicate ankle like a 'promise of happiness', it hints at her seductiveness. An anonymous author wrote a treatise on the fetishism of the foot: 'The Art of Lifting the Skirt'. Moreover, as Taxile Delord explains: 'Look a *parisienne* insistently in the eye and her face will show no emotion. But examine her foot or her hand attentively and she will blush and turn her face away.'[43] This gesture of the lifted skirt became typically Parisian and had great success, especially in the works of Boldini.

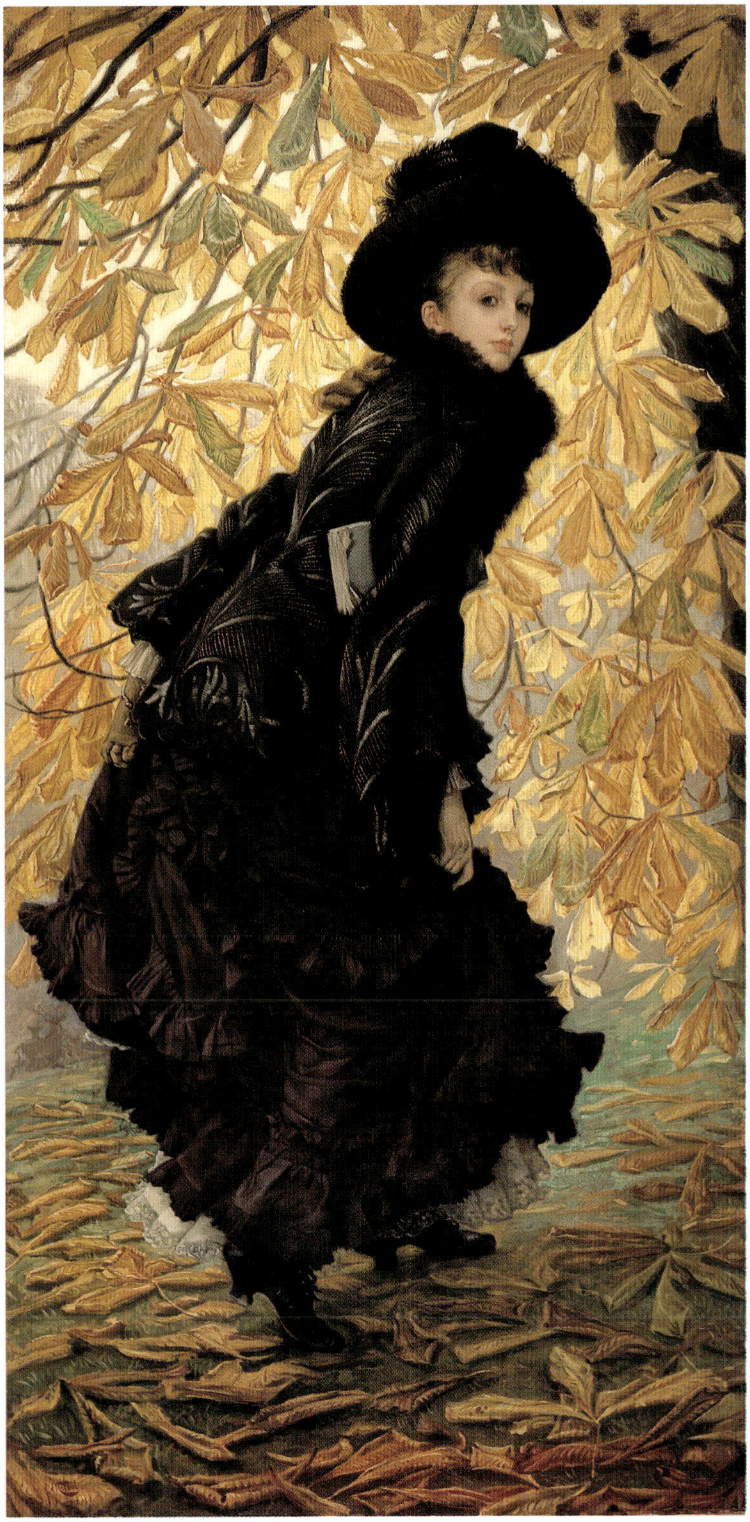

James Tissot, October, *1877.*
Musée des Beaux-Arts,
Montreal.

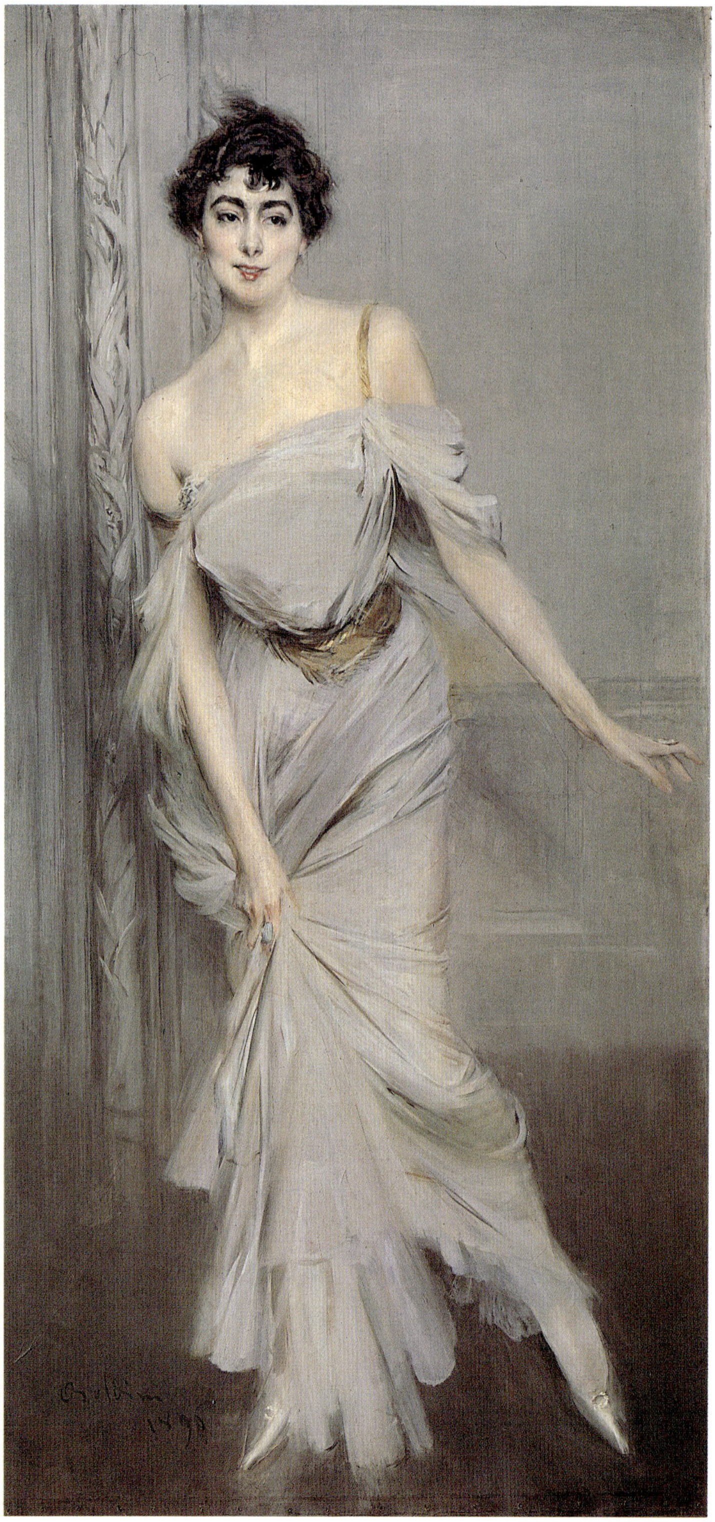

Giovanni Boldini,
Portrait of Madame
Charles Max, *1896.*
Musée d'Orsay,
Paris.

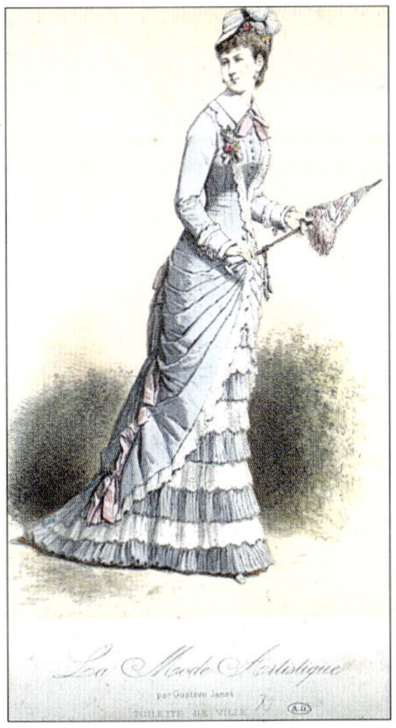

La Mode artistique, *town outfit, 1879 (left).*

Ready-made clothes from the fashion house Steinback Koechin & Cie: *'La Parisienne', 1875 (right).*

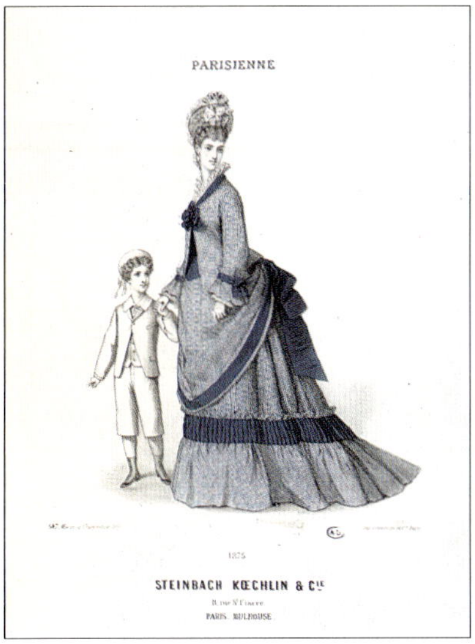

The parasol also plays a part in this coquettish game of concealing and revealing at the same time, as many paintings attest: Manet's *Jeanne*, a portrait of an actress at the Bouffes Parisiens and a renowned *cocotte*; *Madame Valtesse de la Bigne*, alias Louise Delabigne, by Gervex (1879, Paris, Musée d'Orsay), very close to Tissot's *Spring Morning* (1875, private collection) or Helleu's *Woman in white* inspired by Monet. Women knew how to filter their charm through the dappled light cast by the sunshade. Twenty years later Charles Blanc, quoted here by Octave Uzanne, the author of humorous books on women, took up the study of the parasol again in *Les Ornements de la femme*: 'How resourceful they are in their need to cast a penumbra over their faces!... In the work of art called a woman's costume, the parasol plays the part of chiaroscuro.'[44]

The parasol is the exact opposite of the umbrella: whereas the parasol is the weapon of seduction, the umbrella, dry, straight and closed, is the attribute of modesty. What could be more eloquent than a comparison between the *Portrait de Madame Valtesse de la Bigne* and that of *Madame...*, called *Woman with an umbrella* (1874, Paris, Musée National Jean-Jacques Henner). On one hand the flirtatious cocotte, smiling under her spreading parasol, on the other the prudish middle-class woman firmly supported on her strict umbrella, the symbol of her virtue:

> One is surprised that such a vulgar accessory can be reconciled with the severity of the ideal. Such, nevertheless, is the case, and it is my purpose to explain how M. Henner has used mundane objects neglected by fine writers to produce a work in the highest taste.[45]

Taxile Delord was quite clear on this subject: a woman with all the appearance of a

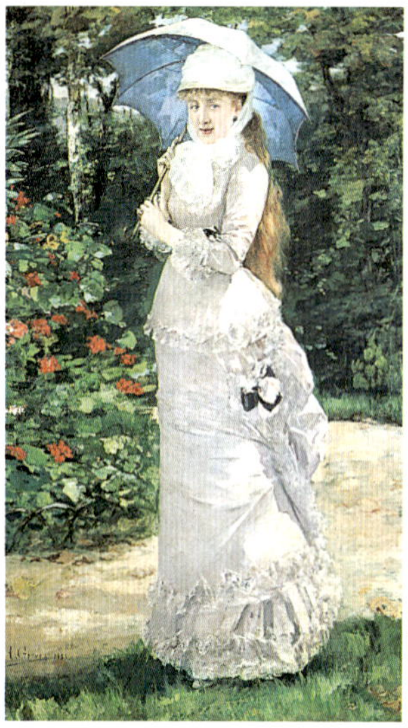

Henri Gervex,
Portrait of Madame Valtesse de La Bigne, *1879. Musée d'Orsay, Paris (left).*

Jean-Jacques Henner,
Woman with an umbrella, *1874. Musée national Jean-Jacques Henner, Paris (right).*

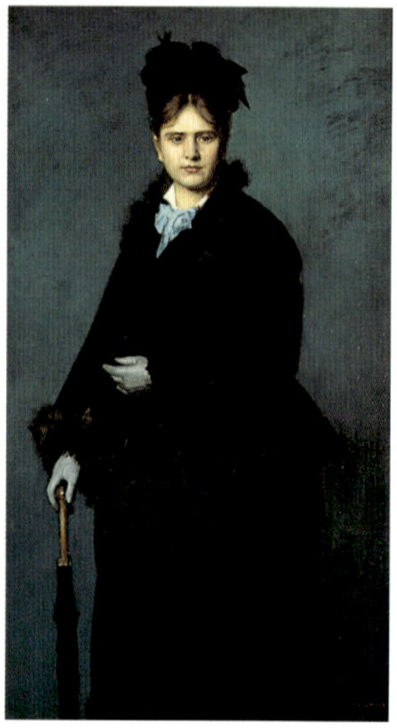

parisienne, caught with an umbrella, reverts to being a mere woman, despite the splendour of her clothes: 'A pretty woman with an umbrella is like a verse that doesn't rhyme.'[46]

If Henner's portrait was a great success and the umbrella made it famous, it was also because it perpetuated a vision of the woman who believed, like the gentle Mme Gonse in the portrait by Ingres, 'that clothing should be decent, not provocative, and that it is impossible for decency to wear the same costume as scandal'.[47]

The portrait redefined

The *Portrait de Madame Valtesse de la Bigne* is evidence that an entire new 'class' of society – that of high-class courtesan – had attained the status of portrait sitters at the same time as they were playing a more active role in fashion.

However, the model for painters in the last quarter of the century was *Woman holding a glove* by Carolus-Duran (1869,Paris, Musée d'Orsay), the archetypal portrait of the *parisienne*. In Giron's *The parisienne* its influence is direct. The composition is the same: a woman in a black dress against a neutral background decorated with an arabesque. This painting by Carolus-Duran is symptomatic of the way the portrait was evolving towards the genre scene. The artist's wife, Pauline Croizette, loses a part of her identity to become an expression of 'elegance'. In this work, according to Paul Mantz, 'a note in the history of the feminine ideal' has displaced the expression of character as the artist's primary concern:[48] 'The portrait of Mme D. by Carolus-Duran has no depth. It's a wholly outward portrayal of the surface, a study of a dress, or rather of an elegant pose.'[49]

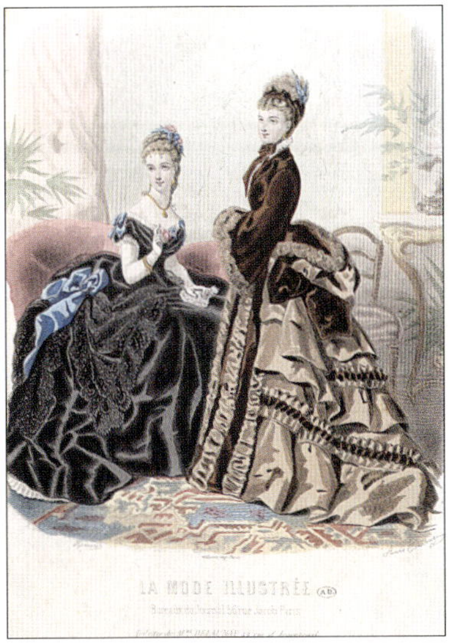

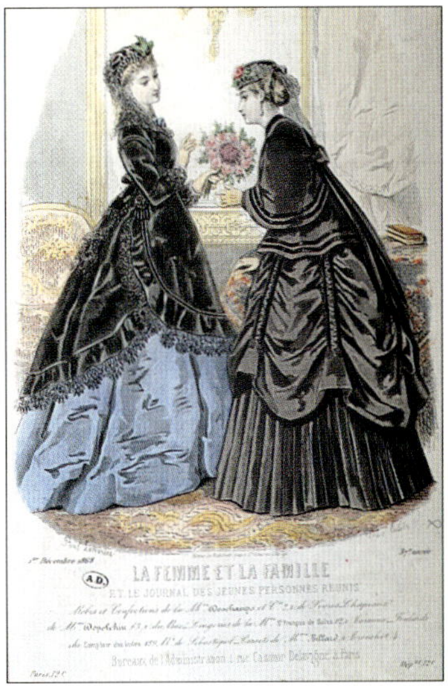

La Mode illustrée, *1874 (left).*

La Femme et la famille, *1 December 1868 (right).*

The portrait shows a woman taking off her gloves in a moment which seems suspended in time. What the public appreciated was the sense of luxurious idleness, the enjoyment of appearances, a new relationship in which seduction was more direct and more open. We know that the glove has had an emblematic significance, from the scandalous pair of gloves in *Les Demoiselles des bords de la Seine*, to Rita Hayworth's glove in *Gilda*.

This new type of portrait had shocked some critics, who were alarmed by the mixing of genres.

> Before M. Carolus-Duran, everyone in France was agreed in believing that the portrait was something interior, intimate, private. Women had themselves painted for their husbands, their children...
>
> M. Carolus-Duran has changed all that. Portraits used to be painted for the inside; now they are painted for the outside, for the street. They used to show discreet, reserved poses – he has turned them into a noisy advertisement... Never has the human element, the cast of features, the thought, been more heedlessly sacrificed to mere clothing.[50]

These portraits of the parisienne show the individual being replaced by the abstract. Artists no longer painted a woman but a human type, a quality. The portrait began to resemble the 'fashion prints' of Stevens or Toulmouche. From this point of view the collection 'Parisian women in pictures', which appeared in *Panorama* in 1895, is revealing: grouped under themes – dress, husbands, betrayals, *soirées* and theatre performances – the evocations of 'feminine grace' are illustrated with works by Deveria, Stevens, Gervex, Béraud, Degas, Manet and Gavarni.[51]

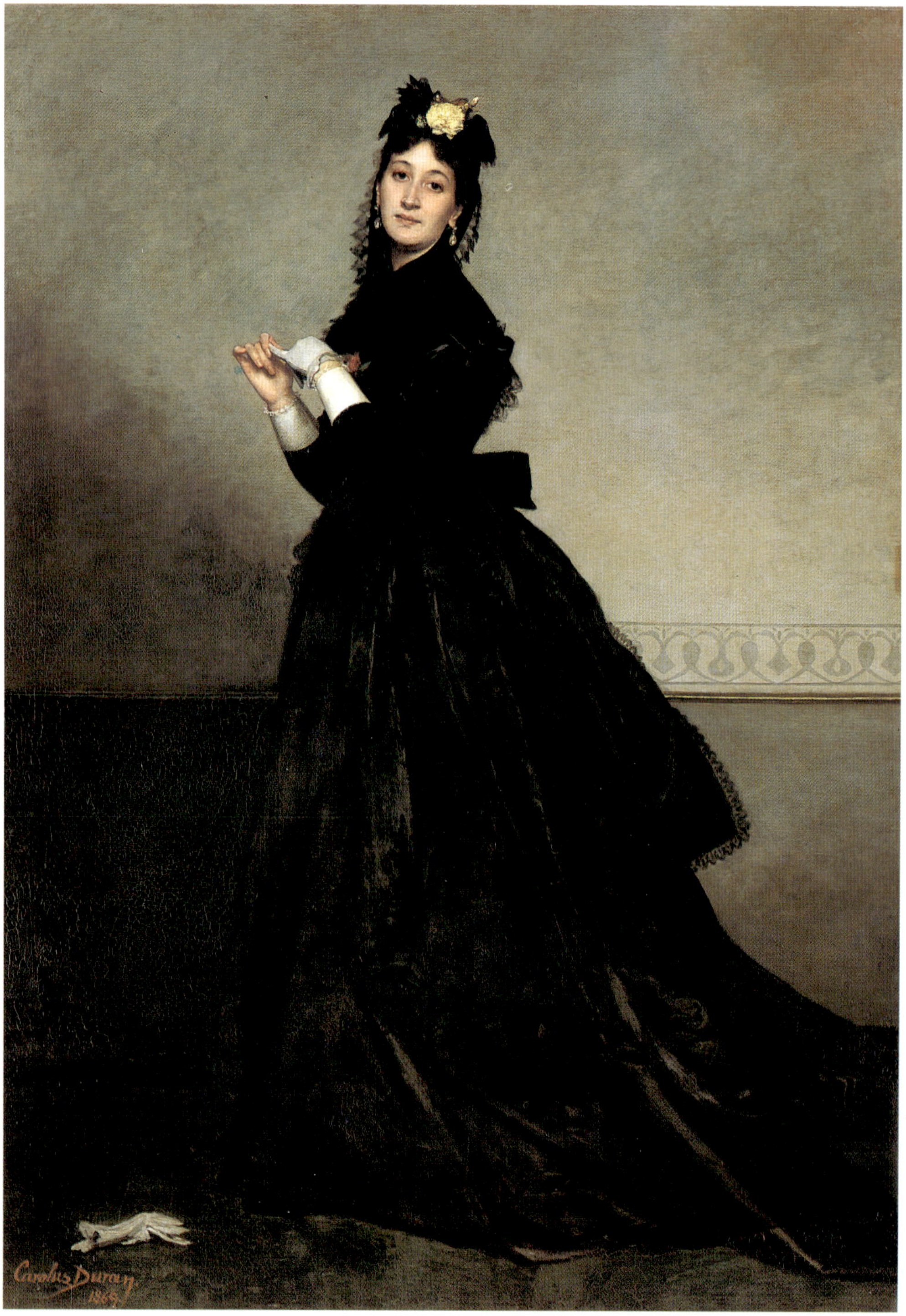

Carolus-Duran, Woman holding a glove, *1869. Musée d'Orsay, Paris.*

Fashion (fashion prints, clothes and accessories) was a material used by painters to create a mirror reflecting a world of heightened luxury. It was a 'lark mirror', a snare, in which the public came to admire itself as if it were trying to escape a reality which was too banal, dreary and industrious. These pictures enable us to distinguish different aspects of fashion's importance for modernity.

Modern painters and 'couturier-painters'

Against the 'couturier painter'

Twenty years after Baudelaire, Huysmans noted that the poet's definition of the 'painter of modern life' had been seriously misconstrued by painters: 'No, the painter is not just an excellent "couturier", like most of those, regrettably, who wrap a mannequin in various silks in the name of modernity.'[52] In his view, painters who thought they were being modern in painting pictures 'which Worth would have painted had he had an artist's temperament', were on entirely the wrong track. He opens the debate on the relation between fashion and modernity with some remarks by Fromentin.

> I shall never be persuaded that a woman reading a letter in a blue dress, a lady looking at a fan in a pink dress, a girl raising her eyes to heaven to see if is going to rain in a white dress, represent interesting aspects of modern life...Ten photos in an album will give me the full quota of modernity contained in such paintings, the more so as the lady and the girl are not taken from 'real life' but are brought to the studio for a hundred sous a session, to wear the above-mentioned dresses and to represent modern life.[53]

These painters, Huysmans argued, liked fashion too much. They thought it saved them the trouble of searching for the 'heroism of modern life'. They mistook the outward envelope for the contents. By removing it from its context and from its support, they had perverted it, emptied it of meaning. Fashion, he said, emanates from an individual, her habits, her feelings. It is impossible to cheat: to dress a tart as a society woman is as incongruous as to clothe a statue from antiquity in nineteenth-century costume.

Only the Impressionists – among whom Huysmans included Pissarro, Monet, Sisley, Morisot, Guillaumin, Cézanne, and the 'independents', Degas, Cassatt, Raffaëlli, Caillebotte and Zandomeneghi, to whom we should add Renoir (who adopted and abandoned the Impressionist formula by turns) and Manet (who was the head of the movement) – only they understood the correspondence between dress and social class. In their works 'a tart is a tart and a society woman is a society woman'.[54]

Fashion and morals

Manet's *Street singer* (1862, Boston, Museum of Fine Arts) provokes a similar comment from a journalist: 'Doesn't his street singer make you feel pity, mingled with a slight apprehension? For under this dress with its loops her underclothes are shabby and drab, poor girl! She must be wearing bulky, elastic-sided boots – men's boots'.[55]

The young woman's elegance has often been noted: her paletot is trimmed all round in black and the details are carefully done–collar, little round pockets and sleeves with cuffs. We are far from the wretchedness captured by Gavarni, but the dark tone, the soft folds, the simplicity of the dress embellished only with a small flounce on the sleeves, lifted up over a greyish-white petticoat, do give the impression of a shabby, much-worn garment.

The source of this painting was a scene witnessed by Manet in the rue Guyot. Struck by the singer's appearance as she emerged from a seedy cabaret, 'lifting her dress and clutching her guitar', Manet asked her to come and pose for him. She refused and Victorine Meurent took her place. Her face echoes her dress. Critics were shocked by the effect of pallor, with the eyes and eyebrows as dark punctuation marks. Nevertheless, Manet succeeds in capturing both the absent-mindedness in her face, due to extreme fatigue, and a certain determination in her sadness which reveals her true nobility. The 'heightening' seen in her dress is applied until it 'reveals the soul', until elegance is entirely extinguished by wear. One could say the same of Manet here as Huysmans says of Degas: 'He was one of the first to explore feminine elegance among the populace.'

In a life-size format Manet seeks only to express the truth of an individual and of an everyday scene, without sentimentality and without engaging in social realism. This was his modernity, which critics found so disturbing.

In 1866 *Woman with a parrot* (New York, Metropolitan Museum of Art) appeared as a kind of pendant to the *Street singer*. Victorine is in much the same pose, but this time is wearing an indoor garment, a pink peignoir with a simple V-neck, decorated with six buttons. She has the black velvet ribbon from Olympia around her neck. Here, too, we find the same rejection of preconceived ideas. Pink does not have the qualities with which it is generally associated: gentleness, purity, virginity. It is 'false and louche',[56] and critics once again excoriated the painting. However, this work does belong to a pictorial tradition, and is less novel than the *Street singer*. Under the July Monarchy, the peignoir was often shown in popular prints,[57] and the woman with a parrot was a common subject for engravings and photographs. In the second half of the nineteenth century the peignoir was part of the wardrobe of the 'couturier-painters' (Stevens, Toulmouche, Tissot), but was far less commonly found in that of portrait painters. Nevertheless, Winterhalter painted a woman in a *déshabillé* twice in 1864: *Empress Elizabeth of Austria* (location unknown) and *Madame Rimsky-Korsakov*

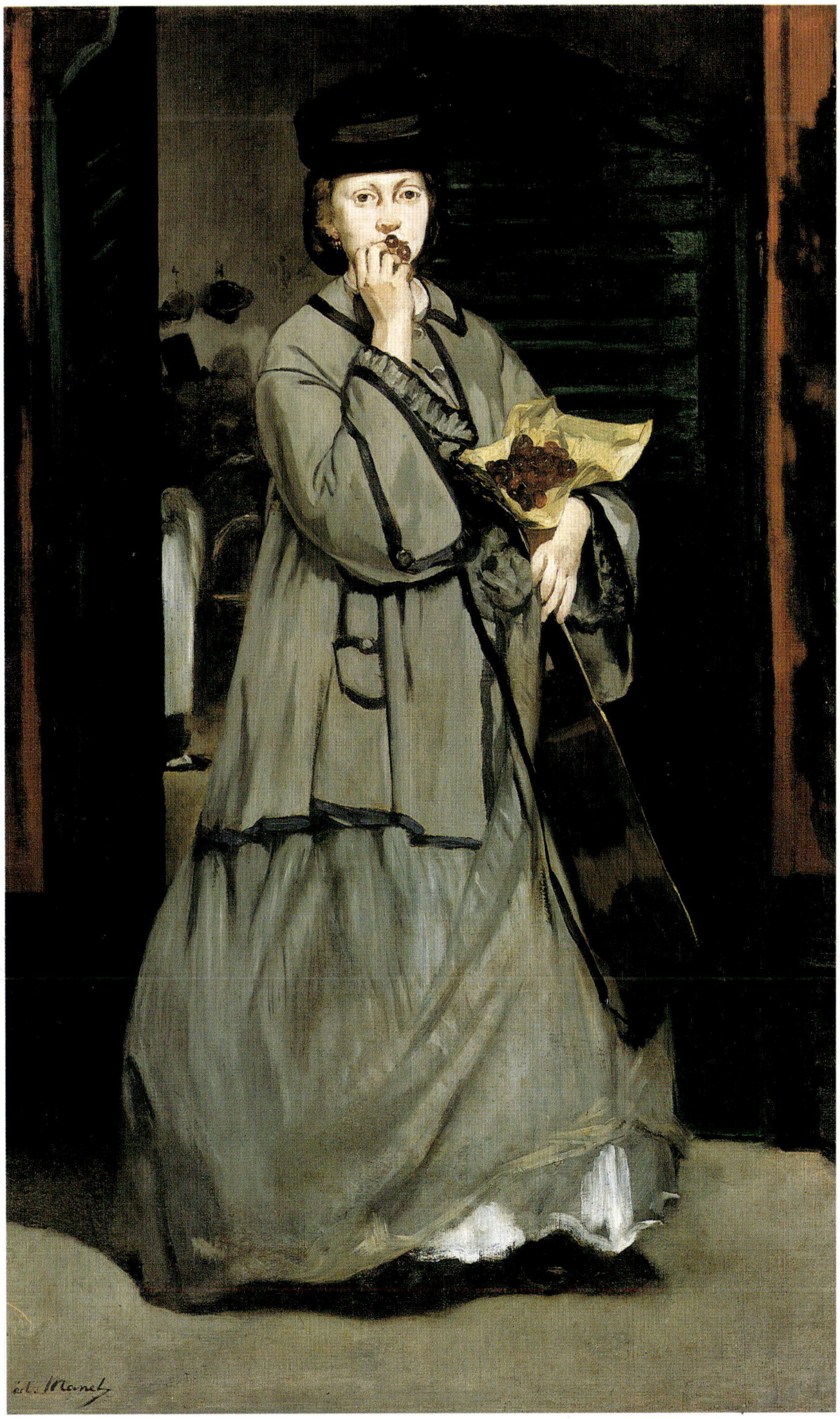

Edouard Manet, Street singer, *1862. Museum of Fine Arts, Boston.*

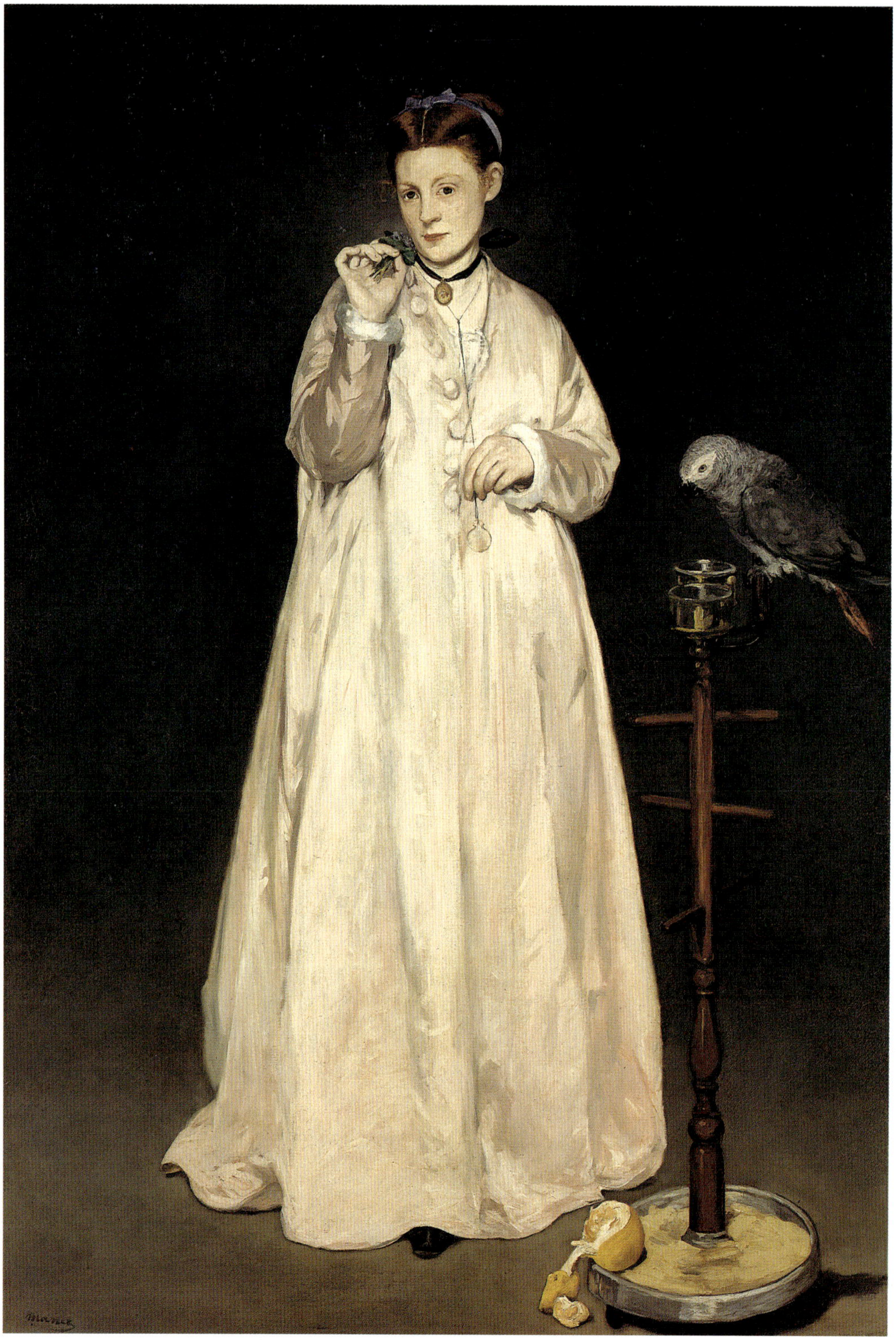

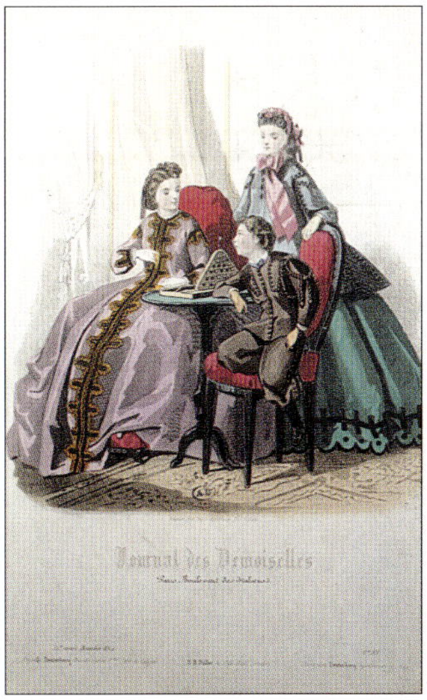

Edouard Manet, Woman with a parrot, *1866. The Metropolitan Museum of Art, New York. (facing page).*

Le Journal des demoiselles, *peignoir, December 1864 (left).*

La Mode illustrée, *1868 (right).*

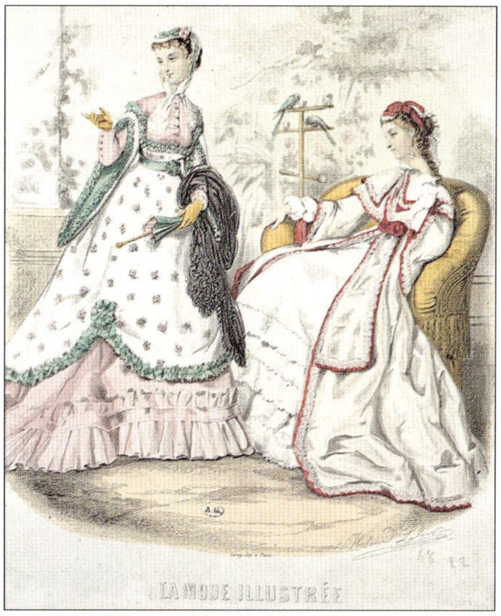

(Paris, Musée d'Orsay). The term *déshabillé* referred to a garment worn at home, alone or possibly with intimate friends, which combined several different elements: the peignoir, which could be quite simple, in the same style as those in Degas and Manet, and the *matinée*, a sumptuous garment worn with a corset, just like an indoor dress.

Madame Rimsky-Korsakov's dress has elements of both the latter. Very luxurious, embellished with ribbons and lace, made of delicate muslin and worn over a crinoline, it is as far removed from Victorine's peignoir as a ball gown is from a town dress. It can be compared, rather, to those found in Tissot (*The staircase*, 1869, private collection) and in Stevens (c.1865, *Woman in pink*, Brussels, Musées Royaux des Beaux Arts, or *The farewell note*, 1867–8, Paris, Musée d'Orsay).

To have one's portrait painted with untidy hair and wearing a *négligé* slipping from the shoulders certainly showed considerable audacity, but that was in keeping with the person in question. Mme Rimsky-Korsakov, a famous St Petersburg beauty, had fled to Paris with her lover, an officer of the horse-guards, after the Emperor Alxander II had refused to grant her a divorce. In France her eccentricities caused a sensation (she appeared disguised as Salammbo at various balls, and took the waters at Biarritz). Her choice of this garment for her portrait was doubtless another of the eccentricities of one who was said to be inordinately proud of her figure.[58]

A comparison of the paintings by Winterhalter and Manet shows how different their treatment of clothing is. It is clear that Victorine and Mme Rimsky-Korsakov come from two worlds which are diametrically opposed. Whereas Winterhalter declines to exploit the audacity of the *déshabillé*, Manet does not abandon the modernity of his pictorial technique in trying to convey elegance of fashion. In his work the correspondence between the girl and her dress is complete in its raw truth.

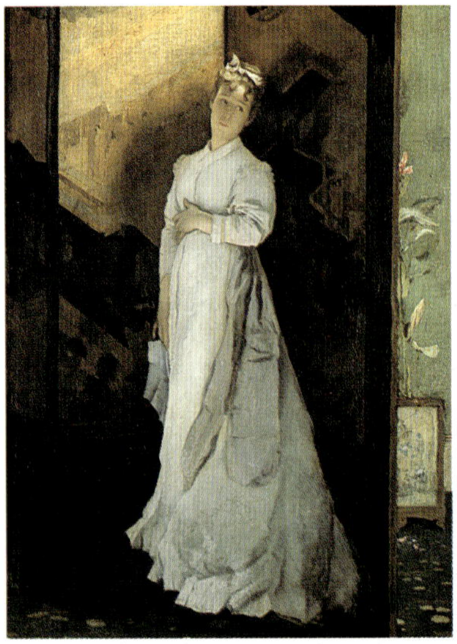

Alfred Stevens,
The farewell note,
c.1867. Musée d'Orsay, Paris (left).

La Vie parisienne:
'The peignoir', February 1875 (right).

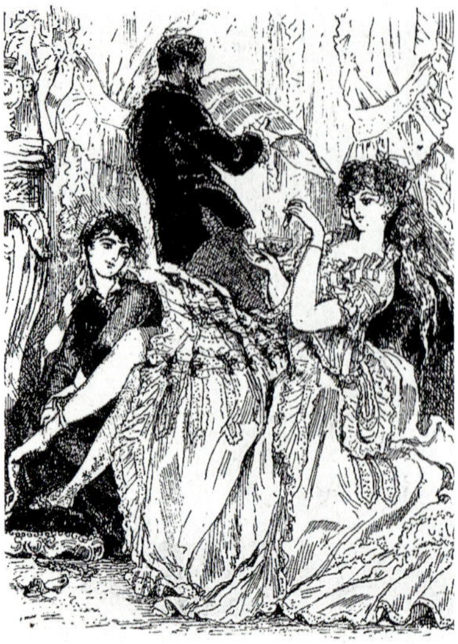

Victorine Meurent's personality was an obstacle to the representation of 'high life'. Manet therefore turned to Berthe Morisot and her friends when he painted *The balcony* (1868–9, Paris, Musée d'Orsay). This scene from modern life is full of contradictions which baffled even the most well-disposed. The most flagrant was the way in which a contemporary scene had been painted 'from life', seen and re-transcribed in the manner of Constantin Guys's sketches in Spain – which may have inspired Manet – in contrast to the artificial manner of a studio composition. The amusing contrast between the dresses of Berthe Morisot and Fanny Claus reveals the same ambiguity. Berthe Morisot has a white dress made of a kind of transparent striped organdie, with pagoda sleeves. This dress, which is very similar to Mme Manet's in *La lecture* (Paris, Musée d'Orsay, 1865–c.1873), is very probably an indoor dress, whereas Fanny Claus is in a town costume with the inevitable parasol and a small flat hat worn high on the forehead, in keeping with the 'latest fashion', and gloves. 'One of them is seated and seems to have simply placed herself so that she can enjoy the spectacle of the street; the other is putting on her gloves as if she were going out. These contradictory attitudes baffle me.'[59]

Manet had chosen the two dresses himself, as he had the blue cravat of Antoine Guillemet. The most extraordinary thing is that Fanny Claus's dress is short (ankle-length). At that time and up to the beginning of the present century, a short dress was very modern. Ten years after *The balcony* a debate about the use of the short dress was still being carried on in the Press. It is extremely uncommon to find one in a nineteenth-century painting, and it appears that there were no other portraits of women in short promenade costumes in France. Manet is a precursor in this, as he

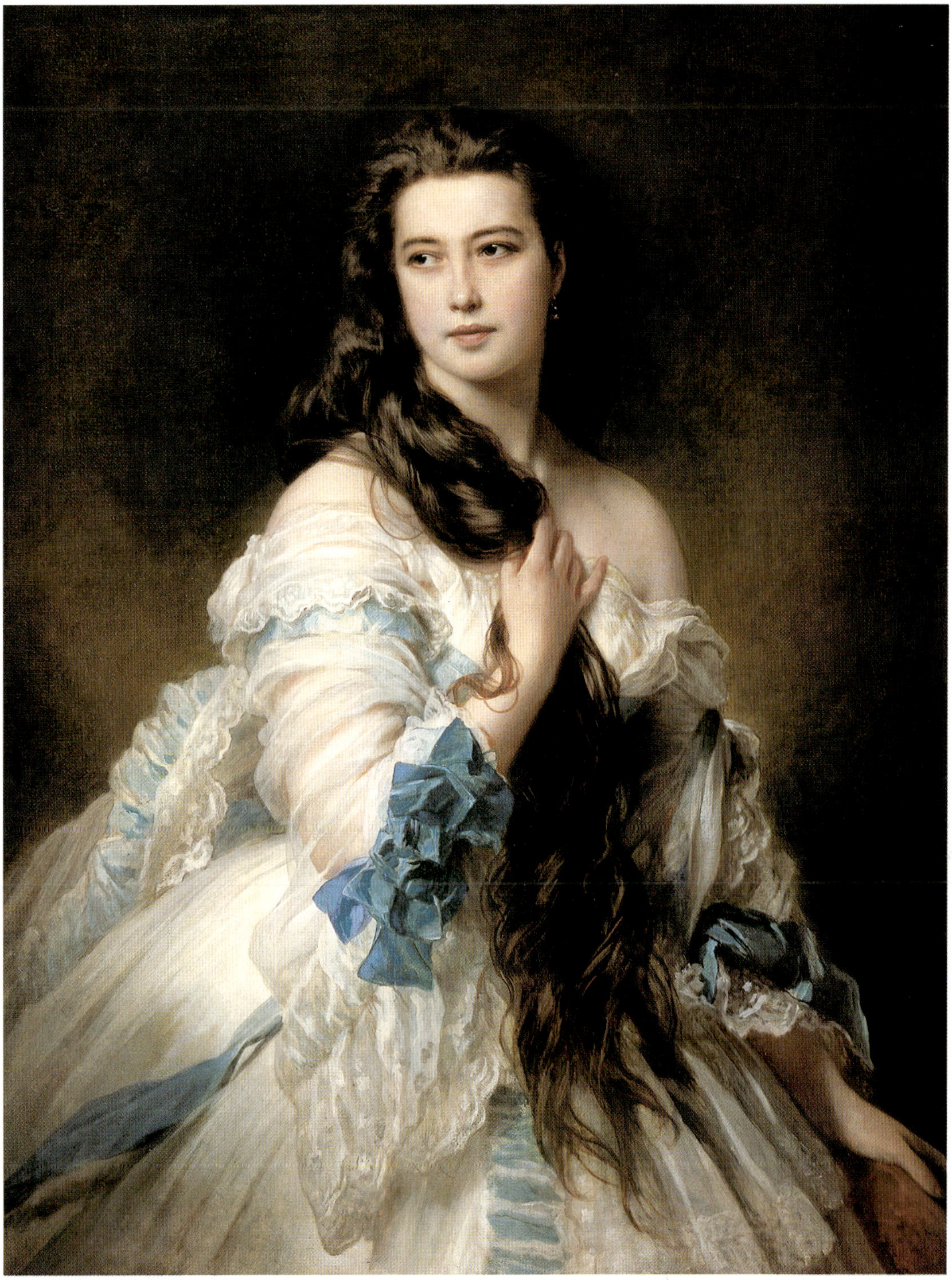

Franz-Xaver Winterhalter, Madame Rimsky-Korsakov, *1864. Musée d'Orsay, Paris.*

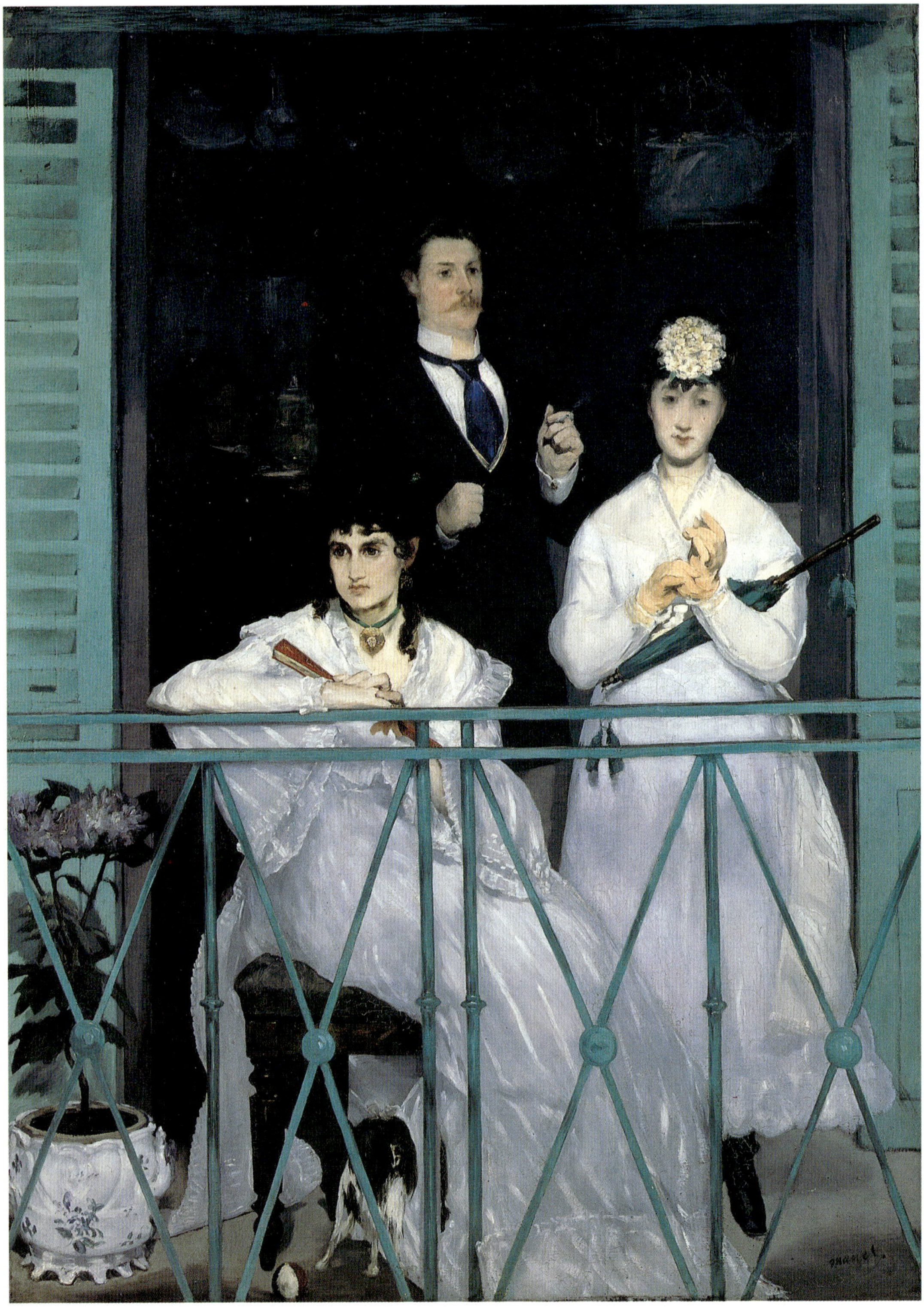

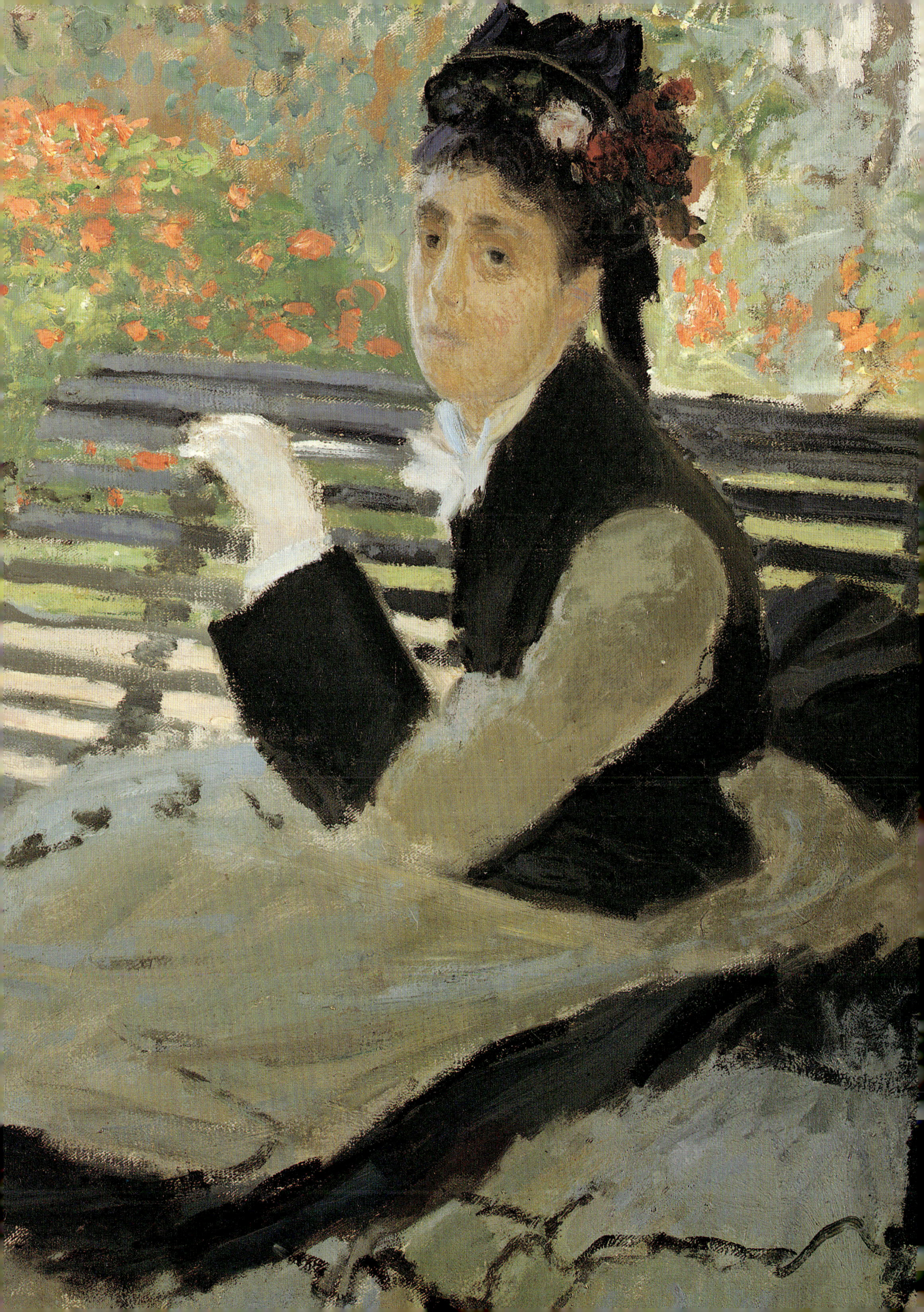

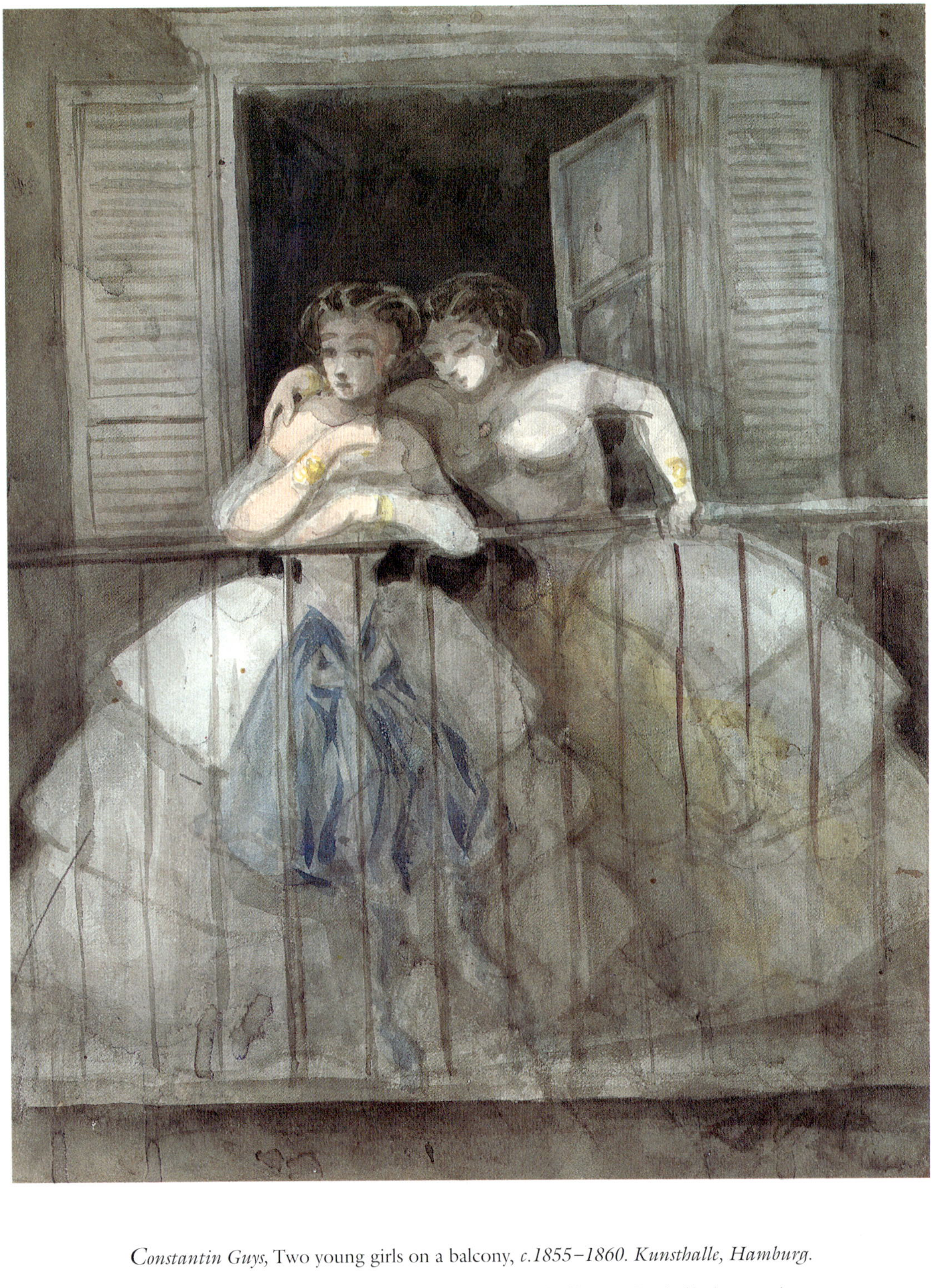

Constantin Guys, Two young girls on a balcony, *c.1855–1860. Kunsthalle, Hamburg.*

Edouard Manet, The balcony, *c.1868–1869. Musée d'Orsay, Paris (facing page).*

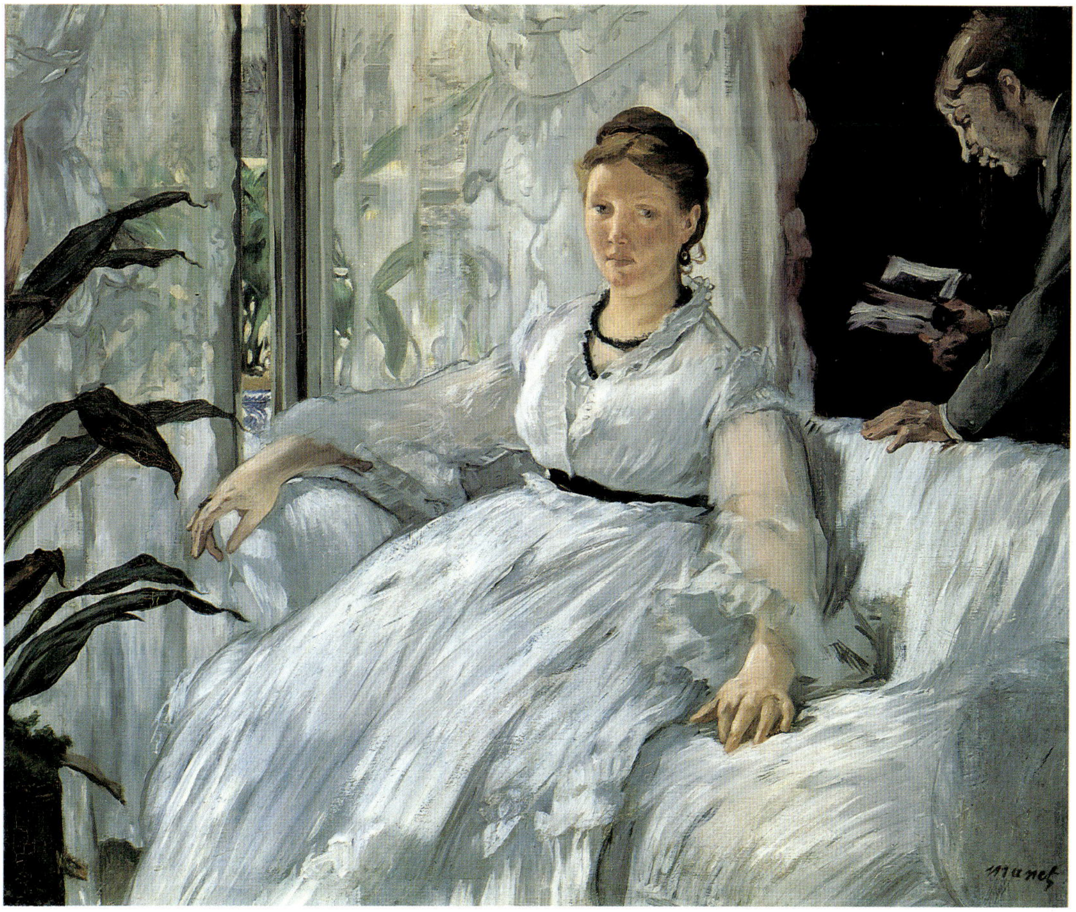

Edouard Manet, La lecture, *1868. Musée d'Orsay, Paris.*

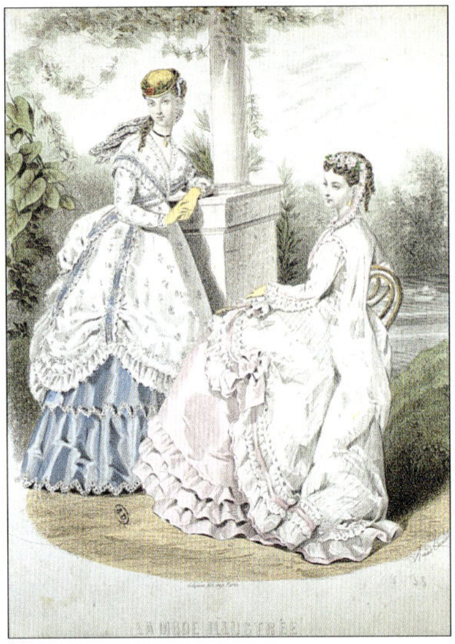

La Mode illustrée, *1868 (left)*.

La Femme et la famille, *1 July 1869 (right)*.

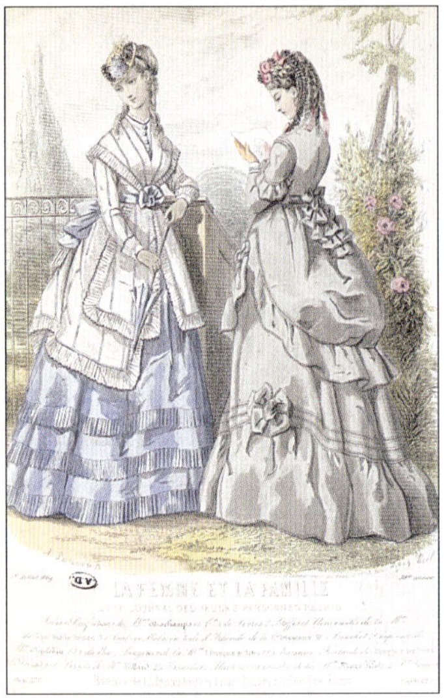

showed such skirts as early as 1867, in *The Exposition Universelle of 1867* (Oslo, Nasjonalgalleriet). It was precisely on account of the fatigue caused by long visits to the exhibition that the fashion press hotly defended the short dress that year.

'Plein-air' painters and the promenade costume

In 1859–60 Degas had the idea of painting 'a portrait of a lady with her hat on, ready to go out and putting on her gloves',[60] as one of his notebooks reveals. This implies the audacious paradox of posing his model in an attitude – 'ready to go out' – which contradicts the essence of the pose: immobility. In 1863 he had painted his sister Thérèse (*Thérèse de Gas, the artist's sister*, Paris, Musée d'Orsay) with a shawl bordered with black lace and a hat in fashion in the years 1860-65: a small bonnet showing the top of the head and decorated with flowers, with a pink taffeta bavolet held by a superb bow under the chin – the hat worn by all women out of doors. Degas turns it into a very subtle still life, prefiguring a whole series of works under the title *Chez la modiste.*

The same Thérèse posed six years later in a yellow summer dress trimmed in black, this time with her hat in her hand: *Madame Edmond Morbilli, née Thérèse de Gas* (1869, pastel, New York, Private collection). But she is still indoors, like the models in *The balcony*, and the presence of her hat is somewhat surprising, even if we suppose she is going out.

Degas took this paradox further in *Madame Jeantaud in front of a mirror* (c.1875, Paris, Musée d'Orsay). Madame Jeantaud is in town costume, with a dolman over her shoulders, and wearing a hat and a muff. She seems to be caught at the moment just

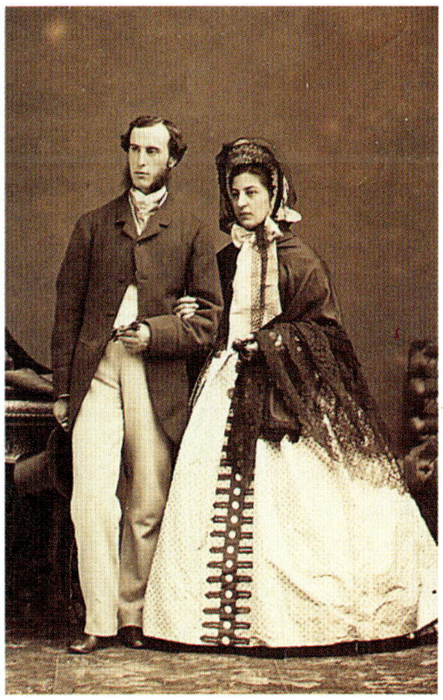

Disdéri,
Monsieur and Madame Scaramanga, *1863. Musée d'Orsay Paris (left).*

Les Modes parisiennes, *20 June 1863 (right).*

Edgar Degas,
Portrait of Thérèse de Gas, the artist's sister, *1863. Musée d'Orsay, Paris (facing page).*

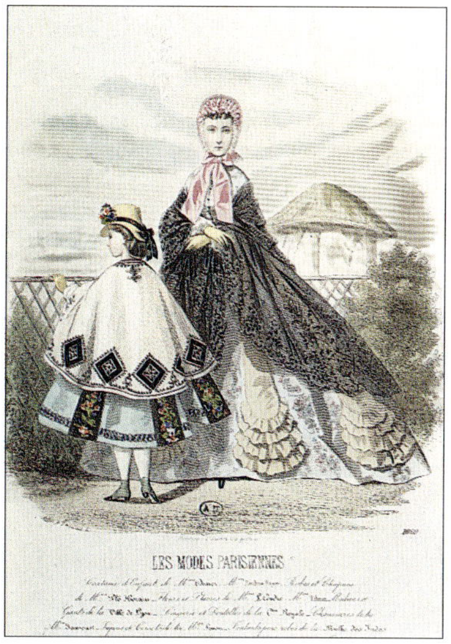

before going out, taking a last 'verifying' glance into the mirror. She is in profile, half-length; her reflection is static, while she herself seems to be moving; indeed, her reflection seems like her portrait. Through this artifice Degas completely renews the genre: the imperative of the pose is abolished and the beholder has the impression that the model is submissive before his gaze. As soon as he turns away, the model will have gone out.

By playing with the woman and her double in this way Degas destroys the uniqueness of the portrait: the reflection is no longer a means of completing the definition of an individual, but of showing a different image, another aspect of the person.[61] The parallel with the portrait of the same woman, by Henner, also painted in 1875, *Madame Jeantaud* (Paris, Musée du Petit Palais), shows the gulf between two aesthetic conceptions. Here too, however, Mme Jeantaud is wearing a town costume very close to that of Degas, but against a uniform background, with nothing connecting her to life.

In fact, Degas is not interested in the model in herself. What he loves is this moment suspended in time when the woman is concentrating all her attention on an image of herself that she is composing, when she is immersed in this search for perfection. One may think of the 'Baudelairean idol' who 'must gild herself to be adored', and of the beauty of a gesture both timeless and ephemeral, the act of looking into a mirror.

Chez la modiste (1882, New York, Metropolitan Museum of Art), in which a woman admires the effect of a hat before a full-length mirror, is part of the same search. In a whole series of pastels on this theme Degas shows clients and working-class women without discrimination. He told Mme Strauss, whom he often

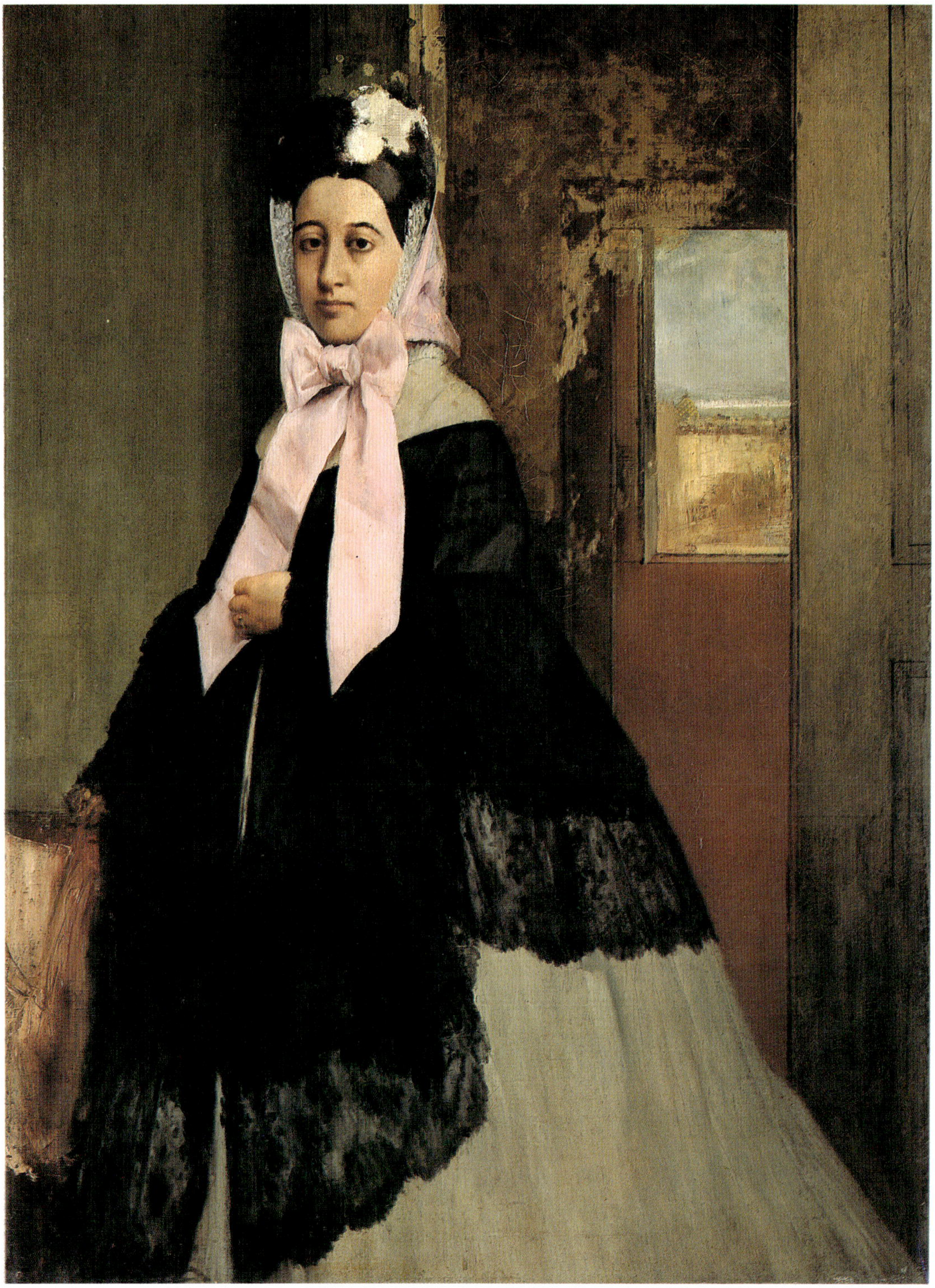

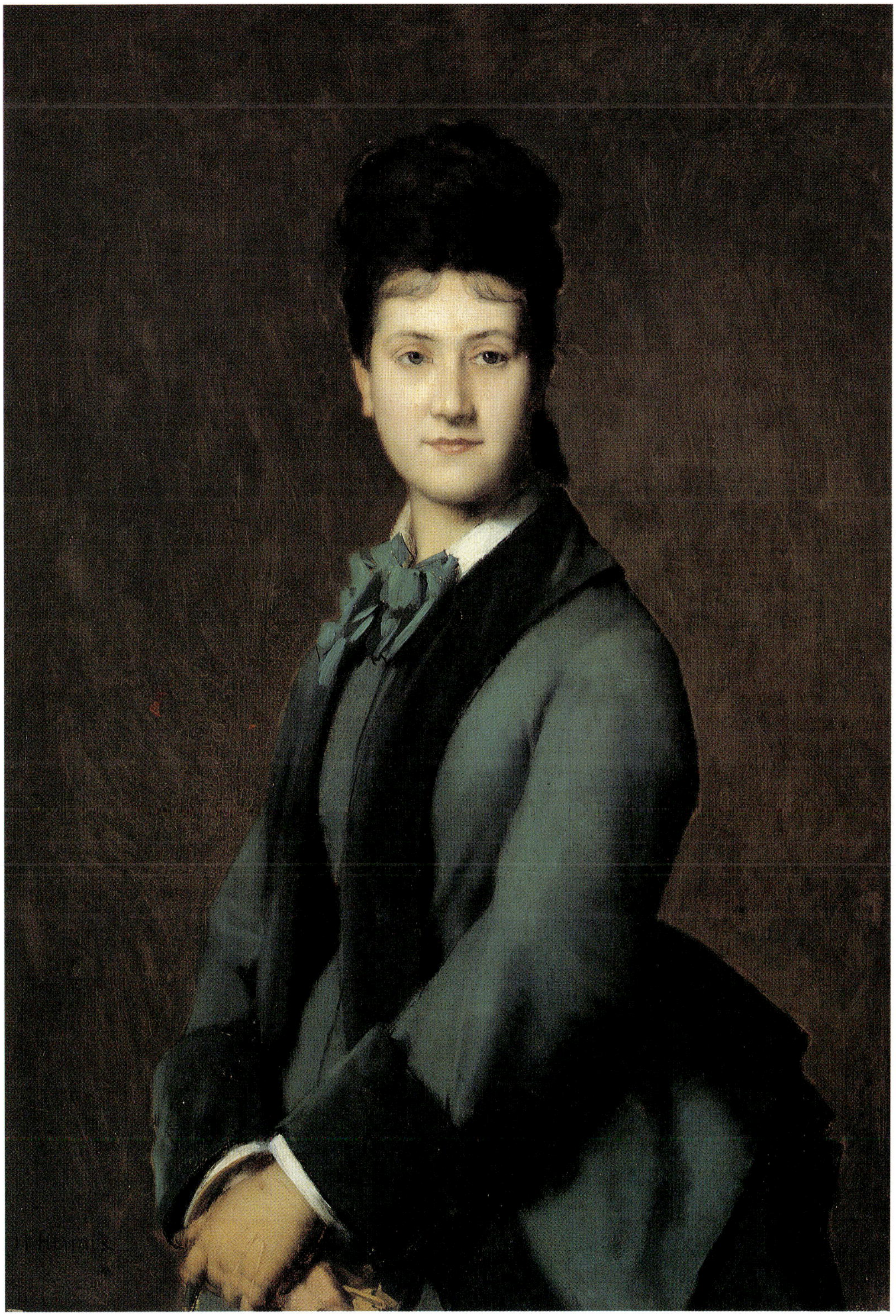

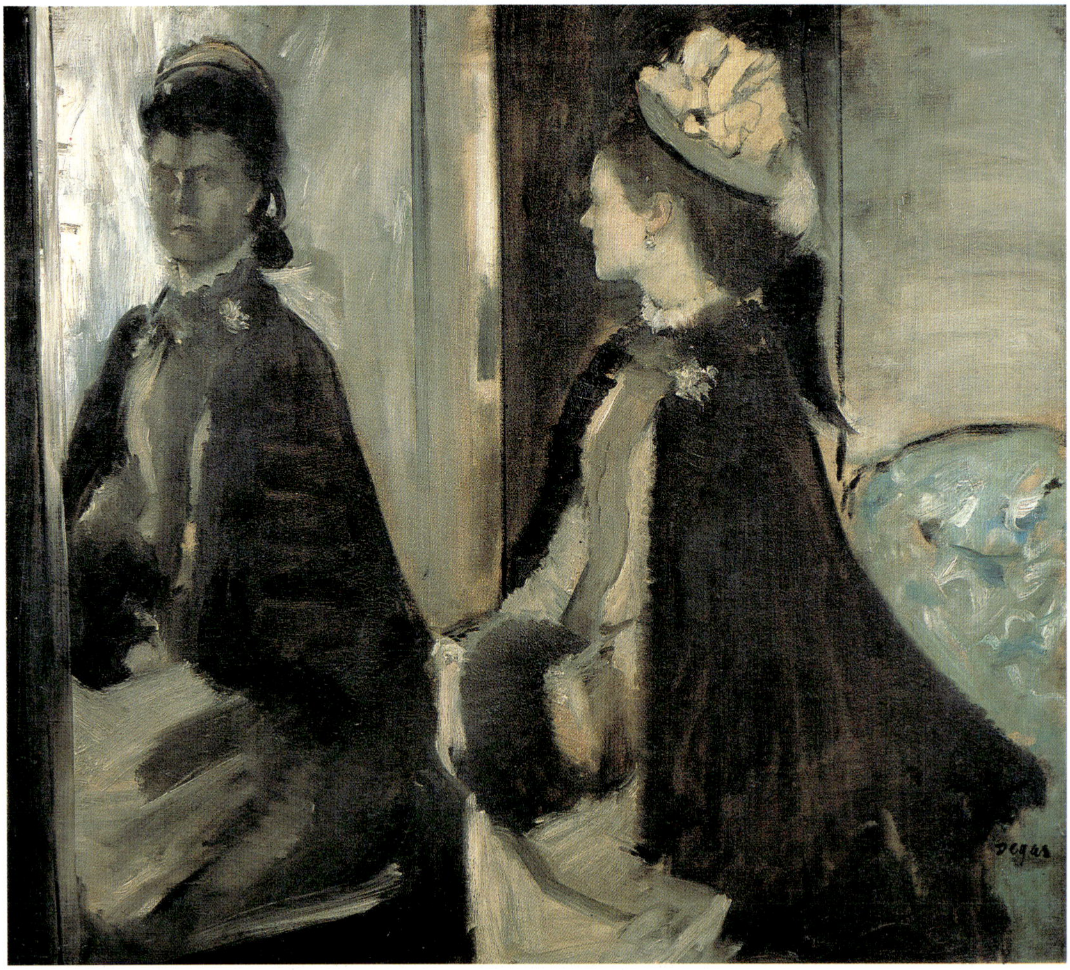

Edgar Degas, Madame Jeantaud in front of a mirror, *c.1875. Musée d'Orsay, Paris.*

Jean-Jacques Henner, Madame Jeantaud, *1875. Musée du Petit Palais, Paris (facing page).*

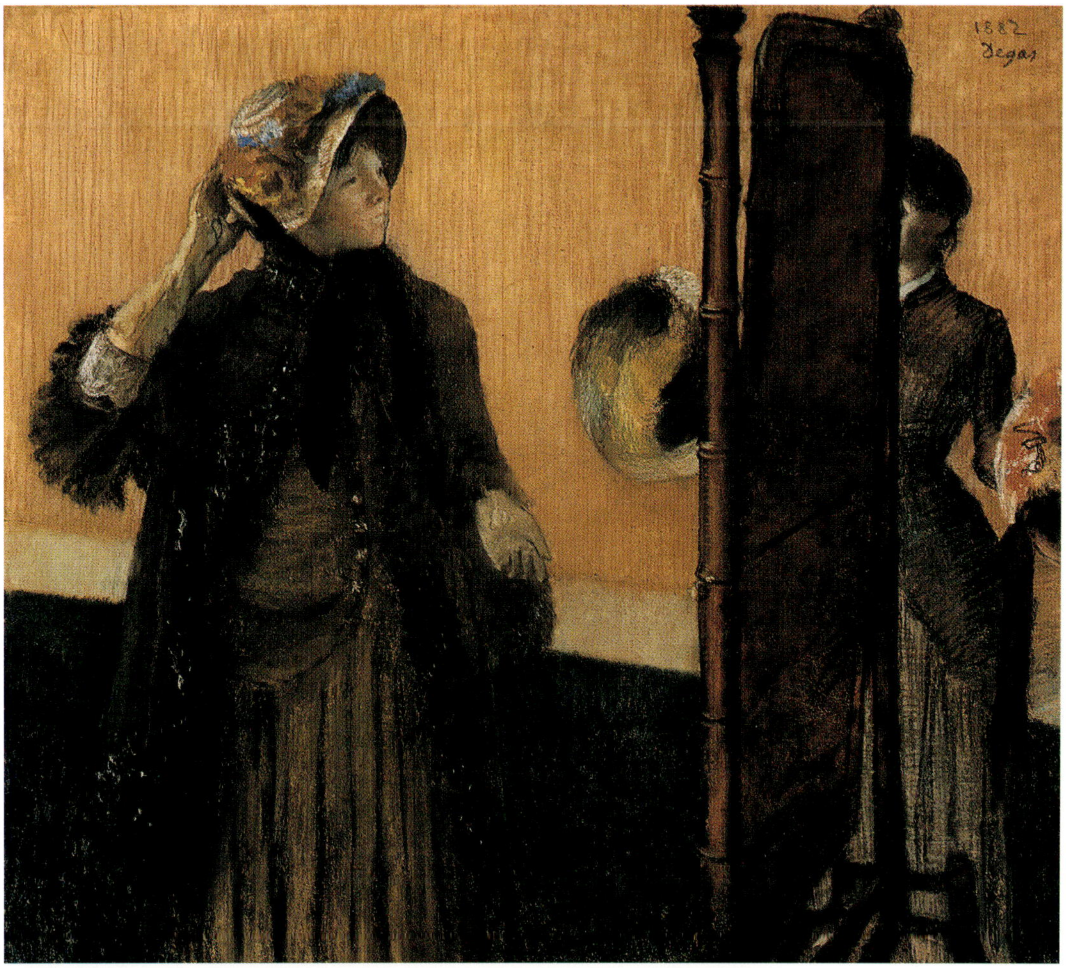

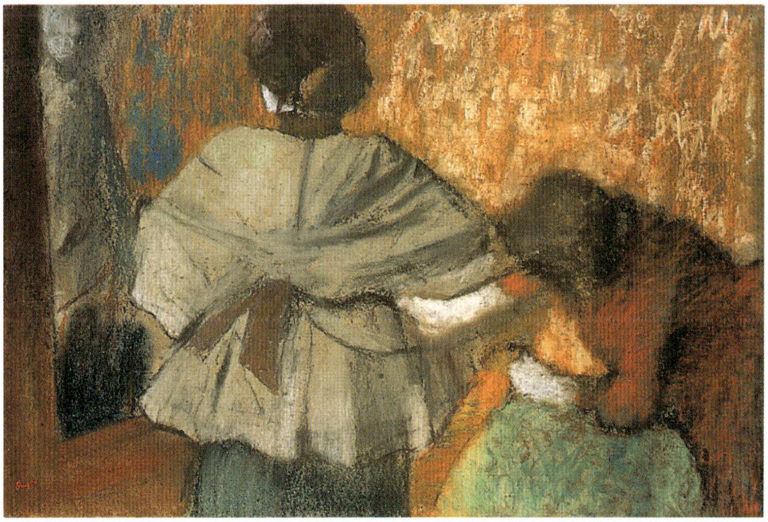

Edgar Degas,
Chez la modiste, *1882.*
The Metropolitan Museum of Art, New York (above).

Edgar Degas,
Chez la couturière,
c.1882 (left).

accompanied to her *modiste* or her couturière, that he liked these fitting sessions because of 'the red hands of the little girl holding the pins'.[62] What he shows of fashion is the world beyond the shop-window – the laborious making of a hat, the mechanical action of the laundresses as they iron, the scene as the fitting is prepared. In all these preludes to elegance he finds a kind of repertory of attitudes that are individual, intimate and true. Fashion, like dancing, instils movements which have something of mimicry, a feminine choreography made up of studies reworked over and over again, attitudes suspended in mid-gesture, in which the natural vies with the artificial: the whole hidden face of ostentation. This is what passionately excites the painter. Unlike his contemporaries, he does not use fashion as a means of depicting elegance, of conveying that abstract film of distinction and chic which enveloped the *parisienne*. On the contrary, he uses it to dissect human reality. Fashion is a pretext, not an end in itself.

We can gauge the whole distance separating him from Stevens, for example, by comparing the portrait of Mme Jeantaud with *Departure for the promenade* (1859, Philadelphia Museum of Art). In the latter work, too, the woman is in a promenade costume: her hand on the door, ready to leave, she turns towards her dog; but Stevens's preoccupations are quite different. He wants to paint a picture in which the woman is as elegant as a fashion print (she is even in a room furnished in the eighteenth-century style, as in a print), and in which attention is caught by the details, the accessories, especially the white poodle.

In 1873 Monet also chose a town costume for his mysterious portrait of *Camille on a bench*, or *The bench* (New York, Metropolitan Museum of Art, Annenberg Collection). Camille is very elegantly dressed in a grey-green and black dress, closely resembling one which was shown in *La Mode illustrée* of spring 1873. It is possible to see it as a mourning dress, since the black velvet was in keeping with the rules of etiquette. Half-mourning was worn by a daughter in the second half of the year of her father's death.

Camille's father had died in September 1873. By showing his model out of doors, not in a natural scene *à la* Chaplin or *à la* Winterhalter, but in a park with flower borders and sitting on a public bench, and by surrounding her with two figures (a man behind the bench, a woman in the distance), Monet satisfies Duranty's requirement that the subject should be seen in the context of her daily life. But if he thereby combines the preoccupations of Degas and Manet, Monet seems to be hesitating between a portrait, an anecdote (the presence of the man in black is very enigmatic) and even a landscape. At any rate, this is not an outdoor scene of the kind that might have been painted by Tissot (*The garden bench* 1882, private collection, painted from photo-graphs); for although, like him, Monet aims to paint an elegant scene, he does not abandon the rapid brushstroke. Neither, however, is this a portrait like Manet's *In*

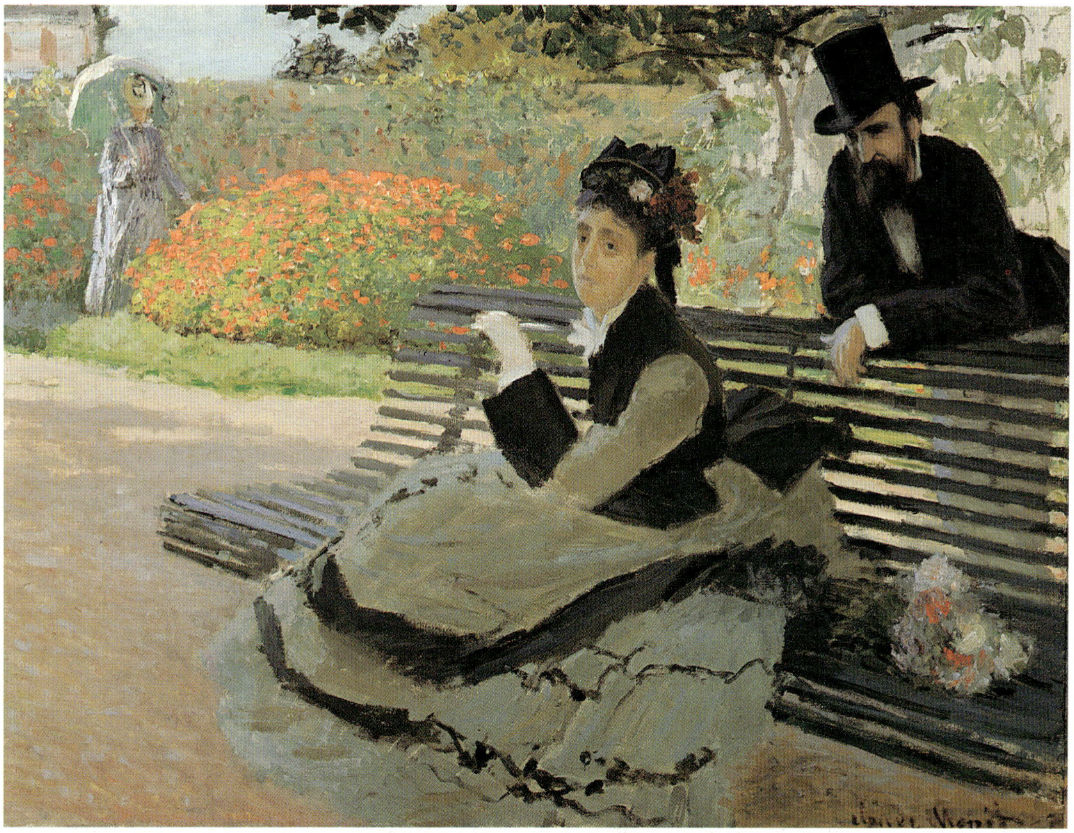

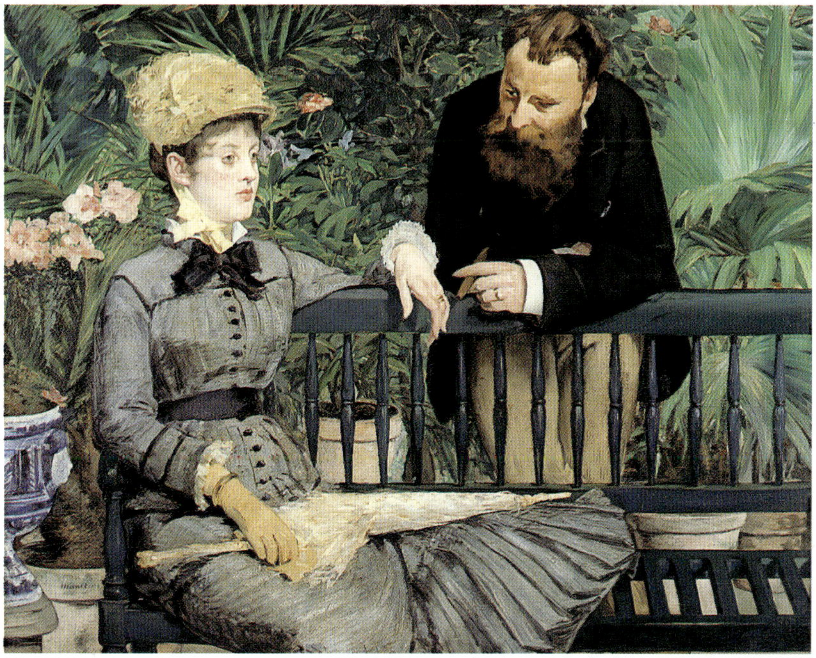

Claude Monet,
Camille on a bench
or The bench, *1873.*
The Metropolitan Museum of Art, New York (above and detail, facing page).

Edouard Manet,
In the conservatory,
1879. Staatliche Museen Preussischer Kulturbesitz, Nationalgalerie, Berlin (left, and detail, overleaf).

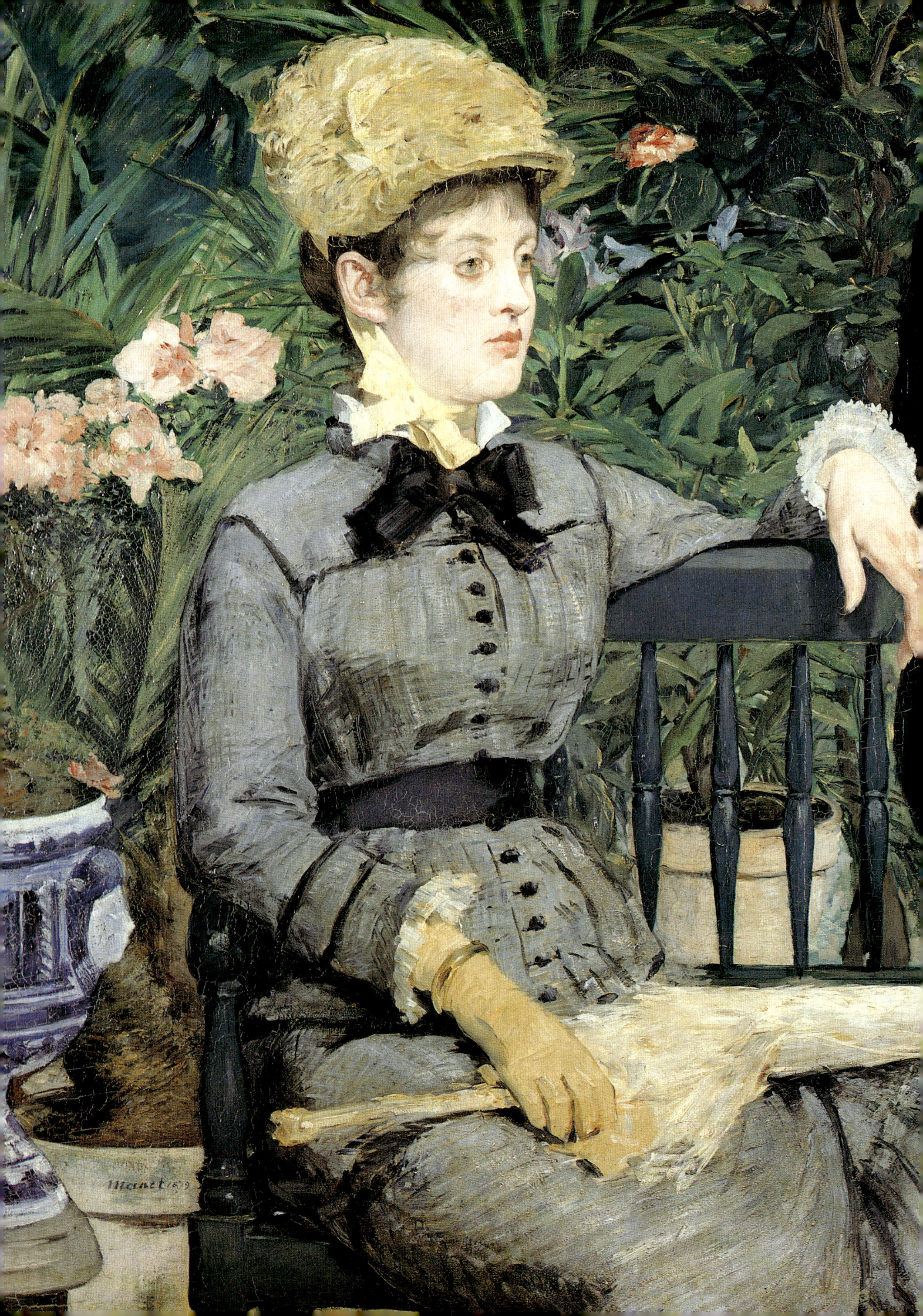
Manet 1879

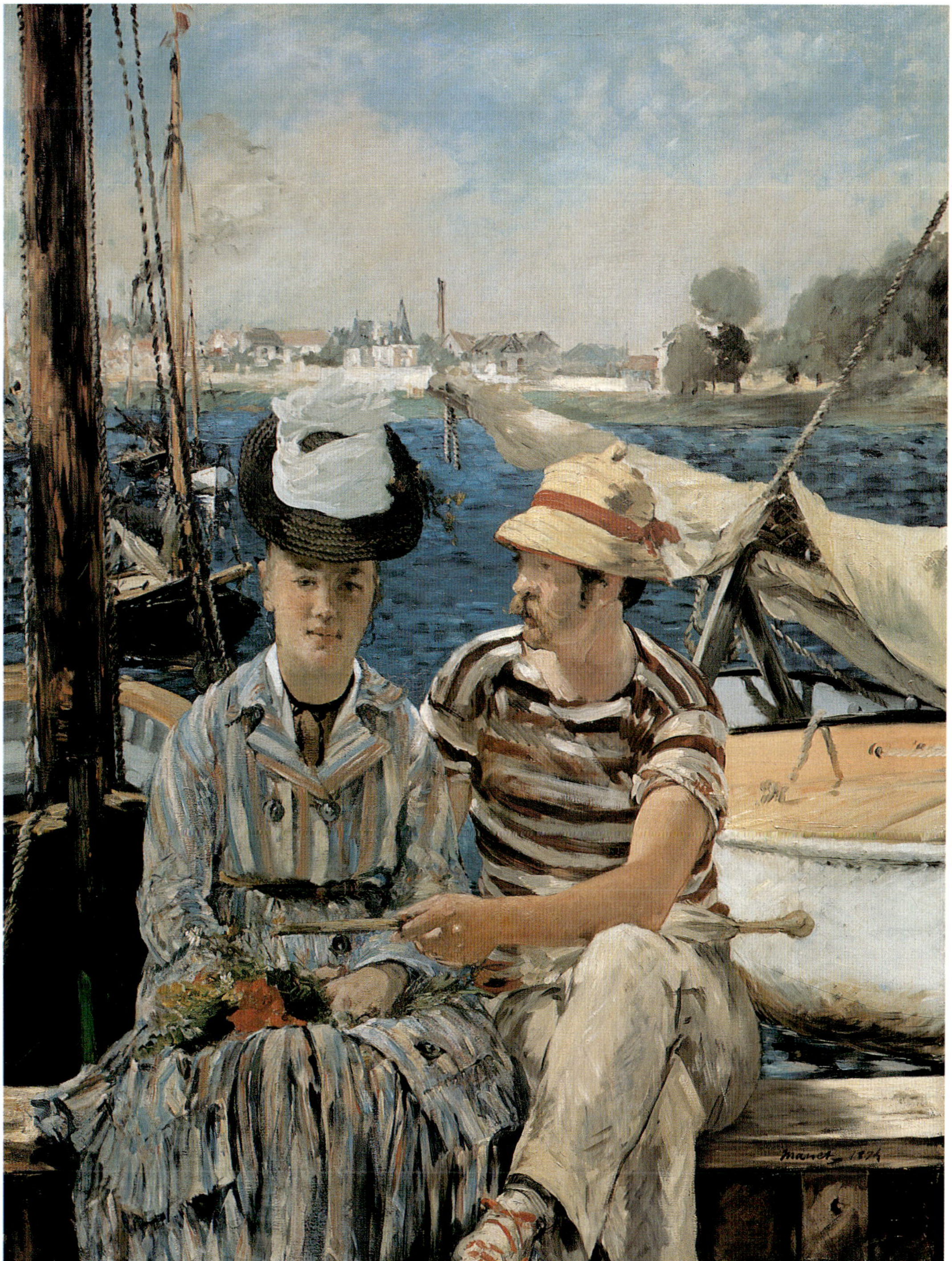

Edouard Manet, Argenteuil, *1974. Musée des Beaux-Arts, Tournai.*

the conservatory (1879, Berlin, Staatliche Museen Preussischer Kulturbesitz, Nationalgalerie). That portrait of M. and Mme Jules Guillemet shows the same concern for elegance: Mme Guillemet's costume is highly tasteful, in exactly the same spirit as in a print in *La Mode artistique*. How could it have been otherwise for a woman who was proprietor of a fashion magazine? The framework is just as modern as Monet's garden at Argenteuil (the conservatory was a typical architectural product of the nineteenth century), but the relationship between the two people is much more natural and apparent.

Huysmans applauded the painting: 'It is a very attractive modern work, a battle joined and won against the cliché of sunlight which is never observed in nature.'[63] We feel that Manet has taken pleasure in punctuating his composition with the yellow patches of the gloves, the parasol and the hat (just as he had done with the green accessories in *The balcony*); and the pleats and darts of the cotton dress, 'done with broad strokes', are like an echo of the Japanese-style grille of the bench. Manet was often criticized for showing materials empty of bodies, and here too critics spoke of an 'empty lobster'. These ideas may reveal indirectly that the painter was interested in clothing as a 'surface' before seeing it as a volume – or was it just a protest against the ubiquitous academic nude?

In *Argenteuil* (1874, Tournai, Musée des Beaux-Arts), Manet had also related the structure of his composition (the horizontals and verticals of the boats) to the clothes of the two people: the striped jersey of the man and the vertical stripes on the dress. This time, perhaps under Monet's influence, the scene is truly *al fresco*. The painting attracted the usual sarcasm: the intense blue of the sea was much criticized, but so was the couple's triviality, especially the apathy of the woman. Théodore Duret enlightens us on the boating manners faithfully transcribed by Manet: 'The oarsmen came from different social groups, but the women they brought with them were undistinguished women of pleasure.'[64] Once again, Manet is concerned to show a face without expression, as he had done so often with Victorine Meurent. His model here seems like the spiritual daughter of Victorine (who had also bequeathed to him her little black velvet bow). The stripes on the dress and the clear-cut shape of the jacket and the tailored collar add a certain extravagance to the effect of the painting, a vividness which heightens the apathy of the face. 'Bright as this person's costume may be, her expression is insignificant and blank...'.[65]

The Impressionists and the intimist dress

By painting life in this 'unemphatic' way, the Impressionists were renewing the portrait in a different sense: no longer being subject to the social conventions of the Salon, they very often painted close relations, producing portraits which were far more intimist.

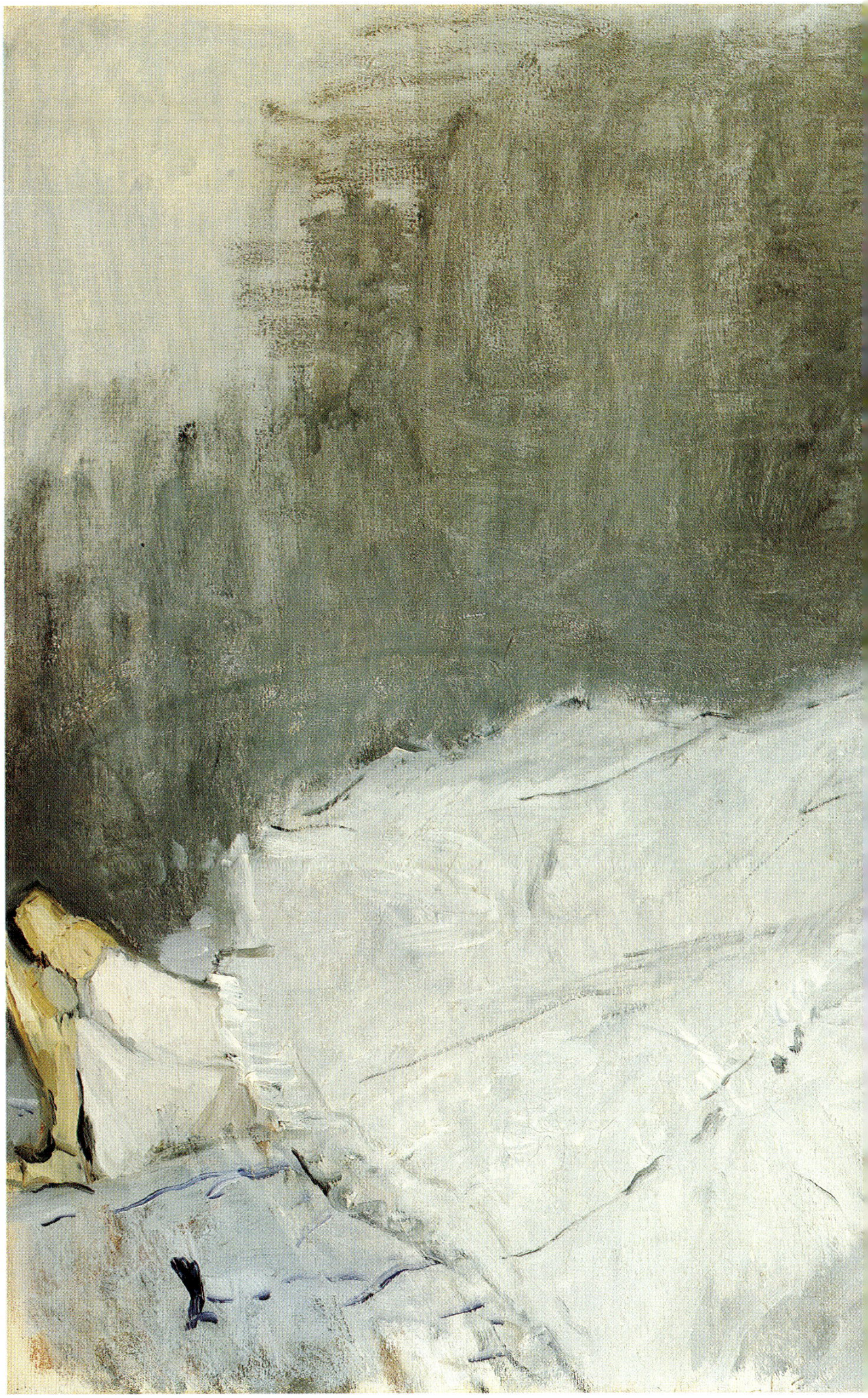

Berthe Morisot,
Madame Hubbard, *1874.*
Ordrupgaardsamlingen,
Copenhagen.

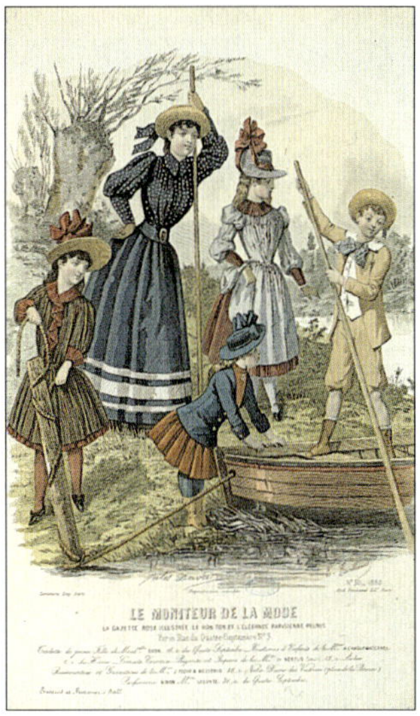

Le Moniteur de la mode, *1888* *(left)*.

Le Follet, *1876* *(right)*.

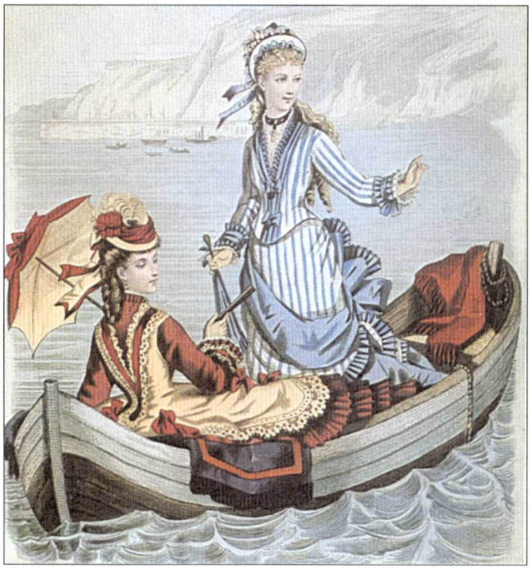

Perhaps influenced by Manet's *Rest* (a portrait of Berthe Morisot on a sofa, 1870, Providence, Museum of Art, Rhode Island School of Design), depictions of reclining women are found frequently in Monet, Renoir, Mary Cassatt and Berthe Morisot. The laxness of such a pose was seen as morally improper and far too free at the time. Nevertheless, the dividing line between the Salon and the Independents was not clear-cut: Clairin's *Portrait of Sarah Bernhardt* (1876, Paris, Musée du Petit Palais) and that of *Mademoiselle de Lancey* by Carolus-Duran (1876, Paris, Musée du Petit Palais) are of two women reclining on couches. The critique of the latter is revealing: 'His recumbent woman is a thousand times less at ease than if she had been standing up, for one does not put on a white satin dress in order to muse on a sofa...We feel that her corset is causing her discomfort. Why does she not go off to the ball?'[66] Unlike the situation in Clairin's portrait, where the actress is wearing a peignoir, Mlle de Lancey's dress is not congruent with her pose. Carolus-Duran was undoubtedly seeking to emulate Boucher (*Madame Boucher*, New York, Frick Collection) rather than modernity.

According to Bernard Dorival, Manet had been inspired by a lithograph by Gavarni (*The siesta*, 1835) in *The rest*, just as the Portrait of Jeanne Duval, Baudelaire's mistress, of 1862, had its source in a drawing by the same lithographer, the *Portrait of Madame Ancelot*, illustrating the article 'Une Femme à la mode' in *Les Français peints par eux-mêmes*.[67] In this way Manet turned to the two modern heroes of Gautier and Baudelaire respectively, Gavarni and Guys, in creating some of his portraits (including *The balcony*, as we have seen). Curiously, in neither of these portraits does Manet show a perfect mastery of the pose, the postures being marred by a certain stiffness, even clumsiness. But perhaps this was a way of avoiding the simpering coquettishness hitherto associated with the *grandes horizontales* (as the high-class courtesans were

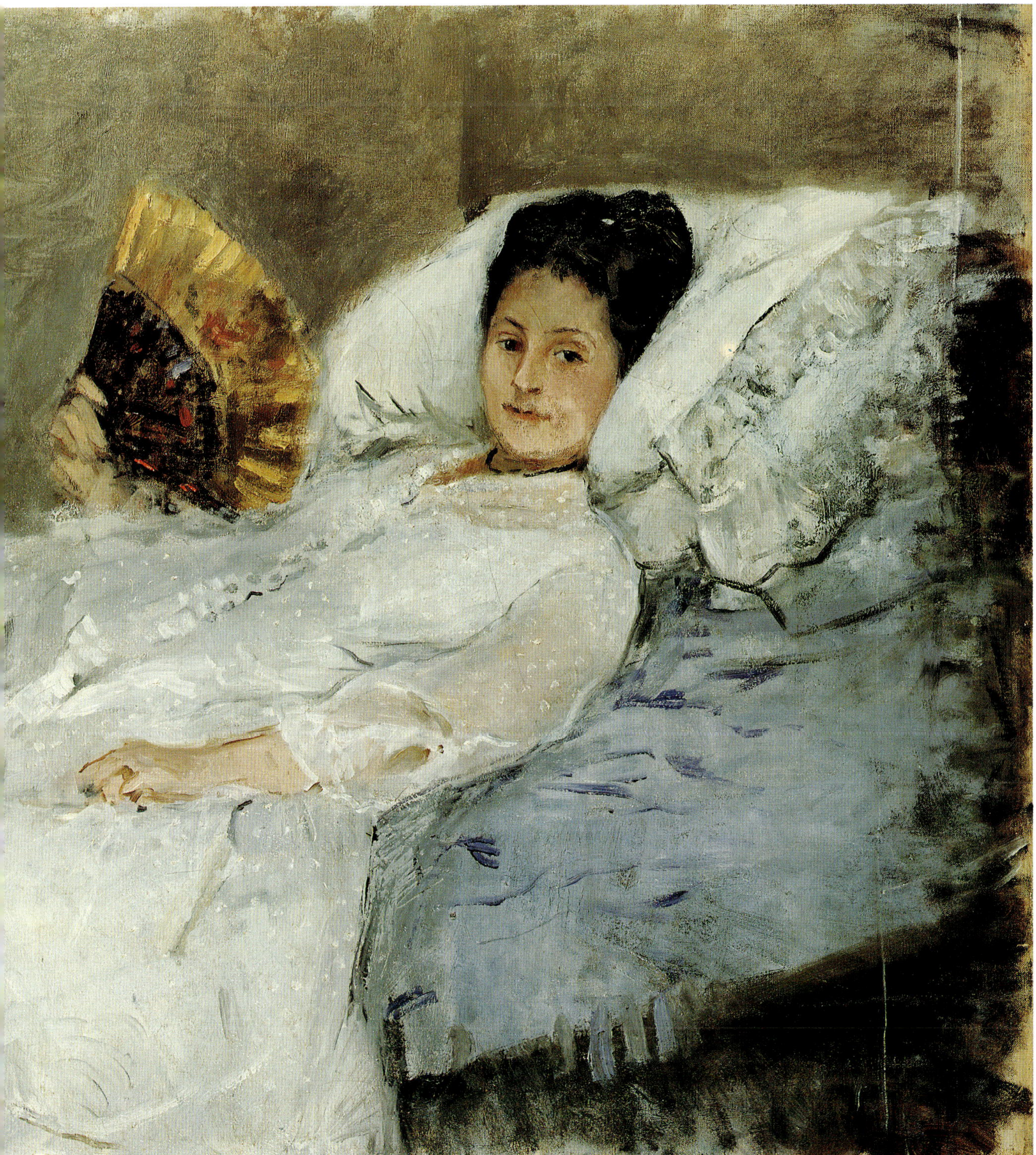

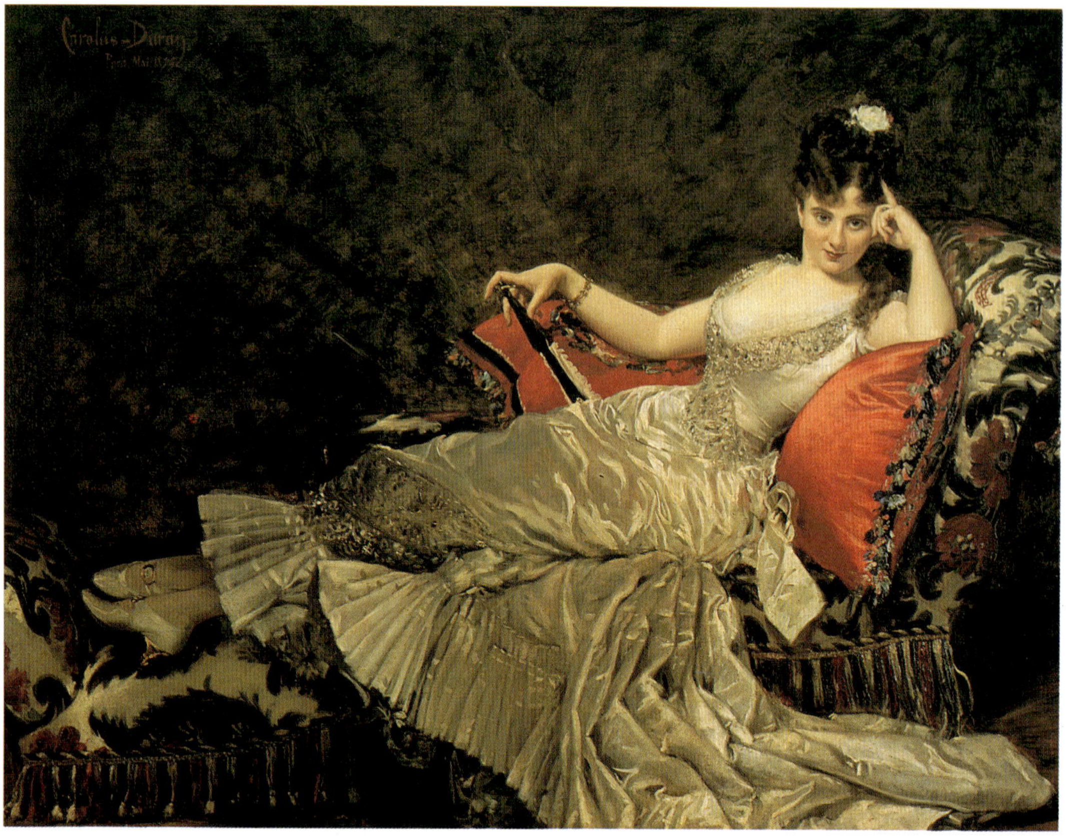

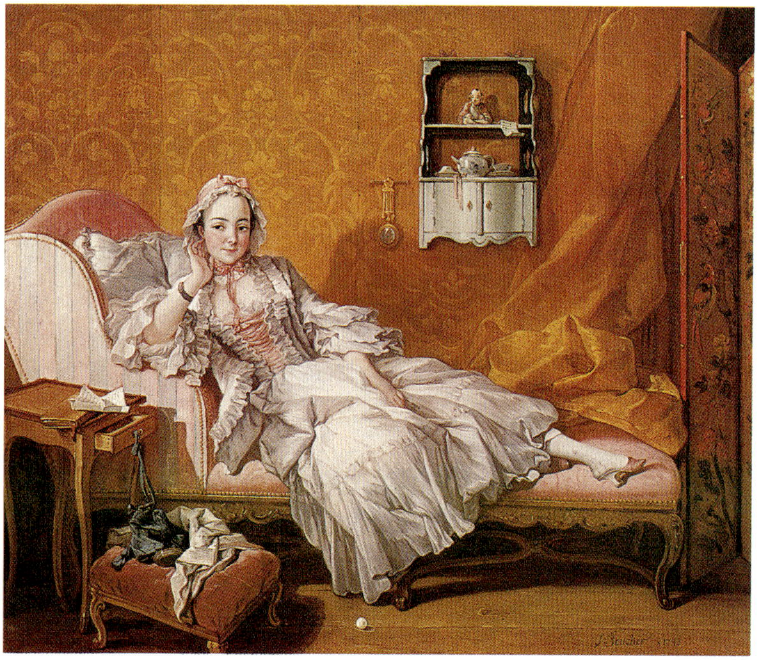

Carolus-Duran, Mademoiselle de Lancey, *1876. Musée du Petit Palais, Paris (above).*

François Boucher, Madame Boucher, *1743. Frick Collection, New York (left).*

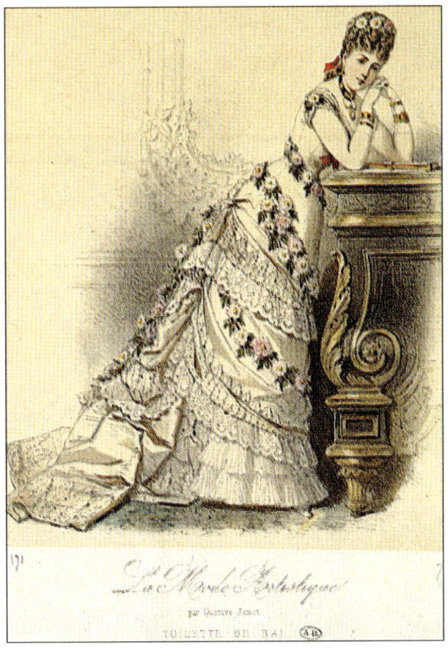

La Mode artistique: *Ball-gown, 1876* *(left).*

La Mode artistique, *no date* *(right).*

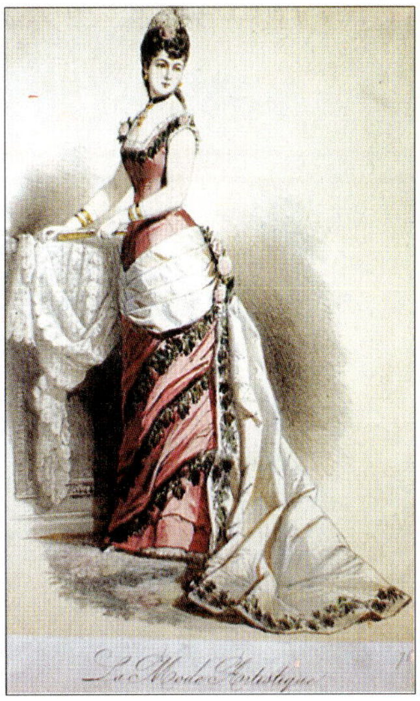

called). Apart from that, with her leg folded beneath her simple white dress, Berthe Morisot seems like the emblem of the modern young woman.

Portraits by the Impressionists often have this freedom; the women become autonomous while the pose is effaced; the momentary vision triumphs, but at the same stroke the portrait disappears. It becomes the image of a silhouette, resembling in this the 'portraits of costumes' by the second-generation society painters. In these silhouettes, rendering of the dress is never avoided but is done, above all, through the play of light. This is undoubtedly one of the reasons why the Impressionists did not use dark colours – aubergine, garnet, pine green – although these were much in vogue in the 1880s. It may also explain a fact which at first sight seems strange. These revolutionary painters never depicted the most modern clothes – those which, like their painting, provoked scandal or at least disapproval: sporting costumes like the tailored suit and the pantaloon. Nor were they interested in another of the symbols of modern life, despite its dazzling, picturesque quality: the great store.[68] If we exclude Degas – although even his paintings contain only allusive descriptions of *modistes*' interiors – the consumerist eye can admire only *The shopgirl* by James Tissot (Toronto, Art Gallery of Ontario, in the series *Women in Paris*, 1883–5), and the *Shop window of the couturier Doucet* (1889, private collection) by Jean Béraud. It was Felix Vallotton's extraordinary triptych *Le Bon Marché* (1898, Switzerland, private collection) which finally penetrated these temples of fashion.

We can now measure the full extent of fashion's paradoxical role. Praised as the key to a new art, its repertoire of subjects was exploited both by the moderns and by people of fashion – and sometimes more so by the latter. It was both a source of renewal in art and the starting-point of a new academicism. While the works of the

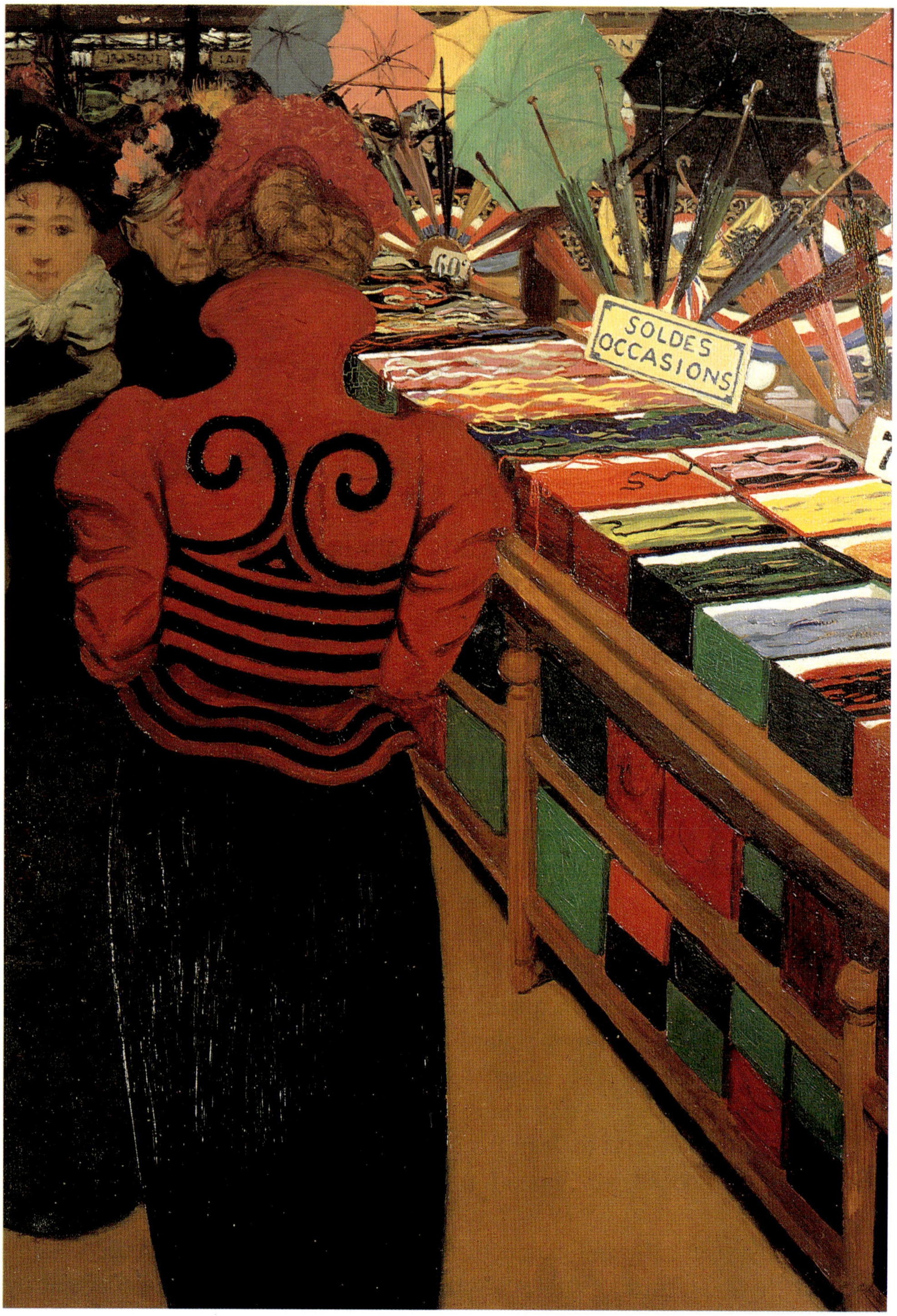

Félix Vallotton, Le Bon Marché, *triptych, left section, 1898. Private Collection, Switzerland.*

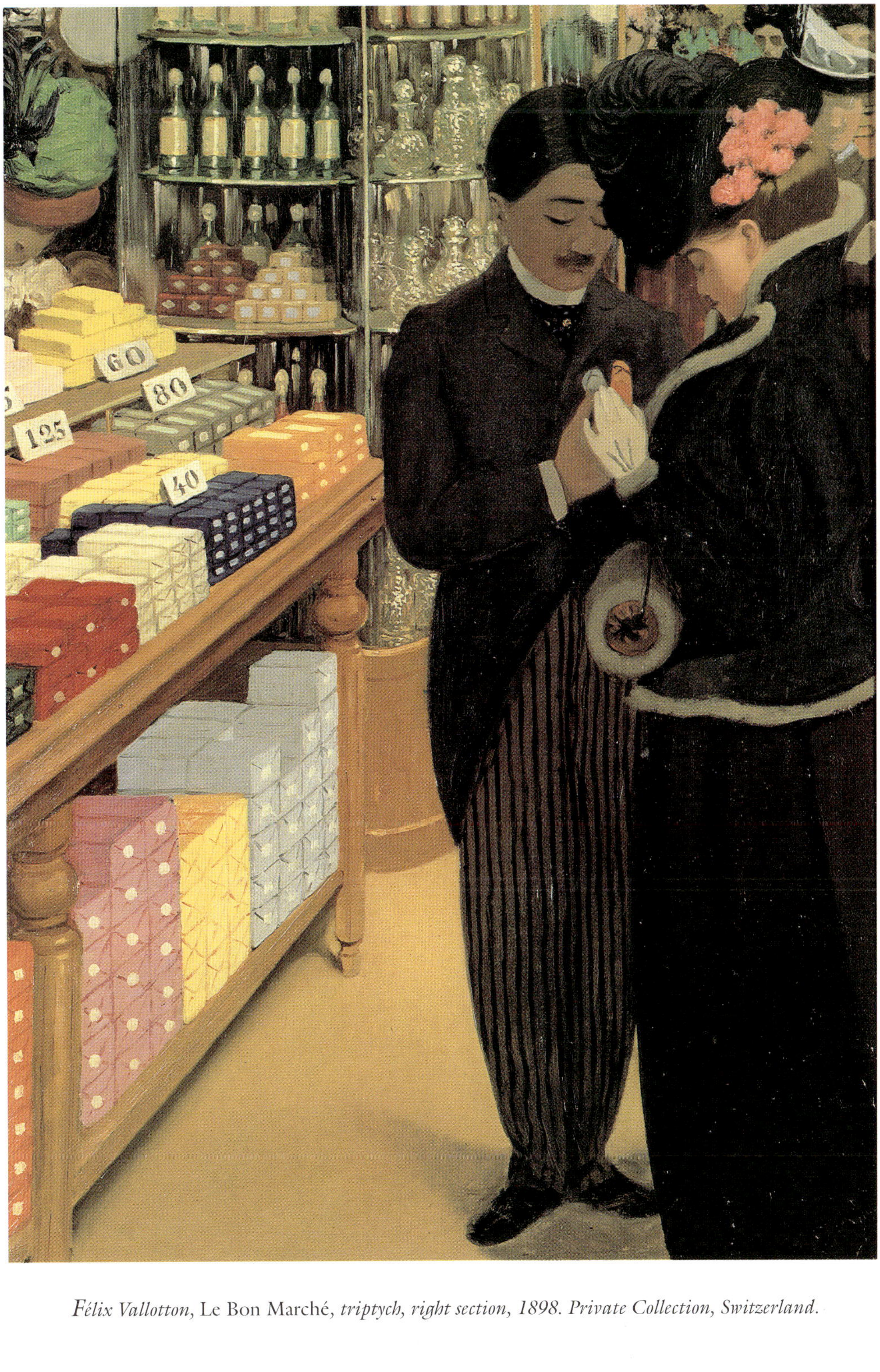

Félix Vallotton, Le Bon Marché, *triptych, right section, 1898. Private Collection, Switzerland.*

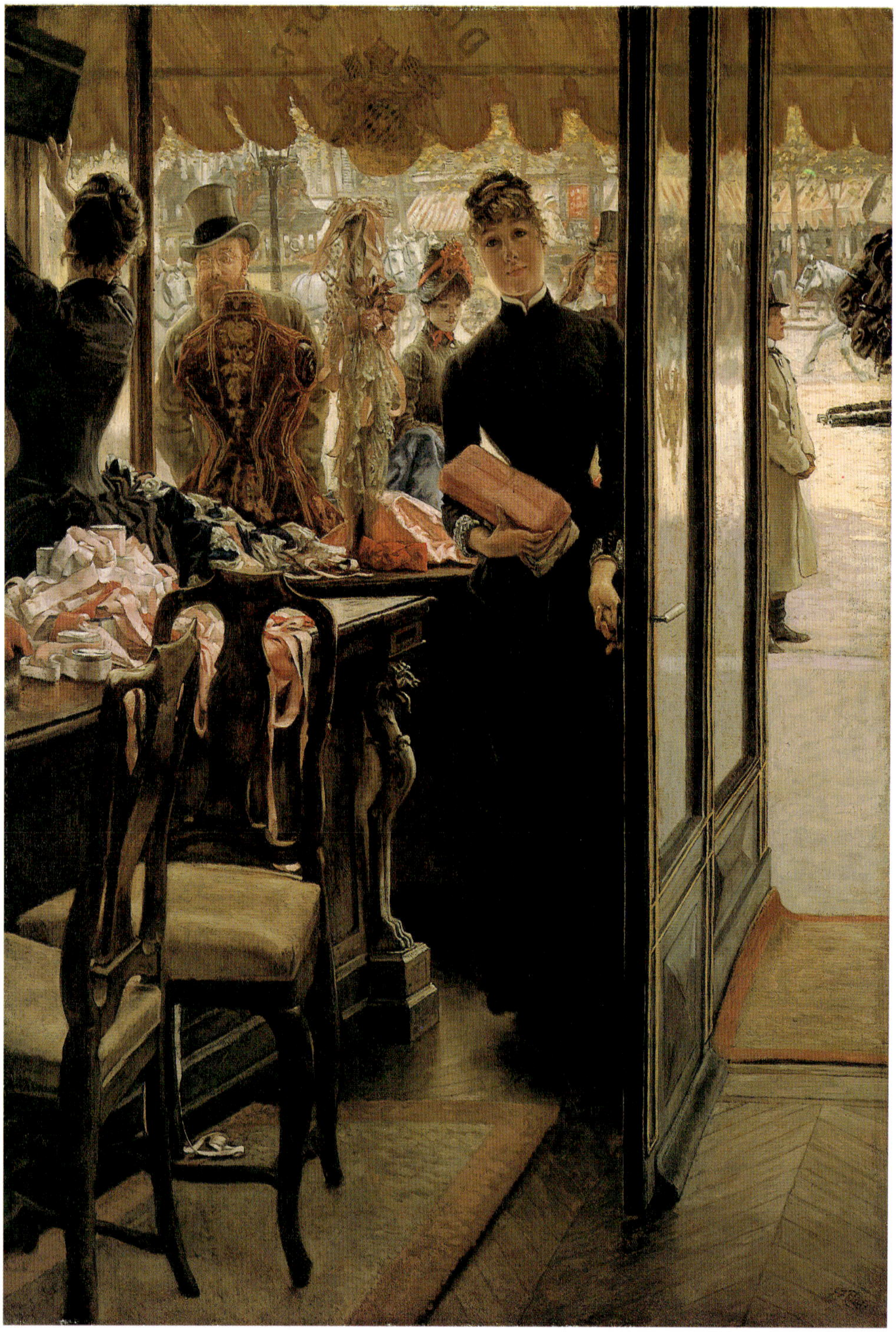

James Tissot, The Shopgirl, *1883–1885. Art Gallery of Ontario, Toronto.*

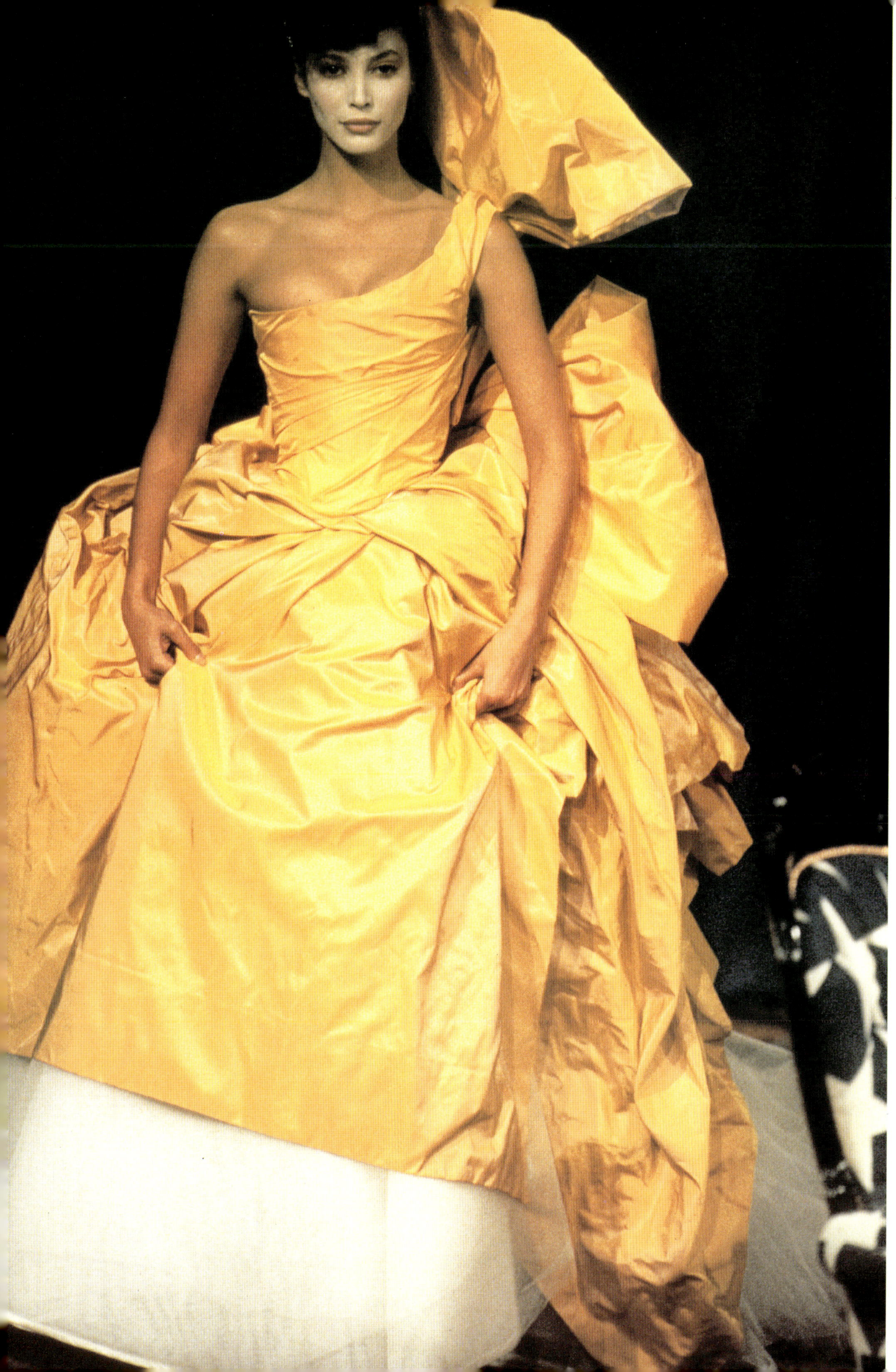

society painters, the Toulmoucheries, flattered the public's narcissism and allowed them to escape into a beautifying mirror, fashion as reflected in the moderns seemed dull and trivial. Manet's women were called 'dressed-up monkeys' by one commentator,[69] his pictorial technique distancing them irrevocably from the fashion prints. For,

> if the others set their satin ablaze, he does not try to make his sparkle. If they carefully distinguish tulle from muslin, foulard from crape, he passes quickly through the draper's shop, looks at the effect and renders it by a simple, clear, vivid tone. He jostles his folds instead of painstakingly counting them one by one.[70]

This unselfconsciousness of Manet and Degas, this sharp perception which goes beyond appearances, was needed in the treatment of fashion, to show how far clothing could sustain an ideal of modernity. In the work of these two painters the choice of a garment is never without purpose, but they never present clothing as other than it is.

Conclusion

Silk taffeta Winterhalter gown in yellow "Cafe Society", Vivienne Westwood. Collection spring-summer 1994.

Fashion appears to have been essential to nineteenth-century man because of its close link with the advent of modernity. Through fashion, beauty was tied to the ephemeral, eternal beauty was seen to be a chimera and the secular conception of the ideal was radically undermined. However by the start of the twentieth century fashion was losing its vitality as a source of artistic inspiration. Only the Nabis, and especially Vuillard, with his childhood memories of a couturier's workshop, revived it to some extent. The interest these painters showed in materials endowed fabrics with a symbolic value they had gradually lost. Rediscovering the rich brocades of the Middle Ages and the Renaissance, they depicted rich, enveloping textiles which imprisoned the wearer in a mesh of motifs, creating an intense, disturbing effect.

Throughout the twentieth century the symbiosis of fashion and painting continued, but in a way which reversed their respective positions. At the beginning of the century the couturier Poiret proposed to Dufy that he should create textile patterns for his models; this was the start of a close collaboration between artists and couturiers. In the 1920s, the Delaunays applied the principles of Orphism, which they had created, to their clothing. Robert Delaunay composed brightly coloured, mismatched costumes for himself, while Sonia invented 'simultaneous dresses' and 'spinning-top costumes'. More generally, artists throughout Europe took to designing clothes as well as consumer goods with the aim, proclaimed earlier by William Morris and members of the Arts and Crafts movement, of bringing art into daily life. In Vienna, within the framework of the Secessionist movement, the Wiener Werkstatte opened in 1910, equipped with a studio for fashion design. After the Russian Revolution several 'modern clothing workshops' were formed in Russia, and the Constructivist painters of the review *Lef* themselves created costumes. In Germany, students at the Bauhaus drew up designs for a 'new type of dress'.

The Surrealists were fascinated by the world of fashion (especially the wax mannequin). They collaborated fruitfully with the couturière Schiaparelli, who worked in France; in some cases they were directly involved in the creation of accessories – André Breton's 'aspirin' necklace, Dali's 'Roi Soleil' perfume bottle – or their works provided Schiaparelli with her main source of inspiration: the 'crayfish dress' inspired by Dali's lobster telephone, the 'tailored suit with drawers', the 'shoe hat'.

In the 1960s Yves Saint-Laurent's Mondrian dress, and later his Braque jackets, were among the best-known examples of fashion taking its inspiration from painting. More recently, Popy Moreni's tachist fabrics, alluding to Pollock, and Yohji Yamamoto's neo-Constructivist jackets in plywood have continued their homage to, and their borrowing from, the domain of pictorial art. In this way the balance of influence of the nineteenth century has been reversed: painting now inspires fashion, while fashion has ceased to be a souce of inspiration for painters, poets and writers.

In recent years it is perhaps the British designer Vivienne Westwood who has

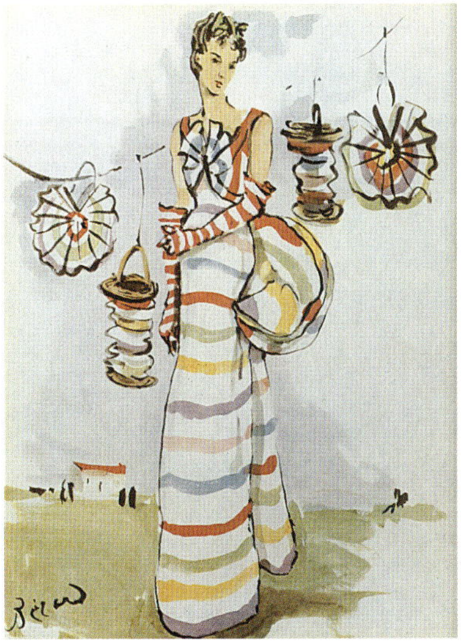

Evening dress with bustle, signed Schiaparelli. Illustration by Christian Bérard, 1939 (left).

Silk taffeta Winterhalter gown in lilac "Cafe Society", Vivienne Westwood. Collection spring-summer 1994 (right).

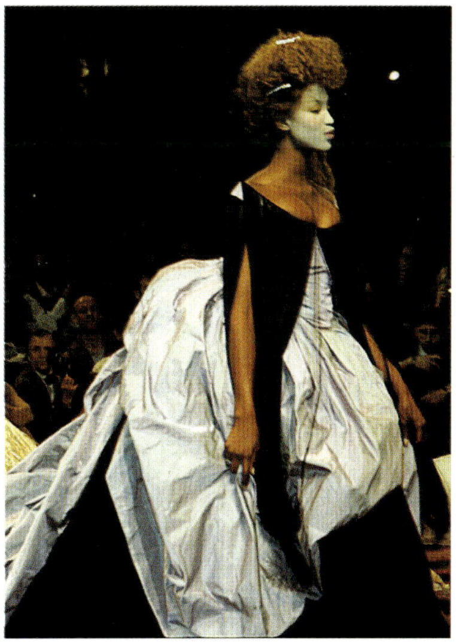

succeeded in interpreting the pictorial tradition most audaciously, in collections sparkling with idiosyncrasy. Ambassadress of Boucher, Ingres and Tissot in turn, she resurrects the corset, the crinoline and the bustle. Encumbering and feminine symbols of a life of idleness, they had been assumed to be tucked away forever in the catalogues of the history of costume and only displayed in the showcases of museums. Yet here they are again, freshly dusted down, flaunting themselves on the catwalks of the Cour Carrée. 'Mini-crinis' and bustles steady the tottering walk of tall, slim girls perched on platform soles and crowned with unruly ringlets. They parade themselves before our astounded eyes, defying logic, time and rationality. For fashion, frivolous and changeable, blithely spins its threads between periods and people. And to gather up and stitch together the scattered pieces, as it saunters on its way, it leaves behind, in Cocteau's words: 'History, sitting and plying her needle'.

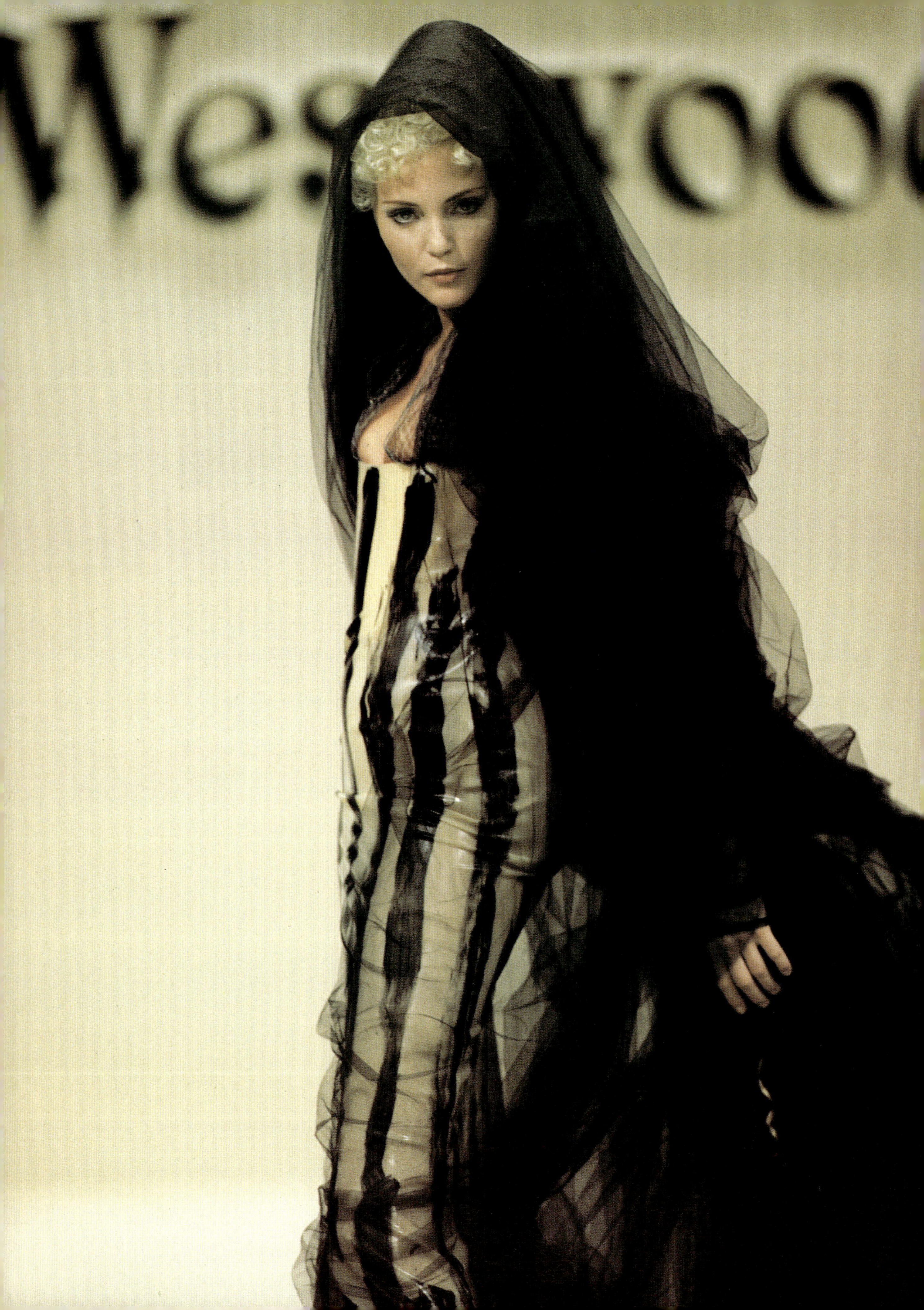

Portrait painters exploit clothing to enhance and emphasize the character of the sitter. This 'language of clothing' is complex and subtle. Uzanne (page 129 above) says: 'Dress for a woman is the first of the arts... her harmonious palette.' Picture galleries are essential to my work, and not merely paintings containing costumes but also landscape and still-life, in which harmonies of colour, design and movement can germinate so many fashion ideas. Great artists radiate this inspiration.

The Industrial Revolution established mass-production permanently in our world. This had the paradoxical result of making couture *equally necessary, because without such a criterion, ready-to-wear degenerates into characterless and ugly rubbish. (Some might say that it frequently does so.) Worth and Doucet emphasized their* couture *because they understood this reciprocal symbiosis. Or think what would become of men's ready-to-wear if Savile Row were abolished.*

Orthodoxy is the grave of intelligence. Today we have no avant-garde like the one in nineteenth-century France which rejected the stagnation of official and academic views. We live under a tyranny of orthodox beliefs which threatens us with another Dark Age.

Perhaps our worst orthodoxy is the notion of 'modernity' when this concept is used to discredit the past. This is a false idea which undermines true progress. Since about 1910 history has been denounced en bloc, *exemplified in Henry Ford's silly dictum 'History is Bunk'. Then, in all fields of applied art, a mania for 'minimalism' and extreme simplicity became established. However this over-simplification is usually only the fear of committing bad taste. (I prefer to allow some choice, and rely on the* chic *of the wearer.)*

It is time to heed Bacon's warning: 'Words are wise men's counters but they are the money of fools.' The words 'modern' and 'progress' were recycled in the late eighteeth century in order to promote utopian promises of a future millenarian pay-off. This put the theorists in business and they still thrive by making their dupes believe in a distant future paradise in exchange for tolerating present evils. Marxism was an example of this, although the very well-informed and intelligent were not taken in by it. However, theorists of the other side are still promoting populist conformity – of which (in fashion) 'grunge' is a deplorable result.

Epilogue

Vivienne Westwood

Hand-painted latex sheath dress and silk tulle Gainsborough coat "On liberty", Vivienne Westwood. Collection autumn-winter 1994–95.

One can see why these economic theories appeal to 'market experts', managers and accountants: these business pragmatists might be labelled 'anti-colbertian' because they insist on undermining style and quality, thereby guaranteeing eventual failure.

Fashion requires a rich and full gamut of ideas. An almost theatrical principle governs dress, because clothes can express and subtly emphasize qualities of personality and sentiment. Fashion is applied art, but also a living art which, ideally, can achieve the 'unity and harmony of a toilette *with a soul (p. 130 above). Such was the aim of the great* cocottes *who set the fashion last century. This spirit must be upheld – pride in refining form and style, the search for a 'language of clothing', the verve and* joie de vivre. *Even if fashion is an applied art, perhaps it is not inappropriate to quote what Gide said about 'pure art': 'L'art est né de contrainte, vit de controverse, et meurt de liberté.'*

The existence of couture guarantees the continuing healthy life of fashion.

Glossary

DRESS

Bavolet: A bavolet was originally a hat extended by a flap intended to protect the neck. By the nineteenth century the term referred only to a strip of material sewn to the hat and covering the nape of the neck.

Berthe (bertha): Ornamental strip of material, lace or fringe bordering the *décolleté* of the corsage of a ball-gown or placed over the corsage of a town costume. A 'bertha' may be flat, draped, or in the form of a fichu (small shawl).

Casaque: Originally a military garment worn over armour; in the nineteenth century the casque simply denoted an overgarment. It had no special characteristics and took various forms, such as an over-blouse or loose jacket.

Collet (collar): The part of the garment enclosing the neck; in the late nineteenth century the collet very often took the form of a collar covering the shoulders or forming a small cape.

Dolman: Hussar's jacket closed by frogs and loops; it was imitateed in short women's jackets decorated with trimmings (braid).

Guimpe (wimple, chemisette): Earlier, a piece of light material used to surround women's faces and falling in bands over the breast and shoulders. In the nineteenth century it was a blouse of fine material with a collar, used to cover the *décolleté* like a shirt front.

Mantelet (manteletta): Derived from the shawl, the manteletta encloses the arms and upper body. Practically without seams, it took various forms with differing lengths throughout the nineteenth century.

Paletot: Like mantelet, this is a rather vague term referring to jackets or short overcoats. The word *paltok* originated in the fifteenth century and defined an unfitted overgarment with loose sleeves. It was first a man's garment, but became part of the feminine wardrobe in the nineteenth century. It can be distinguished from the mantelet through having attached sleeves (although there were exceptions).

Passe: Brim of hat framing the face

Pélerine (cape, cloak): The name comes from the sleeveless cloak worn by pilgrims. It is a kind of cape which can be of various lengths.

Redingote (fitted coat): Another adaptation of a masculine garment – the man's redingote was a long coat with wide lapels. For women it became a robe or overcoat. It was always long, with fitted waist and open from top to bottom.

Tablier (apron): Separate front of a skirt or dress, draped or decorated to contrast with the skirt it covers.

Talma: Long circular cape.

Visite: Jacket closely fitting the body, with sleeves tight-fitting as far as the elbows, but wider below.

FABRICS

Blonde (blond-lace): Very fine silk lace.

Brocade: Silk damask material with woven designs in gold or silver.

Broché (brocaded): Refers to relief designs produced by superimposing an additional weft, in the shape of the design, over the base weft.

Faille: Coarse-grained silk material with fine fluting, belonging to the taffeta group of textiles.

Foulard: Very fine silk or cotton material which has been repeatedly pressed in a fulling mill. Foulard is often printed.

Jaconas (jaconet): Fine, light cotton fabric closely related to muslin or percale.

Poult-de-soie: Delicate, grained silk, also part of the taffeta group but much lighter than faille.

Serge: Woollen material the weave of which gives an effect of close, diagonal ribs.

Sicilienne: A kind of wool or silk poplin.

Surah: Light, supple silk material, formerly produced at the textile centre of Surat.

Taffeta: Silk material distinguished from faille by the absence of grain.

Vicuña: Light material of vicuña wool. The vicuña is an animal related to the lama, living in the mountains of South America.

Zibeline (sable): Siberian marten with precious fur. Sable is an extremely luxurious form of trimming.

Notes

Introduction

1. The sewing machine, invented by a Frenchman, M. Thimonier, in 1825, was patented in 1851 by an American, Mr Singer.

2. The Second Empire continued the building of communications networks, the opening of frontiers and progress in means of transport.

3. The success of this official costume was rather limited, and Jane d'Enval's comment on the *Portrait of Princesse Mathilde* by Edouard Dubufe (1861, Versailles, Musée National du Château), whom she found to be 'dressed in tulle spangled with gold, a costume composed of strident colours disagreeable to the eye', may have expressed an opinion widely shared. Jane d'Enval, 'Salon de 1861', *La Mode en France*, 1861, p. 12.

4. Vicomtesse de Trois Etoiles, 'Modes et toilettes de Fontainebleau', *La Vie parisienne*, 1863, pp. 246–7; description of a Louis XV-style *toilette* worn by the Princesse de Metternich, and of an outfit at the latest races. 'One makes careful enquiries about the author of a good painting; we also wanted to know the author of these little masterpieces of silk and lace. We expected the name of a couturière, but were given the name of an English artist: M. Worth.' Signed.

5. It is worth emphasising the importance of ready-made men's clothes which, although aimed primarily at a popular market, quickly developed to reach a wider clientèle. Tailors understood that their fierce resistance to this new mode of production risked losing the m clients; they had no choice but to adapt:'It is announced today [1850] that M. Jules Dusautoy, a tailor of reputation in the rue d'Amboise, is to open an immense new shop for ready-made men's clothing which will have no rival... Up to now this type of shop had been set up only for use by the people, but *les hommes du monde* [society men] are beginning to understand that nothing is more convenient, or even more in the interests of their elegance, than to have to hand a considerable choice of clothes that they can try on to judge their effect.' The term *homme du monde* needs to be defined more closely. Ready-made men's clothes were primarily addressed to a public extending from the upper working class to the middle bourgeoisie. They enabled people of the lower orders to have access to a middle-class style of dress, thanks to a system of low, fixed prices that were brought within reach by the rising standard of living. One of the inventors of the fixed, marked price was the draper Parisot, who produced work clothes. He decided to rationalize production by a division of manual labour, and in 1824 opened La Belle Jardinière, where he was able to sell clothes at the lowest prices. Later, imitating the novelty shops, he extended his range to ordinary middle-class clothes.

6. *La Mode nouvelle* of 1 January 1857, p. 18, gives some examples of this early publicity. Regarding La Maison Delsalle, rue du Bac, which supplied the faubourg Saint-Germain, we read of 'Good taste, distinction, extreme honesty, good and genuine elegance, combined with a moderateness of price which cannot be sufficiently noted.' Further on, the journal praises the corset-makers Mesdemoiselles Des Vertus at 26 rue de la Chaussée d'Antin, who have made a serious 'study' of 'statuary'.

7. Exh. cat. *Aux Paradis des dames*, Paris, Musée de la Mode et du Costume, Palais Galliéra, 1992–3, p. 24.

8. *La Chronique de Paris*, 30 January 1850, quoted by Henriette Vanier, *La Mode et ses métiers - Frivolités et luttes des classes* 1830–70, Paris, Armand Colin, 1960, p. 131.

9. Bertall, *La Comédie de notre temps*, Paris, Plon, 1874, p. 140: 'When a couturière has managed to launch a few eccentricities among her clientèle the ready-made garment houses immediately get hold of the patterns and, in less than a month, the boulevards are crowded with identical women.' The time-lag of a month is doubtless optimistic, but the essential point is that ready-made trade permitted the mass diffusion of a pattern that had been copied.

Notes on Chapter One

1. Henriette Vanier, op. cit., pp. 198–9, extract from illustration, 26 April 1962.

2. Octave Uzanne, *La femme et la mode–Métamorphose de la parisienne de 1792 à 1892*, Paris, Librairies et Imprimeries Réunies, May et Motteroz, 1892, p. 195.

3. On this subject see the study by Rose Fortassier, *Les Erivains français et la mode. De Balzac à nos*

jours, Paris, Presses Universitaires de France, 1988, p. 99.

4. Charles Baudelaire, *Oeuvres Complètes: Le Peintre de la vie moderne*, vol. II, p. 714.

5. H. Despaignes, *Le Code de la mode*, Paris, publ. by author, 1866.

6. Comtesse de Tamar, *La Mode et l'élégance*, Paris, V. Havard et Cie Editeurs, 1906, p. 287.

7. Comtesse de Bassanville, *La Scène du monde: Politesse, usage, bien-être*, Paris, J. Lecoffre, 1859, p.16.

8. *La Mode illustrée*, 3 March 1860, p. 73.

9. Elisabeth-Félicie Bayle-Mouillard, pseud. Mme Celnart, *Manuel de la bonne compagnie ou guide de la politesse et de la bienséance dédié à la société française*, Paris, Roret, 1836, p. 102.

10. Vicomtesse de Renneville, *La Corbeille*, no. 7, vol. 14, 1 July 1853.

11. Marguerite d'Aincourt, *L'Art de la femme*, Paris, Rouveyre et Blond, 1883, p. 8; description of a visiting or riding costume, as compared to town dress: 'The dress is of satin or broché'.

12. Ibid., p. 45.

13. Jules Claretie, *L'Art et les artistes français contemporains.* Salons of 1873–1874–1875, Paris, Charpentier, 1976, p. 116.

14. Bertall, *La Comédie de notre temps,* Paris, Plon, 1874, p. 412.

15. Marguerite d'Aincourt, op. cit., pp. 46–7.

16. Théophile Gautier, *Portraits contemporains,* Paris, Charpentier, 1874, extract from *Le Figaro,* 9 November 1837.

17. Catherine, Jacques, Annie Lebas, *La Coiffure en France du moyen-âge à nos jours*, Paris, Delmas int., 1979, p. 230.

18. Cf. article on bathing dress in *La Mode*, 6 July 1889.

19. Middle-class women bought two or three dresses each year. Bodices with removable sleeves served alternately as day and evening garments. With a matching jacket they became part of a 'town' costume. Costume museums in France are full of examples of this type. Likewise, the literature of the nineteenth century: La Comtesse Dash, *Comment on fait son chemin dans le monde,* Paris, M. Lévy, 1868, p. 287: 'Have two or three dresses per season; if they are choice, not too profusely adorned, and fresh, you will be able to go anywhere and will not be noticed.'

20. *La Mode universelle*, 1 January 1878.

21. Theatres also had their 'days': *La Mode actuelle*, 1870, p. 60: 'Do not go to the Opéra on Sunday, go on Thursday to avoid "a sad spectacle which is provincial and funereal at once".' The 'day' at the Italiens was Tuesday.

22. Emile Zola, *La Curée*, [1871] Paris, Gallimard, 1981, pp. 39, 41.

23. Cf. the description, in the appendix, of the costume of Mademoiselle Favart on p. 8 of *La mode actuelle* of 1 January 1870.

24. Bertall, op. cit., p. 23.

25. Elisabeth-Félicie Bayle-Mouillard, pseud. Mme Celnart, op. cit., Ch. IV 'De La Bienséance envers soi-même' §1 'De la Toilette'.

26. Marcel Proust, *Le Côté de Guermantes I,* Paris, Gallimard (Folio), 1986, p. 34. Cf. also *Un Amour de Swann,* Paris, Gallimard (Folio), 1990, p. 80; Odette's disappointment on seeing the black woollen dress of the Marquise de Villeparisis, the dress of a 'theatre attendant or a concierge'.

27. Emile Zola, *Nana*, Paris, Presses Pocket, 1978, p.293.

28. Vicomtesse de Trois Etoiles, *La Vie parisienne,* 1863, pp. 377-8. In this connection cf. article in *La Vie parisienne,* 1877, p. 260: 'Au Bois hier et aujourd'hui': 'the five or six *grandes cocottes* who sprinkle the scene without spoiling it; these people, chosen and perfumed, are tacitly accepted here.' (same clothing supplier, same parade grounds), or again: 'De la mode et du goût', *Le messager des modes et de l'industrie,* 1853, vol. 1, no. 2, p. 30.

29. 'De la mode et du goût', *Le Messager des modes et de l'industrie,* 1853, vol. 1, no. 2, p. 30.

30. Edmond About, *Voyage à travers l'exposition des Beaux-Arts de 1855*, Paris, Hachette, 1855, p. 134.

31. Balzac, *Les Parisiens comme ils sont*, 1830–1848, Neuchâtel, Paul Altinger, 1957, pp109, 119.The book brings together several articles: 'Les français peints par eux-mêmes', 6th instalment, 1839, includes 'La femme comme il faut' (The well-bred woman) from which the quotations are taken.

32. Madame de Girardin, *Lettres parisiennes*, 27 April 1839, cited by Perrot, op. cit., p. 318. Le Marais 'executes and buries' because the Faubourg Saint-Antoine was a working-class district traditionally the preserve of second-hand clothes dealers up to 1863, when it was renovated. The market at Carreau du Temple had been a major centre for the sale of second-hand clothes since the eighteenth century and throughout the nineteenth. It was customary in high society for clothes to be passed on to the servants, who eventually sold them to the second-hand dealers (which also explains why so few garments from that period have been preserved). With the advent of ready-made clothing, this market was soon abandoned by the populace, who preferred to buy cheap new clothes, and at the time of its renovation in 1863 it was used primarily as a transit site for exports, particularly to colonial Africa.

33. Ibid., p. 311.

34. Proust, *Le Côté de Guermantes I*, Paris, Gallimard, 1986, p. 63.

35. Philippe Perrot, *Les Dessus et les dessous de la bourgeoisie.Une Histoire du vêtement au XIXe siècle*, Paris, Librairie Arthème Fayard, 1981, p. 318.

36. *L'Art de la mode*, July 1882, p. 2: 'Nowadays the taste for finery has found an inviolable sanctuary in all classes of society. Equality in dress is part of our century's progress; the dresses of the rich bourgeoise and of the princess are indistinguishable in their elegance.' This 'equality' is repeatedly noted in the press. Standardardization is on the march.

37. Cf. *Le Magasin des demoiselles*, November 1850: 'I'm sure that in some provincial towns it is being sold as the latest novelty.' Also cf. September 1854, p. 372, on the difference between the Parisian and the provincial woman.

38. Edmond and Jules de Goncourt, *Journal, Mémoires de la vie littéraire*, Editions de l'Imprimerie Nationale de Monaco, 1956, vol. 22, 1 January 1865, p. 119.

39. Charles Baudelaire, *La Fanfarlo*, op. cit., vol. I, pp. 567–8.

Notes on Chapter Two

1. Proust, *Un Amour de Swann*, Paris, Gallimard, Folio, March 1990, p. 9, on fashion in Odette's time.

2. *Lettres de Degas recueillies et annotées par Marcel Guérin*, Paris, Grasset, 1945, no. XXVIII. According to Marcel Guérin, this letter was not sent. Two pastels show Mme Dietz-Monnin with her boa and a pink hat.

3. Quoted by James Laver, *Costume and Fashion: A Concise History*, London, Thames & Hudson, 1986, p. 206.

Notes on Chapter Three

1. Cf. François Gasnault, 'Les Salles de bal du Paris romantique: décors et jeux des corps', *Romantisme*, 1982, no. 38, p. 12.

2. *Journal des demoiselles*, 'Correspondance', 1854.

3. *L'Artiste*, 1862, p. 117.

4. Ibid.

5. *Le Magasin des demoiselles*, Oct. 1850, no.128, p. 23; Nov. 1853, no. 131, p. 52.

6. Diana de Marly, *Worth, Father of Haute Couture*, London, Elm Tree Books, 1980, p. 63.

7. Marguerite d'Aincourt, op. cit., p. 10. 'Couturières of genius study their models in museums or in the portrait galleries of their aristocratic clients.'

8. *Le Magasin des demoiselles*, vol. II, 1854–5, pp. 185, 346.

9. *La mode actuelle*, 15 March 1870, p. 4.

10. *Le Magasin des demoiselles*, vol. 9, Dec. 1853.

11. *Le Magasin des demoiselles*, Jan. 1855, p. 120: 'I am surprised that the curly hair to be seen in a

portrait of Marie de' Médicis by Rubens is not in favour. It consists of nine or ten rows of crimped ringlets on each side...They start at the middle of the forehead and are rolled towards the ear...They have as much volume as a ruff.'

12. Théophile Gautier, *Contes et récits fantastiques*, 'La Toison d'or', 1839, Paris, Librairie générale française, 1988, pp. 184–5.

13. Théophile Gautier, *L'Artiste*, 1857, p. 226. Some pages earlier (p. 128) the reporter on 'the modes of the season', Vicomtesse de Renneville, devotes an article to satin: 'Satin is back in power, and as I was the first to speak ill of it I am obliged to humble myself before satin.'

14. *Journal des jeunes-filles*, Nov. 1868: 'Watteau will be worn in cashmere or a light black material.'

15. Cited by Marguerite d'Aincourt, op. cit., pp. 81, 88.

16. *Le Magasin des demoiselles* published Schiller's biography of Mary Stuart in 1849–50. *La Vie parisienne*, 1863, p. 79, gave an extract from *La Femme au XVIIIe siècle*: 'Le Petit Lever', *L'Art de la mode*, vol. I, 1881, shows on pp. 60–63 'The costume of the man and woman of the eighteenth century' by Edmond de Goncourt.

17. E. and J. de Goncourt, *Journal*, op. cit., 21 Jan. 1863, 1957, vol. VI, p. 14.

18. *Manet raconté par lui-même et par ses amis*, Geneva, P. Cailler, 1945, p. 172.

19. Uzanne, *La Femme et la mode*, op. cit., 1894, p. 238.

20. Le Magasin des demoiselles, May 1858, p. 248.

21. In *Le Magasin des demoiselles*, 1849, we read: 'The forms of dresses do not change and I much regret having to repeat the same thing, as I cannot pass off dresses with open corsages as novelties, whether they are called *à la* Leiczinska or *à la* Dubarry'.

22. Challamel, *Histoire de la mode en France*, Paris, A. Hennuyer, 1881, p. 265.

23. *La Revue illustrée*, 1893, vol. 2, pp. 34–6. It is worth pointing out that these are, after all, costumes for masked balls.

24. *Le Moniteur de la mode*, July 1863.

25. *Le Journal des dames*, Jan. 1855. The Crimean War began on 26 March 1854.

26. Marguerite d'Aincourt, op. cit., p. 9.

27. *Au Paradis des dames*, op. cit., p. 96.

28. *Le Magasin des demoiselles*, May 1854.

29. Marguerite d'Aincourt, op. cit., p. 7 refers to the 'Japanese peignoir...in one of those marvellous materials woven for the mikado'.

Notes on Chapter Four

1. In an article in *Sunday World*, March 1895, reported in *Femmes fin de siècle*, p. 97.

2. *L'Art de la mode*, 1882, vol. 3, p. 126.

3. Quoted by Huysmans in *L'Art moderne*, Paris, 10/18, 1975, p. 282, in the chapter on Whistler.

4. *L'Artiste*, 1857, p. 128: The Vicomtesse de Renneville on men's waistcoats created by the tailor Becker senior: 'Becker senior's scissors never copy anyone – they are as fanciful as Delacroix's brush.' *La Vie parisienne*, 1867, p.228, on M. Humann, tailor for men and for ladies' riding costumes: 'He is an artist who, in the absence of marble and paint, creates upon the human body he dresses an ideal of proportions dreamed of, but not always achieved, by professional painters and sculptors.'

5. Uzanne, *La Femme à Paris, nos contemporains, notes successives sur les Parisiennes de ce temps en leurs divers milieux, états et conditions*, Paris, May & Motteroz, 1894, p.30. Here Uzanne paraphrases the quotation from Balzac: 'Fashion for women is the first of the arts.'

6. *L'Art de la mode*, 1881, vol. 3, p. 113: 'a woman who knows how to dress is more artistic than many who have the vanity but not the talent to call themselves by that title. To know how to dress...is by no means as easy as is supposed, and the middle-class woman brought up far from museums and elegant society does not know the first word of the high art of pleasing – with due propriety, of course.'

7. It is interesting to note that the chemist had formulated his theory after observations made at the

Gobelins manufactory where he worked, and that his book, published in 1839, was addressed both to artists and to manufacturers, printers and others working in the decorative arts.

8. Ibid., p. 172: 'In a garment conceived in a serious spirit any frivolity can make it seem ridiculous. Unity is needed not only between soul and attire, but within the garment itself.'

9. Charles Blanc, *L'Art dans la parure et dans le vêtement*, Paris, Librairie Renouard, 1875, pp. 90–91. 'We have stated what is expressed, in the human head, by vertical, horizontal and oblique lines (*Grammaire des arts et du dessin*). These inexorable laws also apply to hats. Worn horizontally, a hat reflects a feeling of order and calm; if it is tilted more or less over the forehead to show only the eyes, as if to make them more brilliant, it betrays an independent disposition and an individual fantasy, since there is only one horizontal,while the oblique lines change in appearance according to their degree of obliqueness.'

10. Charles Blanc, op. cit., p. 28–9.

11. Ibid., p. 279.

12. Ibid., p. 187. It is interesting to note that Monet's study of the play of light and colour produced by light reflected on to a face by a sunshade, in the *Woman with a parasol* (1866, Paris Musée d'Orsay) were also investigated in fashion magazines: 'Out of doors she shows the effects of a parasol lined with mauve or violet cloth, which alters the complexion and always seeks light tones which, matching the dress, efface the shadows on the face' (P. Perrot, op. cit., pp. 188–9). In 1862 there was even a theory of colour which offered amusing parallels to that of Chevreul: 'A woman of indolent temperament...should dress in very bright and varied colours; flower beds only have charm for our eyes because they are motionless...A pretty girl, as light and vivacious as a bird, needs soft, almost plain nuances; the cloud fleeting towards infinity only plunges us in a gentle reverie because of its vaporous form, its uncertain, almost uniform colour' (Sérieul, *Le Diable rose*, no. 6, Sept. 1862, quoted by P. Perrot, op. cit., p. 221).

13. Ibid., p. 118.

14. Ibid., p. 174.

15. Ibid., p. 179.

16. *L'Art de la mode*, 1881, vol. 2, p. 77. The author of this article is Arsène Houssaye. He, like Ernest Hoschedé, the editor of the journal, was a defender of the Impressionists. He was even one of their first purchasers, buying *Camille in a green dress* from Monet in 1866. But here he was flattering his fashionable readers rather than trying to convert them.

17. Ibid., Epilogue.

18. Ibid., p.131: 'Yes, he is a deep artist who makes the garment of a human creature into a decoration by helping her to dress, or dressing her, in accordance with her nature and form, with the colour of her hair and her skin, with her degree of distinction and even her particular cast heart.'

19. *La Vie parisienne*, 1864, p. 235.

20. Théophile Gautier, *De La Mode*, Poulet Malassis et de Broise, 1858, pp. 19, 30, 31.

21. Charles Baudelaire, op. cit., ch.: 'Le peintre de la vie moderne' *(L'Eloge du maquillage), Oeuvres Complètes,* p. 715.

22. Ibid., p. 716.

23. Joris-Karl Huysmans, op cit., pp. 27, 101.

24. For a history of the journal see Jean-Pierre Lecercle, *Mallarmé et la mode*, Paris, Librairie Seguier, 1989.

25. *L'Art de la mode*, 1881, vol. I, p. 19. A trace of this direct involvement of painters in fashion can be found in 1905, in a Fémina presenting dresses painted by the same Madeleine Lemaire, still a *styliste*.

26. Baudelaire, *Salon de 1859*, 'Le portrait', op. cit., vol. II, p. 658.

27. Bertall, op. cit., p. 314.

28. Zola, 1868, *Mon Salon*, Paris, Garnier, Flammarion, 1970, p. 134.

29. G. Loquiot, quoted by J.P. Crespelle, *Les Maîtres de la belle époque*, Paris, Hachette, 1966, p. 17.

30. *L'Art de la mode*, 1882, p.126: 'A large, brilliant crowd at the Salon, which is now the daily meeting-place for elegant *parisiennes!*'

31. A.J. du Pays, 1852, quoted in the exhibition catalogue *Dubufe*, p.24.

32. Victor Cherbaliez, 'Le Salon de 1876', *Revue des deux mondes*, 1 and 19 June, 1 July 1976, p. 528.

33. Ibid., p. 528.

34. Baudelaire, *Salon de 1859*, 'Le portrait', op. cit., p. 654.

35. Cherbaliez, op. cit., pp. 34, 35.

36. Henry Lapauze, *Ingres, sa vie et son oeuvre*, 1780-1867, drawing on unpublished documents, Paris, Georges Petit, 1914, p. 444.

37. *Manet raconté par lui-même et par ses amis*, Geneva, P. Cailler, 1945, p. 172.

38. Moreau Vauthier, *Les Chefs-d'oeuvre des grands maîtres*, Hachette, 1903.

39. Crespelle, op. cit., p. 97.

40. Winterhalter: most probably *The Princesse de Metternich* (1860, private coll.), *The Duchesse de Morny* (1863, Château de Compiègne, and various portraits of the Empress Eugénie; Carolus-Duran, *Mrs Astor* (New York, Metropolitan Museum of Art); Bonnat, *Mrs Leland Stanford* (1881, Stanford University Museum); Debat-Ponsan: *The Comtesse Edmond Récopé* (1888, Paris, Musée du Petit Palais).

41. Michel Robida, *Les bourgeois de Paris, trois siècles de chronique familiale de 1875 à nos jours*, Paris, Juillard, 1955, p. 55.

42. Antonin Proust, 1897, in exh. cat. *Manet*, Paris, Galeries Nationales du Grand Palais, April-August 1983, p. 489.

43. William A. Coles, *Alfred Stevens*, The University of Michigan Museum of Art, Ann Arbor (12 Sept.-12 Oct. 1977).

44. Zola, op. cit., p. 255.

45. *Le Magasin de demoiselles*, p. 4, Oct. 1857.

46. Mallarmé, *La Dernière mode*, 'La mode', 15 November 1874, p. 42.

47. Zola, op. cit., p. 139.

48. Alain Daguerre de Hureaux, *Catalogue des peintures du XIXe siècle du Musée des Beaux-Arts; Jules Chéret, Mémoire de maîtrise d'histoire d'art*, University of Paris IV.

49. Zola, op. cit., p. 294.

50. Marguerite d'Aincourt, op. cit., p. 45.

51. Jules Claretie, *L'art et les artistes français contemporains: Salons de 1873–1874–1875*, Paris, Charpentier, 1876, p. 114.

Notes on Chapter Five

1. Charles Blanc, op. cit., p. 94.

2. Théophile Gautier, *De La Mode*, op. cit., pp. 6, 7.

3. The critical outcry caused by Courbet's *Bathers* included the following two defences which illustrate the redefinition of the modern nude: Théophile Silvestre, *Histoire des artistes vivants, français et étrangers, études d'après nature*, Paris, Blanchard, 1856, pp. 275, 177: 'Matrons of sixty, suffocated by their corsets and bundled up in satin dresses from the last century re-dyed reddish black, are incensed about the realist painter in the name of the Venus of Milo...' Pierre Joseph Proudhon, *Du Principe de l'art et de sa destination sociale*, Paris, Garnier, 1865, pp. 178–80: 'Society is full of belles femmes who, in a négligé, would certainly not merit that title.'

4. Zola, op.cit., p. 269.

5. M. d'Aincourt, op. cit., p. 11, apropos of the 'conjugal nightdress': 'do not describe it to young girls, out of respect for their exquisite modesty.'

6. Zola, op cit., p. 69.

7. J.K. Huysmans, op. cit., p. 36: 'What would a real framework mean for a conventional subject? Let us at least be logical', p. 37.

8. Eric Darragon, *Manet*, Paris, Hachette, 1989, p. 281.

9. Cf. V. Steele, *Fashion and Eroticism*, New York, Oxford University Press, 1985, p. 43.

10. Champfleury, 'Du réalisme, Lettre à Madame Sand', *L'Artiste*, 2 Sept. 1855.

11. Baudelaire, *Salon de 1846*, 'De l'héroïsme de la vie moderne', op. cit., p. 496.

12. Théophile Gautier, op. cit., pp. 11, 12.

13.Ibid., pp. 14, 13.

14. Zola, op. cit., p. 235.

15. Ibid.

16. Baudelaire, *Salon de 1859*, op. cit., p. 655.

17. Duranty, *La Nouvelle Peinture, à propos du groupe d'artistes qui exposent à la galerie Durand Ruel*, Paris, E. Dentu, 1876, p. 24.

18. Baudelaire, *Le Peintre de la vie moderne*, op. cit., p. 684.

19. Ibid., pp. 694–5.

20. Théophile Gautier, op. cit., p. 23.

21. Baudelaire, 'De l'héroïsme de la vie moderne', op. cit., p. 493.

22. Baudelaire, op. cit., p. 685.

23. Ibid., p. 695.

24. Gérald Froidevaux, *Baudelaire - Représentation et Modernité*, Paris, José Corti, 1989, p. 39.

25. Baudelaire, *Le peintre de la vie moderne*, op. cit., p. 718.

26. Ambroise Vollard, *En Ecoutant Cézanne, Degas, Renoir*, Paris, Grasset, 1950, p. 62.

27. Cf. V. Steele, *Paris Fashion*, New York, Oxford University Press, 1988, pp. 126–7.

28. Cf. Mount, *Monet*, New York, 1968, pp. 110, 405.

29. Edmond About, *Salon de 1866*, Paris, 1867, pp. 101–2.

30. F. Martin, *Lettre du 6 octobre 1868*, Orsay information sheet.

31. Zola, op. cit., p. 167.

32. Quoted by William A. Coles, op. cit.

33. Taxile Delord, *Physiologie de la Parisienne*, Paris, Aubert & Cie, 1841, p. 70.

34. Ibid, p. 24.

35. Octave Uzanne, *La Femme à Paris*, op. cit., p. 5.

36. Taxile Delord, op. cit., p. 24.

37. J. Prouvaire, in *Le Rappel*, in exh. cat. *Renoir*, Paris, Galeries Nationales du Grand Palais, 14 May–2 Sept. 1985, p. 122.

38. Eric Darragon, op. cit., pp. 308, 389.

39. Ibid., p. 389.

40. P. Demery, *La Jeune France*, 1 June 1882, quoted by Darragon, op. cit., p. 390.

41. L. de Fourcaud, *Le Gaulois*, 4 May 1884, quoted by Darragon, op. cit., p. 390.

42. Taxile Delord, op. cit., p. 28.

43. Ibid., p. 111.

44. Charles Blanc, *L'Art dans la parure et dans le vêtement*, quoted by Uzanne, *Les Ornements de la femme*, May & Motteroz, 1892, p. 190.

45. Paul Mantz, in *Feuilleton du temps*, 14 May 1874. Also cf. Ariste in *L'Indépendence Belge* (A.H., no date): 'M. Henner has depicted an unforgettable bourgeois sphinx which makes one think of another *Mona Lisa*, imperious and more modest.'

46. Taxile Delord, op. cit., p. 19.

47. Lapauze, Henry, *Ingres*, sa vie et son oeuvre, op. cit., p. 460.

48. P. Mantz, *Gazette des Beaux-Arts*, 1869.

49. Castagnary, *Salon de 1869.*

50. Castagnary, *Salon de 1872.*

51. Jean Robiquet, *La Parisienne par l'image, trois siècles de grâce féminine*, Le Panorama, Paris, Ludovic Baschet, 1896.

52. Huysmans, op. cit., *Le Salon de 1879*, p. 50.

53. Ibid., p. 48.

54. Ibid., p. 50.

55. A. Pinard, *Le Radical*, 10 Jan. 1884, 'L' exposition Monet', quoted by Eric Darragon, p.72.

56. T. Gautier, *Le Moniteur universel*, 11 May 1868, quoted by Darragon, p. 153.

57. Also in 1866 Degas painted the same subject, still, it seems, using Victorine Meurent, in his *Young woman in a red peignoir* (New York, private coll.). The effect is rather different. The firm structure of the folds and the rigidity of the collar, clearly separating the head from the body, give the figure a certain religiosity. Curiously, for the second half of the nineteenth century, these examples are almost unique. The peignoir is very rare in portraits, if we disregard Japanese peignoirs which were painted for their exoticism.

58. On her life: Maurice Parturier, *Une Amitié littéraire*, Paris, Hachette, 1952, pp. 116, 117.

59. Castagnary, 1869, quoted in exh. cat. *Monet*, op. cit., p. 307.

60. Degas, notebook of 1859/60, exh. cat. Degas, Paris, Galeries Nationales du Grand Palais, Feb.–March 1988, p. 43.

61. The mirror appears very frequently in fashion prints. It introduces the ideas of seduction and narcissism inseparable from the feminine world, or reflects the back of a costume to complete its definition, sometimes in defiance of logic, as in Manet or Degas.

62. *Lettres de Degas recueillies et annotées par Marcel Guérin*. Les Cahiers verts, 1931, ed. Bernard Grasset, p. 147.

63. J.K. Huysmans, op. cit., p. 52.

64. T. Duret, 1906, pp. 170–71, quoted by Darragon, op. cit., p. 241.

65. T. Véron, De l'art des artistes de mon temps, Salon of 1875, Paris, 1875, p. 69-70, quoted by Darragon, p. 242.

66. 'Un Salon composite: Le Salon de 1877', in *L'Artiste*, July 1877.

67. Bernard Dorival, *Quelques Sources méconnues de divers ouvrages de Monet*, B.S.H.A.F. 1975, pp. 315, 329.

68. Nevertheless, art critics suggested this theme. In 1876 Duranty, in *La Nouvelle Peinture*, cited the 'novelty shop' among the urban settings in which a painter ought to pose his figures. In 1880, on the occasion of the Exposition de Indépendants, Huysmans exclaimed: 'The whole of modern life has yet to be studied. Hardly any of its multiple facets have been perceived and noted. Everything still has to be done: official galas, salons, balls, obscure corners of family, artisan and bourgeois life, shops...' Georges Lafenestre, in *La Gazette des Beaux-Arts* of March 1883, gives a long architectural description of the Le Printemps stores, rebuilt by M. Paul Sédille, which might have been a field for painters.

69. Extract from a critique of the Salon of 1870 concerning *The music lesson* in *La Mode actuelle, journal des modistes et des couturières*, 1 May 1870, p. 11. This term might be a recollection of a comment by Ingres on a woman whose portrait he was painting: 'What pain it causes me to paint this costumed monkey.'

70. Duranty, 'Salon de 1870' (still in connection with *The music lesson*) Paris – *Journal*, 5–18 May 1870.

List of illustrations

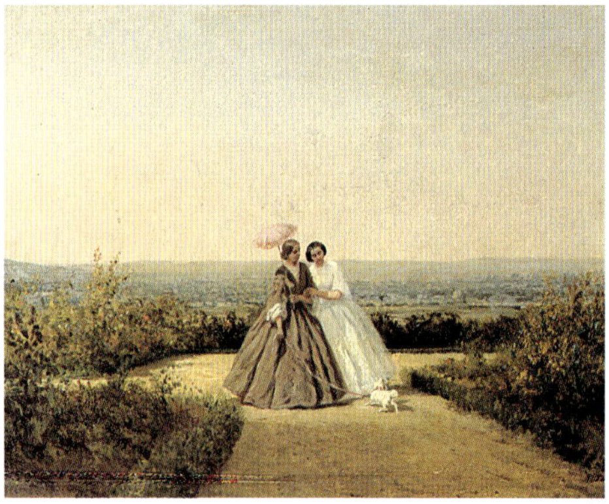

Martial Potemont, Women in a Garden *(detail page 55, left).*

Edouard Manet, Masked Ball at the Opera, *detail page 83 (right).*

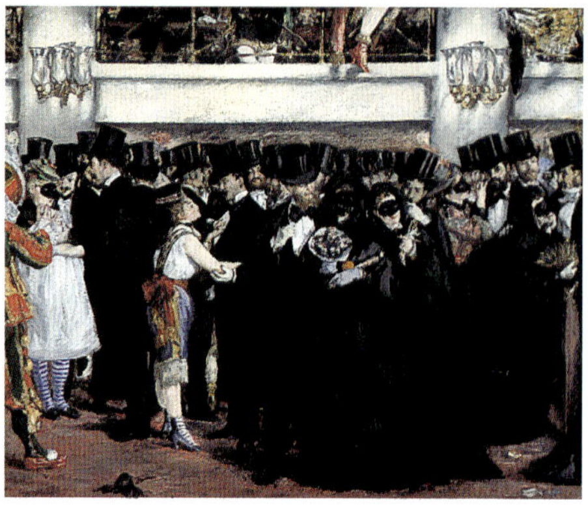

de Rothschild, *1844–1848, oil on canvas, 141.8 x 101.5 cm. Private Collection, Paris (pages 36–37).*

James Tissot, The Sportswomen, *1883–1885, oil on canvas, 147.2 x 101.6 cm. Museum of Fine Arts, Juliana Cheney Edwards Collection, Boston (page 42).*

La Foulhouze, La Cocodette, *no date, lithograph. Bibliothèque des Arts décoratifs, Paris (page 43, left).*

Le Moniteur de la mode, *ball outfit and visiting clothes, 1853, engraving. Bibliothèque des Arts Décoratifs, Paris (page 43, right).*

Franz-Xaver Winterhalter, The Empress Eugénie and her maids of honour, 1855, *detail, oil on canvas, 300 x 420 cm. Musée du Second Empire, Château de Compiègne (page 44)*

Duchâteau petticoat, detail, 1858, engraving, Bibliothèque nationale, Paris (page 47, top left).

Pompadour underskirt with train, 1866, engraving. Bibliothèque nationale, Paris (page 47, top right).

Afternoon dress in plaid taffeta, c.1856. The Metropolitan Museum of Art, Costume Institute, gift of Mrs Edwin R. Mitcalf, New York (page 47, bottom).

Le Magasin des demoiselles, *town fashions for ladies and young girls, 25 May 1858, engraving. Union française des arts du costume, Paris (page 48).*

Honoré Daumier, 'Ladies of the demi-monde without demi-skirts', *drawing no. 190 of the series 'Actualités' for* Le Charivari, *11 May 1855 (page 49, top).*

Honoré Daumier, 'Charming lady, should one sweep you away?', *drawing no. 1 of the series 'Winter sketches' for* Le Charivari, *13 November 1858 (page 49, bottom).*

Brown dress, c.1860–1865. Union française des arts du costume, Paris (page 50, top left).

Grey dress, c.1860–1865. Union française des arts du costume, Paris (page 50, top right).

Dress of grey threaded moiré and brown moiré, 1860–1865. Union française des arts du costume, Paris (page 50, bottom).

Disdéri, Madame Aubert, *undated photograph, 8.5 x 6 cm. Musée d'Orsay, Paris (page 51, left).*

A crinoline shop, c.1862, photograph (page 51, right).

Franz-Xaver Winterhalter, The Empress Eugénie and her maids of honour, *1855, oil on canvas, 300 x 420 cm. Musée du Second Empire, Château de Compiègne (pages 52–53).*

Claude Monet, Le Déjeuner sur l'herbe, *central part, 1865–1866, oil on canvas, 248 x 217 cm. Musée d'Orsay, Paris (page 54).*

Martial Potemont, Women in a Garden, *detail, no date, oil on canvas. Musée du Second Empire, Château de Compiègne (page 55, left).*

After Auguste Toulmouche, Forbidden Fruit, *engraving, Salon de 1865. Bibliothèque des Arts décoratifs, Paris (page 55, right).*

Dress of green-grey shot taffeta, c.1870–1875. Union française des arts du costume, Paris (page 56).

James Tissot, The Branch of Lilac, 1875, oil on canvas, 54 x 37.5 cm. Private Collection, London (page 57).

Pierre Auguste Renoir, Portrait of a Woman, *or* Portrait of Madame Hartmann, *1874, oil on canvas, 183 x 123 cm. Musée d'Orsay, Paris (page 59).*

Le Magasin des demoiselles, *25 November 1856, engraving. Bibliothèque des Arts décoratifs, Paris (page 91, left).*

Harper's Bazar, *1872, engraving. Bibliothèque Forney, Paris (page 91, right).*

Peter Paul Rubens, Hélène Fourment in a carriage, *c. 1631, oil on wood, 198 x 128 cm. Musée du Louvre, Paris (page 92).*

Antoine Watteau, L'Enseigne de Gersaint, *detail, 1720, oil on canvas, 163 x 308 cm. Palais de Charlottenbourg, Berlin (page 93).*

Paul Lacroix, French costumes from their origin to our day: *Louise Labé, vol. II, 1834–1839, engraving. Bibliothèque Forney, Paris (page 94, left).*

La Mode illustrée, *black ensemble in neo-Mary Stuart style, 1871, engraving. Bibliothèque des Arts décoratifs, Paris (page 94, right).*

Les Modes parisiennes, *pleated négligé in the style of Watteau, 8 August 1863, engraving. Bibliothèque des Arts décoratifs, Paris (page 95, left).*

La Galerie des modes, *woman dressed in Polish style, 1778, engraving. Bibliothèque des Arts décoratifs, Paris, (page 95, right).*

Pierre Auguste Renoir, Monsieur and Madame Sisley, *1868, oil on canvas, 100 x 75 cm. Wallraf-Richartz Museum, Cologne (page 97).*

Alexis Axilette, Madame Dubois-Mouchet, *no date, pastel on paper, 200 x 122 cm. Musée des Beaux-Arts, Angers (page 98).*

Franz-Xaver Winterhalter, The Empress Eugénie in 18th-century costume, 1854, *oil on canvas, 92.7 x 73.7 cm. The Metropolitan Museum of Art, New York (page 99).*

Edouard Debat-Ponsan, Countess Edmond de Récopé, *1888, oil on canvas, 210 x 120 cm. Musée du Petit Palais, Paris (page 100).*

L'Art et la mode, *spring outfit in neo-Louis XVI style, 1889, engraving. Bibliothèque des Arts décoratifs, Paris (page 101, left).*

Neo-Directoire dress, 1887–1888. The Victoria and Albert Museum, London (page 101, right).

Anthony Van Dyck, Henriette de Lorraine, *1634, oil on canvas, 213.4 x 127 cm. London Country Council Trustees of the Iveagh Bequest, Kenwood (page 102, left).*

Dress for a reception in neo-17th-century style, signed Worth, c.1895. The Brooklyn Museum, gift of the Princesse Viggo, New York (page 102, right).

Carolus-Duran, Mrs William Astor, *1890, oil on canvas, 212.1 x 107.3 cm. The Metropolitan Museum of Art, New York (page 103).*

La Mode artistique, *outfit for the races, 1874, engraving. Bibliothèque des Arts décoratifs, Paris (page 104).*

After Anthony Van Dyck, Béatrice de Cusance, *sans date, engraving. Bibliothèque nationale, Paris (page 105, left).*

Peter Paul Rubens, Rubens, his wife Hélène Fourment and their son Peter Paul, *detail, 1639, oil on board, 203.8 x 158.1 cm. The Metropolitan Museum of Art, New York (page 105, right).*

Edouard Toudouze, The Swing, *no date, oil on canvas, 65 x 50 cm. Musée des Beaux-Arts, La Rochelle (page 106).*

La Revue de la mode, *neo-Empire ball-gowns, 1888, engraving. Bibliothèque des Arts décoratifs, Paris (page 107, left).*

La Mode illustrée: *neo-18th-century dress and neo-17th-century dress, 1871, engraving. Bibliothèque des Arts décoratifs, Paris (page 107, right).*

Disdéri, The Baron and Baroness de Walmont, *1861, photographs, 9.5 x 5.5 cm each. Musée d'Orsay, Paris (page 108, left and right).*

Gustave Courbet, Mademoiselle Aubé *or* The Lady with a parasol, *1865, oil on canvas, 92 x 73 cm. Art Gallery, Glasgow (page 110).*

La Mode illustrée: *bathing costumes, 1864, engraving. Musée de la Mode et du Costume, Paris (page 111, left).*

Les Modes parisiennes: *indoor outfit and town outfit, 31 October 1863, engraving. Bibliothèque des Arts décoratifs, Paris (page 111, right).*

Edouard Manet, Emilie Ambre in the role of Carmen, *1879–1880, oil on canvas, 91.5 x 73.5 cm. Philadelphia Museum of Art, Philadelphia (page 112).*

John Singer Sargent, La Carmencita, *1890, oil on canvas, 228.6 x 138.4 cm. Musée d'Orsay, Paris (page 113).*

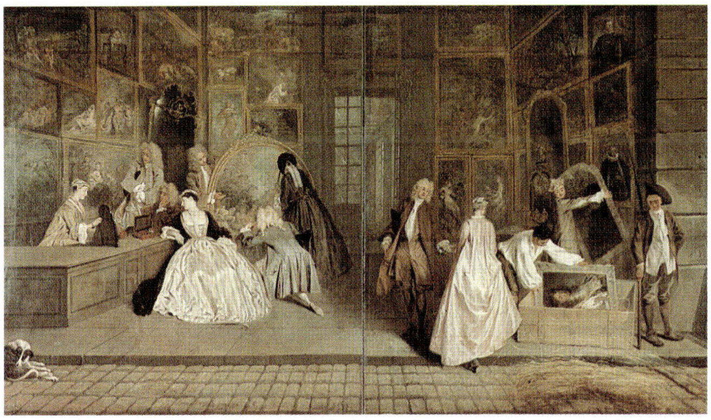

Antoine Watteau L'Ensiegne de Gersaint *(left) detail, page 93.*

Peter Paul Rubens, Rubens, his wife Hélène Fourment and their son Peter Paul, *(right) detail, page 105.*

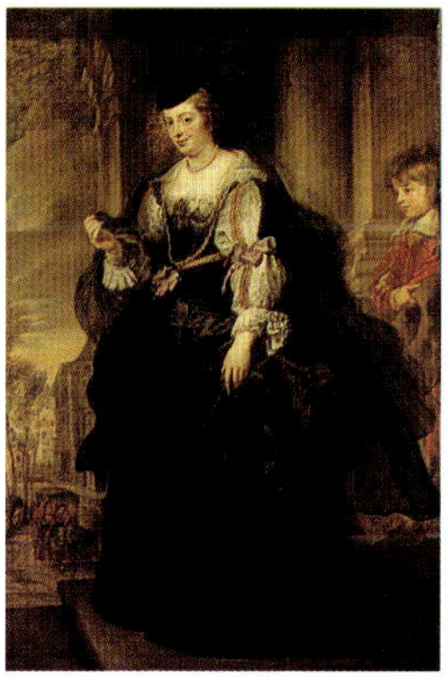

La Dernière Mode, *cover of 4 October 1874. Bibliothèque nationale, Paris (page 135, left).*

La Mode pour tous, *town fashions, cover of 21 May 1893. Bibliothèque Forney, Paris (page 135, right).*

La Revue illustrée, *Jean-Paul Sinibaldi, 'Coat from chez Félix', 1886. Bibliothèque historique de la Ville de Paris (page 136, left).*

L'Art de la mode, *two women in a museum, 1882, p. 175, engraving. Bibliothèque Forney, Paris (page 136, right).*

La Vie parisienne, *'At a picture exhibition, Designer fashions and ready-made clothes for the year 1877', 1877 pp. 258–259, engraving. Bibliothèque Forney, Paris (page 137).*

Disdéri, Baroness d'Heutze, *1860, photograph, 5 x 5.2 cm. Musée d'Orsay, Paris (page 138).*

Le Petit Courrier des dames, *two women at the Salon, 4 June 1853, engraving. Bibliothèque des Arts décoratifs, Paris (page 139, left).*

Bertall, La Comedie de notre temps, '*When I tell you that it is a dress from Worth, it is because I recognize the style', Vol. II, p. 307, engraving. Bibliothèque Forney, Paris (page 139, right).*

Jean-Auguste-Dominique Ingres, Portrait of Madame Moitessier, 1851, oil on canvas, *146.7 x 100.3 cm. National Gallery of Art, Washington (page 141).*

Dress with velvet arabesques on a satin ground, signed Worth. The Metropolitan Museum of Art, Costume Institute, gift of Mrs Eva Drexel Dahlgren, New York (page 143).

Pierre Auguste Renoir, Madame Charpentier and her children, *1878, oil on canvas, 154 x 190 cm. The Metropolitan Museum of Art, New York (pages 144–145).*

Edgar Degas, Portrait of Princesse Pauline de Metternich, *c. 1861, oil on canvas, 41 x 29 cm. The National Gallery, London (page 146).*

Disdéri, The Prince and Princesse de Metternich, *1860, photograph (page 147, left).*

Disdéri, Madame Ferran, *1861, photograph, 9.5 x 5.5 cm. Musée d'Orsay, Paris (page 147, right).*

Georges Clairin, Sarah Bernhardt, *1876, oil on canvas, 250 x 200 cm. Musée du Petit Palais, Paris (page 149).*

Alexandre Cabanel, The Comtesse de Keller, *1873, oil on canvas, 99.2 x 76 cm. Musée d'Orsay, Paris (page 150).*

Léon Bonnat, Madame Pasca, *1874, oil on canvas, 222 x 132 cm. Musée d'Orsay, Paris (page 151).*

Albert Besnard, Madame Roger Jourdain, *c. 1886, oil on canvas, 200 x 153 cm. Musée d'Orsay, Paris (page 152).*

Alexandre Cabanel, Madame Édouard Hervé, *1884, oil on canvas, 75.5 x 102 cm. Musée du Petit Palais, Paris (page 153).*

L'Art et la mode, *'Theatres of the present day', detail, 11 October 1884, engraving. Bibliothèque des Arts décoratifs, Paris (page 154, left).*

La Revue de la mode, *1884, engraving. Bibliothèque Forney, Paris (page 154, right).*

Le Moniteur de la mode, 1888, engraving, Bibliothèque Forney, Paris (page 155, left).

Le Moniteur de la mode, *1882, engraving. Bibliothèque Forney, Paris (page 155, right).*

Georges Seurat, Les Poseuses, *detail, 1886–1887, oil on canvas, 200 x 250 cm. The Barnes Foundation, Merion (page 156).*

Paul Gauguin, Study of a Nude *or* Suzanne sewing, *1880, oil on canvas, 115 x 80 cm. Ny Carlsberg Glyptotek, Copenhagen (page 159).*

Georges Seurat, Les Poseuses, *1886–1887, oil on canvas, 200 x 250 cm. The Barnes Foundation, Merion (page 161).*

Gustave Courbet, Les Demoiselles des bords de la Seine, *1856, oil on canvas, 174 x 206 cm. Musée du Petit Palais, Paris (pages 162–163).*

Edouard Manet, Nana, *1877, oil on canvas, 154 x 115 cm. Kunsthalle, Hamburg (page 164)*

Le Moniteur de la mode, *fashions for taking the waters and for full-dress occasions, September 1863, engraving. Bibliothèque nationale, Paris (page 169).*

Constantin Guys, Woman in a crinoline, *no date, watercolour. Musée du Petit Palais, Paris, (page 170, left).*

Constantin Guys, Two women in flowered dresses, *no date, watercolour. Musée Carnavalet, Paris (page 170, right).*

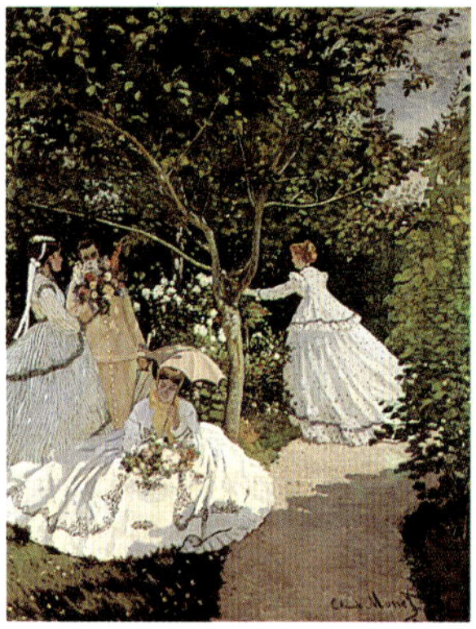

Claude Monet, Women in a garden *(left), detail, page 179.*

Edouard Manet, La Musique aux Tuileries *(right), detail, page 174.*

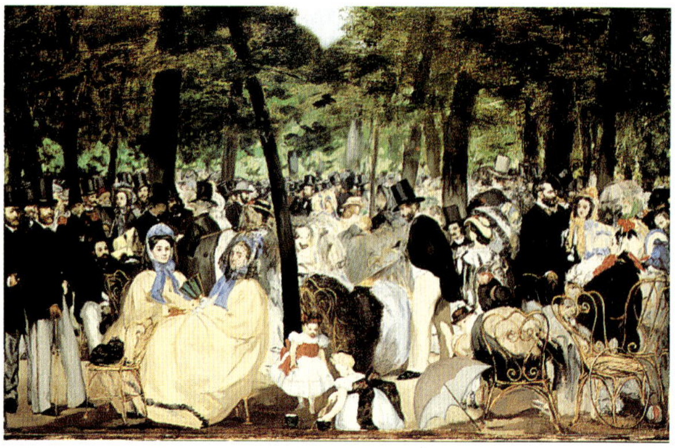

L'Art et la mode: *'Sa majesté la Parisienne', facsimile by Desjardin after Alfred Stevens, 1880. Bibliothèque nationale, Paris (page 192, right).*

Charles Giron, La Parisienne, *1883, oil on canvas, 200 x 91 cm. Musée du Petit Palais, Paris (page 193).*

Édouard Manet, La Viennoise. Portrait of Irma Brunner, *c.1880, pastel on card, 54 x 46 cm. Musée d'Orsay, Paris (page 194, left).*

La Revue de la mode, *hats, 1882, engraving. Bibliothèque des Arts décoratifs, Paris (page 194, right).*

James Tissot, October, *1877, oil on canvas, 216 x 108.7 cm. Musée des Beaux-Arts, Montreal (page 195).*

Giovanni Boldini, Portrait of Madame Charles Max, *1896, oil on canvas, 205 x 100 cm. Musée d'Orsay, Paris (page 196).*

La Mode artistique, *town outfit, 1879, engraving. Bibliothèque des Arts décoratifs, Paris (page 197, left).*

Ready-made clothes from the fashion house Steinback Keochlin & Cie: *'La Parisienne', 1875, engraving. Bibliothèque des Arts décoratifs, Paris (page 197, right).*

Henri Gervex, Portrait of Madame Valtesse de La Bigne, *1879, oil on canvas, 190 x 149 cm. Musée d'Orsay, Paris (page 198, left).*

Jean-Jacques Henner, Woman with an umbrella, *1874, oil on canvas, 143 x 81 cm. Musée national Jean-Jacques Henner, Paris (page 198, right).*

La Mode illustrée, *1874, engraving. Bibliothèque des Arts décoratifs, Paris (page 199, left).*

La Femme et la famille, *1 December 1868, engraving. Bibliothèque des Arts décoratifs, Paris (page 199, right).*

Carolus-Duran, Woman holding a glove, *1869, oil on canvas, 228 x 164 cm. Musée d'Orsay, Paris (page 200).*

Edouard Manet, Street singer, *1862, oil on canvas, 175 x 118.5 cm. Museum of Fine Arts, Boston (page 203).*

Edouard Manet, Woman with a parrot, *1866, oil on canvas, 185.1 x 128.6 cm. The Metroplitan Museum of Art, New York (page 204).*

Le Journal des demoiselles, *peignoir, December 1864, engraving. Bibliothèque des Arts décoratifs, Paris (page 205, left).*

La Mode illustrée, *1868, engraving. Bibliothèque des Arts décoratifs, Paris (page 205, right).*

Alfred Stevens, The farewell note, *c.1867, oil on canvas, 74.5 x 54.5 cm. Musée d'Orsay, Paris (page 206, left).*

La Vie parisienne,'The peignoir', *February 1875, engraving. Bibliothèque Forney, Paris (page 206, right).*

Franz-Xaver Winterhalter, Madame Rimsky-Korsakov, *1864, oil on canvas, 117 x 90 cm. Musée d'Orsay, Paris (page 207).*

Edouard Manet, The balcony, *c.1868–1869, oil on canvas, 170 x 124.5 cm. Musée d'Orsay, Paris (page 208).*

Constantin Guys, Two young girls on a balcony, *c.1855–1860, watercolour and crayon, 29 x 24 cm. Kunsthalle, Hamburg (page 209).*

Bibliography

Fashion

AINCOURT, Marguerite d', *L'Art de la femme. Études sur le costume féminin*, Paris, Rouveyre et Blond, 1883.

BALZAC, Honoré de, *Les Parisiens comme ils sont, 1830-1848*, Neuchâtel, Paul Altinger, J. A., 1957.
BASSANVILLE, Comtesse de, *La Scène du monde, politesse, usage, bien-être*, Paris, J. Lecoffre, 1859.
BERTALL (Charles-Albert d'Arnoux), *La Comédie de notre temps*, Paris, Plon, 1874.
BLANC, Charles, *L'Art dans la parure et dans le vêtement*, Paris, Librairie Renouard, 1875.
BLUM, André and CHASSE, Charles, *Histoire des costumes, les modes au XIXe siècle*, Paris, Hachette, 1931.
BLUM, Stella, *Victorian Fashion and Costume from Harper's Bazar*, New York, Dover Publications, 1974.
BOUCHER, François, *Histoire du costume en Occident de l'Antiquité à nos jours*, Paris, Flammarion, 1965.
BURMAN BAINES, Barbara, *Fashion Revivals from the Elizabethan Age to the Present Day*, London, Batsford, 1981.
BUTAZZI, Grazietta, *La Mode, art, histoire et société*, Paris, Hachette, 1983.

CELNART (Élisabeth-Félicie Bayle-Mouillard), *Manuel de la bonne compagnie ou guide de la politesse et de la bienséance dédié à la société française*, Paris, Librairie Roret, 1836.
CHALLAMEL, J. Augustin, *Histoire de la mode en France*, Paris, A. Hennuyer, 1881.
COLEMAN, Elizabeth Ann, *The Opulent Era, Fashions of Worth, Doucet and Pingat*, New York, Thames and Hudson–Brooklyn Museum, 1989.

DASH, Comtesse, *Comment on fait son chemin dans le monde, code de savoir-vivre*, Paris, Michel Lévy, 1868.
DELBOUR-DELPHIS, Marylène, *Le Chic et le look : Histoire de la mode féminine et des mœurs de 1850 à nos jours*, Paris, Hachette, 1981.
DELORD, Taxile, *Physiologie de la Parisienne*, Paris, Aubert & Cie, 1841.
DELPIERRE, Madeleine, « Ingres et la mode de son temps », *Bulletin du musée Ingres*, juillet 1975, pp. 21–26 ; *Le Costume de la Restauration à la Belle Époque*, Paris, Flammarion, 1990.
DESLANDRES, Yvonne, *Le Costume, image de l'homme*, Paris, Albin Michel, 1976.

FORTASSIER, Rose, *Les Écrivains français et la mode de Balzac à nos jours*, Paris, P.U.F., 1988.

GAUDRIAULT, Raymond, *La Gravure de mode féminine en France*, Paris, Éditions de l'Amateur, 1983.
GERNSHEIM, Alison, *Fashion and Reality*, London, Faber & Faber, 1963.
GIBBS SMITH, Charles H., *The Fashionable Lady in the 19th Century*, London, Victoria and Albert Museum, 1960.

HUART, Louis, *Physiologie de la grisette*, Paris, Aubert & Cie, s.d.

JOANNE, Adolphe, *Le Guide parisien*, Paris, Librairie Hachette & Cie, 1863.

LANGLAY MORE, Doris, *Fashion through Fashion Plates 1770-1970*, London, Ward Lock, 1971.
LAVER, James, *Costume and Fashion: A Concise History*, London, Thames & Hudson, 1986; *Costume Illustration, the Nineteenth Century*, London, Victoria and Albert Museum, 1947.
LEBAS, Catherine et JACQUES, Annie, *La Coiffure en France du Moyen Âge à nos jours*, Paris, Delmas, 1979.
LECERCLE, Jean-Pierre, *Mallarmé et la mode*, Paris, Librairie Seguier, 1989.
LELOIR, Maurice, *Dictionnaire du costume*, Paris, Gründ, 1951.
LEVI-STRAUSS, Monique, *Cachemires*, Paris, Adam Biro, 1987.

MEILHEURAT, Alfred de, *L'Art de se conduire selon les usages et les convenances du monde*, Paris, Desloyes, 1852.

PERROT, Philippe, *Les Dessus et les dessous de la bourgeoisie. Une histoire du vêtement au XIXe siècle*, Paris, Librairie Arthème Fayard, 1981 ; *Le Travail des apparences. Le corps humain XVIIIe-XIXe siècle*, Paris, Le Seuil, 1984.

ROBIQUET, Jean, *La Parisienne par l'image, trois siècles de grâce féminine*, Paris, Ludovic Baschet, 1896.

STEELE, Valérie, *Fashion and Eroticism : Ideals of Feminine Beauty from the Victorian Era to the Jazz Age*, New York, Oxford University Press, 1985 ; *Paris-Fashion, a Cultural History*, New York, Oxford University Press, 1988.

TAINE, Hippolyte, *Notes sur Paris, vie et opinions de M. Frédéric-Thomas Graindorge recueillies et publiées par Taine*, Paris, Hachette, 1867.

UZANNE, Octave, *La Femme et la mode, Métamorphoses de la Parisienne de 1792 à 1892*, Paris, May

& Motteroz, 1892 ; *Les Ornements de la femme, l'éventail, l'ombrelle, le gant, le manchon*, Paris, Quantin, 1892 ; *La Femme à Paris, nos contemporaines, notes successives sur les Parisiennes de ce temps en leurs divers milieux, états et conditions*, Paris, May & Motteroz, 1894.

VANIER, Henriette, *La Mode et ses métiers. Frivolités et luttes des classes 1830-1870*, Paris, Armand Colin, 1960.
VEDRES, Nicole, *Un siècle d'élégance française*, Paris, éditions du Chêne, 1943.

WORTH, Gaston, *La Couture et la confection des vêtements de femmes*, Paris, Imprimerie Chaix, 1895.

Fiction

BAUDELAIRE, Charles, *Œuvres complètes*, Paris, Gallimard, La Pléiade, 1985, v.I.

GAUTIER, Théophile, *Contes et récits fantastiques*, Paris, Librairie générale française, Le Livre de poche, 1988.

PROUST, Marcel, *A l'ombre des jeunes filles en fleurs*, Paris, Gallimard, Folio, 1954 ; *Le Côté de Guermantes I & II*, Paris, Gallimard, Folio, 1986 ; *Le Temps retrouvé*, Paris, Gallimard, Folio, 1954 ; *Un amour de Swann*, Paris, Gallimard, Folio, 1990.

ZOLA, Emile, *Au bonheur des dames*, Paris, Librairie générale française, Le Livre de poche, 1980 ; *La Curée*, Paris, Gallimard, 1981 ; *Nana*, Paris, Presses Pocket, 1978.

Painting

BAUDELAIRE, Charles, *Œuvres complètes*, Paris, Gallimard, La Pléiade, 1985, v.II.

DARRAGON, Eric, *Manet*, Paris, Hachette, 1989.

FOUCART, Bruno, *Courbet*, Paris, Flammarion, 1977.
FROIDEVAUX, Gérald, *Baudelaire, représentation et modernité*, Paris, José Corti, 1989.

GAUTIER, Théophile, *De la mode*, Paris, Poulet-Malassis et de Broise, 1858 ; *Portraits contemporains*, Paris, Charpentier, 1874.
GONCOURT, Emile et Jules de, *Journal. Mémoires de la vie littéraire*, Editions de l'Imprimerie nationale de Monaco, 1956.

HUYSMANS, Joris-Karl, *L'Art moderne*, Paris, Charpentier, 1883 ; new edn., Paris, UGE Poche/10/18, 1975.

LAPAUZE, Henry, *Ingres, sa vie et son œuvre 1780-1867, d'après des document inédits*, Paris, Georges Petit, 1914.
LETHÈVE, Jacques, *La Vie quotidienne des artistes français au XIXe siècle*, Paris, Hachette, 1968 ; *Manet raconté par lui-même et par ses amis*, Geneva, Pierre Cailler, 1945.

PILES, Roger de, *Cours de peinture par principes*, Paris, Gallimard, 1989.

ROBIDA, Michel, *Les Bourgeois de Paris, trois siècles de chronique familiale de 1785 à nos jours*, Paris, Julliard, 1955.

STERLING, Charles and SALINGER, Margaretta, *French Paintings, a Catalogue of the Metropolitan Museum of Art, 19th Century*, The Metropolitan Museum of Art, New York, 1966.
SUTHERLAND BOGGS, Jean, *Portraits by Degas*, Berkeley University of California Press, 1962.

VALERY, Paul, *Degas, Danse, Dessin*, Paris, Gallimard, 1965.
VOLLARD, Ambroise, *En écoutant Cézanne, Degas, Renoir*, Paris, Grasset, 1950.

WENTWORTH, Michael Justin, *Tissot, catalogue raisonné*, The Minneapolis Institute of Art, 1978.

ZOLA, Emile, *Mon Salon, Manet, Ecrits sur l'art*, Paris, Garnier-Flammarion, 1970.

Articles and salons

ABOUT, Edmond, *Voyage à travers l'Exposition des beaux-arts de 1855*, Paris, Hachette, 1855 ; *Salon de 1866*, Paris, 1867 ; « Le costume français vu par les artistes du XVIIe, du XVIIIe et du XIXe siècle », *Art et style*, n° 11 June 1949.

CASTAGNARY, Jules-Antoine, *Salons de 1857-1879*, Paris, Charpentier et Fasquelle, 1892.
CHERBULIEZ, Victor, « Le Salon de 1876 », *La Revue des deux mondes*, 1 June–19 June, 1 July 1876.
CLARETIE, Jules, *L'Art et les artistes français contemporains. Salons de 1873-1874-1875*, Paris, Charpentier, 1876.

DORIVAL, Bernard, « Quelques sources méconnues de divers ouvrages de Manet », *Bulletin de la Société d'histoire de l'art français*, 1975.
DU CAMP, Maxime, *Salon de 1857*, Paris, 1857 ;

Les Beaux-Arts à l'Exposition universelle et aux Salons de 1863-1864-1865-1866-1867, Paris, Jules Renouard, 1867.
DURANTY, Louis-Edmond, *La Nouvelle Peinture, à propos du groupe d'artistes qui expose à la galerie Durand-Ruel,* Paris, E. Dentu, 1876.

ENVAL, Jane d', « Salon de 1861 », *La Mode de France,* 1861.

GASNAULT, François, « Les salles de bal du Paris romantique : décors et jeux des corps », *Romantisme,* n° 38, 1982, p. 12.

LEVINE, Steven Z., « The Crisis of Resemblance : Portraits and Paintings during the Second Empire », *Art Magazine,* n° 53, December 1978, pp. 90-93.

MANTZ, Paul, *Le Feuilleton du Temps,* 14 May 1874.

ROSKILL, Mark, « Early Impressionism and the Fashion Print », *The Burlington Magazine,* June 1970, pp. 391-395.

OUVRAGE COLLECTIF, *La Promenade du critique influent. Anthologie de la critique d'art en France, 1850-1900,* Paris, Hazan, 1990.

Fashion magazines

L'Art de la mode, Journal de la vie mondaine, later *L'Art et la mode* (1880-1967).
Le Bon Ton, Journal des modes (1834-1884).
Le Conseiller des dames et des demoiselles (1847-1892).
La Dernière Mode, Gazette du monde et de la famille (1874-1875).
Le Follet (1829-1882).
Le Journal des demoiselles (1833-1922).
Le Journal des jeunes filles (1868-1871).
Le Magasin des demoiselles (1844-1896).
Le Messager des modes et de l'industrie (1853-1862).
La Mode (1829-1855).
La Mode actuelle (1869-1888).
La Mode artistique, Revue de toutes les élégances (1869-1892 ; 1895-1907).
La Mode illustrée (1860-1937).
La Mode miniature illustrée (1872-1874).
La Mode nouvelle (1856-1862).
La Mode pour tous (1878-1901).
La Mode universelle (1874-1885).
Les Modes parisiennes (1843-1885).
Le Moniteur de la mode (1843-1913).
Le Petit Courrier des dames (1821-1868).
Revue de la mode (1872-1913).
La Vie parisienne (1863-1939).

Exhibition Catalogues

Great Portraits from Impressionism to Modernism, Wildenstein & Co., New York, March 1938.

Poufs et tournures. Costumes français de femmes et d'enfants 1869-1889, 1954 ; *Costumes français 1725-1925,* April–June 1957. Musée du Costume de la Ville de Paris.

Alfred Stevens, The University of Michigan Museum of Art, Ann Arbor, September–October 1977.

Un témoin de la Belle Époque, Jean Béraud, Musée Carnavalet, Paris, June–July 1979.

A la mode, Women's Fashion in French Art 1850-1990. The Sterling and Francine Clark Art Institute, Williamstown, Massachusetts, 1982.

The House of Worth : the Gilded Age 1860-1918, Museum of the City of New York, 1982.

Dessins de mode : Jules David (1808-1892) et son temps, Mairie du VIe arrondissement, Paris, 1987.

James Tissot, April–June 1985; *Franz-Xaver Winterhalter et les cours d'Europe,* February–May 1988. Musée du Petit Palais, Paris.

L'Art en France sous le second Empire, May–August 1979 ; *Manet,* April–August 1983 ; *Renoir,* May–September 1985 ; *Japonisme,* 1988 ; *Degas,* February–May 1988. Galeries nationales du Grand Palais, Paris.

Claude-Marie, Edouard et Guillaume Dubufe : Portraits d'un siècle d'élégance parisienne, Délégation à l'Action artistique de la Ville de Paris, 1988.

Masterpieces of Impressionism and Postimpressionism, The Annenberg Collection, Philadelphia Museum of Art, Philadelphia, 1989.

Le Monde de Proust, photographs by Paul Nadar, Hôtel de Sully, Paris, February–May 1991.

Secrets d'élégance 1750-1950, 1978 ; *L'Atelier Nadar et la mode 1865-1913,* 1978 ; *Femmes fin de siècle 1885-1895,* 1990 ; *Au paradis des dames,* 1992. Musée de la Mode et du Costume, Palais Galliera, Paris.

Index

Figures in italics refer to illustrations.